Excel 97 Essentials

Annotated Instructor's Edition

Donna Matherly

An imprint of Macmillan
Computer Publishing

Excel 97 Essentials, Annotated Instructor's Edition

Copyright © 1998 by Que® Education and Training.

All rights reserved. Printed in the United States of America. No part of this book may be used or reproduced in any form or by any means, or stored in a database or retrieval system, without prior written permission of the publisher except in the case of brief quotations embodied in critical articles and reviews. Adopters of the textbook for which this manual was prepared are hereby given permission to reproduce this manual in-house for their students. For further information, address Que Education and Training, 201 West 103rd Street, Indianapolis, IN 46290.

Adoption of the accompanying Que Education and Training textbook, *PowerPoint 97 Essentials Level I,* is required for use of the material in the classroom. This material is not for distribution under any other circumstances or for resale.

ISBN 1-57576-871-2

This book is sold *as is*, without warranty of any kind, either express or implied, respecting the contents of this book, including but not limited to implied warranties for the book's quality, performance, merchantability, or fitness for any particular purpose. Neither Que Education and Training nor its dealers or distributors shall be liable to the purchaser or any other person or entity with respect to any liability, loss, or damage caused or alleged to be caused directly or indirectly by this book.

01 00 99 98   4 3 2 1

Publisher: Robert Linsky

Publishing Director: Charles O. Stewart III

Product Development Specialist: Diane E. Beausoleil

Product Marketing Manager: Susan L. Kindel

Acquisitions Editor: Kyle Lewis

Managing Editor: Nancy Sixsmith

Production Editor: Jeff Durham

Cover Designer: Ann Jones

Production Team: Trina Brown, Linda Knose, Maureen West

Composed in *Stone Serif* and *MCPdigital* by Que Corporation

About the Author

Donna Matherly teaches and coordinates the Introduction to Computer Literacy course at Tallahassee Community College. She received her doctorate degree from Indiana University, where she served as a faculty member in the Department of Business Education in the School of Business for five years. She has authored numerous articles on office automation, written more than two dozen textbook instructional manuals, and has authored and co-authored many Que books, including seven of the books in the *Essential* series. She has also conducted training programs for private and public sector organizations.

Trademark Acknowledgments

All terms mentioned in this book that are known to be trademarks or service marks have been appropriately capitalized. Que Education and Training cannot attest to the accuracy of this information. Use of a term in this book should not be regarded as affecting the validity of any trademark or service mark.

Table of Contents

Introduction — vii

Using the Annotated Instructor's Edition — viii
  Personalizing the Manual ix
  Anatomy of a Typical Lesson ix
  Using the Annotated Student's Guide xi

Preparation for Teaching Your Course — xii
  Teaching Experience xii
  Preparing to Teach Excel Checklist xiii
  Presentation Skills xiii
  Resource CD-ROM xiv
  Setting up the Training Room xiv
  Training Resources xiv

Preparing Class Materials — xvi
  Opening the Class xvi
  Closing the Class xvi
  Resource CD-ROM xvi
  The Successful Instructor's Checklist xvii
  Day-of-Course Checklist xviii

Curriculum Guide — xviii
  Excel 97 Essentials I Time Chart xix

Training Tips, Tricks, & Techniques — xx
  Identifying Student Expectations (Why Are They Here?) xx
  Training Tips, Tricks, and Techniques xx
  Give Students Control over the Pace xx
  Body Language xxi
  Educational Entertaining xxi
  Put Differences in Skill Sets to Work xxii
  Dealing with Objections from Students xxii
  Avoiding Disaster: When (Not If) Equipment Fails xxiii

Project 1: Getting Started with Excel	1
Project 2: Building a Spreadsheet	39
Project 3: Creating Formulas	67
Project 4: Calculating with Functions	89
Project 5: Improving the Appearance of a Worksheet	119
Project 6: Using Charts and Maps	151
Project 7: Managing Data	185
Project 8: Using Excel with Other Programs	211
Appendix A: Working with Windows 95	235
Appendix B: Answers	

Introduction

As computer technology advances at lightning speed, more and more people turn to Que Education and Training. It is easy to get lost in the technoshuffle of software releases, hardware upgrades, new operating systems, and on-line technology. We've published over 500 titles written by people who are the absolute best in their field. With a strong network of experts, Que Education and Training knows how to provide readers with support, guidance, and insight they can trust.

You'll find Que books in offices, classrooms, and homes across the United States and abroad. Our books are easy to find. They are the ones that are highlighted and marked with pages turned down. Most likely, you'll find them right beside the computer—ready to help in troubleshooting and problem solving. We do more than just look nice on your book shelf.

We do more than just look nice on your book shelf.

Que Education and Training is quickly becoming the leader in developing instructional materials. Our *Essentials* courseware is anchored in the practical and professional needs of all types of students.

We were founded in the belief that people want to learn from experts. Just as your students expect you to be a pro, you should demand that the courseware you use is top of the line. You deserve expert advice and professional techniques, as well as thorough annotations, classroom exercises, and supplements that make your job easier while allowing you to teach the best possible course. You can trust Que Education and Training to deliver what you and your students need to take you wherever technology goes.

Excel 97 Essentials is designed for use by college, independent, or corporate instructors. The authors have made every effort to give you useful and practical information to ensure your teaching success. Our *Essentials* courseware and accompanying *Annotated Instructor's Edition* (AIE) are designed by professional instructors who understand the special challenges of providing computer instruction. The questions, tips, and examples used throughout the AIE provide students with instruction adapted to their needs, interests, and experience.

Our Essentials courseware and accompanying Annotated Instructor's Edition are designed by professional instructors who understand the special challenges of providing computer instruction.

The *Annotated Instructor's Edition* can be used by instructors in various settings and with varying teaching experience. New instructors will make good use of the teaching tips and discussion questions that help them teach successfully the first time. Experienced instructors will value the fresh approaches and ideas for teaching familiar topics.

The *Annotated Instructor's Edition* includes several sections that will help you prepare for teaching the course, plan classes with the amount of time available, assess the student's skill level before and after the course, and generally show you interesting and effective ways to present the information. Following is a brief description of the sections of the *Annotated Instructor's Edition*:

- ◆ **Preparation for Teaching Your Course.** This section suggests organization techniques, preparation ideas, teaching tips, and ideas for handouts and visuals.
- ◆ **Curriculum Guide and Project Summary.** This section provides guidance on how to teach the material within certain time constraints. You can easily adapt the material to two-, three-, four-, six-, or eight-hour training sessions for the most effective use of the material.

- **Bonus Section.** This section gives you practical techniques and tactics from the *Computer Instructor's Personal Training Guide*. You'll get tips on dealing with student's expectations, objections, and hardware failure, as well as advice on body language and delivery.

- **Annotated Student's Guide.** The largest section of this manual, the Annotated Student's Guide provides running commentary, assistance, and guidance during the class. The commentary provides tips, suggestions, and ideas for enhancing teaching. Annotations are marked clearly so that you can refer to them readily during class. Answers to all the questions and exercises at the end of each project are also included in the guide. You may want to customize and further annotate this part of the Annotated *Instructor's Edition* by adding your own tips in the margin.

- **Test Questions and Answers.** Additional true/false, multiple choice, and completion questions and answers are included in a special section. You may make photocopies of the tests, or print the tests from the CD-ROM provided at the back of the *Annotated Instructor's Edition*.

- **Transparencies/Slides.** Transparencies of key points, objectives, and other information are included to supplement the text.

Using the Annotated Instructor's Edition

We believe that immersion in a topic is the best way to learn. Students prefer to be active doers rather than passive recipients of information.

The *Annotated Instructor's Edition* (AIE) is built around the corresponding *Essentials* courseware, which assumes a classroom or training-room setting. The AIE reflects many hours of real-world teaching experience on the topic, offering you invaluable ideas, guidance, and advice to support your efforts in the classroom.

Each *Essentials* workbook is designed to provide a great deal of hands-on use by the students. We believe that immersion in a topic is the best way to learn. Students prefer to be active doers rather than passive recipients of information. Whether you're a new or experienced instructor, the *Annotated Instructor's Edition* can help you provide effective instruction for all students in your class.

This section describes how best to use the AIE for teaching adults some of the more advanced features of Excel.

Discovery-Based Training

Students cannot be expected to respond to the basic "Instructor Lectures—Student Learns" training. Instead they respond to discovering answers during hands-on exercises and practice. Don't just tell your students the answers. Allow them to find them with your support and guidance. Discovery-Based Training isn't rocket science. You provide the road map and let them reach their destination. If you are driving the entire time, they may get there—but they will have no idea how they did it.

Give them the freedom to make mistakes while you facilitate the learning experience. It's quite a difference from the "Do This, Do That" school of training, but it works. Just let the *Annotated Instructor's Edition* show you how.

Using the Annotated Instructor's Edition

Personalizing the Manual

In addition to the numerous supplied examples and pointers, you'll want to add your own ideas to the material to make it your own. We encourage you to customize and personalize the *Annotated Instructor's Edition* as you adapt the material to your teaching style, experiences, and preferences.

Additionally, consider the following points as you teach and prepare to teach these lessons:

- **What was that?** When an unusual comment or question arises in class, make a note in the annotated area (margin) of the AIE for future reference.

- **Take notes.** Mark or make note of any methods of explaining a topic that work for you.

- **Prepare for the next time around.** Make copies of additional examples you have used and insert them into the AIE.

- **Mark it up.** Circle and highlight points that are important to you.

- **Once upon a time...** Note anecdotes about classroom experiences or personal experiences you have had with the program you're teaching—things that you can draw on in class to make your training more genuine.

- **Tell us about it.** Share your experiences with us so that all instructors using our materials can grow through each other's learning experiences.

- **Don't forget:** Relax and have fun!

Anatomy of a Typical Lesson

Each *Essentials* book typically is divided into six to eight projects, concerning topics such as creating a database, querying your database, creating and printing reports, and so on. Each project is then divided into a number of lessons related to that topic. For example, a project on entering and editing data in *Excel 97 Essentials* is divided into lessons explaining how to build spreadsheets, create formulas, calculate with functions, use charts and maps, and manage data.

All Essentials books include specific elements that help the student understand why the lesson is important and what to do if things go wrong.

Each element in *Excel 97 Essentials* was designed to maximize learning and facilitate instruction. All *Essentials* books include specific elements that help the student understand why the lesson is important and what to do if things go wrong. Included are shortcuts, tips, key terms, and jargon. Additionally, step-by-step instructions make it easy for the student to complete tasks and follow procedures.

Following is a list of the *Essentials* project elements and a description of how each element can help the student:

- **Project Objectives.** Starting with an objective gives a student a short-term, attainable goal. Using project objectives breaks the overwhelming prospect of learning all of some of the more advanced features of Excel into small, attainable, bite-sized tasks.

  Project objectives give the instructor a chance to stay focused and not get sidetracked. If questions come up that take away from the overall learning experience of the class, ask yourself whether the question relates to the project objective. If it does not, write down the question and save it for "off-line" time later.

> ### Using Off-Line Time
>
> Getting sidetracked by answering the wrong questions at the wrong time can leave you playing catch-up later. At the time, it may seem that swaying from your agenda won't be that big of a deal. If it happens enough, you'll find yourself so far from the topic at hand that you'll end the class without covering all the important material.
>
> Creating "Off-Line" time is a great way to minimize the time you spend answering questions that don't relate to the topic you are covering or that apply to future lessons.
>
> Explain to the class that there will be times that they will ask questions that you will label as off-line. Tell them that these questions will be written down and covered later. Then, as they pop up, write them on a white board or poster board. As you cover them, check them off. If you don't get to them, you can respond in a follow-up letter after the class. If they understand why it is important that you stick to the agenda, they can help you control getting sidetracked.
>
> **Warning:** Do not confuse a "clarifying question" with an "off-line question." You always want to provide answers to the questions that directly relate to the subject matter in order to help students understand the material.

- ◆ **Why Would I Do This?** This section gives the student the reason these tasks or procedures are important to him/her. What can the student do with the knowledge? How can it be applied to everyday tasks?

- ◆ **Step-by-Step Tutorial.** These numbered instructions guide the student to perform the procedures step-by-step. Additionally, the student can refer to the stepped instructions later, when working back at the office.

- ◆ **Inside Stuff.** Inside Stuff provides the student with tips, shortcuts, and special hints about using the software. It's one thing to show someone how to do something; it's another issue to show them something "neat." Inside Stuff might be lost on some of the more remedial students in the class; however, many students will take to this section as their favorite. They will walk away with a "better" way, a different insight.

- ◆ **Key Terms.** The book includes a limited number of vocabulary words and definitions that the student will find useful, such as *Query By Example (QBE)*, *criteria*, *fixed-width fields*, *data form*, *delimiters*, and *dynaset*. These key terms are shown in bold in the text and defined in the margin when they first appear.

- ◆ **Jargon Watch.** Offers a layperson's view of "technobabble" in easily understandable terms. Examples include terms such as *relational database*.

- ◆ **If You Have Problems...** These short troubleshooting notes help students anticipate or solve common problems quickly and effectively.

- ◆ **Project Summary Tables.** This end-of-project element summarizes the instructions and procedures in short, easy-to-follow steps that the student can use for future reference.

It's one thing to show someone how to do something; it's another issue to show them something "neat."

Using the Annotated Instructor's Edition

- ◆ **Checking Your Skills.** This section offers optional True/False, multiple choice, and completion exercises designed to check comprehension and assess retention.

- ◆ **Applying Your Skills.** This section enables students to check their comprehension, evaluate their progress, and practice what they've learned. The exercises in this section build on and reinforce what has been learned in each project.

Using the Annotated Student's Guide

The Annotated Student's Guide provides the instructor with the same text and elements as the student, but with a number of additions. Each project contains a wide variety of margin notes to assist the instructor in conducting a successful class. These notes give the instructor tips on directing the class, provide helpful tips and shortcuts on using the program, point out when slides should be shown, suggest questions to ask attendees, and provide additional guidance to new as well as experienced instructors.

Included within the Annotated Student's Guide are the following elements:

- ◆ **Lesson Time.** At the start of each project is an estimation of the typical time it takes to complete this module.

Kickoff questions keep the instructor from just diving into a topic and help students gain an understanding of what they are about to learn. They create some association with and context for the topic.

- ◆ **On Your Mark.** Kickoff questions are provided that you can use to get students talking about what they expect to learn. These questions are useful for getting feedback from students on the connections they see between the topic and their "real work." They keep the instructor from just diving into a topic and help students gain an understanding of what they are about to learn. It is the intent of the kickoff questions to create some association with and context for the topic.

- ◆ **Tip for Instructors.** Each lesson in the AIE also contains tips to aid the instructor in presenting the topic. Their content includes such items as pedagogical tips; ideas on how to suggest other applications for a particular feature; deeper examples than those in the student courseware; real-life examples to connect a program feature or operation with a business scenario that students will recognize; discussion, where relevant, of how things are done in other programs (exporting data to WordPerfect instead of Word and QuattroPro instead of Excel); wrap-up discussion ideas ("Can you see yourself using this feature? How? In what situations?"); and suggestions for transition to next topic.

One key to students accepting your ability to teach is their belief that you are providing them more than what is in their book.

- ◆ **Tip for Students.** These provide shortcuts for the instructor to share with the students. This gives the instructor the opportunity to share a new and unique tidbit of information not contained in the courseware. One key to students accepting your ability to teach (and therefore their learning acceptance threshold) is their belief that you are providing them more than what is in their book. Many students leave traditional courseware-driven classes with the feeling that they could have read the book on their own—so why go to class? These sections provide tips for you to share to supplement the class. They make the class appear more of your own design until the time when you have made the class fully your own.

- ◆ **Quicksand.** These notes provide a "heads up" for the instructor to things that are likely to cause problems such as how to get out of a record when you don't understand what a particular error message means. Quicksand sections point out software problems and other things that might seem easy to you as the instructor, but won't seem easy or intuitive to students.

- ◆ **Concept Notes.** These notes shed new light on difficult or challenging concepts; and present opportunities for trying out different analogies, metaphors, and examples.

- ◆ **Speedy Class.** Ideas for expanding on the material are provided in the Speedy Class notes, which contain comments and additional information to share with a class that is moving quickly and has the time and the ability to grasp the topic in more depth.

- ◆ **Q&A.** These sections offer questions designed to check for understanding concepts or procedures at critical junctures.

The elements provided in the AIE work in conjunction with the elements in the workbook to contribute to a well-rounded, easy-to-understand and use course of study for students. From planning and preparation to the evaluation of the course, the *Essentials* method ensures a successful training experience for the instructor and the student.

Preparation for Teaching Your Course

Whether you're wondering if you can be an instructor, or you know you can do the job but would appreciate some guidance, this section can help. Even if you're a seasoned instructor, you'll find some useful ideas in this section for teaching *Excel 97 Essentials*. This section provides suggestions for preparing to teach the course, ideas for class organization and planning, and some tips and hints for teaching the class to your specific audience.

Experiment with the program and make sure that you're comfortable with it before you ever enter the training room; then you'll be ready to help others learn Excel.

Even if you've never conducted a class before, you can successfully teach this course if you follow the guidelines in the AIE. The most important thing you need to know is your application. Become familiar with Excel 97 and Windows 95 prior to class, go through the exercises as the student will, and read along in the Annotated Student's Guide. Experiment with the program and make sure that you're comfortable with it before you ever enter the training room; then you'll be ready to help others learn Excel.

Teaching Experience

As part of the *Essentials* series, *Excel 97 Essentials* provides basic skills in application training. You should expect your students to have a working knowledge of Windows 95. You may find, however, that some of your students may need a refresher on some aspects of Windows 95. You should be able to provide a basic understanding of Windows 95, as needed.

You will need to be very comfortable with Excel 97. It will be a definite plus if you're also familiar with basic tables design, along with the fundamental processes involved in developing queries, forms, reports, and macros. Although this class is appropriate for an entry-level instructor, we highly recommend that every instructor be well-versed in adult training principles and in the operating system.

Teaching a GUI (graphical user interface) class is much different from teaching a class on a character-based application or operating system such as MS-DOS. It is very important that the instructor become sensitive to the

Preparation for Teaching Your Course

motor skills required of the students that might be new to them. We recommend that an instructor be familiar with using and teaching a GUI interface before teaching this class.

Obviously, the first step to being a successful instructor is to be prepared. Gather all the materials on the subject, organize them, and know where to find the answers to difficult questions. You don't have to know all the answers; no one does. But you should be able either to find the answer to a question or problem, or know where the student can go to find the answer. Reference materials, on-line Help, and the assistance of other experts in the field are invaluable. Do your research well before your class so that you feel prepared.

Your goal is to take advantage of those "teachable moments" and "aha!" experiences that every class contains.

Accordingly, the more you know about your subject, the easier it will be to break down things and explain them on a very basic level for those who don't understand a concept or procedure. You also need to practice explaining things in a different way, trying various comparisons or correlations, for example. Your goal is to take advantage of those "teachable moments" and "aha!" experiences that every class contains.

Preparing to Teach Excel Checklist

- ☐ **Know your application.** Become familiar with the Excel 97 topics to be covered prior to class, go through the exercises as the student will, and read along in the Annotated Student's Guide.

- ☐ **Experiment with the program.** Make sure that you're comfortable with it before you ever enter the training room; then you'll be ready to help others learn Excel 97.

- ☐ **Do your homework.** Research on a variety of topics will help prepare you to teach.
    - ○ Get familiar with how the session's Excel 97 topics are used in the "real world."
    - ○ Be well-versed in adult training principles and in the operating system.
    - ○ Be familiar with using and teaching a GUI interface before teaching this class.

Presentation Skills

This course is best taught with a projection system hooked up to the instructor's computer. The instructor can show the class what they are about to do, and the class can emulate what they see on the screen. Projection systems can represent a sizable investment on the part of the training center. The instructor should have practice using overhead projection systems, or practice in teaching from printed materials. The cheapest alternative to large-screen projection of the actual program is to use transparencies on an overhead projector, but this not nearly as effective. If you don't have access to a projection system, plan on doing a lot of roaming around the training room and examining screens.

If you are new to delivering training with this type of media, we highly recommend several dry runs with no audience so that you can become familiar with the equipment.

There are considerations in teaching a GUI application that are not usually considered in training a character-based application. Be aware that the quality of most projection systems is geared for character-based displays. You will need to spend more time pointing to the screen, telling the students what they are looking for. The mouse pointer will frequently "get lost" on many of the less-expensive projection systems, forcing the instructor to pay additional attention to what is happening on the screen, not just

Resource CD-ROM

to what is on the instructor's monitor. If you are new to delivering training with this type of media, we highly recommend several dry runs with no audience so that you can become familiar with the equipment.

Included on the Resource CD-ROM is a set of PowerPoint slides you can display on-screen within Windows or use as overhead transparency masters. These slides include summaries of important points, explanations of concepts, and support for discussion of significant interface features such as toolbars or dialog boxes. Show these overheads as you teach each project and refer to them occasionally to vary the class.

You may want to create your own visuals to add to the class. Visuals can include posters, documents, overheads, slides, or any other props to help you get the point across.

Setting up the Training Room

When teaching adults, enable and encourage them to "look at each other's work" for extra support, confirmation, and peer learning.

The way your classroom is configured can have an impact on the learning process.

Each workstation must have Excel 97 loaded on it, or available on a network. We highly recommend one student per PC, but have successfully taught the class with two per PC, when necessary. Make sure that the computers are grouped together so that you can easily move from one to another for individualized help during training, and so that each student can view at least one other student on his/her computer. When teaching adults, enable and encourage them to "look at each other's work" for extra support, confirmation, and peer learning.

The grouping of computers should face the same direction, toward any screen or board you might use to demonstrate or present visuals. Make sure that the distance from overhead screens, for example, is right for comfortable viewing. Make certain that the room is comfortable as far as temperature and lighting are concerned. All these issues make for a successful training session.

You will need to install the student data files on the server (or on each student's PC if the training room is not networked), create subdirectories on the server (or local hard drive) for each workstation, and then put a set of sample files in each subdirectory for each student. Check each computer to make sure that the program works and the files are where you say they will be.

Because each student has access to the PC, there is a constant problem of each PC looking different at the end of the class. You will need to reset each system for the same consistent look and feel to prepare to teach a new class. We strongly recommend that you do not teach classes without resetting the screens at the beginning of each class. Doing so will reduce any student confusion about screens that may not match.

Training Resources

Even with excellent courseware and a thorough *Annotated Instructor's Edition*, you must have basic teaching ability to succeed as a computer instructor. Many people have a deep-seated fear of public speaking; you can overcome this fear only with practice. The more comfortable you are in front of an audience, the better you will be perceived by your students, and the more receptive they will be to learning. It is beyond the scope of this book to teach you the art of teaching or of public speaking. You might want to turn to the following resources if you are new to the teaching profession or want to improve your existing skills (much of the following list was downloaded from the CompuServe DPTRAIN forum):

Preparation for Teaching Your Course

- ***The Complete Computer Trainer.*** Clothier, Paul. McGraw-Hill, New York, NY. One of the outstanding authors of Que E&T's *The Computer Trainer's Personal Training Guide,* Paul Clothier helps veteran and novice instructors alike develop the interpersonal skills needed to be a successful computer instructor.

- ***The Complete Guide to Certification for Computing Professionals.*** Drake Prometric. McGraw-Hill, New York, NY. This comprehensive reference describes what certification is and isn't, and gives you full details on more than 25 certification programs nationwide.

- ***The Computer Trainer's Personal Training Guide.*** Brandon, Bill, et al. Macmillan Computer Publishing, 201 W. 103rd Street, Indianapolis, IN 46290 (1-800-428-5331). Cutting-edge training advice on traditional as well as "hot" topics from a team of experts.

- ***The Computer Training Handbook.*** The MASIE Center, P.O. Box 397, Saratoga Springs, NY 12866-0397 (1-800-98-MASIE or 518-587-3522). You can reach the MASIE Center on the World Wide Web at **http://www.masie.com**. Advice from a training visionary and the founder of the Computer Training & Support Conference.

- ***Games Trainers Play/More Games Trainers Play/Still More Games Trainers Play.*** Scannell, Ed. McGraw-Hill, New York, NY. This series contains icebreakers and other exercises.

- ***Instructional Design Strategies and Tactics.*** Leshin, Cynthia; Pollock, Joellyn; and Reigeluth, Charles. Educational Technology Publications, 700 Palisade Avenue, Englewood Cliffs, NJ 07632. A good primer on the basics of instructional design.

- ***The Internet Trainer's Guide.*** Kovacs, Diane K. Van Nostrand Reinhold Computer, New York, NY. From creating course outlines and conducting presentations to teaching methods and evaluation procedures, this book covers everything readers need to design Internet courses (including seminars, lectures, and hands-on labs).

- ***The Mager Six-Pack***, a collection of basic books by Robert Mager, et al. You can purchase the following books individually or collectively from Lake Publishing Company, 500 Harbor Blvd., Belmont, CA 94002.

    Making Instruction Work: Planning, developing, teaching, and improving.

    Analyzing Performance Problems (with Peter Pipe): To train or not to train.

    Preparing Instructional Objectives: Mager's best-known work.

    Measuring Instructional Results: Criterion testing.

    Developing Attitudes Toward Learning: Motivating students.

    Goal Analysis: Why, when, and how to conduct educational goal analysis.

- ***101 Ways to Improve the Quality of Training.*** The MASIE Center, P.O. Box 397, Saratoga Springs, NY 12866-0397 (1-800-98-MASIE or 518-587-3522). You can reach the MASIE Center on the World Wide Web at **http://www.masie.com**. More advice from a training visionary and the founder of the Computer Training & Support Conference.

Preparing Class Materials

Typically, a class will be set up with students having their own courseware book and their own PC. You'll find it helpful also to have name tags for them to put on top of the monitors.

You may want to review any of the additional exercises and Speedy Class tips in the *Instructor's Manual*, and then add some exercises of your own.

Consider preparing your own visual aids in addition to the slides and transparency masters included with the AIE.

If you need additional equipment, such as an overhead projector, flip chart, or chalkboard, make sure that it is in the room before class and working. Before each class, review discussion questions and other materials so that the subject is fresh in your mind. Gather your materials and organize them so that you can quickly find overheads, reference notes, or any other supplementary items while you teach.

Develop and give your own presentation that introduces the class and instructor, and gives the basic agenda for the day. Pop in and out of it during the day as you introduce each project. Build some of the features that the class uses into your presentation.

You need to keep in mind the hardware that the presentation will be running on.

Opening the Class

At the beginning of class, introduce yourself, and list some of your credentials and background. Even if you work with the students or know them personally, you should take a few minutes to give them some of your qualifications. You could mention other classes you teach and any other information pertinent to this class. Keep this introduction short but informative.

How will Excel 97 make their work easier, faster, and more efficient? How will mastery of Excel 97 enable them to succeed professionally and academically? Tie the application to the student's situation as much as possible. The AIE offers some "kickoff" questions ("On Your Mark") at the beginning of each project to encourage the student to make these associations.

Now you're ready to begin your class.

Closing the Class

You can come full circle with the opening class discussion by asking the students how they see themselves using their new skills on the job.

At the end of each class, ask questions to make sure that the students have understood the key topics covered. The AIE includes "Q&A" sections at the end of each project. You can also add your own questions and comments. You can come full circle with the opening class discussion by asking the students how they see themselves using their new skills on the job. You should also give students an evaluation form to fill out before leaving the classroom. A sample form is included in this manual.

Resource CD-ROM

A Resource CD-ROM has been included with your *Annotated Instructor's Edition*. This CD-ROM contains data files (Proj files) that are intended to be used by students as they work through the text. Also included on the CD are the solution files, which show the end result of students' work on the Proj files. In addition, there is a PowerPoint presentation, which can also be printed and used as handouts. The CD also includes additional teaching tips and test questions and answers.

Preparing Class Materials

The CD-ROM is set up with the following directories:

- SOLUTION FILES:, which contains the solution files that show how a student's file should look at the end of a tutorial. These files are named with the logical name the student was asked to assign at the beginning of a tutorial. Solution files are also provided for the "Applying Your Skills" exercises at the end of each tutorial.

- POWERPOINT SLIDES These slides include project objectives, concepts, and other information to augment your instruction.

- STUDENT DATA FILES, which contains the data files your students will use to complete the tutorials in the textbook and the "Applying Your Skills" exercises provided at the end of each textbook project. The file names correspond to the file names called for in the textbook, such as PROJ0101, PROJ0102, and so on.

- INSTRUCTOR MANUAL, which includes additional teaching tips, along with test questions and answers.

The Successful Instructor's Checklist

- ☐ **Get organized.** Gather all the materials on the subject, organize them, and know where to find the answers to difficult questions.

- You should be able either to find the answer to a question or problem, or know where the student can go to find the answer. Reference materials, on-line Help, and the assistance of other experts in the field are invaluable.

- ☐ **Do some research.** Do your research well before your class so that you feel prepared.

- ☐ **Practice.** Try explaining things in a different way, trying various comparisons or correlations.

- ☐ **Prepare your classroom.** Hook your projection system up to the instructor's computer. Set up the classroom so the computers face your projection area. Make sure that the distance from overhead screens, for example, is right for comfortable viewing.

- If you don't have access to a projection system, plan on doing a lot of roaming around the training room and examining screens.

- Make sure additional equipment, such as an overhead projector, flip chart, or chalkboard, is in the room before class.

- ☐ **Test the equipment.** Make sure the above mentioned equipment is in working condition.

- ☐ **Conduct dry runs.** We highly recommend several dry runs with no audience so that you can become familiar with the equipment.

- ☐ **Create your own supplements.** You may want to create your own visuals to add to the class. Visuals can include posters, documents, overheads, slides, or any other props to help you get the point across.

- ☐ **Prepare the equipment.** Do not wait until the last minute to install software and check the equipment.

- Load Excel on each workstation. Make sure each application works.

- Install the Resource Disk sample files on the server (or on each student's PC if the training room is not networked).
- Create subdirectories on the server (or local hard drive) for each workstation.
- Put a set of sample files in each subdirectory for each student.
- Check each computer to make sure that the program works and the files are where you say they will be.
- Reset each system for the same consistent look and feel to prepare to teach a new class.
    - ☐ **Get ready for the class.** Having your classroom ready for students involves more than having equipment up to speed. The more comfortable your students are the more they will be prepared to learn. Anticipate their needs so that you aren't scrambling for pens and paper during valuable class time.
- Make certain that the room is comfortable as far as temperature and lighting are concerned.
    - ☐ **Refresh your memory.** Don't wait until it's too late to make one last run through.
- Review discussion questions and other materials so that the subject is fresh in your mind.
- Gather your materials and organize them so that you can quickly find overheads, reference notes, or any other supplementary items while you teach.

Day-of-Course Checklist

☐ At the beginning of class, introduce yourself, and list some of your credentials and background.

☐ Refer often to and be familiar with the Annotated Workbook as you facilitate Discovery-Based Training.

Curriculum Guide

The Curriculum Guide will enable you to give your class the best information in the amount of time available. Whether you are conducting an abbreviated class or using all the lessons, you won't have to walk out of the class kicking yourself for skipping an important component. We've clearly noted which projects and exercises are core units. You'll also be able to quickly see which projects are good to know, but not absolutely vital.

Excel 97 Essentials I Time Chart

Chapter	One Day of Instruction*	Twelve Hours of Instruction	Twenty-Five Hours of Instruction
1	Lessons 1-9	Lessons 1-9; Applying Your Skills 1-2	Lessons 1-9; all activities
2	Lessons 1-7	Lessons 1-7; Applying Your Skills 1,5	Lessons 1-7; all activities
3	Lessons 1-4	Lessons 1-5; Applying Your Skills 1	Lessons 1-4; all activities
4	Lessons 1-3	Lessons 1-5;	Lessons 1-7; all activities
5	Lessons 1-4, 8	Lessons 1-4, 8; Applying Your Skills 1,3,5	Lessons 1-8; all activities
6	Lessons 1, 5-6	Lessons 1-6;	Lessons 1-6; all activities
7	Lessons 1-3	Lessons 1-5	Lessons 1-5; all activities
8	Lessons 1-4	Lessons 1-5;	Lessons 1-5; all activities

Note: In the shorter sessions, it is advisable to omit topics rather than to rush through more topics than students can possibly comprehend. The primary objective of the shorter sessions should be to acquaint students to Excel 97 concepts, terminology, and elementary worksheets.1

Training Tips, Tricks, & Techniques

Even a seasoned pro can benefit from the experience of others. The following section was condensed from The Computer Trainer's Personal Training Guide written by Bill Brandon and a host of training experts. In this section, you'll hear practical advice about a variety of topics.

- Identifying student expectations
- Establishing a comfortable pace for the students
- Using body language to your advantage
- Making the learning process enjoyable
- Making differences in skill sets work
- Dealing with objections
- Avoiding disaster: When (not if) equipment fails

Identifying Student Expectations (Why Are They Here?)

It is critically important for you to ask the students what they expect to gain from the course. The easiest, most natural time to do this is at the beginning of the first class session.

When you ask students what they expect to gain, there are several ways to have the students answer:

- Each student calls out his or her expectations and objectives.
- Students take two minutes to list their expectations and objectives individually, then combine lists with their immediate neighbor, and finally combine the list of that pair with the list of another pair of students. A spokesperson for the group then reads the list out loud.
- Each student writes down on a small piece of paper one thing he or she hopes to learn in the class and crumbles it into a small ball. On a signal, each student tosses his or her paper across the room to another student (this can be done several times to get good mixing). After everyone has somebody else's objective, the items are read off the notes one at a time.

The last two methods generate much more activity than the first. They model the level of participation desired and generate a sense of fun and cooperation. The third method has the added benefit of protecting group members who may be shy about saying what they think is important. On the other hand, the first method is good to use when the group is comfortable together or already has a good sense of play and team spirit.

In each case, the instructor (or an assistant selected from the group) should record the expectations on a large piece of newsprint or a flipchart at the front of the room. When the list is complete, tear it off and tape it to the wall so that it remains visible throughout the class.

Give Students Control over the Pace

There is no reason why the instructor should feel solely responsible for regulating the flow of the class.

During a class, it is often hard for the instructor to judge whether people are satisfied with the pace of the class.

One interesting way to give control of the pace to the students is to hand out small paper ballots just before a break. On each ballot, students mark whether they feel the class is moving too slowly, too quickly, or about right. Collect these in a small receptacle at the door. Tally them on the marker board or on the newsprint pad so that students can see the results of the vote. Adjust your pace accordingly.

If you are lucky enough to be working in a classroom equipped with responder units, you can do the same thing without having to wait for a break. (In fact, you can use the responder units to ask whether students want to take a break.) A responder unit is a small box at the student's station that provides a variety of buttons for responding to true/false and multiple-choice questions. The results of the responses to a question are automatically tallied and displayed to the instructor on a separate monitor. Similar systems are sometimes used in distance-learning classrooms to give feedback to instructors who may be located miles away from their students.

Body Language

Proper body language can not only help the class understand the message you are conveying, it can help you stay in control and appear confident—even when you aren't!

Have you ever looked out in a class only to find a sea of blank faces? Have you ever wondered why the students aren't with you? Sometimes how you say something is as important as what you say.

- When you stand, keep your feet about shoulder-width apart, one foot slightly toward the students to whom you are speaking.
- Turn your whole head to look at students as you speak to them, not just your eyes.
- Use your hands to gesture and emphasize points; keep your elbows loose, not tucked into your ribs. Relax your shoulders and make your hand movements large and free.
- Move into the group of students as much as possible, rather than staying up behind a lectern or your own terminal.
- If you are using overhead slides or projected images, say a few words related to what is on the next image before you display it.
- Choose short words, action verbs, and active voice when you talk.

Educational Entertaining

An appropriate amount of fun helps people learn without making them consciously aware of the fact that they are learning.

There is a fine line between being entertaining and being entertainment. You cross that line only when the students cease to be involved as active participants in the learning process. If you had the video camera running when the line was crossed, you would see students' behavior go from "using the software" to "watching the instructor" and stay there.

So how does an instructor stay entertaining, yet keep the focus and the activity out among the students?

Do the expected in unexpected ways. For example, if you need to "borrow" somebody from the class for a demonstration or to lead a group, ask for a volunteer. Say only that you need this person to do a very important job. Eventually someone will volunteer. Then tell this person that his or her important job is to pick the actual person who will be involved in the demonstration or lead the group. This is a very safe way to get a big laugh—much better than using a joke. It may also help you manage the person who would like to be the "teacher's pet" (you know—the one who always has his hand up first to answer a question).

Do things in a way that requires people to move around. When you review a step-by-step procedure, use a Koosh ball. Toss the ball to one of the students. This person must give the first step in the procedure and then toss the ball to another student. The second person gives the second step and throws the ball to someone who hasn't given a step yet. If someone misses a step, anyone who knows what comes next calls it out and gets the ball to pass on. This continues until the procedure is complete. Not only does this wake everyone up, it gets the know-it-alls to stop playing solitaire.

Periodically award "fabulous prizes." (Award prizes such as coffee mugs, mouse pads, imprinted ball-point pens, whatever for correct responses or performances. You should have a group that is fairly evenly matched if you plan to use this approach fairly.

The key word is appropriate. Should your classroom look like a three-ring circus? Absolutely not. Should people be smiling and looking as if they are having a great experience? Absolutely yes!

Put Differences in Skill Sets to Work

Use the fact that there is a mixture of skill levels in the room to increase the level of participation by students.

Most courseware is created with the assumption that everyone is at the same level. However, it is far more often the case that the group's skill levels are mixed. A strategy that works well is to deliberately place two people at one computer during the exercises that follow demonstration of a procedure. An effective way to do the pairing is to use a totally arbitrary personal characteristic. For example, individuals can only partner with someone who was born in the same season of the year or on the same day of the week as themselves.

It is neither necessary nor desirable to pair people up according to ability.

While paired up for an exercise, each partner must complete the exercise, with coaching as necessary from his or her "buddy." Questions may be asked of the instructor, but both partners must each raise a hand, indicating that collectively they could not solve the problem. Change partners after each exercise.

Dealing with Objections from Students

Even in a well-planned, well-run course, everybody won't always be totally satisfied. In some classes, you will have a student who seems to have some problem with everything you are teaching. In other sessions, all is well until—bang! You get blindsided by a protest from a student.

What's important isn't that you got an objection, it's how you handle it.

This happens to every instructor. For any objection or question from a student, you have more than one way to respond so that everybody wins. The choice is yours.

Meet the Objection. The most basic, and perhaps natural, response is to meet the objection head on. Stick to your story and explain how your idea works. Sometimes this is effective. Sometimes it just starts a fight, makes you look defensive, and alienates class members.

If you decide to use the head-on response, consider using Ben Franklin's method: "It seems to me..." or "In my opinion..." helps to soften the response. It's better if you turn to face the other person squarely when you do this, but don't take a step toward or away from the person. Stepping toward the person can seem aggressive. Stepping back weakens your point.

Consider using the word and in your reply instead of but. For example, saying, "I understand how it might seem that way to you and I believe you are overlooking..." keeps the other person listening to you and seems much less harsh than, "I understand what you're saying but you haven't considered..." By using "It seems to me..." or substituting "and" for "but," everybody wins.

Accept the Objection. Another basic response is to back off your point. Let the objector have it his or her way. If you realize that you were wrong, say so. The positive side of this choice is that you can come off looking better in the long run. The down side is that it may invite further attacks or undermine your credibility. Face the person squarely when you back off the point. If the other person is emotional about the objection, take a step back as you say, "You know, you're right." Then drop it and move on. Everybody wins.

Deflect the Objection. A third response is good to use when someone has made an objection you'd either like to check out or to discredit totally. Throw out a related question "overhead" to the group: "Has anyone else had an experience like this?" Take note of the answers and respond accordingly. If the question is discounted by the group, face the objector and say, "I'd like to understand the problem better. Are you willing to meet me on the break about this?" In most cases, this will be the last you'll hear about it, and you have helped the person save face. Everybody wins.

Defer the Objection. The fourth response is reserved for those times when you want to deal with the objection later. Perhaps someone brings up a point that you plan to address in another part of the program. Perhaps someone raises an objection that has an "agenda" attached. Smile, say you think that's a great question but you want to deal with it a little later in the course, and then write the objection on a piece of newsprint and hang it on the wall. You have acknowledged the point. You can get back to it when (and if) you want to. You are being fair and the objector has had his or her say. Everybody wins.

Avoiding Disaster: When (Not If) Equipment Fails

In most classrooms, the weak link is the hardware. After that, the weakest link is the software on the instructor's system.

Were Ben Franklin alive today, he would have to amend his famous saying about death and taxes. "Hardware failure" is now the third certain thing in life.

In most classrooms, the weak link is the hardware. After that, the weakest link is the software on the instructor's system. As you plan your classes, keep this in mind. It is wise to have a Plan B for any eventuality.

The most commonly needed Plan B has to do with projector bulbs. If you are using an overhead projector or an LCD projector, have a spare bulb in the classroom where you can get to it quickly. Know how to replace the bulb. Remember to turn off the power to the projector before you make the replacement.

The most serious Plan B is the one that deals with the classroom network shutting down during the class. This is a Plan B you must think through carefully before every class. Will you cancel the course? Will you bring in a freestanding PC and a big monitor and continue to demonstrate until the system is restored? Will you shift to alternative media (a videotape or overheads)? You have plenty of choices, but they must be in place before disaster strikes.

Project 1

Getting Started with Excel

Creating a List of Office Expenses

In this project, you learn how to:
- Start Excel
- Use the Excel Window
- Get Help
- Move around a Worksheet
- Enter Data
- Save a Worksheet
- Prepare for Printing
- Print a Worksheet
- Close a File and Exit Excel

On Your Mark ✓

What are the advantages of using a spreadsheet program rather than a calculator, pencil, and paper?

Data
The information that you work with in a spreadsheet, including text, numbers, and graphic images.

Workbook
An Excel file that contains one or more worksheets.

Worksheet
One page of your work in an Excel workbook.

Default
The settings a program uses unless you specify another setting. For example, in an Excel 97 worksheet, the default column width is 8.43 characters. Generally, you can change a default setting.

Why Would I Do This?

Computer spreadsheet software is the application software that started the personal computer revolution. That's because electronic spreadsheets, such as Microsoft Excel, are versatile tools for both personal and business use. As you work through the projects in this book, you will find that spreadsheet technology enables you to calculate and display your business applications easily and flexibly. Spreadsheets, as you will see, aid your thought processes and save you time.

Basically, spreadsheet software turns your computer into a business analysis tool. Many people compare spreadsheets to pocket calculators, but spreadsheets, such as Excel, have capabilities that are many times more powerful than even the most high-tech calculator. At the most basic level, Excel enables you to decide what *data* you want to see and how it is to be displayed—a capability no pocket calculator can duplicate. You will explore these features of Excel first.

In this project, you begin to learn how spreadsheets work and what you can do with them by starting the software and taking a tour of the Microsoft Excel 97 screen. You also get a taste of how spreadsheets can help you by creating a list of office expenses. After you create the list, you learn how to save your work, prepare the list for printing, and, finally, print it.

Lesson 1: Starting Excel

The first thing you need to know about Excel is how to start the software. Windows 95 must be running on your computer before you can start Excel. If you are not familiar with Windows 95 or using the mouse, ask your instructor for assistance.

When you first start Excel 97, the program displays a blank *workbook* titled `Book1`, which displays a blank *worksheet*, titled `Sheet1`. In Project 2, "Building a Spreadsheet," you learn to create a new worksheet and work on an existing worksheet. In this lesson, you use the blank *default* worksheet supplied by Excel.

To Start Excel

Tip for Instructors
Remind students that their screens may look different from the classroom screen due to screen resolution, software configuration, and so on.

❶ Turn on your computer and monitor.

If Windows 95 is installed on your computer, the computer should automatically start Windows 95, and the Windows desktop should appear on your screen, as shown in Figure 1.1. (Your screen may appear slightly different, depending on how Windows is set up on your computer.) When you see the Windows desktop, you are ready to start Excel.

**Project Time
75 minutes**

Lesson 1: Starting Excel

> **Tip for Instructors**
> Some students may use Excel as part of the Office suite rather than as a stand-alone program. Remind students that they can access Excel from Microsoft Office by clicking the Excel icon in the Office shortcut bar.

❷ **Click the Start button on the taskbar (see Figure 1.1).**

The Start menu opens on the desktop (see Figure 1.2). From the Start menu, you can start programs and open documents, get help, find files or folders, change settings, and shut down Windows 95. For more information on using the Start menu or the taskbar, ask your instructor.

Figure 1.1
The Windows 95 desktop.

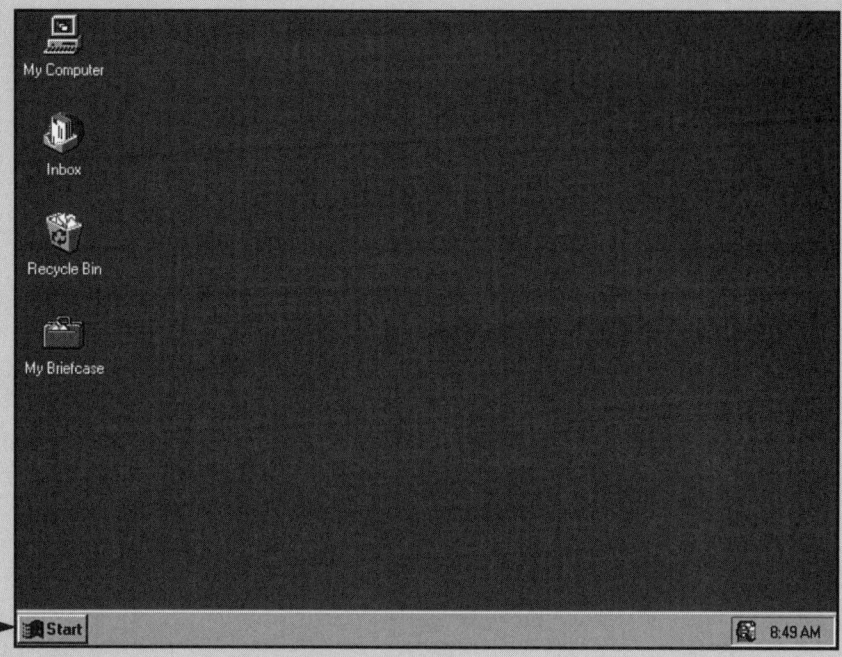

Start button

Figure 1.2
When you move the mouse pointer to the **P**rograms item on the Start menu, a submenu of installed programs appears.

The Start menu
Point here to see a list of programs
Click here to start Excel

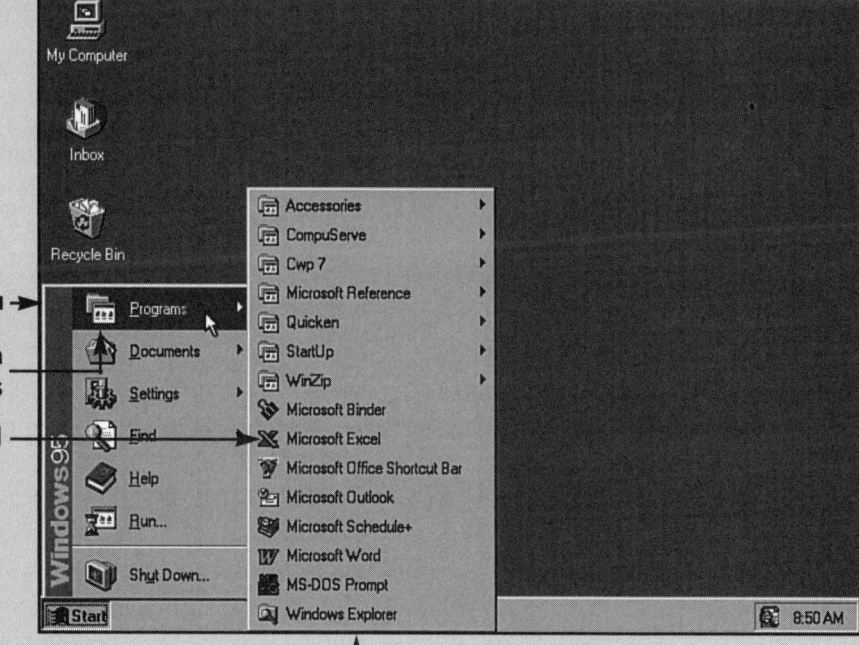

The Programs submenu

> **Tip for Students**
> Recently used documents are listed on the Documents option of the Start menu of Windows 95. If the Excel document that you want to use is listed here, then clicking its name will start Excel and open that document.

continues

To Start Excel (continued)

3 **Move the mouse pointer to the Programs item at the top of the Start menu.**

A *submenu*, listing the programs installed on your computer, appears on the desktop to the right of the Start menu, as shown in Figure 1.2.

Submenu
A list of options that appears when you point at some menu items in Windows 95 and in applications designed for use with Windows 95. A small, right-pointing arrowhead appears to the right of menu items that have submenus.

If you have problems...

Because you can customize Windows 95, your desktop may look different from the one shown in the illustrations in this book. Your **P**rograms submenu may be different than that illustrated in this book, depending on the programs that are installed on your computer. For example, you may have to point at the Microsoft Office item on the **P**rograms submenu to display another submenu from which you can select Microsoft Excel.

Concept Note
A spreadsheet is made up of rows and columns. The intersection of a row and a column is a cell, and each cell has a unique name made up of the column letter and the row number. Besides working with numbers and formulas, spreadsheets can be used to create columns of text, such as inventory catalogs or employee lists.

4 **Choose Microsoft Excel from the Programs submenu.**

Excel starts, and the Excel screen appears with the default workbook and worksheet displayed, as shown in Figure 1.3. Now you can begin using Excel.

Keep this worksheet open to use in the next lesson.

Figure 1.3
The Excel default workbook and worksheet.

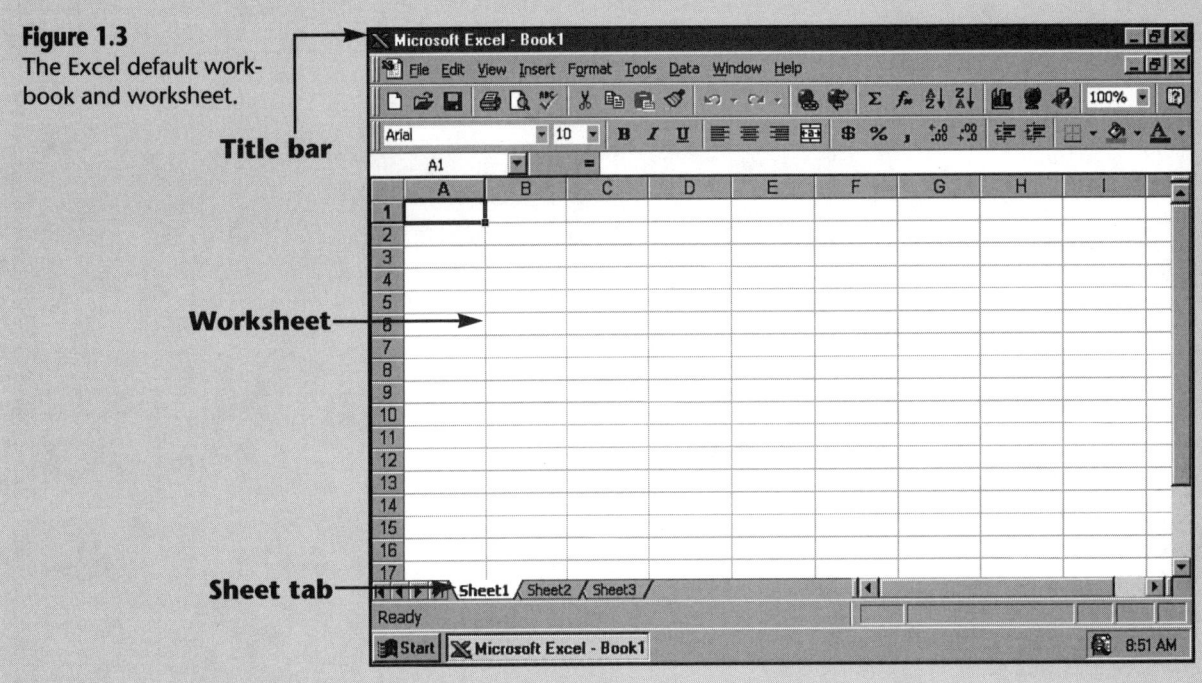

Lesson 2: Using the Excel Window

 If a Microsoft Excel icon appears on the Windows desktop, you can double-click it to start Excel. If you have the Microsoft Office suite of applications installed, you may have an Office toolbar in the upper right-hand corner of your screen. If the Office toolbar appears, you can click the Microsoft Excel button to start Excel.

The very first time you start Excel 97, the Office Assistant may appear in the upper right-hand corner of your screen. The Office Assistant is an animated graphics image included with Microsoft Office 97. (By default, it assumes the appearance of a paper clip called Clippit.)

The Office Assistant is designed to help you learn how to use the Microsoft Office applications quickly and easily. If the Office Assistant appears when you start Excel 97, simply click the button next to the statement, `Begin working in Excel 97 right away`. The Office Assistant will close, and you can continue using Excel. You learn more about using the Office Assistant in Lesson 3 of this project.

Lesson 2: Using the Excel Window

On Your Mark

Why is it important to know all the elements of a computer program that are displayed on-screen?

Now that Excel 97 is running on your computer, it's time to learn about the Excel window. You may recognize some of the elements from other Windows programs, such as the Minimize and Maximize buttons, the Control menu icon, scroll bars, the title bar, the menu bar, and so on. Other elements of the window are features of Excel that will help you complete your work quickly and efficiently. The formula bar, sheet tabs, and toolbars are convenient tools that you will use in most of the projects throughout this book.

To get to know the elements of the Excel window, take a look at Figure 1.4.

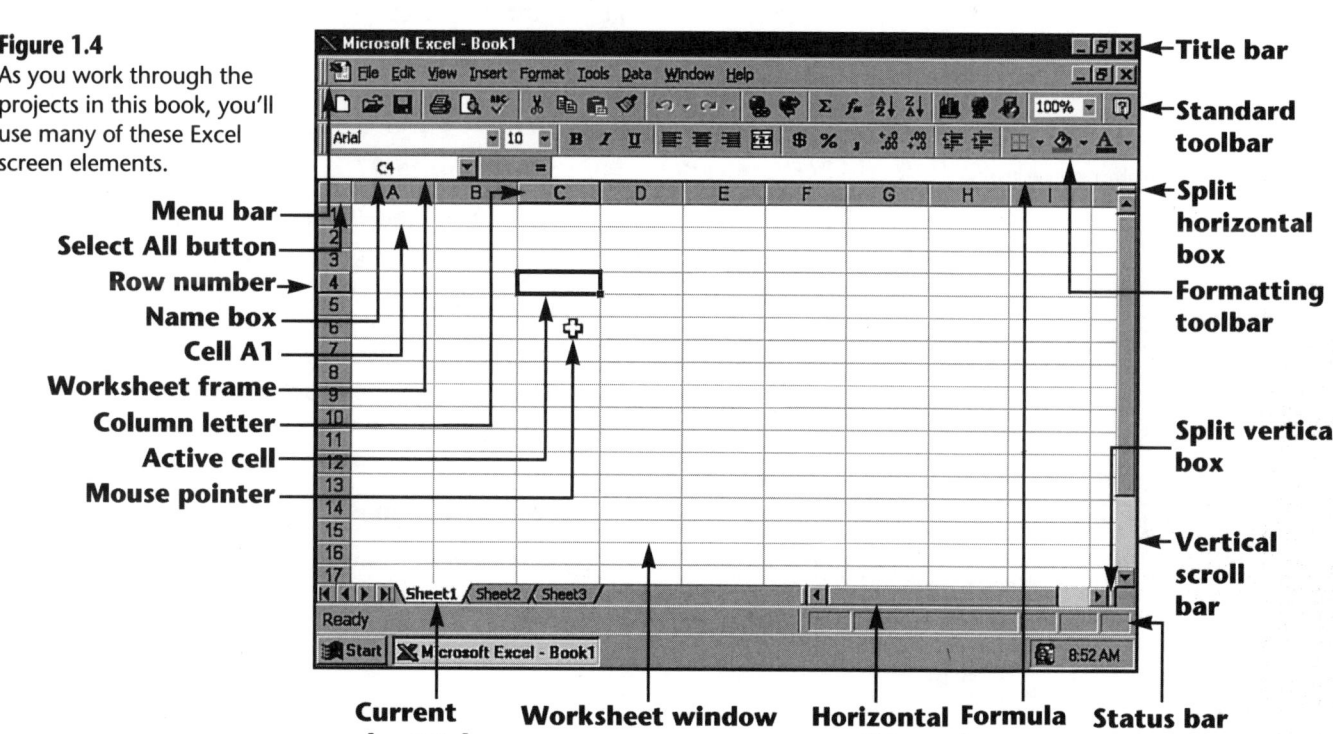

Figure 1.4
As you work through the projects in this book, you'll use many of these Excel screen elements.

In the following exercise, you practice finding your way around the Excel screen on your computer. (If you need help, refer to Figure 1.4.)

To Use the Excel Window

> **Tip for Instructors**
>
> Rather than pointing out each area of the Excel screen, consider asking students to name the various parts of the screen and see how many items they can identify.

> **Tip for Students**
>
> What happens if a menu is displayed and you press [Esc] only once? You can't regain use of your keyboard until you press [Esc] again. Check whether Ready is displayed on the Status bar: It tells you when you're able to perform your next Excel task.

> **Quicksand**
>
> Make students aware of the different mouse pointer shapes and operations for these shapes. Students often move cell contents by mistake and do not realize what they have done. They also may attempt to select cells and use the fill handle by mistake, resulting in a copy operation.

> **Quicksand**
>
> If students click the mouse while on the Formula bar, they will be in Edit mode. The insertion bar (I-beam) appears on the Formula bar, ready for them to type. If this happens, they should press [Esc], or click the worksheet to leave Edit mode.

❶ Using the mouse, click File on the menu bar.

This opens the File menu. Notice that Excel menus appear the same as menus in any Windows program. In Excel, you can open menus and choose commands to perform actions. You can cancel a menu by clicking the menu name again, by clicking anywhere in the window outside of the menu, or by pressing [Esc]. Press [Esc] again to deactivate the menu bar.

❷ Click the word File again to cancel (close) the menu.

❸ Move the mouse pointer to the title bar.

The title bar contains the names of the program and the workbook, and other common Window 95 elements, such as the Maximize, Minimize, and Close buttons, and the Control menu icon.

❹ Move the mouse pointer to any cell of the worksheet, then click the left mouse button.

An outline appears around the *cell* to indicate that the cell is the *current* or *active* cell. The cell's *address*—such as A1 or B1—appears in the *name box* to let you know which cell is *selected*. The cell address refers to the row and column that intersect to form the cell. The selected cell is where any typing or new action takes place.

❺ Move the mouse pointer around the edges of the selected cell.

Notice that the mouse pointer changes from a white plus sign to an arrow when you are near the cell boundary. In later projects, you will see that as you perform different actions on the selected cell, the mouse pointer assumes different shapes.

❻ Click the column letter for column A.

The entire column becomes selected. Every cell in the column, except for the first (cell A1) is highlighted. You can select any column or row by clicking the column letter or row number in the worksheet frame. You select a column or row to perform an action—such as copying or deleting—on the information in the selected area. When you select more than one cell, such as a column or row, the entire *range* is highlighted, but the first cell is still the active cell; data that you type is entered into the active cell.

❼ Click cell B1 (the first cell in column B).

Cell B1 is now the active cell, and column A is no longer highlighted. To *deselect* cells, simply click outside the highlighted area.

Lesson 2: Using the Excel Window

8 Move the mouse pointer to the Bold button on the Formatting toolbar.

The fourth line of the Excel screen is the *Formatting toolbar. Buttons* on the toolbars are small pictures that represent actions you can perform—generally, the most common actions you perform are menu commands you choose when using Excel. If you click a button only once, you trigger the action that the button represents. Remember, you need only single-click the toolbar buttons, not double-click.

Leave Excel open on your computer. In the next lesson, you learn how to get help with common Excel features while you are working.

 To find out what any button does, position the mouse pointer over the button and leave it there for a moment. In a second or two, a ScreenTip appears that contains a description of that button.

If you have problems...

If the ScreenTips don't appear, you must enable them. Open the **V**iew menu and point at the **T**oolbars command to display the Toolbars submenu. Click **C**ustomize to open the Customize dialog box. In the dialog box, click the **O**ptions page tab, then click the **S**how ScreenTips on toolbars check box. Choose Close to clear the dialog box from the screen. The ScreenTips should now appear when you point at a toolbar button.

Jargon Watch

 **Key terms** *are defined for you throughout this book where they are first used. When a number of computer terms are introduced in the same lesson, you will see a Jargon Watch box like this one to help take some of the mystery out of the words.*

In this lesson, you have had to wade through a lot of computer jargon. Because you have just been introduced to a number of spreadsheet basics, Table 1.1 lists and describes all the screen elements that are shown in Figure 1.4, and defines all the key terms used in this lesson.

Table 1.1 Parts of the Microsoft Excel Screen

Element	Description
Active cell	The selected cell where the next action you take, such as typing or formatting, happens.
Address	Describes which column and row intersect to form the cell; for example, A1 is the address for the first cell in the first column (column A) and the first row (row 1).
Cell	The intersection of a column and a row.

continues

Table 1.1 Continued

Element	Description
Cell A1	The first or top-left cell of a worksheet.
Column heading	Lettered A through Z, then AA through AZ, and so on, through IV—up to 256 columns.
Formatting toolbar	Represents various shortcuts to the Format menu commands, such as Font, Bold, Italic, Underline, Alignment, Numeric display, and so on, in button form.
Formula bar	Displays the address and contents of the current or active cell.
Menu bar	Contains common menu names that, when activated, display a list of related commands; the Edit menu, for example, contains such commands as Cut, Copy, Paste, and Clear.
Mouse pointer	Selects items and positions the insertion point (cursor).
Name box	Displays the cell address of the current (selected) cell or a named range.
Range	Multiple adjacent cells
Row heading	Numbered 1 through 65,536.
Scroll bars	Enable you to move the worksheet window vertically and horizontally so that you can see other parts of the worksheet.
Sheet tab	Displays tabs representing each sheet in the workbook. Click a sheet tab to quickly move to that sheet.
Select All button	Selects all cells in the current worksheet.
Split horizontal box	Enables you to split the worksheet window horizontally to display two window panes of the same worksheet so that you can view two different areas at the same time.
Split vertical box	Enables you to split the worksheet window vertically to display two window panes of the same worksheet so that you can view two different areas at the same time.
Standard toolbar	Represents various shortcuts to menu commands, such as Open File, Save, Print, Cut, and so on, in button form.
Status bar	Contains information about options you have on or off, such as (Num Lock) and (Caps Lock).
Title bar	Displays the name of the software and the name of the active workbook—either a default name, such as Book1, or a saved file.
Workbook	An Excel file that contains one or more worksheets.
Worksheet frame	The row and column headings that appear along the top and left edge of the worksheet window.
Worksheet window	Contains the current worksheet—the work area.

Lesson 3: Getting Help

On Your Mark

Where do you turn for help when you have a question about a computer program? What are some of the resources available to you when you need assistance with your spreadsheet?

By now you have probably realized that you may run into problems as you work with your computer and Excel. If you find that you need a quick solution to a problem, you can use any one of Excel's help features. For example, you can use the Office Assistant to help you find the answer to a specific question or when you can't remember how to complete a task. You can use the Help Contents or Index to find additional information about any of Excel's features, or you can use the What's This? pointer to display a description of any feature on the screen.

In this lesson, you use the Office Assistant to learn more about getting help while working with Excel.

To Get Help

❶ Click Help on the menu bar.

The **H**elp menu displays a number of options that you can use to get help information.

❷ Choose the Microsoft Excel Help command.

The Office Assistant appears (refer to Figure 1.5). A balloon instructs you to `Type your question here` and then click Search. The balloon may also include a list of topics.

If you have problems...

Sometimes the Office Assistant opens offering a list of topics because it tries to figure out what you need help with before you actually ask. Don't worry if your Office Assistant opens looking different from the one in Figure 1.5—the steps work the same.

❸ Replace the text in the text box by typing `Get Help`, then click the Search button.

Office Assistant displays a new balloon listing related topics, as shown in Figure 1.5. You can select a topic, type a different question, display more topics, display tips or options, or close the Office Assistant without getting any help.

continues

10 Project 1 Getting Started with Excel

To Get Help (continued)

Figure 1.5
When you need help, you can ask the Office Assistant a specific question.

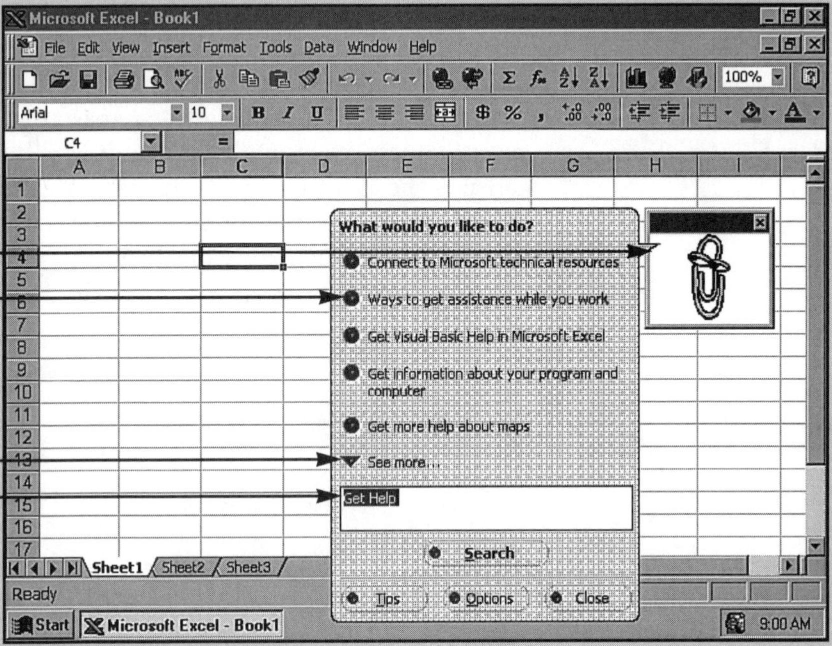

Office Assistant
Balloon
Click here to see additional related topics
Type a question or keyword here

If you have problems...

If the Office Assistant can't find topics related to the question you type, a balloon appears telling you so. Check to be sure you typed the question correctly, or try being more specific, then click **S**earch again.

❹ Click See more, then click the topic: Get Help, tips, and messages through the Office Assistant.

The Excel Help program starts, and a Help Topics window is displayed on your screen, as shown in Figure 1.6. This window provides information about the many ways you can use the Office Assistant.

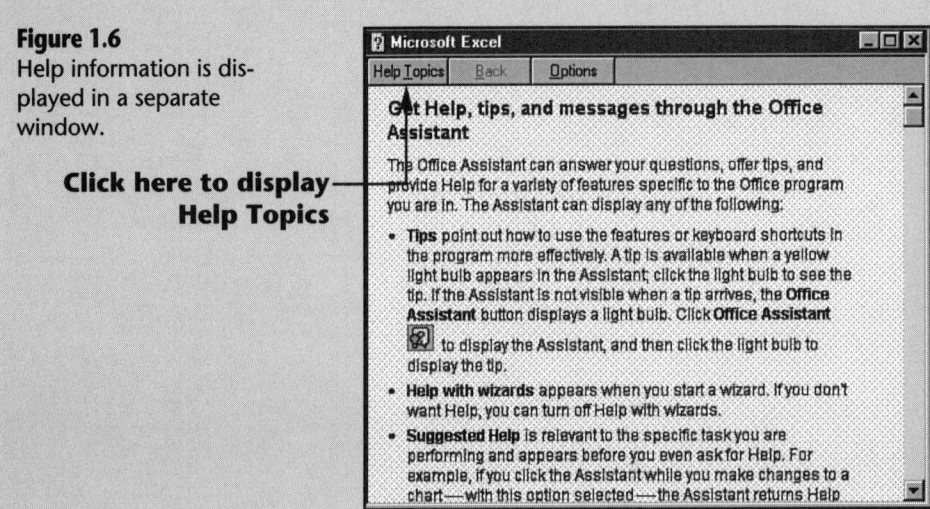

Figure 1.6
Help information is displayed in a separate window.

Click here to display Help Topics

Lesson 3: Getting Help

❺ Click the Help Topics button in the Help window.

The Excel Help Topics dialog box appears (see Figure 1.7). Here you can choose from three Help functions to find the information you need: Contents, which displays a list of general topics; Index, which displays a comprehensive, alphabetical list of all topics; and Find, which enables you to search through all topics for a word or phrase.

Figure 1.7
Excel offers many ways to access useful help information.

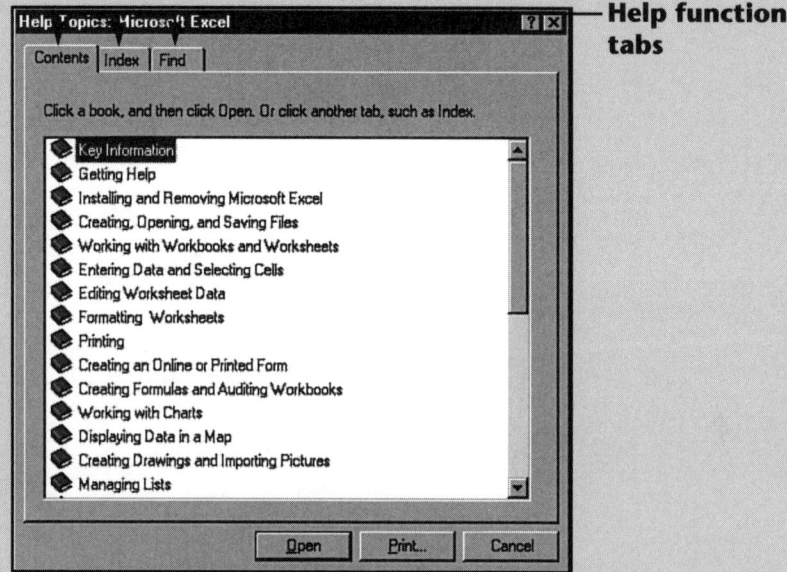

Help function tabs

❻ Click the Contents tab to make sure the Contents page is displayed.

Clicking the Contents tab ensures that the list of general help topics is displayed (refer to Figure 1.7). The help information in the Contents tab is similar to a book with chapters: you display the chapter and read the pages.

❼ In the list of topics, click Getting Help, then click the Open button.

This opens the topic Getting Help. Specific tasks related to getting help appear in the topic list, as shown in Figure 1.8.

continues

Project 1 Getting Started with Excel

To Get Help (continued)

Figure 1.8
You can click any topic for more information.

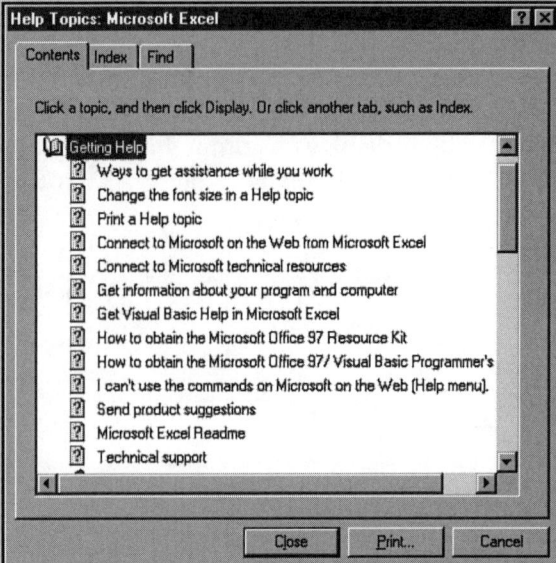

8 **Click the topic Ways to get assistance while you work, and then click the Display button.**

A Help screen appears, providing access to information about how to get assistance while you work in Excel (see Figure 1.9). Some help topics, like this one, provide at-a-glance information as well as labels that you can click for more information.

Figure 1.9
In some Help screens, you can click labels for additional information.

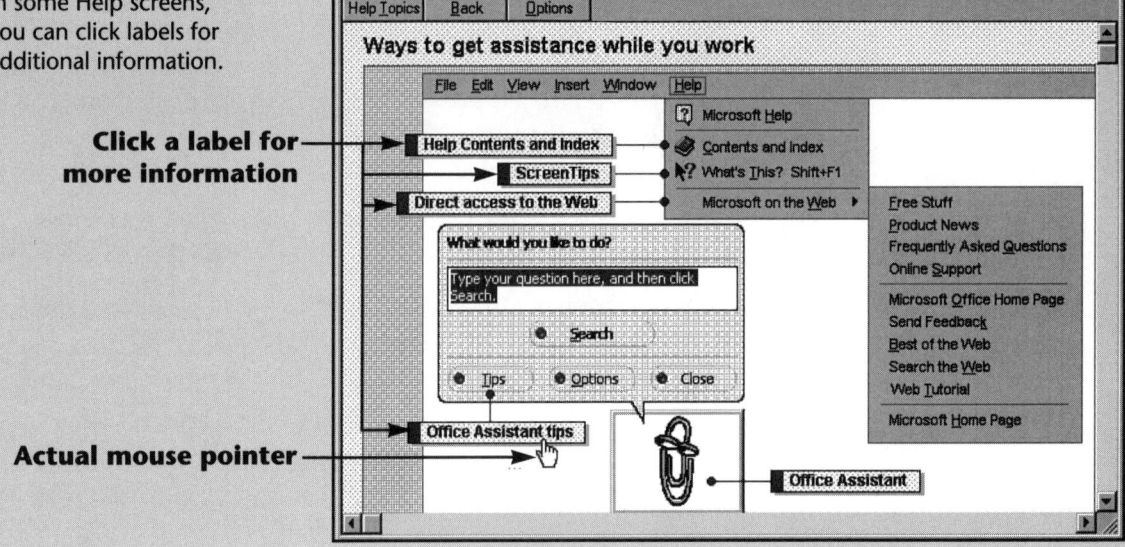

Lesson 3: Getting Help

Tip for Students
Press F1 or click the Office Assistant button at any time to display the Office Assistant.

9 Click the label Office Assistant tips.

A help box appears, providing information about how to use the Office Assistant while you work, as shown in Figure 1.10. Notice that when you move the mouse pointer to a label, the pointer becomes a hand with a pointing finger. This mouse pointer indicates that more information is available. Click any label on the Help screen to get information about using that feature.

Figure 1.10
Excel displays the specific information you require.

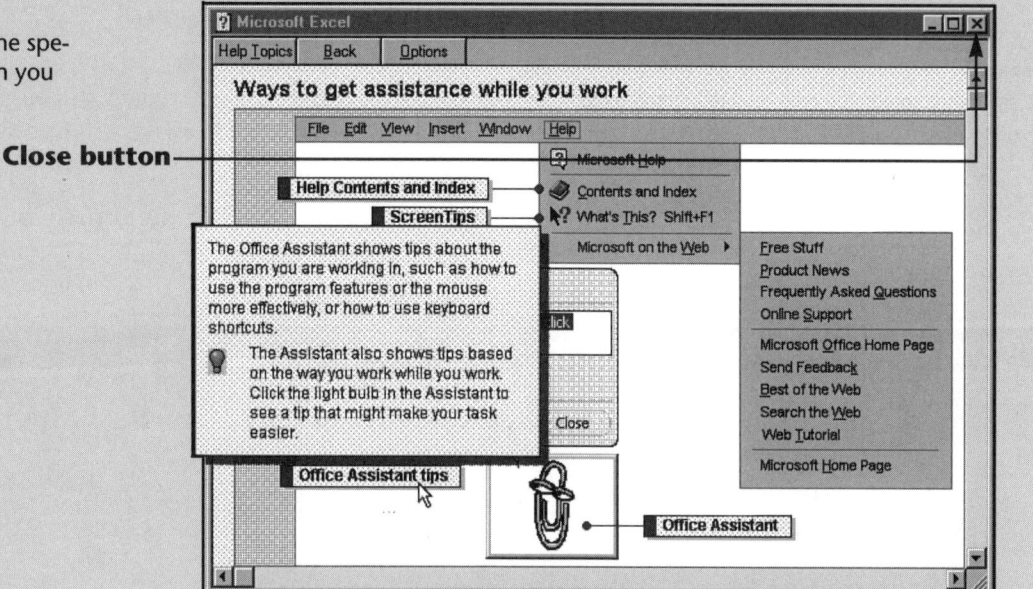

Close button

10 Click the Close button at the right end of the Help Topics window's title bar.

This closes Help and returns you to the worksheet. If necessary, click the Close button in the Office Assistant to clear it from the screen. You are now ready to continue learning about how to use an Excel worksheet.

To quickly open the Office Assistant, press F1 at any time or click the Office Assistant button on the Standard toolbar. If the Office Assistant icon is on the screen, simply click it to open the balloon where you can type a question.

To change the icon used to represent the Office Assistant, click the **O**ptions button in any Office Assistant balloon, choose the **G**allery tab, and click **N**ext to display a series of available icons. Select from The Dot, The Genius, Hoverbot, Mother Nature, Power Pup, Scribble (the cat), Office Logo, and Shakespeare, then click OK.

To quickly open the Help Topics dialog box, choose **H**elp, **C**ontents and Index. To print any Help Topics window, choose **O**ptions, **P**rint in the Help Topics window.

To use the What's **T**his? pointer to display a ScreenTip about anything on the screen, choose **H**elp, What's **T**his?, or press Shift+F1. When the pointer resembles a question mark with an arrow, point and click at the item for which you need information.

Project 1 Getting Started with Excel

Hypertext links
Text that, when you click, displays additional text.

In the Help program, keywords and phrases that appear highlighted in green and underlined are *hypertext links*. When you point at a hypertext link, the mouse pointer changes to a hand with a pointing finger. When you click on a hypertext link, Excel displays additional information.

Lesson 4: Moving around a Worksheet

✓ On Your Mark
Why is it important to be able to move around your worksheet, especially beyond the part of the screen that is visible?

To use Excel, you need to learn how to move from one part of a worksheet to another. You can move around a worksheet using either the keyboard or the mouse. You probably will use a combination of these two methods.

Format
To change the appearance of text or numbers.

When you move around the worksheet, you usually go to a specific cell. When you get to that cell, it becomes the active cell so you can enter or edit information, *format* information, or otherwise change the contents of the cell.

Now use the default worksheet on your screen to practice moving around Excel.

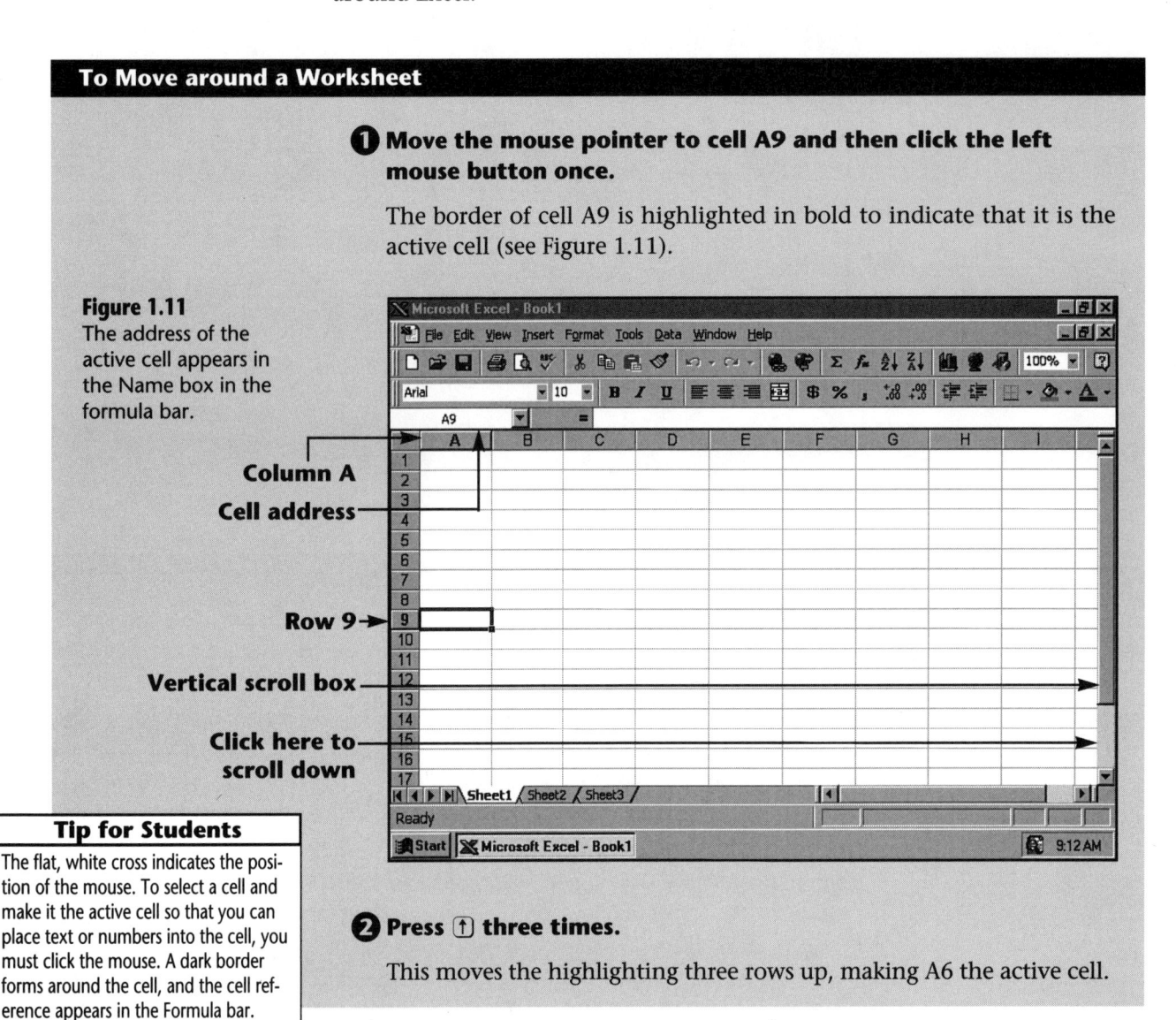

To Move around a Worksheet

❶ Move the mouse pointer to cell A9 and then click the left mouse button once.

The border of cell A9 is highlighted in bold to indicate that it is the active cell (see Figure 1.11).

Figure 1.11
The address of the active cell appears in the Name box in the formula bar.

Column A
Cell address
Row 9
Vertical scroll box
Click here to scroll down

Tip for Students
The flat, white cross indicates the position of the mouse. To select a cell and make it the active cell so that you can place text or numbers into the cell, you must click the mouse. A dark border forms around the cell, and the cell reference appears in the Formula bar.

❷ Press ↑ three times.

This moves the highlighting three rows up, making A6 the active cell.

Lesson 4: Moving around a Worksheet

3 **Press → three times.**

This moves the highlighting three columns to the right, making D6 the active cell.

4 **Use the mouse to click in the vertical scroll bar below the scroll box (refer to Figure 1.11).**

Your view of the worksheet changes so you can see rows that appear further down. Use the vertical scroll bar to move up and down in the worksheet; use the horizontal scroll bar to move left and right. No matter which view of the worksheet is displayed on-screen, if you begin typing before you click a new cell, the text you enter appears in the last active cell—in this case, cell D6.

5 **Click cell A19.**

Cell A19 becomes the active cell.

6 **Press Ctrl+G.**

The Go To dialog box appears, as shown in Figure 1.12. In the Go To dialog box, you can specify the exact cell that you want to make active. The key combination Ctrl+G means that you press and hold down Ctrl while you press G. This convention is used to show key combinations throughout this book.

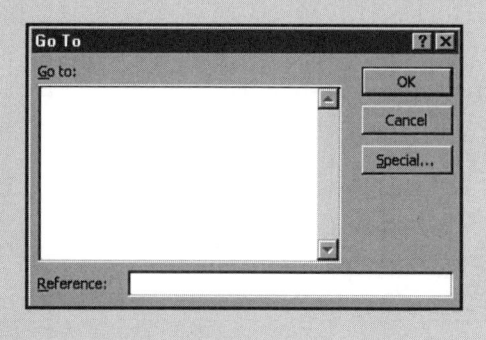

> **Tip for Instructors**
> The F5 function key invokes the Go To function. This is a universal use of the key, found in all the major spreadsheet programs, as well as in Word 97.

Figure 1.12
Use the Go To dialog box to make a specific cell active.

7 **In the Reference text box, type r12 and then press ↵Enter.**

The active cell is now R12.

8 **Press Ctrl+G again.**

The Go To dialog box appears. When you open the Go To dialog box again, the address of the last active cell appears in the **G**o to list box, with dollar signs ($) added before the row number and column letter. To go back to a cell that you had been working in, simply click it in the **G**o to list, then choose OK.

> **Tip for Students**
> You can always press ↵Enter in lieu of clicking OK to accept the dialog box information. Similarly, you can press Esc to close the dialog box without executing the Close command.

9 **In the Reference text box, type aa6 and choose OK.**

Cell AA6 becomes the active cell. As in other dialog boxes, you can also choose OK in the Go To dialog box to make the specified cell active.

continues

Project 1 Getting Started with Excel

> ### To Move around a Worksheet (continued)
>
> **⑩ Press** Ctrl+H.
>
> Your view of the worksheet changes, and A1—the first cell in the worksheet—becomes the active cell again.
>
> Keep this worksheet open for the next lesson, in which you begin entering data. Table 1.2 lists other keystrokes for moving around a worksheet.

Table 1.2	Moving around a Worksheet Using the Keyboard
Press	To Move
↑, ↓, ←, and →	One cell in the direction of the arrow (up, down, left, or right).
PgUp or PgDn	One screen up or down.
Home	To the first cell of the current row.
Ctrl+Home	To the first cell of the active worksheet: A1.
Ctrl+→	To the last or first cell in a range of contiguous cells—to the right—stopping at Column IV (256 columns).
Ctrl+←	To the first cell in a range of contiguous cells—to the left—stopping at Column A.
Ctrl+↑	To the first cell in a range of contiguous cells—to the top—stopping at Row 1.
Ctrl+↓	To the last cell in a range of contiguous cells—to the bottom—stopping at row 65,536—(the bottom row).
Ctrl+PgUp	To the preceding worksheet. You can also click the Sheet tab.
Ctrl+PgDn	To the following worksheet. You can also click the Sheet tab.

> **Tip for Instructors**
>
> Teach students how to use the scroll bar to accomplish the same moves that Table 1.2 demonstrates with the keyboard. Remind students that the cell pointer doesn't relocate when you use the scroll bar to view different parts of the worksheet.

> **Tip for Instructors**
>
> Discuss the use of End in combination with the arrow keys to move around the worksheet, in lieu of using the mouse and the scroll bars. (This works in Lotus 1-2-3 and Quattro Pro as well.)

> **Tip for Instructors**
>
> Remind former Lotus 1-2-3 and Quattro Pro users that in Excel, you must press Ctrl+Home to move to cell A1. (In Lotus 1-2-3 and Quattro Pro, you just press Home.)

> **Speedy Class**
>
> Use Alt+PgUp and Alt+PgDn to advance the worksheet display one screen right or left.

> **✓ On Your Mark**
>
> What are the three types of information that can be entered into a worksheet? *Answer:* values, text, and formulas.

Lesson 5: Entering Data

Now that you have had a chance to find your way around the Excel window, it's time to create your own worksheet. *Values*, *text*, and *formulas* are referred to as *data*, and can be entered in the cells of your worksheet. Each cell can hold up to 32,000 characters. In this lesson, you set up a simple worksheet to track office expenses. You also use a formula, one of the most powerful features of Excel, to find the total amount of the expenses.

Lesson 5: Entering Data

Jargon Watch

If you are not used to working with numbers, you may not be familiar with some of the terms used to describe spreadsheets. Values and formulas are terms borrowed from math that apply to even the simplest work that you do with a spreadsheet.

The formal terms are used here simply to let you know what they are and what they mean. A **value** is a number you enter in a cell of a worksheet. **Text** is any word or label you enter in the spreadsheet. A **formula** is a specific calculation that Excel performs, such as adding or subtracting two numbers.

To Enter Data

❶ In the default worksheet (Book1) that you used in the previous lesson, click cell A2.

A2 becomes the active cell. Information you that type will appear in this cell. You can now enter the first item on your office expense worksheet.

❷ Type Rent.

Insertion point
A blinking vertical line that appears on screen at a location where you can enter data. The insertion point is sometimes called a *cursor*. Characters that you type appear to the left of the insertion point.

I-beam
The shape of the mouse pointer when you move over a screen area in which you can edit text.

As you type in the cell, a blinking vertical cursor, or *insertion point*, appears, indicating that you are in edit mode. Characters that you type appear to the left of the insertion point. Also, as you type in the worksheet cell, the word also appears in the formula bar (see Figure 1.13). You can type directly in the formula bar by selecting the cell where you want the data entered, then clicking in the formula bar. You can also start edit mode by selecting the cell and pressing (F2).

Notice that when the mouse pointer is positioned within the formula bar or within the cell while you are typing, it changes to an *I-beam*. You can use the I-beam to position the insertion point for entering or editing data.

Notice that three buttons appear on the formula bar. The red *X* is the Cancel button. Clicking the Cancel button is the same as pressing (Esc) when you are typing data into a cell; that is, Excel stops accepting the entry, and the cell's previous contents reappear. The green check mark is the Enter button. Clicking the Enter button accepts the data you entered as complete. The equal sign is the Edit Formula button, which you learn about in Project 3, "Creating Formulas."

Speedy Class

On the Formula bar, click anywhere within the text, numbers, or formulas to position the I-beam for editing. Double-click a word or number in the Formula bar to select it, then type to replace everything within the selected area.

continues

Project 1 Getting Started with Excel

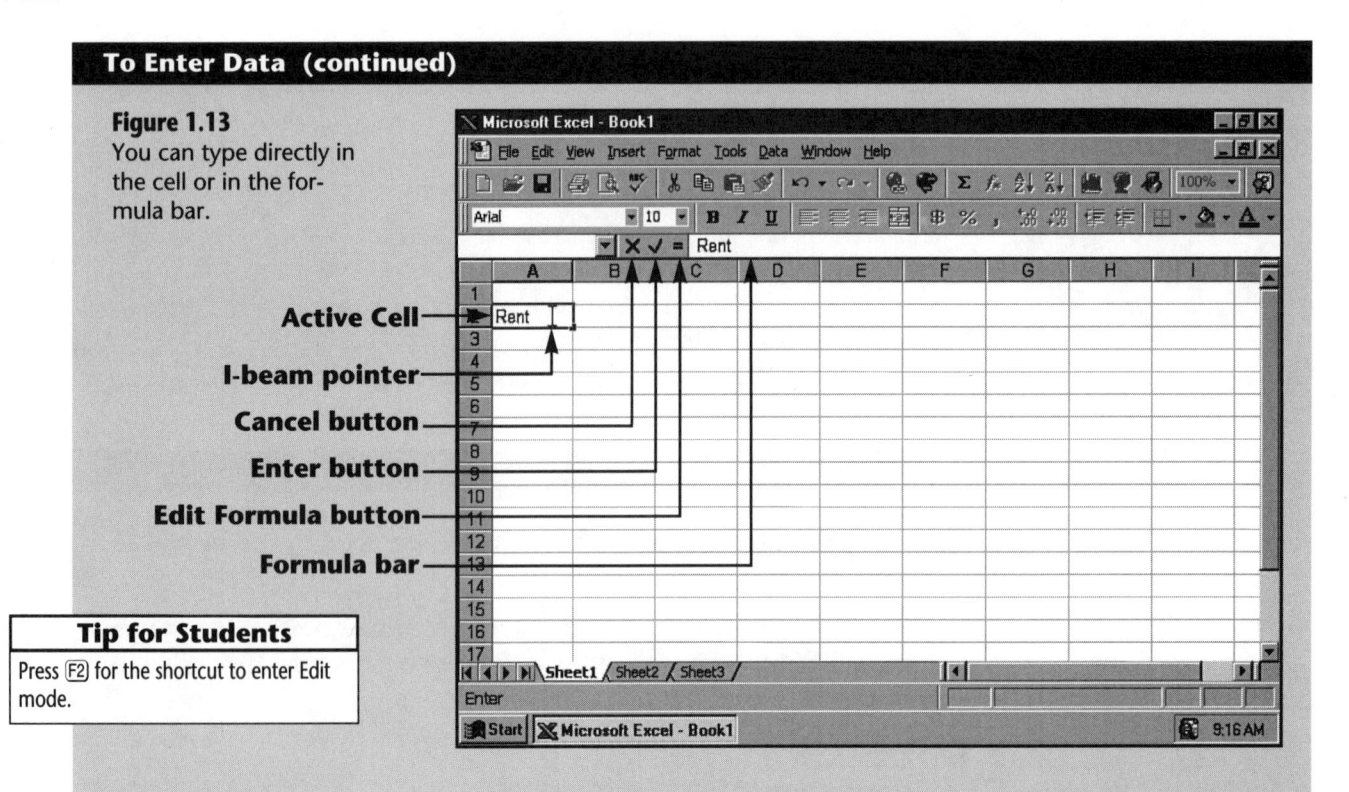

To Enter Data (continued)

Figure 1.13
You can type directly in the cell or in the formula bar.

Labels pointing to the screenshot:
- Active Cell
- I-beam pointer
- Cancel button
- Enter button
- Edit Formula button
- Formula bar

> **Tip for Students**
> Press F2 for the shortcut to enter Edit mode.

> **Quicksand**
> When editing a cell, press Enter or Tab to finish editing. Using the right or left arrow keys doesn't take you out of Edit mode.

> **Tip for Instructors**
> Remind students that typing replaces the contents of the cell. Sometimes it's quicker to type over a cell's contents than to edit it.

> **Speedy Class**
> Some users don't like the feature that moves the cell pointer down one cell following the use of Enter. This feature can be turned off. Choose **T**ools, **O**ptions, then click the Edit tab and uncheck the **M**ove Selection after Enter check box. Click OK to accept this change.

If you have problems...

If you make a mistake while typing, press Backspace to delete the error, then continue typing. If you discover a mistake after you've moved to another cell, click the mouse or use the arrow keys to select the cell that contains the mistake, double-click the cell to change to edit mode, then use the arrow keys, Backspace, or Del to correct the mistake. If you want to replace the entire contents of the cell, select the cell and then begin typing; the new text you enter replaces the cell's previous contents.

❸ Press ↓.

The text you typed is entered in cell A2, and A3 becomes the active cell. You can now enter the other expenses in your worksheet. You can also press Enter to enter information and move to the next cell down the column, or you can click the Enter button on the formula bar to enter the information and remain in the same cell.

❹ Enter the following additional expenses in your worksheet. Press ↓ or Enter after typing each word to enter the data and move to the next cell down the column.

```
Supplies
Phone
Cleaning
Insurance
Total
```

Lesson 5: Entering Data

Each time you press ↓ or ↵Enter, the text is entered in the active cell and the cell below becomes the active cell. By default, text appears flush with the left border of the cell. Don't worry if it looks as if there is not enough room in the cell for the text. You can enter up to 32,000 characters in each cell! If the column is not wide enough to display all of the characters, the characters are simply hidden; they are not erased. You learn how to adjust cell width in Project 4, "Calculating with Functions."

You have now entered row labels (headings) for all the various expenses you will track in this office expense worksheet. The word Total should appear in cell A7 and cell A8 should be active. Now you can enter the amount paid for the rent last month.

❺ Click in cell B2, type 1200, then press ↓.

Be sure to press ↓ or ↵Enter to enter the information. Now enter the amounts for the rest of your expenses. (Don't worry that your numeric entries don't show dollar signs right now; in Project 5, "Improving the Appearance of a Worksheet," you learn how to format numbers to show dollar signs.)

❻ Type each of the following amounts, and press ↓ or ↵Enter to enter them into the worksheet:

   300

   150

   80

   75

You have now entered a record of your expenses into the worksheet. To see how useful a spreadsheet can be, try entering a simple formula to find the monthly total for the expenses in this example.

❼ In cell B7, type =b2+b3+b4+b5+b6.

You have now typed the formula for adding all the expenses in column B. The equal sign identifies the information as a formula rather than data to be entered in the cell, and the plus signs are the mathematical operators that tell Excel to use addition. (Notice that as soon as you type the equal sign, the Functions button replaces the Name box on the formula bar.) This formula tells Excel to add the contents of the five preceding cells in column B. Because the formula is entered in cell B7, the total is displayed there as well.

continues

Tip for Students

When typing numbers, don't use commas to separate thousands, or dollar signs to designate currency. Type the numbers with no enhancements, then format the numbers to change their appearance. Number formats are presented in Project 3, "Creating Formulas."

Tip for Instructors

Explain the importance of entering cell references instead of amounts in a formula. Thus, if the amounts in the cells change, the formula doesn't have to be rewritten.

? Q&A

What would happen if you didn't begin this formula with an equal sign? *Answer:* The formula itself would appear in the cell (as a text entry), instead of the result.

Is there any way besides the equal sign to start formulas? *Answer:* The plus or minus sign (Excel automatically adds an equal sign to the beginning of the formula for you).

To Enter Data (continued)

8 **Click the Enter button (the green check mark) on the formula bar to enter the formula.**

You can also press ↵Enter or ↓ to enter the formula. Excel adds the numbers and displays the result in cell B7 with the total for the expenses. Notice that as long as cell B7 is active, the formula—not the actual numerical total—appears in the formula bar (see Figure 1.14). If necessary, click cell B7 to make it active so you can see the contents of the formula bar.

Tip for Students
On a spreadsheet prepared by someone else, you can figure out how the answers were derived by clicking a cell containing a formula, then examining the formula itself in the Formula bar.

Figure 1.14
The formula appears in the formula bar, while the formula's results appear in cell B7.

Formula — =B2+B3+B4+B5+B6

Result of formula — 1805

	A	B
2	Rent	1200
3	Supplies	300
4	Phone	150
5	Cleaning	80
6	Insurance	75
7	Total	1805

Q&A
What would happen to the total in cell B7 when you changed the amount in cell B4 if you had used actual amounts in your formula instead of cell references? *Answer:* Nothing! The formula would calculate, but display the same result.

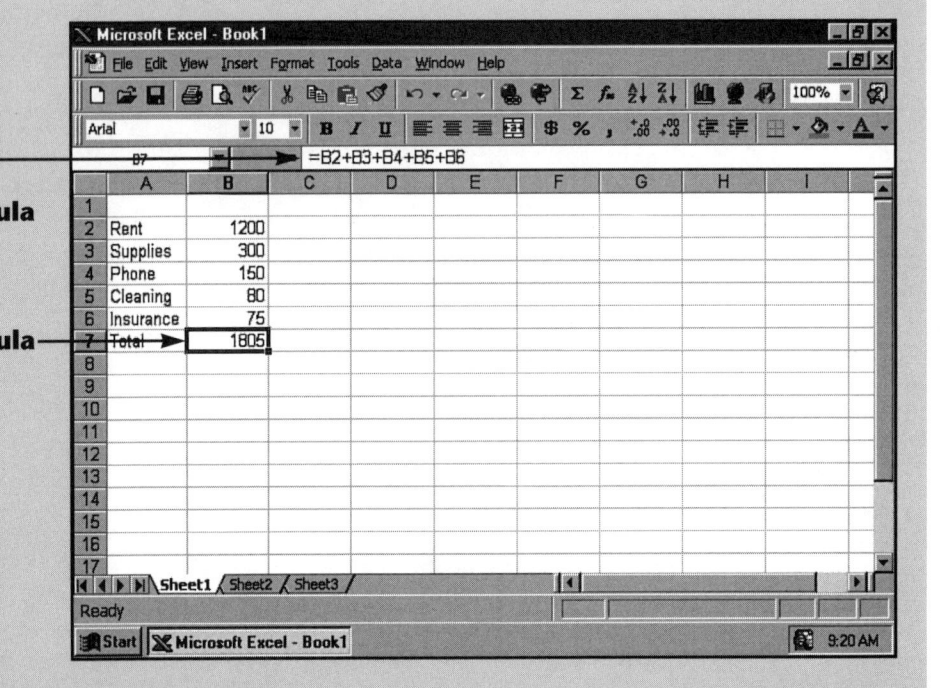

The true power of Excel resides in formulas. If several of your expenses change next month, you can find the new expense total simply by entering the new information in the correct cells. The formula in B7 automatically calculates a new total for you.

Try changing one of the expense values now.

9 **Click cell B4.**

This makes cell B4 the active cell. Its contents appear in the Formula bar.

10 **Type 100 and then press ↵Enter.**

Notice that when you enter the new amount in cell B4, the total automatically changes in cell B7.

Keep this expense worksheet open for the next lesson, where you learn how to save your work.

Tip for Instructors
Discuss ways to make formulas totally dynamic by using cell references instead of values. For example, if you want to multiply a cell by 10 percent, consider putting the 10 percent in a cell by itself, then referring to that cell in your formula. If the value needs to change, you need merely change the value in the cell containing the 10 percent, rather than edit the formula.

Lesson 6: Saving a Worksheet

On Your Mark
What are some ways that you can lose data if you haven't saved your worksheet?

Tip for Instructors
File names in Excel 97 are limited to 255 characters and can include spaces. However, they cannot contain the slash (/), back slash (\), colon (:), asterisk (*), quotation marks (" "), question mark (?), angle brackets (< >), and pipe character (|).

File
Information you enter in your computer and save for future use, such as a document or workbook.

Up to this point, none of the information that you have entered in your expense worksheet has been safely stored for future use. At the moment, your worksheet and the workbook that contains it are stored in the computer's *random access memory* (RAM). If your computer were to crash or shut down for any reason, you would lose your expense worksheet.

For this reason, it is important to save your work every 10 to 15 minutes. You can save your work to the *hard disk* inside the computer or to a *floppy disk* that you insert and can take with you. You may already be familiar with the concepts and terms described above. If not, see the Jargon Watch later in this lesson.

When you save a workbook, or *file*, you assign the file a name and location on a disk. Later, you can retrieve the file, and add to it, edit it, and print it. So that you don't lose any of your valuable work (and your valuable time), save your expense worksheet now.

To Save a Worksheet

Tip for Instructors
Have students discuss any naming conventions that may be in place at their workplaces.

Tip for Students
When the Save As dialog box opens, you don't need to delete the *.*, which shows in the file name location. Because it is already selected, you can begin typing; the file name you type will replace the characters that are there.

❶ **Choose File from the menu bar.**

The File pull-down menu opens.

❷ **Choose the Save command.**

The Save As dialog box opens, as shown in Figure 1.15. The first time you save a file, choosing either **S**ave or Save **A**s opens the Save As dialog box. Notice that the text in the File **n**ame text box is highlighted; this is the temporary file name that Excel assigns to your workbook.

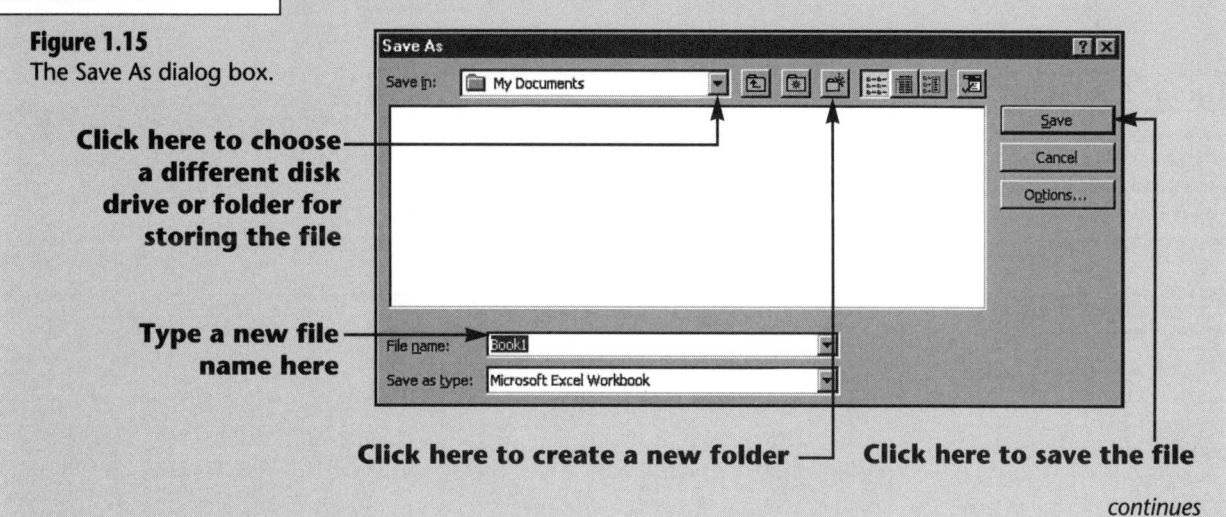

Figure 1.15
The Save As dialog box.

Click here to choose a different disk drive or folder for storing the file

Type a new file name here

Click here to create a new folder — Click here to save the file

continues

To Save a Worksheet (continued)

③ Type OffExp in the File name text box.

The name you type replaces the temporary name assigned by Excel.

You can type any name you want using Windows 95's file-naming rules. You can include spaces as well as upper- and lowercase letters. Excel automatically stores the file in the default Excel 97 file format, adding the XLS file extension, but by default, Windows 95 does not show file extensions.

④ Click the Save in drop down arrow, then click the drive or folder where you want to save your workbook.

In the Save As dialog box, Excel automatically proposes to save the workbook on the current drive (usually C) and in the default folder, My Documents. Ask your instructor where to save the files you create during this course. If you want to save to a different device, such as a floppy disk, select the drive from the Save **in** list. If you want to save the file in a different folder, select the folder from the Save **in** list, or click the New Folder button to create and name a new folder.

If you have problems...

If you try to save to a floppy disk and you get an error message, check two things: First, be sure to select the correct disk drive—most likely drive A. Second, be sure that you are using a formatted disk. If this is the problem, you should see an error message that tells you the disk you selected is not formatted. The error message may ask you if you want to format the disk now. If this is the case and you want to format the disk so you can save files to it, click the **Y**es button and follow the instructions until the disk formatting is complete.

Be careful when formatting disks, and make sure that you don't format your hard disk drive. When you format a disk, all information stored on the disk is erased. If you have any questions about formatting or disk drives, don't hesitate to ask your instructor for help.

⑤ Choose Save.

This saves a copy of your workbook containing the worksheet data as a file named OffExp. The Save As dialog box closes, and the new file name appears in the workbook window title bar. Now practice a shortcut method for quickly saving a file that already has a name, drive, and folder.

Tip for Students
Use the Save toolbar button to save files quickly. This button appears in all Office 97 programs (as well as other programs running in Windows). Also, remember the keyboard shortcut for saving: Ctrl+S.

Tip for Instructors
Excel 97 also assigns a DOS file name when you save a workbook with a long file name. Look for your file names to be truncated and end with a tilde (~) and a numeral, such as office-1.xls for officebudget98.xls, if you want to open files in a program that doesn't support Windows 95.

Speedy Class
Have students create a class folder with a unique name in which to store their class files.

6 Click the Save button on the toolbar.

This method quickly saves your workbook. Alternatively, you can press Ctrl+S. If you want to save an existing workbook with a different name or to a different drive or folder, choose Save **A**s from the **F**ile menu.

Keep the OffExp workbook open for the next lesson, where you learn how to prepare a worksheet for printing.

Jargon Watch

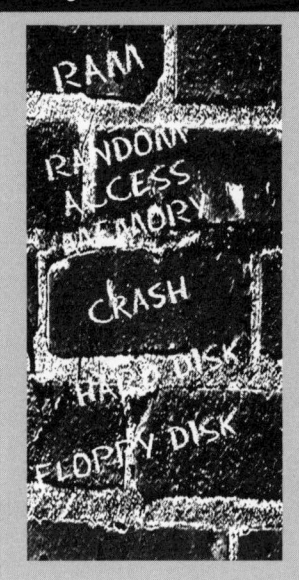

In this lesson, a number of technical terms have been used to describe how computers save information. **RAM** stands for **random access memory**, which simply means the temporary storage space the computer uses for programs and data it's currently working with.

When a computer **crashes**, it means that an error—either in a program the computer is running or in the hardware or power supply—has caused the computer to stop working. Everything stored in RAM is lost when a crash occurs. Remember, it's important to frequently save your work to a **hard disk** or a **floppy disk**.

Floppy disks are small disks that you can carry around with you. They can be either 5 ¼-inch disks or 3 ½-inch disks, and are often used to keep backup copies of important information. Although 3 ½-inch floppy disks have hard outer cases, the disk inside is flexible. Your hard disk is built into your PC and is made up of several rigid platters that look similar to the CDs that you buy in music stores. The bulk of the programs and information that your computer uses is stored on the computer's hard disk.

Lesson 7: Preparing a Worksheet for Printing

Page setup
The way data is arranged on a printed page.

Header
Text or graphics that appear at the top of every page.

Footer
Text or graphics that appear at the bottom of every page.

With Excel, you can quickly print a worksheet using the default *page setup*. However, you can improve the way the worksheet looks when it is printed, and you can add useful information to the printed page by changing the page setup. For example, you can add *headers* and *footers* to help identify the contents of the printed page, and you can adjust the page margins. Now, use Excel's Page Setup features to make sure your worksheet is ready for printing.

✓ **On Your Mark**
What are some of the ways that you can customize the appearance of your printed worksheets? *Answer:* Paper size and orientation, margin sizes, centering, headers and footers, and gridlines.

To Prepare a Worksheet for Printing

Tip for Students

When getting ready to print, find out which bin your paper is stored in, which printer you are using, and whether you are to use portrait or landscape format.

❶ In the OffExp worksheet, open the File menu and choose Page Setup.

The Page Setup dialog box appears (see Figure 1.16). Use this dialog box to adjust the page setup before you print your worksheet. This dialog box provides a wide range of options from which you can choose to customize your printed worksheet. By default, the Page options are displayed. These options enable you to select features pertaining to the actual page on which the worksheet is printed, such as the correct paper size and orientation. For this example, you want to change the margins, center the worksheet on the page, add a header and a footer, and choose to display gridlines for the printed worksheet.

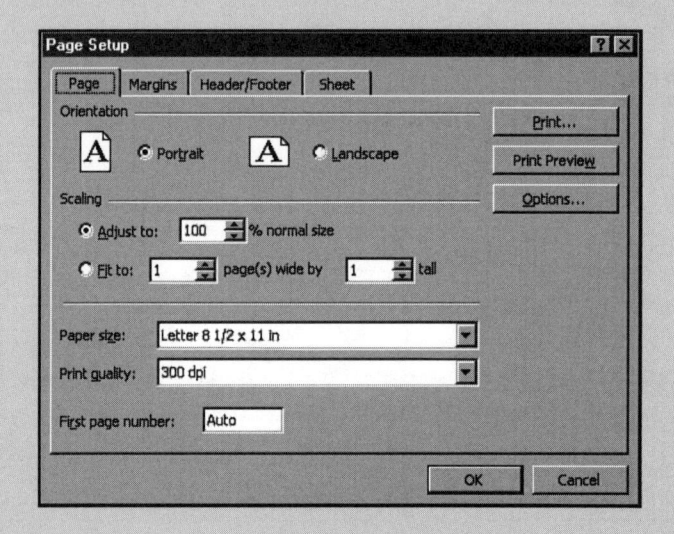

Figure 1.16
The Page options in the Page Setup dialog box.

Tip for Instructors

Students may use multiple printers at their work locations. When the Print dialog box opens, instruct students how to choose a printer if more than one is installed.

Tip for Students

Use the toolbar button to print files quickly. You don't have to access the Print dialog box when you choose this button. Also, remember the keyboard shortcut for printing is Ctrl+P.

Quicksand

By default, Excel prints the entire worksheet. You may want to, however, select a smaller area to print. Project 5, "Improving the Appearance of a Worksheet," explains how to customize print selections.

❷ Click the Margins tab in the Page Setup dialog box.

This displays the Margins options. The default top and bottom margins are one inch. The default left and right margins are 0.75 inch.

❸ In the Top text box, click the up arrow twice.

This changes the top margin to 1.5 inches. Notice the preview page in the dialog box shows you the changes.

❹ In the Bottom text box, click the down arrow once.

This changes the bottom margin to 0.75 inch.

❺ In the Center on page area, select both the Horizontally and Vertically check boxes.

The worksheet is now centered horizontally between the left and right margins and vertically between the top and bottom margins. You can see how the changes affect the preview page in the dialog box, as shown in Figure 1.17.

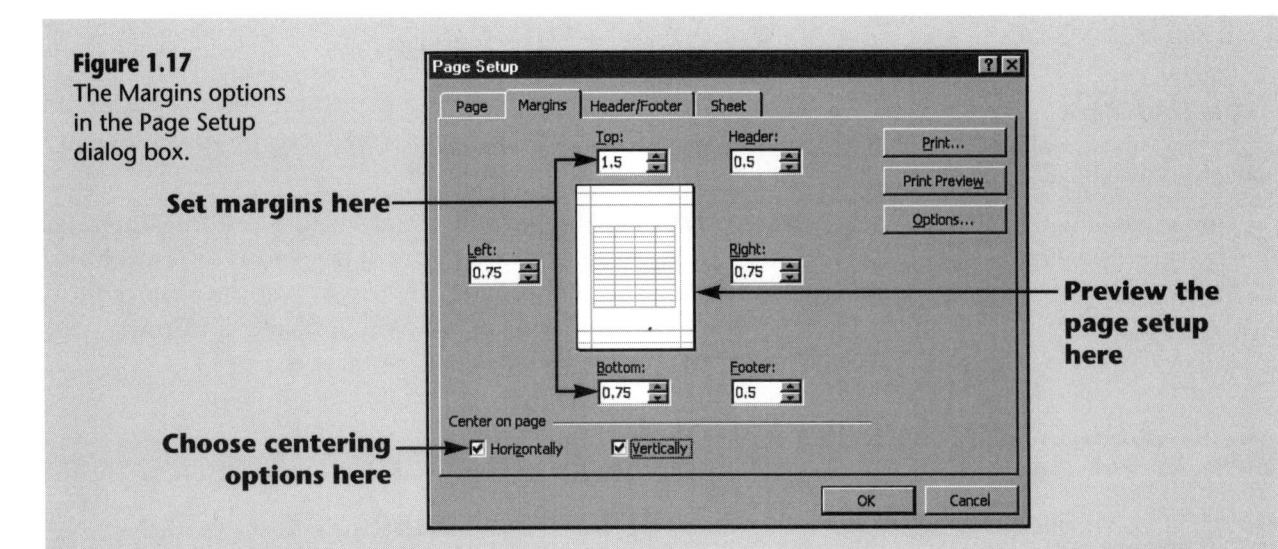

Lesson 7: Preparing a Worksheet for Printing   25

Figure 1.17
The Margins options in the Page Setup dialog box.

Set margins here

Choose centering options here

Preview the page setup here

❻ In the Page Setup dialog box, click the Header/Footer tab.

The Header/Footer options let you specify information to print in the header and footer area of each page. You can choose from pre-defined headers and footers, or you can create your own.

❼ Click the drop-down arrow next to the Header text box, then scroll down through the list of pre-defined headers and select Prepared by {YOUR NAME} MM/DD/YY, Page 1.

This header will print the words Prepared by, followed by your name and today's date in the center of the header and the page number on the right side of the header.

❽ Click the drop-down arrow next to the Footer text box, and select OffExp.

This footer prints the current file name in the center of the footer area.

❾ Click the Sheet tab in the Page Setup dialog box.

On this page, you can choose options that affect the way the data in the worksheet is printed.

❿ Select the Gridlines check box.

When this option is selected, the gridlines between rows and columns are printed. You have now finished setting up the worksheet page for printing.

⓫ Choose OK.

The Page Setup dialog box closes.

⓬ Click the Save button on the Standard toolbar.

This saves the changes you have made to the OffExp worksheet file. Leave OffExp open. In Lesson 8, you learn how to preview and print the worksheet.

Tip for Students

By default, Excel 97 displays worksheet gridlines on your screen, but will print them only when you specify it.

Speedy Class

Choose **S**etup while in Print Preview (or choose Page Set**u**p from the **F**ile menu) to change the following: make a printer selection, make changes to headers and footers, turn on gridlines, change orientation, change the worksheet scale, or set specific margins. Ask students if there are specific printing requirements at their workplaces, and have the class discuss ways to implement those printing specifications.

Project 1 Getting Started with Excel

Lesson 8: Printing a Worksheet

On Your Mark
What are some reasons that you might want to print your worksheets?

Now that you have saved your workbook and worksheet and have adjusted the page setup, you can print a copy of your worksheet for your files or to review while you are away from the computer.

Current worksheet
The worksheet containing the active cell.

It's a good idea to save documents immediately before printing them, as you did in Lesson 7. It's also a good idea to preview on your screen the way the worksheet will look when it is printed. That way, you can make adjustments to the page setup before you print. Now, preview and print your expense worksheet—the *current worksheet*.

To Print a Worksheet

❶ Make sure that the printer is turned on, has paper, and is *online*.

Online
Directly connected to a computer and ready for use.

You can't print if the printer is not turned on, if the printer is out of paper, or if the printer is not online. Printers often have a light that shows whether the printer is online or receiving commands from the computer. If the printer is not online, Excel displays an error message.

❷ From the File menu, choose Print.

The Print dialog box appears, as shown in Figure 1.18.

Figure 1.18
You can change any of the options in the Print dialog box.

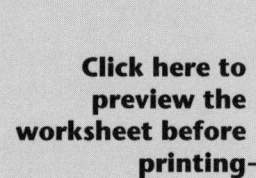

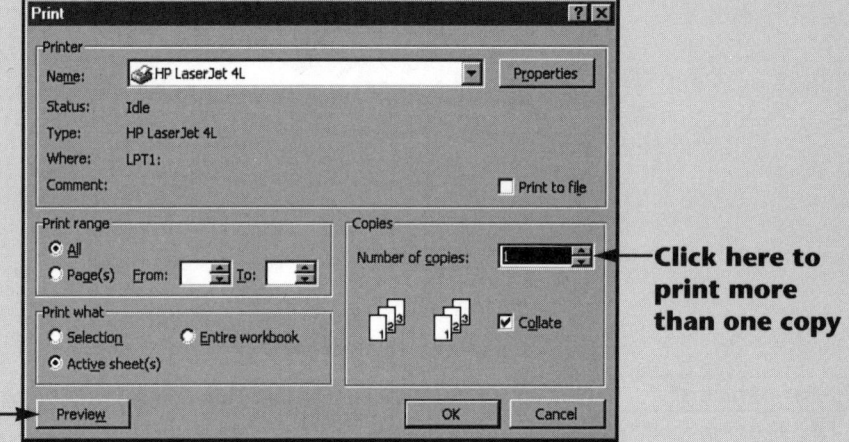

Click here to print more than one copy

Click here to preview the worksheet before printing

❸ In the Number of copies spin box, click the up arrow once.

This changes the number of copies to be printed to two. In a spin box, you use the up and down arrows to change the value in preset increments. You can type a value in the box if you prefer. You can also change other options in the Print dialog box. After the printer is ready, you should check the worksheet you are going to print.

Lesson 8: Printing a Worksheet   27

④ Click the Preview button in the Print dialog box.

The worksheet now appears in the Print Preview window, which enables you to see how the entire worksheet will look when printed (see Figure 1.19). In Print Preview, you can see the effects of the changes you made to the page setup, including the header and footer you have added to the page, as well as the gridlines. When the mouse pointer changes to a magnifying glass, you can click within the window to increase the size of the document being displayed.

Figure 1.19
View the worksheet as it will look when printed to decide if you need to make changes.

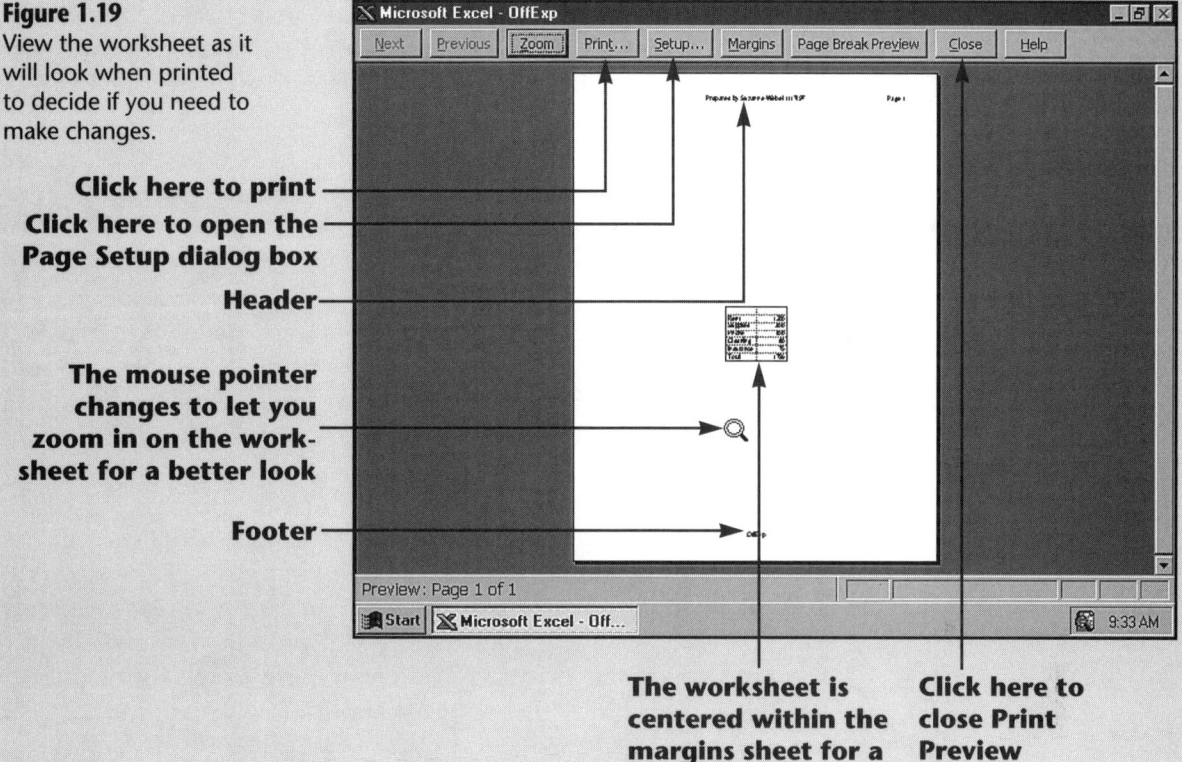

Click here to print
Click here to open the Page Setup dialog box
Header

The mouse pointer changes to let you zoom in on the worksheet for a better look

Footer

The worksheet is centered within the margins sheet for a better look

Click here to close Print Preview

⑤ Click anywhere in the worksheet.

Your view of the worksheet becomes enlarged so that you can more easily read it, but you can't see the entire page. You can click the worksheet again to go back to the view of the whole page. If you decide you want to make a change in the worksheet before you print it, click the **C**lose button to close the view and return to the worksheet in Excel, or click the **S**etup button to open the Page Setup dialog box.

⑥ Click the Print button on the Print Preview toolbar.

Excel sends two copies of your worksheet to the printer. The Print Preview window closes and the OffExp worksheet is displayed in Normal view. Leave the worksheet open in Excel. In the next lesson, you learn how to close it and exit the program.

Project 1 Getting Started with Excel

To quickly open the Print dialog box, press Ctrl+P.

To quickly print the current worksheet without opening the Print dialog box, click the Print button on the Standard toolbar.

To change to Print Preview without opening the Print dialog box, click the Print Preview button on the Standard toolbar, or choose Print Preview from the **File** menu.

Lesson 9: Closing a File and Exiting Excel

> **On Your Mark**
> Have any of you ever exited a program improperly? What happened to your data?

Before you turn off your computer, you should first close the file you have created and then exit Excel so that you don't lose any of your work. Complete this project by closing your file and exiting the Excel and Windows software.

To Close a File and Exit Excel

> **Tip for Instructors**
> Review the Minimize, Maximize, Restore, and Close buttons. Discuss the difference between using the buttons for the spreadsheet as opposed to the entire program.

❶ Choose File, Close.

If you haven't saved your work, Excel displays a dialog box that asks if you would like to save your work. Choosing **Yes** saves the file and then closes it. Choosing **No** closes the file and erases any work you have done since the last time you saved.

❷ Choose File, Exit.

Excel closes. If there are any files left open, Excel displays a dialog box that asks if you would like to save your work. Choosing **Yes** saves all open files, then closes the program. Choosing **No** closes the program without saving the files; any work you have done since the last time you saved is erased. After you close Excel, the Windows desktop appears if no other software applications are running.

If you have completed your session on the computer, proceed with Step 3. Otherwise, continue with the "Applying Your Skills" section at the end of this project.

❸ To exit Windows, click the Start button on the taskbar and choose Shut Down from the Start menu.

The Shut Down Windows dialog box appears, asking you to confirm that you are ready to shut down Windows and your computer.

❹ Verify that the Shut Down the Computer? option button is selected, then choose Yes.

Windows closes and prepares your computer for shut down. When a message appears telling you it is safe to shut off your computer, you may do so.

You have now completed the lesson on getting started with Excel. If you want to continue with the "Checking Your Skills" section at the end of this project, restart your computer and Excel using the information you learned in Lesson 1.

Checking Your Skills 29

> **INSIDE:** To exit any file or program you are currently using, you can also click the Close button at the right end of the window's title. For example, clicking the Close button of a workbook closes the workbook, and clicking the Close button in the Excel title bar closes Excel. Again, you are prompted to save unsaved work before you close any file or software.

Project Summary

To	Do This
Start Excel	Click the Start button on the Windows taskbar, point at **P**rograms on the Start menu, then choose Microsoft Excel from the Programs submenu.
Make a cell active	Click it.
Get help	Open the **H**elp menu and choose Microsoft Excel **H**elp to start the Office Assistant, or choose **C**ontents and Index for general information.
Move to cell A1	Press Ctrl+Home.
Enter data in a cell	Click the cell, type the data, then press Enter.
Enter a formula in a cell	Click the cell, type an equal sign, type the formula, then press Enter.
Save a worksheet	Choose **F**ile, **S**ave. If necessary, type the file name in the File **N**ame text box, choose a disk drive and folder from the Save **I**n list, then choose **S**ave.
Change page setup	Choose **F**ile, Page Set**u**p, select options, then choose OK.
Print a worksheet	Click the Print button on the Standard toolbar.
Preview a worksheet before printing	Click the Print Preview button on the Standard toolbar.

Checking Your Skills

True/False

For each of the following, check *T* or *F* to indicate whether the statement is true or false.

✓T __F **1.** The formula bar of the Excel screen displays the contents of the current cell and the cell's address.

__T ✓F **2.** Pressing F10 starts the Office Assistant.

__T ✓F **3.** The only way to move around a worksheet is by using the mouse.

✓T __F **4.** You can have up to 65,536 rows in a worksheet.

✓T __F **5.** You can press Ctrl+S or click the Save button on the toolbar to save changes to a file that has already been named.

✓T __F **6.** To select an entire column, click the column letter in the worksheet frame.

Project 1 Getting Started with Excel

__T ✓F **7.** When you select more than one cell, the last cell in the range is the active cell.

__T ✓F **8.** A worksheet can have up to 50 columns.

✓T __F **9.** You can use spaces in an Excel file name.

✓T __F **10.** To move to cell A1, press Ctrl + Home.

Multiple Choice

Circle the letter of the correct answer for each of the following questions.

1. Which of the following is *not* a part of the Microsoft Excel screen?

   a. ruler line
   b. sheet tab
   c. status bar
   d. toolbar

2. Which of the following is a valid cell address?

   a. b-12
   b. B:12
   c. B12
   d. B/12

3. What is the address of the top-left cell in a worksheet?

   a. T1
   b. L1
   c. B1
   d. A1

4. Which of the following is an example of an Excel formula?

   a. $240
   b. =B2+B3+B4
   c. January
   d. 1/21/94

5. Which of the following is a method of getting help in Excel?

   a. Office Assistant
   b. Directory Assistance
   c. Help Assistant
   d. Excel Assistant

6. To move up one screen, you press which of the following keys?

   a. PgUp
   b. ↑
   c. Ctrl + ↑
   d. Ctrl + PgUp

7. Each cell can hold up to how many characters?

   a. 24
   b. 100
   c. 10,000
   d. 32,000

8. The red X button on the formula bar does what?

   a. Enters the data into the cell
   b. Cancels the entry
   c. Enables you to edit a formula
   d. Deletes the last character you entered

9. To change to edit mode to correct a cell entry, you do which of the following?

   a. Press F2
   b. Double-click the cell
   c. Right-click the cell
   d. a or b

10. How do you cancel a menu you have selected?

   a. Click the menu name again
   b. Click anywhere in the window outside the menu
   c. Press Esc
   d. any of the above

Checking Your Skills

Completion

In the blank provided, write the correct answer for each of the following statements.

1. Data is entered in the _active_ cell.
2. To use a button on the toolbar, you _click_ the button.
3. The Name box in the formula bar displays the _cell address_.
4. You can add a header or footer to a worksheet using the _Page Setup_ dialog box.
5. To print a worksheet, open the _File_ menu and choose **P**rint, or click the Print button.
6. The _Title bar_ displays the name of the software and the active workbook.
7. The row and column headings that appear along the top and left edge of the worksheet window are called the worksheet _frame_.
8. To check the appearance of the worksheet before printing it, click the _Preview_ button in the Print dialog box.
9. To display a list of general help topics, similar to a book with chapters, click the _Contents_ tab in the Help Topics dialog box.
10. When the mouse pointer is positioned within the formula bar, it displays as a(n) _I-beam_.

Matching

In the blank next to each of the following terms or phrases, write the letter of the corresponding term or phrase.

_e_ 1. To change the appearance of text or numbers.

_g_ 2. Text or graphics that appears at the top of every page.

_j_ 3. Text or graphics that appears at the bottom of every page.

_i_ 4. The intersection of a column and a row.

_a_ 5. Multiple adjacent cells.

_f_ 6. Values, text, and formulas.

_c_ 7. A blinking vertical line that appears where you can enter data.

_h_ 8. A specific calculation that Excel performs.

_d_ 9. A number you enter into a worksheet cell.

_b_ 10. Any word or label you enter into a spreadsheet.

a. range
b. text
c. insertion point
d. value
e. format
f. data
g. header
h. formula
i. cell
j. footer

Project 1   Getting Started with Excel

Screen ID

Label each element of the Excel screen shown in Figure 1.20.

1. *Title Bar*
2. *Menu Bar*
3. *Formula Bar*
4. *Standard Toolbar*
5. *Formatting Toolbar*
6. *Sheet Tab*
7. *Column A*
8. *Row 3*
9. *Mouse Pointer*
10. *Active Cell*
11. *Start Button*

Tip for Instructors
Due to exercise similarity, choose one that best meets your needs, then have students take the Checking Your Skills quiz before preceeding to Project 2.

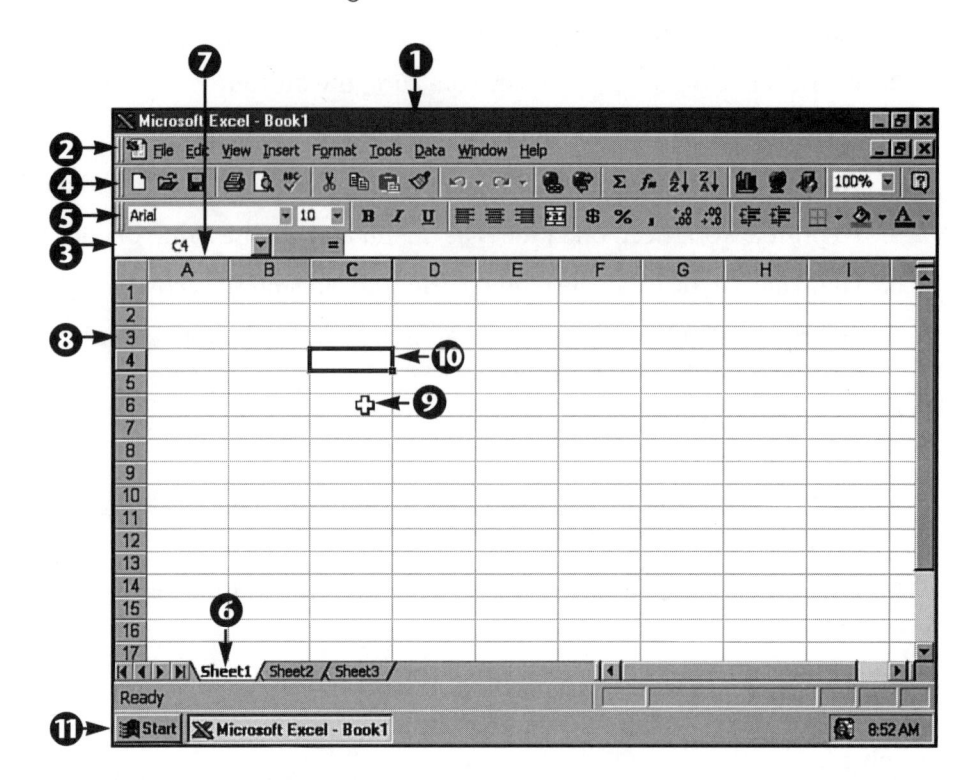

Applying Your Skills

Practice

The following exercises enable you to practice the skills you have learned in this project. Take a few minutes to work through these exercises now.

1. Creating an Employee List

Imagine that you are the owner and hands-on business manager of a new gourmet coffee shop. With Excel, you can keep track of the employees you hire and plan to hire. You can list job descriptions, hire dates, starting salaries, and pay raise information.

To Create an Employee List

1. Start Windows and then start Microsoft Excel.
2. Use the default worksheet.
3. Enter the following row labels, starting in cell A3 and moving down to cell A6:

    ```
    Office Manager
    Sales Clerk
    Stock Clerk
    Cashier
    ```

    You can add your own categories to the list if you want.

4. After you have finished setting up the row labels, enter the following column labels, starting in cell A2 and moving to the right to F2 by pressing `Tab` to move from one column to the next:

   `Position`

   `Description`

   `Salary`

   `Employee name`

   `Start Date`

   `Next Review Date`

5. If you want, enter a formula in cell C7 to calculate your total projected salary costs. Don't worry about entering any data yet.

6. Save the file as `Job List`. If requested by your instructor, print two copies of the file, then close it.

> In this exercise, students insert text in a worksheet. The formula to insert in cell C7 is =C3+C4+C5+C6. The solution file is saved as **Job List** on the Instructor's Resource disk.

2. Creating an Advertising Worksheet

One of your first goals in launching the coffee shop is to let people know about the store and that it is open for business. Create a worksheet to help you manage the costs and benefits of the advertising campaign by listing the various types of advertising, when the ad was run, its cost, and its effect on business.

To Create the Advertising Worksheet

1. Start Windows and then start Microsoft Excel.

2. Use the default worksheet.

3. Enter the following column labels, starting in cell A2 and moving from left to right:

   `Ad Title`

   `Medium`

   `Date`

   `Cost`

   `Effect`

   You can also add your own categories to this list.

4. After you have finished setting up the column labels, enter the following example information, starting in cell A3 and moving from left to right:

   `Grand Opening`

   `Print`

   `9/27/97`

   `$150`

   `$250`

5. Create your own information for a radio ad and a direct market mailing in rows 4 and 5.

6. Save the file as `Advertising`.

Project 1 Getting Started with Excel

7. Add a header to display your name, the page number, and the date, and add a footer to display the file name.

8. Save, preview, and print two copies of the file, then close it.

> In this exercise, students create a simple worksheet by inserting text in columns and rows. To add a header and a footer to the worksheet, students use the **F**ile, Page Set**u**p, Header/Footer tab. The solution file is saved as **Advertising** on the Instructor's Resource disk.

3. Creating an Office Budget

You can also use Excel to keep a handle on office expenses. Create a spreadsheet to help you plan office expenses by listing the costs of typical stationery items that you require to get started.

To Create the Office Budget

1. Start Windows and then start Microsoft Excel.

2. Use the default worksheet.

3. Enter the following row labels, starting in cell A2 and moving down to cell A6:

    Letterhead
    Business cards
    Envelopes
    Mailing labels
    Total

    You can add your own categories to the list if you want.

4. After you have finished setting up the row labels, enter the following costs, starting in cell B2 and moving down to cell B5:

    250
    175
    125
    150

5. Enter a formula in cell B6 to calculate the total costs.

6. Save the file as `Paper Costs`.

7. Change all of the margins for the worksheet to 1.5 inches, and center the worksheet between the margins.

8. Save and preview the worksheet.

9. If requested by your instructor, print two copies of the file, then close it.

> In this exercise, students create a worksheet by inserting text in columns and rows. The formula to insert in cell B6 is =B2+B3+B4+B5. Students use the **F**ile, Page Set**u**p, Margins tab to change all of the margins and center the worksheet between margins. The solution file is saved as **Paper Costs** on the Instructor's Resource disk.

4. Cataloging Your Inventory

You can use an Excel worksheet to create a catalog of store inventory that you can use to schedule reordering. List each product in column A of your worksheet, then add columns for a description, vendor name, and price per pound.

To Catalog Your Inventory

1. Start Windows and then start Microsoft Excel.

2. Use the default worksheet.

3. In column A, enter the labels and information to create a list of store inventory. Use as many of the suggested categories as you want, and feel free to add your own.

4. In column B, enter the information about the Arabica coffee beans you purchased from Coffee Importers for $1.50 per pound. You can also enter the information about the Kona coffee purchased from Aloha Coffee, Inc. for $1.99 per pound, and the French Roast you purchased from Coffee Importers for $1.50 per pound.

5. Use Page Setup to add a header and footer to the worksheet.

6. Save the file as Inventory.

7. Preview the worksheet; if requested by your instructor, print two copies, then close it.

This exercise provides students an additional opportunity to insert text and values in a worksheet. To add a header and a footer to the worksheet, students use the **F**ile, Page Set**u**p, Header/Footer tab. The solution file is saved as **Inventory** on the Instructor's Resource disk.

---

5. Using the Excel Window

In this project, you learned to use various elements of the Excel window. In this exercise, you practice using these elements.

To Use the Excel Window

To practice using the Excel window, complete the following exercise. Use a new, blank worksheet for this exercise.

1. Open the F**o**rmat menu by clicking this menu option.

2. Open the **T**ools menu by moving the mouse pointer to this menu option.

3. Remove the menu from your screen by clicking the **T**ools menu option again.

4. Click cell D12 to activate it.

5. Click the number for row number 10. This selects the entire row.

6. Click the Sheet2 tab at the bottom of the Excel window. This activates worksheet 2.

7. Click the column letter for column D in this worksheet. The entire column is selected.

8. Click the Sheet1 tab at the bottom of the Excel window to return to the first worksheet in the workbook. Notice that row 10 is still selected in this worksheet.

9. Click cell A1 to activate this cell.

Leave this workbook open for the following exercise.

Project 1   Getting Started with Excel

> Students gain familiarity with the Excel screen in this exercise as they review menu options and move around the Excel screen and worksheets. The solution file, saved as **Medical Expenses 97** on the Instructor's Resource disk, reflects Exercise 5, Challenge 1, 2, and 3 additions.

Challenge

The following challenges enable you to use your problem-solving skills. Take time to work through these exercises now.

1. Moving around Excel Worksheets

You have decided that you want to become more familiar with moving around Excel worksheets. Practice moving around a worksheet using the keyboard and mouse. Use the Go To dialog box to move from one worksheet to another.

> Students gain practice moving around the worksheet screen in this activity. In addition to using the mouse and the keyboard, students use the Go To dialog box to move around workbook components. The solution file, saved as **Medical Expenses 97** on the Instructor's Resource disk, reflects Exercise 5, Challenge 1, 2, and 3 additions.

2. Entering Data into a Worksheet to Track Medical Expenses

Now that you are ready to create a worksheet, you decide to enter data into the worksheet currently on your screen. Because you want to use the worksheet to track the current year's medical expenses for your family, enter the following information:

Family Medical Expenses—1997				
Name	Date	Description	Amount	Applied to Deductible
Joe	5-Jan	Dr. visit	45	
Joe	15-Feb	Dr. visit	45	
Erica	31-Jan	Dr. visit	45	
Erica	31-Jan	Blood test	25	
Lisa	15-Mar	Dr. visit	50	
Joe	28-Feb	Dentist	80	

Leave the worksheet open for the following exercise.

> Students enter data in an existing worksheet. The solution file, saved as **Medical Expenses 97** on the Instructor's Resource disk, reflects Exercise 5, Challenge 1, 2, and 3 additions.

Applying Your Skills

3. Saving the Medical Expenses Worksheet

Now that you have entered data into the worksheet, you need to save the file to protect your data and so that you can access the information at a later time. You also want a printed copy of your worksheet. Save the worksheet created in the previous exercise as `Medical Expenses 97`; then print the worksheet in landscape orientation.

> Students save and print a copy of the open worksheet. The solution file, saved as **Medical Expenses 97** on the Instructor's Resource disk, reflects Exercise 5, Challenge 1, 2, and 3 additions.

4. Exploring the Excel Help System

Explore the Help System by locating the help topics titled `Enter a Formula` and `Selecting Cells`. Use the Contents tab to find these topics. If your instructor requests it, you can print the help topics by choosing **O**ptions, **P**rint Topic from the help window. When the Print dialog box displays, click OK to print a copy of the help topic.

> Students gain another opportunity to use Excel 97 Help features in this activity. Students use the **H**elp, **C**ontents feature to learn about entering a formula and selecting cells. Instructors may encourage students to use the Help **O**ptions, **P**rint Topic command to print the information.

5. Creating a Checking Account Worksheet

Now that you are learning to use Excel, you decide it would be easier to keep track of your checking account on the computer. Enter the following data and then save the worksheet as `Checking Account`; you use this worksheet in a later project.

1. In cell A2, type `Checking Account`.

2. In row 4, starting in column A, type the following. Each entry should be in a separate column. Don't worry if the entire entry won't display in a column; you fix it in a later project.

    ```
    Check #
    Date
    Description
    Deposits
    Check Amount
    Balance
    ```

3. In cell F5, enter a starting balance.

4. Starting in cell A6, type information for the last 10 checks you have written. You can use actual information, or just create the information for the file.

5. Leave column F blank. In a later project, you enter a formula to calculate the balance.

> This activity provides students an additional opportunity to insert text and values in a worksheet. Although solutions will vary, a solution file is saved as **Checking Account** on the Instructor's Resource disk.

Project 2

Building a Spreadsheet

Creating an Office Expense Budget

In this project, you learn how to:
- Open an Existing Worksheet
- Select Worksheet Items
- Use AutoFill
- Add and Remove Rows and Columns
- Undo and Redo Actions
- Copy Information
- Move Information

Project 2 Building a Spreadsheet

Why Would I Do This?

Now that you are familiar with the Excel screen and the basics of entering data and saving files, it's time to work with some of Excel's more powerful editing tools. In Project 1, "Getting Started with Excel," you learned how to create a simple worksheet. In this project, you learn to use Excel to create a budget worksheet that includes office expense information for several months.

Using the sample budget information, you learn how to control the structure of a worksheet by adding and deleting columns and rows. You also learn how to use Excel's editing features to make your work faster and easier.

Lesson 1: Opening an Existing Worksheet

After you create a workbook and save it to your hard disk or floppy disk, you can reopen the workbook and resume working with its data. With Excel, you can open a new workbook file, open an existing workbook file, or work with the default workbook. The default worksheet appears on-screen whenever you start Excel, or when you create a new file using the General Workbook file template.

> **On Your Mark**
> Who needs to be able to open an Excel file that you've created? What are the advantages of being able to work on a spreadsheet you've already created?

To Open an Existing Worksheet

> **Tip for Instructors**
> A *new workbook* is a blank or empty workbook. When you start Excel, a new workbook appears on the screen.

1 **Start Excel if it is not already running, and in the default workbook file, click the File menu.**

The File menu opens to display a number of commands.

2 **Choose the Open command.**

The Open dialog box appears, as shown in Figure 2.1. The files and folders stored in the default folder, My Documents, are displayed. You can also click the Open File button on the Standard toolbar to get to the Open dialog box.

Figure 2.1
The Open dialog box lists all files in the default folder.

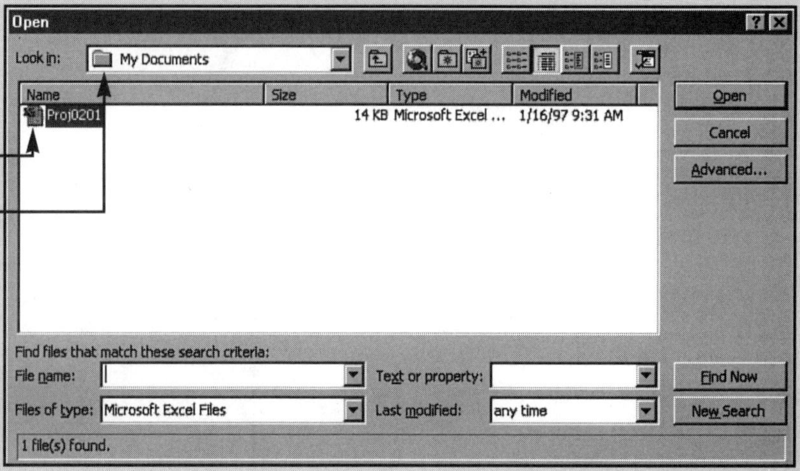

Select a file here
Default folder

> **Speedy Class**
> Mention the concept of *template*, and indicate that the standard template contains the defaults you see in the blank workbook (column widths, row heights, number formats, and so on).

**Project Time
90 minutes**

Lesson 1: Opening an Existing Worksheet   41

Tip for Students
The second icon on the Standard toolbar is a shortcut for opening files.

Tip for Students
Excel looks for Excel files by default: *.XL*, *.XLS, and *.XLA. (See the Files of **T**ype option at the bottom of the dialog box.) Other kinds of files can be opened in Excel, and found quickly by choosing another file type from the Files of Type drop-down list.

Tip for Instructors
Discuss the procedure for changing folders and/or drives when searching for a file.

❸ In the list of files and folders, click the Proj0201 file icon to select it.

This file may already be selected. If you don't see Proj0201 in the list, try opening another folder from the Look **in** drop-down list, or try looking on another drive. The file may be stored in a different location on your system. If you can't find the file on your computer, ask your instructor for the location of the data files you will use with this book.

> **If you have problems...**
>
> If, when you click the file to select it, the characters in the file name become highlighted instead of the entire file name, it means you changed to Rename mode. In Rename mode, you can change the name of an existing file or folder. To select the file, make sure you click its icon.

Tip for Students
Instead of clicking **O**pen, you can select the file and press ↵Enter, or just double-click the file name.

❹ Choose Open.

The office budget sample worksheet (Proj0201) appears on-screen, as shown in Figure 2.2. Now use the Save **A**s command to save a copy of this sample file under a more descriptive file name. The original data file will be stored intact.

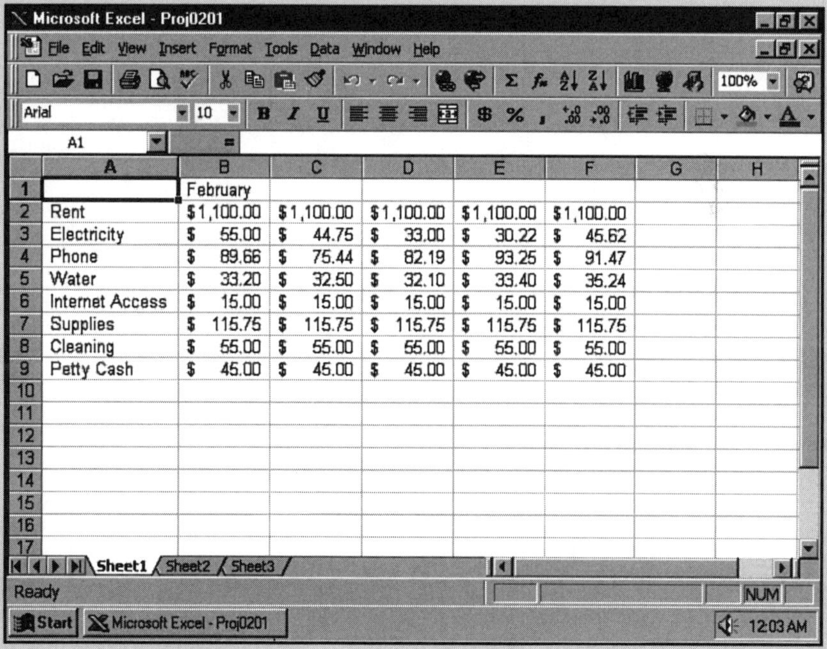

Figure 2.2
Save the sample file Proj0201 as **Budget** to use in this project.

Tip for Instructors
This book refers to a default folder called My Documents. The students' default folders may be different on their machines.

Speedy Class
Discuss defaults: what they are, why you may want to change them (such as the default folder), and how to set a default (by choosing **T**ools, **O**ptions).

Tip for Students
By using Save As, you keep the original file intact on the disk and save a copy of the file with a new name or in a new location. Therefore, you can make changes to the new file without affecting the original.

Tip for Instructors
Consider some situations in which you might want to use Save As instead of simply saving the changes to a file.

❺ Choose the File menu again, then choose the Save As command.

The Save As dialog box appears.

continues

Project 2 Building a Spreadsheet

To Open an Existing Worksheet (continued)

Tip for Students
When saving a file in Excel, an .XLS extension is attached to the file name. Unless you've changed the default settings, you won't see this file extension when viewing the files in My Computer or in Windows Explorer.

6 **In the File name text box, type** Budget **to replace** Proj0201.

Budget is the workbook file name that is used throughout this project.

7 **From the Save in drop-down list, select the appropriate drive and folder for saving the new file.**

If necessary, ask your instructor where you should save the new workbook file.

Tip for Students
In the Save As dialog box, the file name is selected when you first open the box. You don't have to delete it; just type over the old name.

8 **Choose Save.**

Excel saves the workbook as Budget and automatically closes the original data file. Keep the Budget workbook open to use in the next lesson.

INSIDE To open a file quickly from the Open dialog box, double-click the file's icon in the list of files. If you double-click the file name, however, you may end up in Rename mode.

✓ On Your Mark
How do you select one cell or several on the worksheet? What can you do to a worksheet item once you've selected it?

Selecting
Designating an item on-screen so you can do something with it. Also called *highlighting*.

Lesson 2: Selecting Worksheet Items

In order to build a worksheet, you must learn how to *select* items in the worksheet. When you select an item, you highlight that item so you can make changes to it. You select a cell, for example, so you can copy the cell's content into another cell. You must select a column so that you can change the column's width.

In this lesson, you learn how to select items in the Budget worksheet.

To Select Worksheet Items

SLIDE 2–1

? Q&A
What's a quick way to get to cell A1?
Answer: Press Ctrl+Home.

Tip for Students
Select an entire row by clicking a number. Select more than one column or row by dragging across column letters or row numbers.

Range
A cell or a rectangular group of adjacent cells.

1 **Click cell B1 in the** Budget **worksheet.**

You have selected cell B1 by clicking in it. Once you select a cell, the cell's border is highlighted in bold, the cell's address appears in the name box of the formula bar, and the cell's content appears in the contents area of the formula bar. In addition, the letter heading of the column and the number heading of the row in which the cell is located appear in bold.

2 **Click cell A2, press and hold down the left mouse button, then drag the mouse pointer to cell G2. Release the left mouse button when the mouse pointer is in cell G2.**

Several adjacent cells—called a *range*—are now selected (see Figure 2.3). As you drag the mouse, the name box on the formula bar shows you how many rows and columns you are selecting. Dragging the mouse is an easy way to select a range of cells. After you finish

Lesson 2: Selecting Worksheet Items   43

Speedy Class
To select cells with the keyboard, use ⇧Shift and the arrow keys.

Tip for Instructors
The active cell in the selected range has a white background, even though it is still selected.

selecting the range, the entire range of selected cells is highlighted, but only the address of the first cell—in this case, A2—appears in the name box, and only the content of the first cell appears in the Formula bar. That's because only the first cell is the active cell.

Now practice selecting an entire column of the worksheet.

Figure 2.3
The first cell in the selected range is active while the rest of the selected cells are highlighted.

- Active cell address
- Column and row headings are bold
- Selected cells

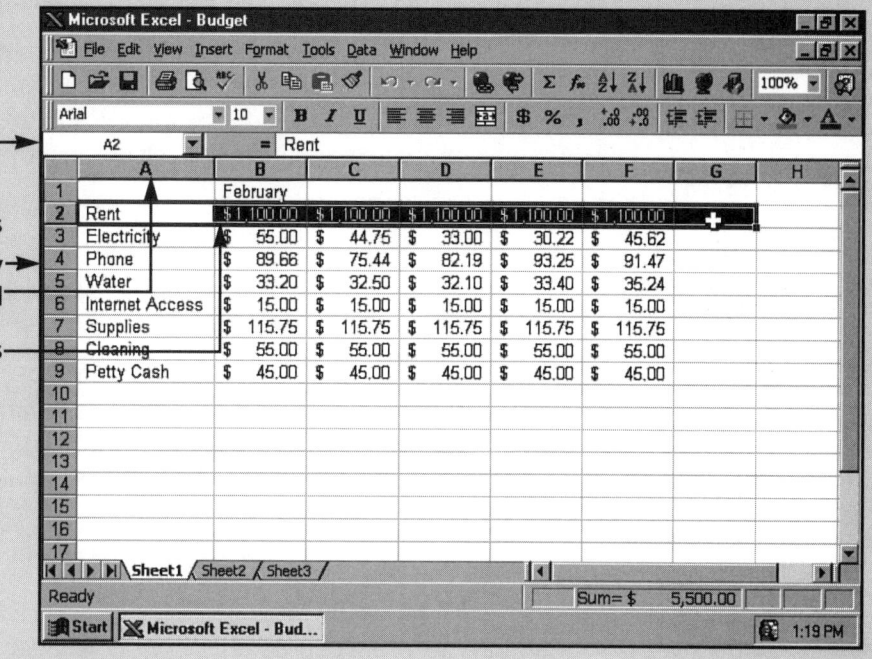

Speedy Class
Select the entire row with ⇧Shift+Spacebar.
Select the entire column with Ctrl+Spacebar.

Worksheet frame
The horizontal bar containing the column letters and the vertical bar containing the row numbers, located in the worksheet area.

❸ **Click column heading B in the *worksheet frame*.**

This selects the entire worksheet column B, as shown in Figure 2.4. Keep the Budget worksheet open to use in the next lesson.

Figure 2.4
You can quickly select a column or row by clicking the column or row heading in the worksheet frame.

- Worksheet frame
- Click the Select All button to select the entire worksheet
- Selected column

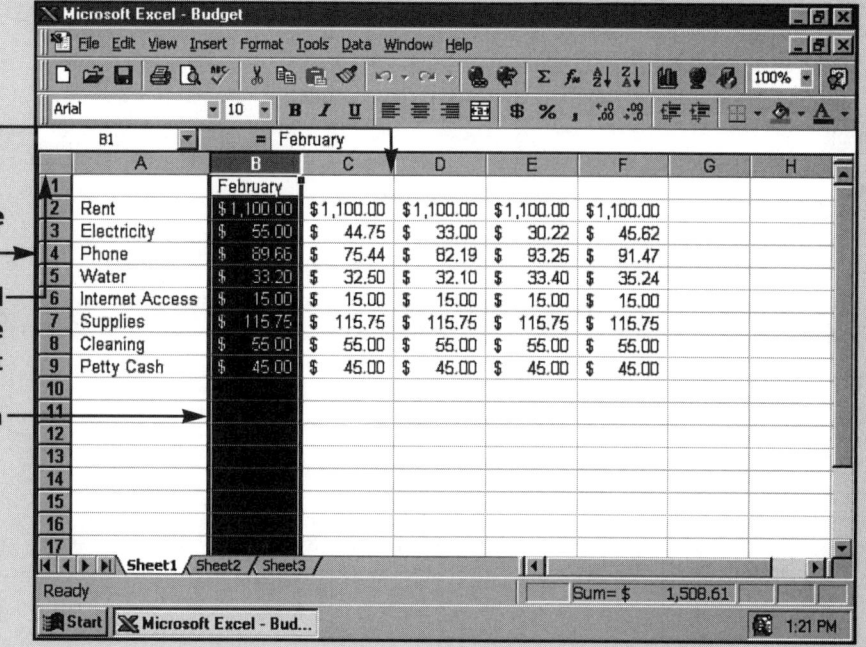

Quicksand
Selecting rows is tricky. Students often accidentally resize or delete rows altogether. Make sure that the mouse pointer is a white cross when students select. Be ready to show them how to reset the range of rows to the default height.

Q&A

Under what circumstances would you want to select non-adjacent cells?
Answer: When you want to perform the same operation on the group of cells (data entry, copying and pasting, formatting, and so on).

Tip for Students

To make global changes (such as changing number format or column width) select the entire worksheet by clicking the Select All button.

Tip for Instructors

Select a block of cells in which you want to enter data. As you press ↵Enter after each entry, the active cell pointer moves from one cell to another within the block. Press ↵Enter to move the cell pointer forward down through the block; press ⇧Shift+↵Enter to move it backward; press Tab to move it forward across; and press ⇧Shift+Tab to move it across and backward. Caution: Using arrow keys deselects the block.

On Your Mark

What kinds of headings can be used to create incremental sequences (such as months of the year)?

SLIDE 2–2

You can select two or more rows, columns, or cells by pressing and holding down Ctrl while you click the individual elements. This way, you don't have to select rows, columns, or cells in succession.

To select the entire worksheet, click the Select All button, the rectangle in the top-left corner of the worksheet frame.

To select non-adjacent cells, click the first cell, then press and hold Ctrl and click additional cells. The last cell that you click is the active cell, but the others remain selected.

To select just the content or part of the content of a cell, you can click in the active cell to display the I-beam mouse pointer, then drag the I-beam across any part of the text or data in the cell or the formula bar to select it.

To select cells with the keyboard, select the first cell in the range, press and hold down ⇧Shift, then use the arrow keys to select additional cells.

To select data with the keyboard, position the insertion point where you want to start selecting, press and hold down ⇧Shift, then use the arrow keys to move the insertion point to the last item you want to select.

In Excel, the standard notation for identifying ranges is to list the first cell in the range, then a colon, then the last cell in the range. For example, if you are referring to the range of cells from A1 to F9, you would type `A1:F9`.

Lesson 3: Using AutoFill

You have now opened the Budget worksheet and practiced selecting items in the worksheet. The Budget worksheet has information on various expenses over several months, but before the worksheet is complete, a few items need to be changed.

As you can see, row 1 of the Budget worksheet should have column headings for each month of expenses you track. Using the AutoFill command, you can easily select a range of cells to have Excel fill the range with a sequence of information.

In this case, by selecting the cell containing the label February and then selecting a range of cells, you can add a sequence of months (February, March, April, and so on) to the range you select. You can also set up a sequence of numbers, letters, and days of the week by using the AutoFill command.

To Use AutoFill

Q&A

If cell B1 isn't visible on the screen, what is a quick way to get to that cell?
Answer: Press F5 (Go To).

❶ Click cell B1 in the Budget worksheet.

Cell B1 contains the column heading for the month of February. To build column headings for the rest of the worksheet, you select this cell as the starting value for the fill. This tells Excel the type of series you want to create—in this case, a series of consecutive months.

Lesson 3: Using AutoFill

Tip for Instructors
AutoFill works only on adjacent cells (either horizontal or vertical).

Tip for Students
Format the first cell (bold and centered, for example) before dragging. When you fill the adjacent cells, the format is copied as well.

❷ **Move the mouse pointer to the *fill handle* (the small, black box in the lower right corner of cell B1) until the pointer changes to a thin, black plus sign.**

When the mouse pointer changes to a black plus sign, Excel is ready to select a range of cells to be filled (see Figure 2.5).

❸ **Press the left mouse button and drag right to cell F1, then release the mouse button.**

This action selects the range B1 through F1. As you drag, notice that ScreenTips indicate the data that Excel will use to fill each cell. When you release the mouse button, Excel fills the range with months (starting with February and increasing by one month for each cell in the range), and selects it, as shown in Figure 2.6.

Figure 2.5
The fill handle is a thin black plus sign.

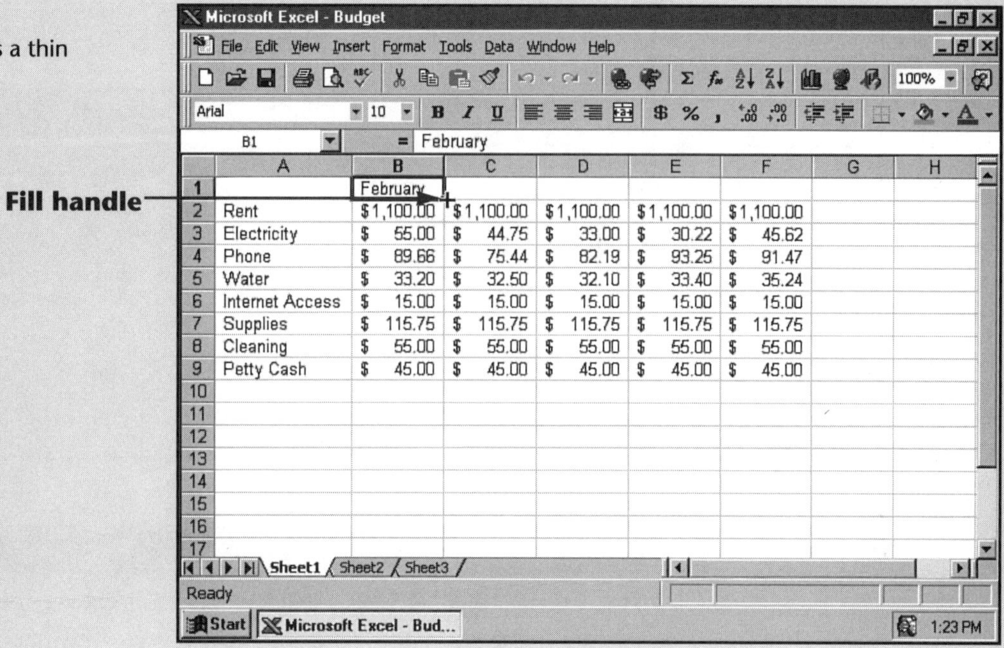

continues

46 Project 2 Building a Spreadsheet

To Use AutoFill (continued)

Figure 2.6
The AutoFill command is used here to create a series of months.

	A	B	C	D	E	F
1		February	March	April	May	June
2	Rent	$1,100.00	$1,100.00	$1,100.00	$1,100.00	$1,100.00
3	Electricity	$ 55.00	$ 44.75	$ 33.00	$ 30.22	$ 45.62
4	Phone	$ 89.66	$ 75.44	$ 82.19	$ 93.25	$ 91.47
5	Water	$ 33.20	$ 32.50	$ 32.10	$ 33.40	$ 35.24
6	Internet Access	$ 15.00	$ 15.00	$ 15.00	$ 15.00	$ 15.00
7	Supplies	$ 115.75	$ 115.75	$ 115.75	$ 115.75	$ 115.75
8	Cleaning	$ 55.00	$ 55.00	$ 55.00	$ 55.00	$ 55.00
9	Petty Cash	$ 45.00	$ 45.00	$ 45.00	$ 45.00	$ 45.00

Speedy Class
To create incremental sequences of numbers, type the first two numbers in two adjacent cells, select both cells, then drag as before. You can use any increment. To create a sequence by one, type the number in the first cell, hold down Ctrl, then drag.

Tip for Students
If you don't want to create an incremental sequence with such a value as months of the year, then hold down Ctrl while dragging: The first cell will repeat itself in all the others.

Speedy Class
Experiment with sequential items: days of the week and months of the year (full names and standard abbreviations), combinations of letters and numbers (such as Week 1, Region 1, and 1st Quarter), and times of the day.

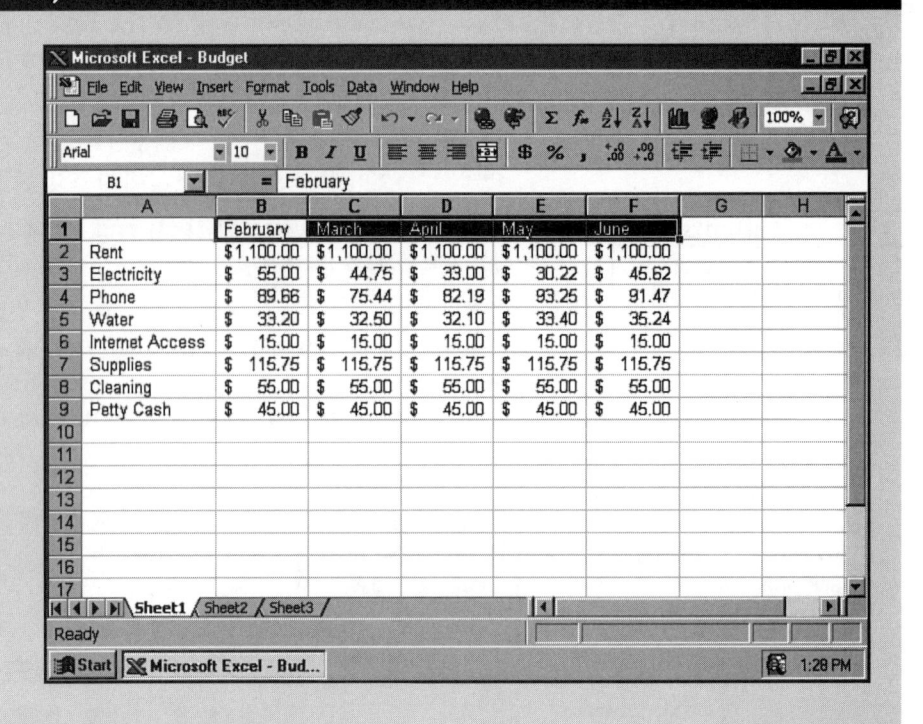

4 Click any cell.

This deselects the range. From here you can take the next step to build your Budget worksheet: adding and deleting columns and rows.

Save your changes and keep the worksheet open for the next lesson.

If you have problems...

When using AutoFill, if you select cells that already contain data, Excel overwrites the data in the cells. You can reverse this action by choosing **E**dit, **U**ndo before performing any other action.

You can fill columns as well as rows. Simply use the fill handle to drag down or up the column the same way you drag left or right to fill a row.

If you want to create a sequence of consecutive increments to fill by example (1, 2, 3, and so on), you enter the first two items in the sequence and select those cells. If you want to create a sequence of values in increments other than 1 (5, 10, 15), you enter the data in two cells and select those cells before filling the range.

You may already have noticed that sometimes Excel seems to anticipate what you are going to enter into a cell. For example, you may start typing a column label, and Excel automatically completes the word you have begun—sometimes correctly, sometimes incorrectly. This is a feature called AutoComplete.

Lesson 4: Adding and Removing Rows and Columns

With AutoComplete, as you enter new data, Excel considers data you have recently entered to see if they seem to match. If so, Excel automatically enters the same data you entered previously. For example, if you enter the label `Winter` in a cell and then start typing `Wi` into another cell, Excel assumes you are entering `Winter` again. If Excel is correct, this saves you some typing. If not, you can edit the entry.

To disable AutoComplete, choose **T**ools, **O**ptions, click the Edit tab, and deselect the Enable Auto**C**omplete for Cell Values check box. Then choose OK.

Lesson 4: Adding and Removing Rows and Columns

If you decide to add more information to your worksheet, Excel enables you to add rows and columns. You may, for example, want to add expense information for the month of January to your worksheet. Also, the cost of insurance, a common expense, is not listed in your worksheet. If you no longer want to include certain information, you can also remove columns and rows.

In this lesson, you learn how to add and remove rows and columns in a worksheet.

> **✓ On Your Mark**
> Under what circumstances might you want to add or remove rows or columns?

To Add and Remove Rows and Columns

> **? Q&A**
> How do you know which area to select when inserting a row or column? *Answer:* Select the row or column that you want to be blank.

> **Tip for Students**
> You also can right-click the selected row or column and choose **I**nsert from the shortcut menu to insert a row or column.

> **Tip for Students**
> After selecting the row or column that you want to be blank, press Ctrl followed by + on your keypad to insert. Each time you press +, another row is inserted. Pressing − with Ctrl deletes the selected row or column.

❶ In the Budget worksheet frame, click the row heading for row 8.

The entire row 8, Cleaning, is highlighted to show that it has been selected.

❷ Choose Insert, Rows.

The content of row 8 and all rows below it move down one row. A new, blank row is inserted as the new row 8 (see Figure 2.7). Notice that all the rows beneath the new row 8 are automatically renumbered. Excel always inserts the new row above the row you select.

continues

To Add and Remove Rows and Columns (continued)

Figure 2.7
A new, blank row is inserted into the Budget worksheet.

Inserted row → (row 8)
Contents move down → (rows 9, 10)

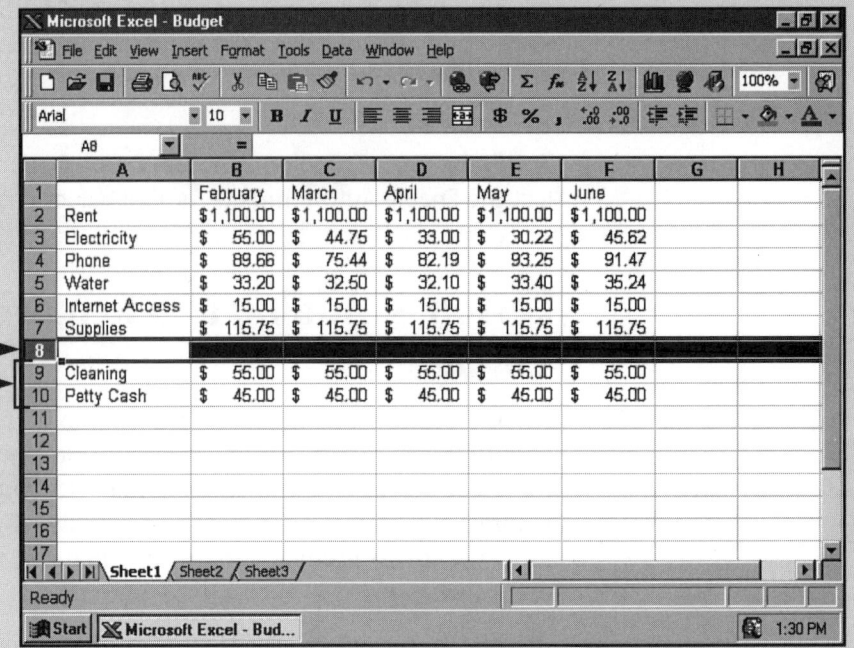

Tip for Students
Inserted rows and columns contain the format attributes of the area you selected when making the insertion.

3 **Click cell A8 and type** Insurance, **then press** ↵Enter.

You have inserted and labeled a new row for insurance expenses. Now insert a new column for January's expenses.

4 **In the** Budget **worksheet frame, click the column heading for column B.**

The entire column B, February, is highlighted to show that it has been selected.

5 **Choose Insert Columns.**

The content of column B and all columns to the right of column B, move to the right and have new letters assigned to them. A new, blank column B is added to the worksheet. Excel always inserts a new column to the *left* of the column you select.

6 **Click cell B1 and type** January, **then press** ↵Enter.

You have inserted and labeled a new row for January expenses. Finally, you decide that you don't want to include petty cash expenses in your worksheet. Delete the entire row 10 to remove Petty Cash data.

7 **In the worksheet frame, click the row heading for row 10.**

The entire row 10, Petty Cash, is highlighted.

8 **Choose Edit, Delete.**

Row 10 is now deleted. When you delete a selected column or row, you also delete any content in that column or row. Your worksheet should now look similar to Figure 2.8.

Speedy Class
Selecting an area, rather than an entire row or column, enables you to insert or delete a group of cells. This operation adjusts cells around the selected area, but doesn't go beyond—thus leaving the rest of the worksheet unchanged. When you insert or delete a group of cells, Excel prompts you to identify the direction in which you want the cells to move.

Lesson 4: Adding and Removing Rows and Columns

Figure 2.8
Use the **E**dit, **D**elete command to remove unwanted columns or rows.

> **Tip for Instructors**
> Discuss the dangers of inserting and deleting entire rows and columns when you can't see what part of your workbook might be off-screen.

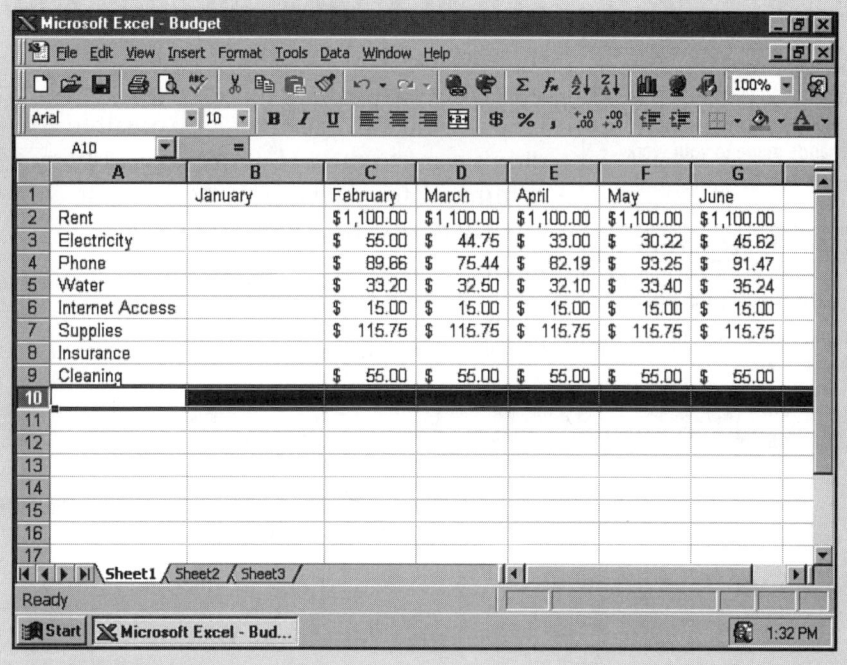

	A	B	C	D	E	F	G
1		January	February	March	April	May	June
2	Rent		$1,100.00	$1,100.00	$1,100.00	$1,100.00	$1,100.00
3	Electricity		$ 55.00	$ 44.75	$ 33.00	$ 30.22	$ 45.62
4	Phone		$ 89.66	$ 75.44	$ 82.19	$ 93.25	$ 91.47
5	Water		$ 33.20	$ 32.50	$ 32.10	$ 33.40	$ 35.24
6	Internet Access		$ 15.00	$ 15.00	$ 15.00	$ 15.00	$ 15.00
7	Supplies		$ 115.75	$ 115.75	$ 115.75	$ 115.75	$ 115.75
8	Insurance						
9	Cleaning		$ 55.00	$ 55.00	$ 55.00	$ 55.00	$ 55.00

Save your changes and leave the Budget worksheet open to use in the next lesson.

If you want to insert more than one row or column at a time, select as many adjacent rows or columns as you need blank rows or columns, then choose **I**nsert, **R**ows or **I**nsert, **C**olumns. For example, if you want to insert five new rows beginning at row 4, select rows 4 through 8 and then choose **I**nsert, **R**ows. The same is true for deleting rows and columns. To delete five columns, select the five columns you want to delete and then choose **E**dit, **D**elete.

You can also delete only the contents of selected cells. Select the cells and press Del, or choose **E**dit, Cle**a**r, Co**n**tents.

You can use shortcut menus to insert or delete columns, rows, and cell contents. Select the item you want to insert or delete, move the mouse pointer to it, and click the right mouse button. Choose the appropriate command from the shortcut menu that appears.

> **Tip for Students**
> Undo is especially important when undoing the deletion of a row or column. You can't put the row or column back by inserting a new one (unless you deleted a blank area).

If you change your mind about what you added or deleted, choose **E**dit, **U**ndo. Undo reverses the last action you performed.

If you have problems...

If the Delete dialog box appears when you choose **E**dit, **D**elete, it means that you didn't select the entire row or column before choosing the command. You can either cancel the dialog box and try selecting the row again, or select Entire **R**ow or Entire **C**olumn in the dialog box, and choose OK to complete the deletion. The same is true for inserting and deleting rows and columns.

Project 2 Building a Spreadsheet

On Your Mark
In what situations would you choose to reverse a change to your worksheet? In what situations would you want to repeat a change made to your worksheet?

Tip for Instructors
Point out to students some of the worksheet actions that *cannot* be undone such as saving to disk, opening and closing files, and so on.

Lesson 5: Undoing and Redoing Actions

By inserting and deleting rows and columns, you have changed the structure of your worksheet. However, when you use insert and delete commands, you can see that it is possible to accidentally make changes you didn't want to make. Luckily, Excel is very forgiving: You can use the Undo command to quickly reverse the last action and the Redo command to quickly reverse the Undo command.

Excel even lets you undo or redo a series of actions; if you don't realize you made a mistake right away, you can still recover the data you need. In this lesson, you practice undoing and redoing actions in your Budget worksheet.

To Undo and Redo Actions

1 In the worksheet frame, click the heading for row 9, then choose Edit, Delete.

This selects, then deletes row 9.

2 Choose Edit, Undo Delete.

Excel reverses the last action you performed, which was the deletion of row 9. The row and all of its contents are put back in the worksheet. Notice that the Undo command includes a description of the last action. The command changes according to the action that will be reversed.

3 Choose Edit, Redo Delete.

Excel reverses the last action of the Undo command. In this case, Excel deletes row 9 again. Like Undo, the Redo command also includes a description of the last action.

4 Click in cell A11, type Miscellaneous and press ↵Enter.

The text is entered in cell A11. At this point, you realize you really need row 9 back in the worksheet. However, the last action you performed was typing text into cell A11. You must use multiple undo to reverse more than one action.

5 Click the Undo drop-down arrow on the Standard toolbar.

A list of the actions that can be reversed is displayed, as shown in Figure 2.9. The most recently performed action is at the top of the list. You can chose to undo as many or as few of these actions as you want.

Lesson 6: Copying Information

Figure 2.9
You can use multiple undo to reverse more than one action at a time.

- Redo button
- Undo button
- List of actions that can be undone

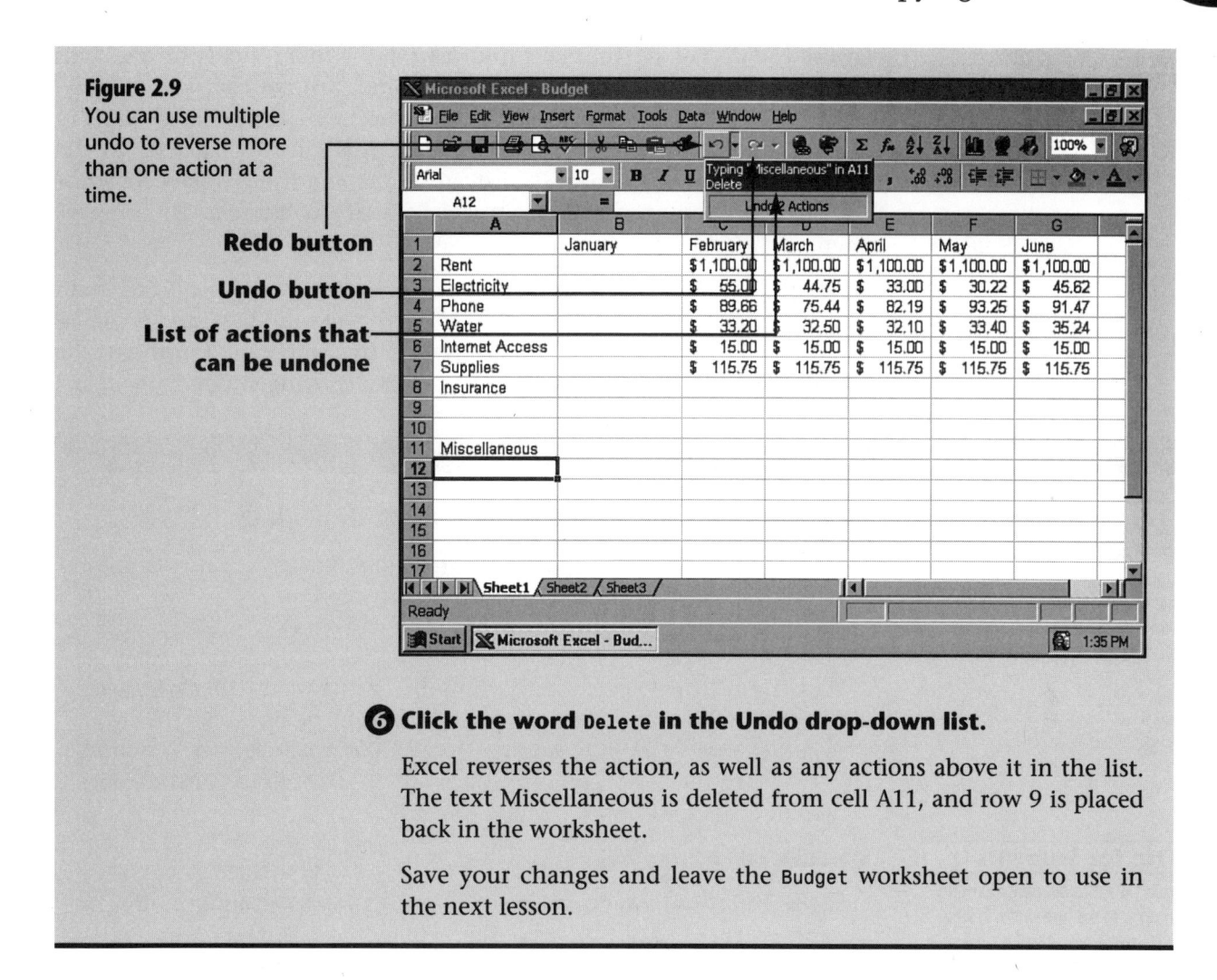

6 **Click the word** Delete **in the Undo drop-down list.**

Excel reverses the action, as well as any actions above it in the list. The text Miscellaneous is deleted from cell A11, and row 9 is placed back in the worksheet.

Save your changes and leave the Budget worksheet open to use in the next lesson.

You can use multiple level Redo to redo more than one action. Click the Redo drop-down arrow on the Standard toolbar to display the Redo list, then click the last action you want to redo. All of the actions above the selected action are reinstated.

To quickly undo the most recent action, click the Undo button on the Standard toolbar, or press Ctrl+Z.

To quickly redo the most recent action, click the Redo button on the Standard toolbar, or press Ctrl+Y.

If an action cannot be undone, the Undo command and Undo button are dimmed. If an action cannot be redone, the Redo command and Redo button are dimmed.

Lesson 6: Copying Information

✓ **On Your Mark**
When would you want to be able to copy information from one cell to another on your worksheet?

By adding and removing columns and rows, you have made some important changes to your Budget worksheet. You still need to insert expense information, however, in the new row for Insurance and the new column for January.

Because you don't have the exact information for your office insurance bills or for your January expenses in this example, assume that you can use information from other parts of your worksheet to estimate these parts of your budget. You might assume, for example, that January expenses are the same as your February expenses. Instead of retyping the February information, you can copy the cells from the February column to the January column.

Copying information from one column to another is much quicker than typing it a second time. You can copy or move text, numbers, and formulas from one cell to another, from one worksheet to another, and from one file to another. Use the Budget worksheet to practice copying and moving data.

To Copy Information

Tip for Students
After you select the range you want to copy, right-click the selected range to open a shortcut menu that includes a **C**opy command.

1 In the Budget worksheet, select cells C2 through C9.

This highlights the expense information that you want to copy from the February column into the January column.

2 Choose Edit, Copy.

A copy of the selected cells' contents is placed in the Windows *Clipboard*. The Clipboard stores information or formulas that you want to move (copy) to another location. (See the Jargon Watch at the end of this lesson for more about the Clipboard.) A flashing dotted line appears around the copied cells.

Tip for Students
If you don't want to overwrite existing cell contents, make sure that the area you are pasting into is blank.

3 Click cell B2.

This selects the location where you want the copied information to appear. You do not have to select a range that is the same size as the range you are copying; Excel automatically fills in the data starting with the one cell you select. Notice that the flashing dotted line still appears around the copied cells, even though the cells are no longer selected. This helps you remember which cells are currently stored on the Clipboard.

Tip for Instructors
The nature of this example (copying to adjacent cells) lends itself to the shortcut of dragging the information using AutoFill.

4 Choose Edit, Paste.

The copied cells' content appears in cells B2 through B9, as shown in Figure 2.10. As indicated by the commands you have chosen, this process is called *copying and pasting*, and is a very common procedure in Windows applications. The flashing dotted line still appears around cells C2 through C9 because they are still stored on the Clipboard.

Tip for Instructors
Remind students that the Clipboard can contain any type of information created in a Windows program, including text and graphics.

Note that the expense information in the January column is exactly the same as the information in the February column. To estimate your office insurance expense, assume for now that your monthly insurance bill is the same as your monthly office rent payment.

Lesson 6: Copying Information 53

Figure 2.10
The January column now contains expense information copied from the February column.

Copied data
Pasted data

Tip for Instructors
Mention the use of the Clipboard to copy and move information from one program to another, and to link data between those programs. Examples of this procedure are covered in Project 7, "Using Excel with Other Programs."

Tip for Students
If you place an extremely large amount of data on the Clipboard, it continues to use your computer's memory while it stays there, even after you've finished the paste operation.

Q&A
How can you quickly relieve the Clipboard of a large selection? *Answer:* Click one cell, then click the Copy button to copy that cell to the Clipboard.

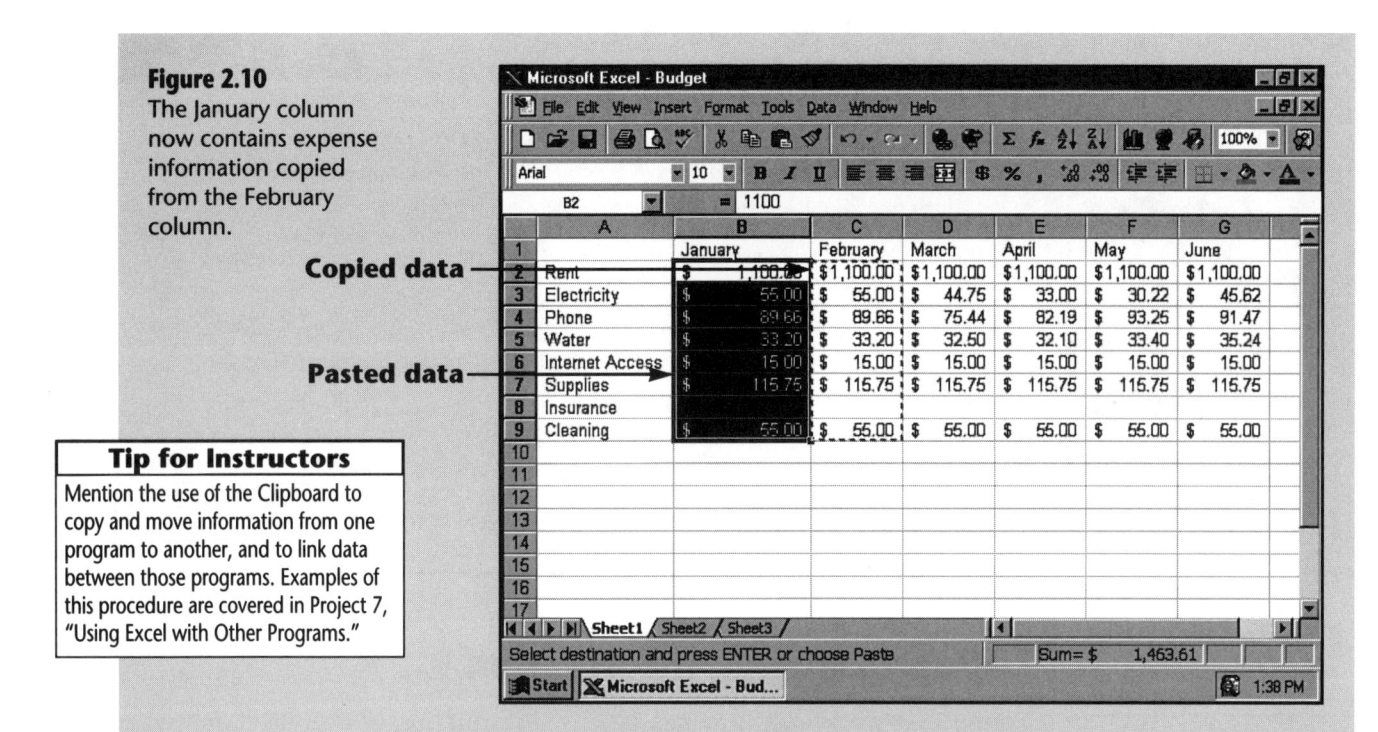

❺ Select cells B2 through G2.

To estimate your insurance expenses, copy the rent expense information that you just selected to the Insurance row.

❻ Click the Copy button on the Standard toolbar.

This copies the selected cells the same way as when you use the **E**dit, **C**opy command. The cells' contents are stored in the Clipboard, ready to be pasted. Now, the flashing dotted line appears around cells B2 through G2.

❼ Click cell B8.

This selects the new location for the copied information.

❽ Click the Paste button on the Standard toolbar.

The contents of the copied cells are pasted into the new location. Again, notice that the Insurance expense information is exactly the same as the Rent information in row 2. In Project 5, "Improving the Appearance of a Worksheet," you use formulas to change the amount you just copied. Save your most recent changes and keep the Budget worksheet open to use in the next lesson.

Jargon Watch

When you **copy** or **cut** information in Excel, it moves to the Windows **Clipboard**—a part of memory set aside for storing data that you want to move or copy to another location. The cut or copied information stays in the Clipboard until you cut or copy something else. Remember that the Clipboard can hold only one item, although that

continues

> **Continued**
>
> item can be quite large. Whenever you cut or copy a new piece of information and place it in the Clipboard, it overwrites any information that is already there. Because information that you cut or copy is stored in the Clipboard, you can **paste** the item many times and in many different places.
>
> One thing to keep in mind while you are working in Excel is the difference between the Edit menu commands **Cut, Clear,** and **Delete**. Edit, Cut removes an item from the worksheet and moves it to the Clipboard where it is stored for later use. Edit, Clear removes the selected information completely. You can choose Clear, Contents to clear cell contents, Clear, Formats to clear cell formatting, or Clear, All to clear both the formatting and the contents. Edit, Delete removes not only the selected information but the cells containing it as well. If you choose the wrong command by mistake, press Ctrl+Z to undo the command, click the Undo button on the Standard toolbar, or choose Edit, Undo.

Lesson 7: Moving Information

> **✓ On Your Mark**
> Under what circumstances would you want to pick up something from one part of your worksheet and move it to another?

Your Budget worksheet now has expense information in every cell, but what if you want to look at a certain type of expense separately? For example, perhaps you want to see how your utility expenses compare to the rest of your expenses.

You can use Excel's Cut and Insert Cells commands to remove cells from one location in a worksheet and place them in another location. You can use these commands to move cells so that you don't have to go to each cell, enter the same information, and then erase the information in the old location.

In this lesson, you move the rows containing utility expenses to another part of the worksheet.

To Move Information

❶ Select rows 3 through 5 in the Budget worksheet frame.

This highlights the rows of your worksheet that contain utility expenses. These are the rows you will move to another part of the worksheet.

> **Tip for Students**
> The dotted outline serves as a reminder of what you've placed on the Clipboard.

❷ Choose Edit, Cut.

The information in rows 3 through 5 moves to the Clipboard (although you can still see it in the worksheet), and a dotted outline appears around the cut text, as shown in Figure 2.11. You can also click the Cut button on the Standard toolbar.

Lesson 7: Moving Information — 55

Figure 2.11
Cut cells appear in the worksheet surrounded by a flashing dotted line until you move them to a new location.

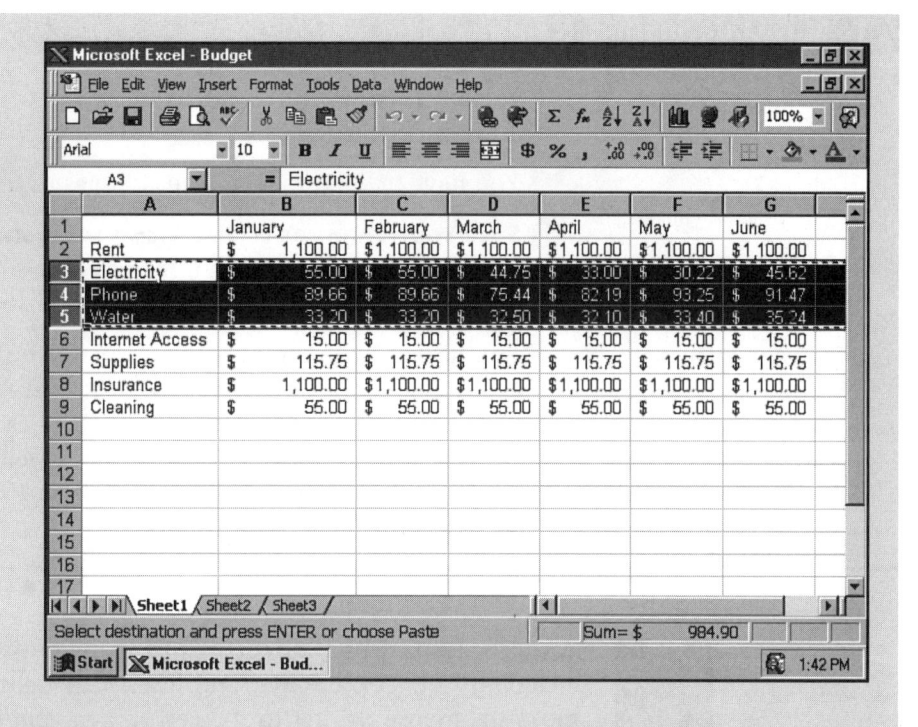

Quicksand
When students are using the shortcut menu, make sure they keep their mouse pointers in the selected cell. Right-clicking over a different cell then selecting **P**aste pastes to the cell that was right-clicked. Remind students of the Undo button, and that the information they cut is still on the Clipboard. They can then try pasting again in the correct location.

❸ Click cell A11 to select it and then choose Insert, Cut Cells.

The rows containing the utility expense information are cut from their original location in the worksheet and are inserted in the new location. The information now appears in rows 8, 9, and 10 (see Figure 2.12).

Figure 2.12
The cut cells are moved to a new location in the worksheet.

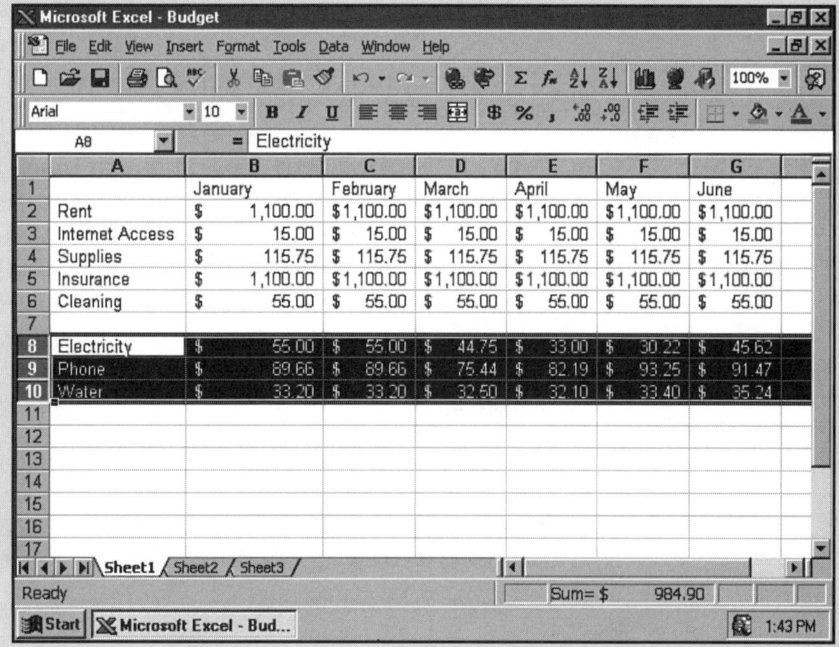

continues

Project 2 Building a Spreadsheet

> **To Move Information (continued)**
>
> Table 2.1 shows some shortcuts for the commonly used C**u**t, **C**opy, and **P**aste commands.
>
> You have now completed the changes to the Budget worksheet.
>
> **④ Save your changes to the Budget worksheet and print two copies, if requested by your instructor. Then close the Budget file.**
>
> You have now completed the lesson on building a spreadsheet. Save the changes you have made to the Budget worksheet. If requested by your instructor, print two copies, then close the Budget file. If you have completed your session on the computer, exit Excel and Windows 95. Otherwise, continue with the "Checking Your Skills" section at the end of this project.

INSIDE

You can use Excel's shortcut menus to perform many common commands, including Cut, Copy, Paste, and Insert Cut Cells. To open a shortcut menu, move the mouse pointer to the cell or area you want to affect, then press the right mouse button. To select a command, click its name in the shortcut menu. Make sure that you move the mouse pointer to the correct cell before you click the shortcut menu command. Shortcut menu commands happen at the location of the mouse pointer, not necessarily in the current cell.

You can also use Excel's Cut and Paste commands to remove information from one cell and place it in another cell. Select the cell or cells you want to move and choose **E**dit, C**u**t. Select the cell where you want to place the information and choose **E**dit, **P**aste. Excel moves the information, but leaves the cells where the information had been intact in the worksheet. You can insert new data, or delete the cells.

> **Tip for Students**
>
> The white arrow mouse pointer can be dangerous. You may find yourself moving data when you intended to merely select cells. Remember the Undo button if you get into trouble!

A handy way of quickly moving one or more cells of data is to select the cells and position the mouse pointer on any border of the cells so that the cell pointer changes to a white arrow. Click and drag the white arrow to the new location. An outline of the cells that you are moving appears as you drag, and a ScreenTip shows you the current active cell where the information will appear when you release the mouse button. If the new location already contains information, a dialog box appears, asking whether you want to replace the current information.

You can also copy data by pressing Ctrl and dragging the cells to the new location.

Table 2.1 Copying, Cutting, and Pasting

Command	Tool	Shortcut Key
Edit, C**u**t	✂	Ctrl+X
Edit, **C**opy	📋	Ctrl+C
Edit, **P**aste	📋	Ctrl+V

Project Summary

To	Do This
Open an existing file	Choose **F**ile, **O**pen, select the file name in the Open dialog box, then choose **O**pen.
Save a file with a new name	Choose **F**ile, Save **A**s, type a new name in the File **n**ame text box, then choose **S**ave.
Select a cell	Click the cell you want to select, or use the arrow keys to move to it.
Select a range of cells	Drag from the first cell to the last cell in the range, or use ⇧Shift and the arrow keys to highlight cells using the keyboard.
AutoFill a range of cells	Select the cell containing the first entry in the series, then drag across the range you want to fill.
Insert rows or columns	Select the rows or columns, then choose **I**nsert, **R**ows or **I**nsert, **C**olumns.
Delete rows or columns	Select the rows or columns, then choose **E**dit, **D**elete.
Reverse the last action	Choose **E**dit, **U**ndo.
Reverse a series of actions	Click the Undo drop-down arrow, then select the last action you want to reverse.
Redo the last undone action	Choose **E**dit, **R**edo.
Redo a series of undone actions	Click the Redo drop-down arrow, then select the last action you want to redo.
Copy cells	Select the cells to copy, then click the Copy button on the Standard toolbar. Select the first cell in the new location, then click the Paste button on the toolbar.
Move cells	Select the cells to move, then click the Cut button on the Standard toolbar. Select the first cell in the new location, then choose **I**nsert, Cut C**e**lls.
Paste cells	Copy or cut the cells, select the new location, then click the Paste button on the Standard toolbar.

Project 2 Building a Spreadsheet

Checking Your Skills

True/False

For each of the following, check *T* or *F* to indicate whether the statement is true or false.

✓T __F **1.** You use the **F**ile, **O**pen command to retrieve a file that has been previously saved.

__T ✓F **2.** Select the entire worksheet by clicking the sheet tab.

✓T __F **3.** To insert two rows, select two rows and then choose the **E**dit, **I**nsert command.

__T ✓F **4.** Use AutoFill to fill the selected cells with a shade of gray.

__T ✓F **5.** Pressing F9 is a shortcut for deleting selected rows.

__T ✓F **6.** To save a file using a different file name, use the **S**ave command on the **F**ile menu.

✓T __F **7.** You can automatically enter a sequence of days of the week using the AutoFill command.

__T ✓F **8.** Excel automatically inserts a new column to the right of the column you select.

✓T __F **9.** To open a file quickly from the Open dialog box, double-click the file's icon.

✓T __F **10.** If you select cells that already contain data when using AutoFill, Excel overwrites the data in the cells.

Multiple Choice

Circle the letter of the correct answer for each of the following questions.

1. What does the mouse pointer look like when Excel is ready to use AutoFill?
   a. an arrow
   b. a hand
   c. A thin, black plus sign
   d. A thick, white plus sign

2. What appears around cells that have been copied or cut to the Clipboard?
   a. A flashing dotted line
   b. A solid double line
   c. A thick red border
   d. A red dotted double line

3. Which of the following cannot be pasted?
   a. Data that has been cut
   b. Data that has been cleared
   c. Data that has been copied
   d. Data you just pasted

4. What command do you use to save an existing file with a new name?
   a. File, **S**ave
   b. File, **O**pen
   c. File, **N**ew
   d. File, Save As

5. What do you click to quickly select an entire row?
   a. The row number
   b. The column letter
   c. The Select All button
   d. The name box

6. To select non-adjacent cells, you hold down which key(s) while you click the cells that you want?
   a. Alt
   b. Ctrl
   c. ⇧Shift
   d. ⇧Shift+Ctrl

Checking Your Skills

7. To identify the range of cells from A1 to Z100, type which of the following?

> **a. A1:Z100**
>
> **b.** A1;Z100
>
> **c.** A1-Z100
>
> **d.** A1,Z100

8. Which Excel feature anticipates what you are going to enter and enters the data automatically?

> **a. AutoFill**
>
> **b.** Automatic Entry
>
> **c.** AutoComplete
>
> **d.** QuickComplete

9. To use the keyboard to select a range of cells, hold down which of the following keys while pressing the arrow keys?

> **a.** Alt
>
> **b.** Ctrl
>
> **c. Shift**
>
> **d.** Shift+Ctrl

10. How do you display a shortcut menu?

> **a.** Double-click any menu option
>
> **b.** Double-click within a range of selected cells
>
> **c.** Choose **E**dit, **S**hortcut
>
> **d. Click the right mouse button**

Completion

In the blank provided, write the correct answer for each of the following statements.

1. To retrieve a file that has already been saved, you open the **F**ile menu and choose the _Open_ command.
2. To select a range of cells, you _drag_ the mouse over the cells.
3. When using AutoFill, the next item in sequence after April is _May_ .
4. Use the _Undo_ command to reverse the last action.
5. Select or _highlight_ a cell when you want to cut or copy the cell content.
6. The command to clear the contents of select cells is located on the _Edit_ menu.
7. The Clipboard can hold _one_ item(s).
8. If an action cannot be undone, the **U**ndo command and Undo button are _dimmed_ .
9. To move entire cells (the cells and their contents) to another location, use the _Insert, Cut Cells_ command.
10. The Copy and Paste buttons are located on the _Standard_ toolbar.

Matching

In the blank next to each of the following terms or phrases, write the letter of the corresponding term or phrase.

 _i_ **1.** Moves an item from the worksheet to the Clipboard.

 _e_ **2.** Removes the selected information from the worksheet, but not the cells.

 _j_ **3.** Removes the selected cells and the information they contain.

 _c_ **4.** Places a duplicate of the information on the Clipboard.

 _b_ **5.** A cell or rectangular group of adjacent cells.

 _d_ **6.** The shortcut for the **E**dit, **Cu**t command.

Project 2   Building a Spreadsheet

_h_ **7.** The shortcut for the **E**dit, **C**opy command.

_f_ **8.** The mouse pointer that displays as a black plus sign.

_g_ **9.** This command reverses the last action you performed.

_a_ **10.** A part of the computer's memory that stores information or formulas you want to copy or move to another location.

- **a.** Clipboard
- **b.** range
- **c.** **E**dit, **C**opy
- **d.** Ctrl+X
- **e.** **E**dit, Clea**r**
- **f.** fill handle
- **g.** Undo
- **h.** Ctrl+C
- **i.** **E**dit, Cu**t**
- **j.** **E**dit, **D**elete

Screen ID

Label each element of the Excel screen shown in Figure 2.13.

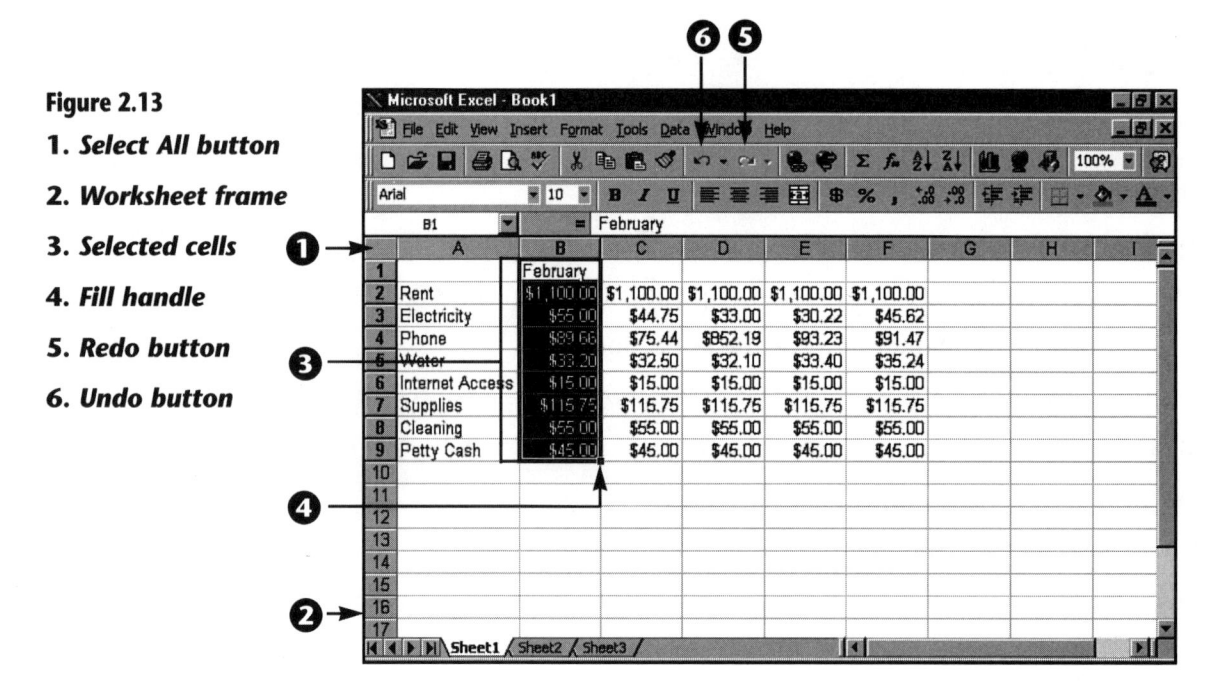

Figure 2.13
1. Select All button
2. Worksheet frame
3. Selected cells
4. Fill handle
5. Redo button
6. Undo button

Applying Your Skills

Practice

Take a few minutes to practice the skills you have learned in this project by completing the following exercise.

1. Reworking the Job List

In this exercise, follow the steps below to rework the Job List worksheet you created in Project 1. To make the worksheet suitable as a list of job positions rather than a list of employees, you want to add a new job position and delete the information about specific employees.

To Rework the Job List

1. Open the file Proj0202 and save it as Job List2.
2. Insert a new row 3 and label it Buyer.
3. Delete columns D, E, and F.
4. Save the changes.
5. If requested by your instructor, print two copies of the file, then close it.

> In this exercise, students use the **I**nsert, **R**ows command to insert a new row 3. The **E**dit, **D**elete command is used to delete columns D, E, and F. A solution file is saved as **Job List2** on the Instructor's Resource disk.

2. Completing a Schedule of Events

In this exercise, follow the steps below to complete a schedule of monthly coffee tastings that you will hold in the coffee shop.

To Complete a Schedule of Events

1. Open the file Proj0203 and save it as Tastings.
2. Insert a new row 1 and enter the title Coffee Tastings in cell A1.
3. Use AutoFill to complete the list of months from cell A3 down to cell A8.
4. Copy the data from cells C3:C8 into cells D3:D8.
5. Save the file. If requested by your instructor, print two copies, then close it.

> In this exercise, students revise a worksheet by using the **I**nsert, **R**ows command to insert a new row 1. AutoFill is used to fill cells with the names of the months of the year. In addition the **E**dit, **C**opy command is used to copy cells. The solution file is saved as **Tastings** on the Instructor's Resource disk.

Project 2 Building a Spreadsheet

3. Organizing the Inventory Worksheet

In this exercise, follow the steps below to organize the Inventory worksheet you created in Project 1.

To Organize the Inventory Worksheet

1. Open the file Proj0204 and save it as Inventory2.
2. Insert a new row 1 and enter the title Inventory in cell A1.
3. Rearrange the columns so the data for French Roast is between the data for Arabica and Kona.
4. Save the changes. If requested by your instructor, print two copies of the worksheet, then close it.

> In this exercise, students use the **I**nsert, **R**ows command to insert a new row 1. The **I**nsert, **C**olumns command, the **E**dit, **C**ut command, and the **E**dit, **P**aste command are used to rearrange columns of data. The solution file is saved as **Inventory2** on the Instructor's Resource disk.

4. Expanding the Paper Costs Worksheet

In this exercise, follow the steps to expand the Paper Costs worksheet you created in Project 1.

To Expand the Paper Costs Worksheet

1. Open the file Proj0205 and save it as Paper Costs2.
2. Insert a new row 6 and label it for fax paper.
3. In cell B6, enter 500 as the amount you spent on fax paper.
4. Rearrange the rows so that the cost of mailing labels and the cost of envelopes are at the top of the worksheet.
5. Label column B Cost.
6. Save the worksheet. If requested by your instructor, print two copies, then close it.

> This exercise provides students an additional opportunity to insert a row using the **I**nsert, **R**ows command. The **I**nsert, **R**ows command, the **E**dit, **C**ut command, and the **E**dit, **P**aste command are used to rearrange rows data. The solution file is saved as **Paper Costs2** on the Instructor's Resource disk.

5. Opening a Workbook and Selecting Worksheet Items

In this project, you learned how to open an existing workbook and how to use various methods to select worksheet items. In this exercise, you practice completing these tasks.

To Open a Workbook and Select Worksheet Items

1. Choose **F**ile, **O**pen to display the Open dialog box.
2. Select your floppy disk drive in the Look in drop-down list box.
3. From the list of files, select Proj0206.
4. Click the **O**pen button to open the file.

5. Save the file under a new name by choosing **File**, Save **As**. The Save As dialog box displays on your screen.

6. In the File **n**ame text box, type `Medical Expenses 2`.

7. Click the Save button to save the file.

8. Select the range of cells from B4:D9 by clicking cell B4, holding down the mouse button, and dragging the mouse down to cell D9.

9. Select row 8 of the worksheet by clicking the row number 8 in the worksheet frame.

10. Select column D by clicking column heading D in the worksheet frame.

11. Leave the workbook open for the following exercise.

> Students gain an opportunity to practice selecting worksheet items by the mouse. Students select entire columns and rows by clicking column and row labels on the worksheet frame. Dragging the mouse is used to select specific ranges of cells. The solution file is saved as **Medical Expenses 2** on the Instructor's Resource disk.

Challenge

The following challenges enable you to use your problem-solving skills. Take time to work through these exercises now.

1. Adding and Removing Rows and Columns

You have decided to add and remove some rows and columns in the `Medical Expenses 2` workbook. Insert two columns to the left of column D and then enter the following information:

1. In cell C3, type `Illness`.

2. In cells C4:C9, type the following descriptions:

    ```
    bronchitis
    ear infection
    check up
    check up
    eye infection
    check up
    ```

You decide that you no longer need column D, so delete it. Insert a blank row above row 6 and enter the following information:

```
Joe     28-Feb   follow-up   Dr. visit   45
```

Save your changes to the workbook and leave it open for the following exercise.

> This activity requires students to use the **I**nsert, **C**olumns command to insert two new columns before column D. In addition, students use the **E**dit, **D**elete command to delete a column. The solution file is saved as **Medical Expenses 2** on the Instructor's Resource disk.

Project 2 Building a Spreadsheet

2. Undoing and Redoing Actions

You know how easy it is to make mistakes while editing a worksheet so you decide to practice undoing and redoing actions in the Medical Expenses 2 workbook. Delete column D and then undo the action. Change the first number in column E to 55, the next number to 60, and the third number to 65. You realize that all three of these changes are incorrect, so use the Undo button on the Standard toolbar to undo the changes. Change the name in cell A4 to Mark and then undo the change. Redo the action by using the Redo button on the Standard toolbar. Save and print the workbook before closing it.

> Students will enjoy this activity as they practice using the Undo and Redo commands. The solution file is saved as **Medical Expenses 2** on the Instructor's Resource disk.

3. Using the AutoFill Command

Because you are short on time, you decide to use the AutoFill command when creating a worksheet. In a new, blank workbook, use the AutoFill command to enter the days of the week in cells A1 to G1. In cells A4 to A15, use the AutoFill command to enter the numbers 1-12. In cells B4 to B15, enter the numbers 5 to 60 in increments of 5. In cells C4 to C15 enter the word Category using the AutoFill command. Save the workbook as AutoFill Practice and leave it open for the next exercise.

> Students revise a worksheet by using the AutoFill command to fill cells with the names of the days of the week and numbers. The solution file is saved as **AutoFill Practice** on the Instructor's Resource disk.

4. Copying and Moving Information

Because you often need to change the location of information in a worksheet, you decide to practice copying and moving information to different locations in the AutoFill Practice workbook. Copy the days of the week in cells A1:G1 to cells A18:G18 and cells A20:G20. Move the data in cells A4:A15 to cells E4:E15; then move that data to cells C4:C15. Save the worksheet. If requested by your instructor, print the file before closing it.

> Students have another opportunity to copy and move text in this exercise. The **E**dit, **C**opy command, the **E**dit, Cu**t** command, and the **E**dit, **P**aste command are used to rearrange data. The solution file is saved as **AutoFill Practice** on the Instructor's Resource disk.

5. Using AutoFill to Balance Your Checkbook

Now that you are familiar with various editing techniques, you decide to balance your checkbook using an Excel worksheet. Open `Proj0207 s` and save it as `Checking Account 2`. Use the AutoFill command to enter the sequence of check numbers, starting with 500, in column A. Insert a blank row above row 12. Add an entry for a $500 deposit on April 26th. Delete column B and then undo the deletion. Save the worksheet. If requested by your instructor, print the worksheet before closing it.

> In this activity students use the AutoFill command to add numbers to a worksheet. The **I**nsert, **R**ows command and the **E**dit, **D**elete commands are used to insert rows and delete a column. The solution file is saved as **Checking Account 2** on the Instructor's Resource disk.

Project 3

Creating Formulas

Expanding the Office Expense Budget Worksheet

In this project, you learn how to:
- ➤ Create Formulas Using Mathematical Operators
- ➤ Create Formulas by Selecting Cells
- ➤ Copy Formulas
- ➤ Use Absolute Cell References

Project 3 Creating Formulas

Why Would I Do This?

Function
A built-in formula that automatically performs calculations.

A formula is a calculation that Excel performs on data entered in a worksheet. You can use formulas to add, subtract, multiply, and divide data with basic mathematical operators. You can also use Excel's built-in *functions* to simplify the number of characters required in a formula. Formulas are the most valuable part of spreadsheet software such as Microsoft Excel. A worksheet full of data would be of little use without built-in ways to perform calculations on the data.

Once you write a formula using cell addresses, you can change the information in one or more of the cells referenced in the formula, and the formula automatically recalculates the result. You can also copy the formula from one location to another in the worksheet, so you do not have to re-enter the formula to perform the same calculation on different data.

In this project, you learn how to create basic formulas in your budget worksheet using mathematical operators. You also learn how to use some of Excel's features for automating formulas—including the Formula palette, which enables you to view the result of a formula before you actually enter it in a cell, and the AutoSum button, which quickly finds the total of a row or column of data. Finally, you learn the difference between relative and absolute cell references, and how to copy formulas from one location in a worksheet to another.

Lesson 1: Creating Formulas Using Mathematical Operators

✓ On Your Mark
What types of formulas do you currently use in workbooks that you create (including pencil-and-paper spreadsheets, if any)?

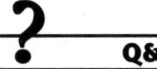

You can easily create a basic formula by typing an equation into a cell, just as you did in Project 1, "Getting Started with Excel," to find the total of a list of expenses. To create the formula, type the actual values you want to use in the calculation or the addresses of the cells that contain the values you want to use, separated by the mathematical operators that specify the type of calculation (a plus sign for addition or a minus sign for subtraction, for example). Table 3.1 lists some common mathematical operators.

In this lesson, you open a version of the budget worksheet you created in Project 2, "Building a Spreadsheet," and create some basic formulas.

? Q&A
Here's a simple math test for students in your class. Put it on the board, and ask them to work it out on paper or in their heads (no fair using Excel!): 48+8/2*4–1=? Use this formula to illustrate the importance of order when discussing math operators. *Answer:* 48+16–1 = 63.

Table 3.1	Common Mathematical Operators
Description	Operator
Addition	+ (plus sign)
Subtraction	– (minus sign)
Multiplication	* (asterisk)
Division	/ (forward slash)
Exponents	^ (caret)

Project Time
45 minutes

Lesson 1: Creating Formulas Using Mathematical Operators

To Create Formulas Using Mathematical Operators

Tip for Instructors
When considering the order of math operators, each level of operation is performed left to right unless parentheses overrule the order.

❶ Open the file Proj0301 and save it as Budget2.

This is an expanded version of the office budget worksheet you created in Project 2.

❷ Select cell B5 in the Budget2 worksheet.

Cell B5 is now the current (active) cell, and it is where you want to create your first formula in this example. After looking at the expense worksheet again, you might decide that estimating insurance expenses to be the same as rent is too high. To change the insurance bill estimate, divide the amount of rent in half using a formula.

Quicksand
Make sure that the cell pointer is located in the cell where you want the formula result to appear!

❸ In cell B5, type the formula =b2/2.

This formula tells Excel to divide the contents of cell B2 by 2. The equal sign (=) tells Excel that you are about to enter a formula. If you do not type an equal sign, Excel enters the values as text data in the cell. B2 is the cell address of the January rent expense: $1,100. The slash (/) is the operator that tells Excel which mathematical operation you want to perform—in this case, division.

Tip for Students
Rather than typing a cell reference in a formula, you can click the cell while creating the formula.

❹ Click the Enter button (the green check mark) on the formula bar.

This tells Excel to enter the formula in the cell and calculate the formula. The result of the formula appears in cell B5, as shown in Figure 3.1. Notice that the formula =B2/2 appears in the formula bar. The formula is entered in cell B5, but Excel displays the result of the formula—not the formula itself. Now try using the Formula palette to create a formula for the February insurance bill.

Tip for Students
Pressing ⏎Enter is the same as clicking the green check mark.

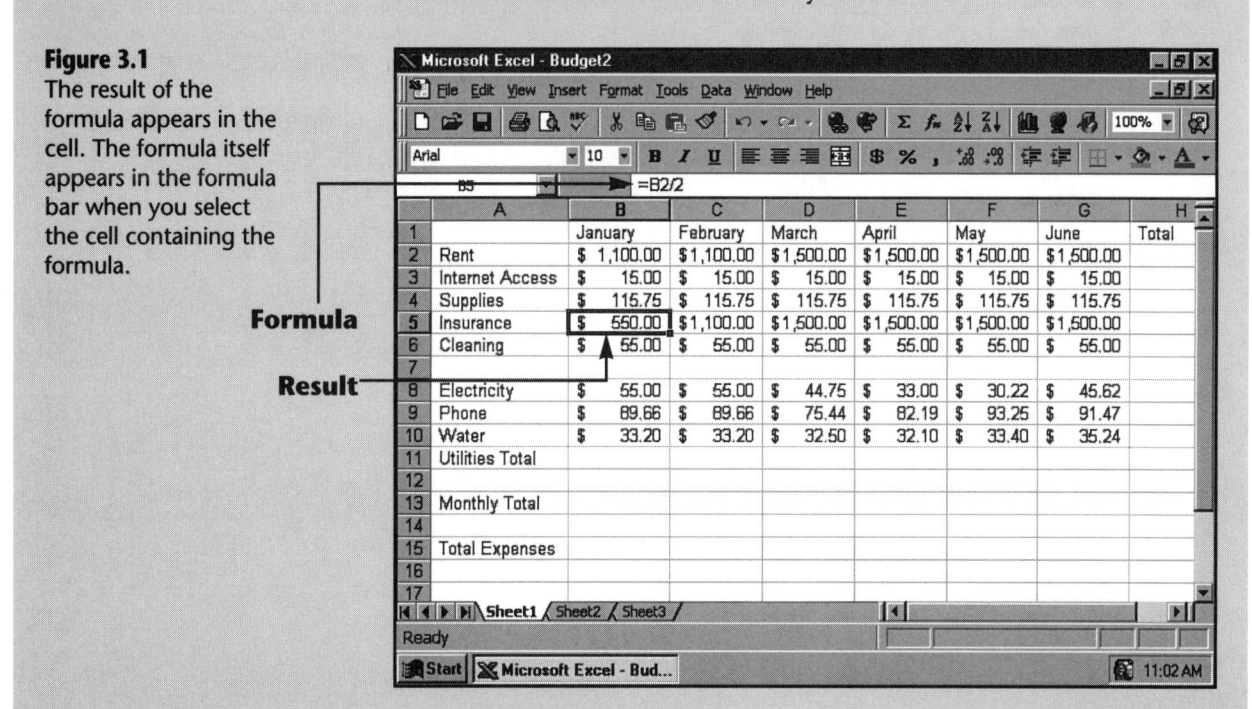

Figure 3.1
The result of the formula appears in the cell. The formula itself appears in the formula bar when you select the cell containing the formula.

Formula
Result

	A	B	C	D	E	F	G	H
1		January	February	March	April	May	June	Total
2	Rent	$ 1,100.00	$1,100.00	$1,500.00	$1,500.00	$1,500.00	$1,500.00	
3	Internet Access	$ 15.00	$ 15.00	$ 15.00	$ 15.00	$ 15.00	$ 15.00	
4	Supplies	$ 115.75	$ 115.75	$ 115.75	$ 115.75	$ 115.75	$ 115.75	
5	Insurance	$ 550.00	$1,100.00	$1,500.00	$1,500.00	$1,500.00	$1,500.00	
6	Cleaning	$ 55.00	$ 55.00	$ 55.00	$ 55.00	$ 55.00	$ 55.00	
7								
8	Electricity	$ 55.00	$ 55.00	$ 44.75	$ 33.00	$ 30.22	$ 45.62	
9	Phone	$ 89.66	$ 89.66	$ 75.44	$ 82.19	$ 93.25	$ 91.47	
10	Water	$ 33.20	$ 33.20	$ 32.50	$ 32.10	$ 33.40	$ 35.24	
11	Utilities Total							
12								
13	Monthly Total							
14								
15	Total Expenses							

continues

Project 3 Creating Formulas

To Create Formulas Using Mathematical Operators (continued)

If you have problems...

If your formula results in #NAME? instead of a value, it means you made a mistake entering the formula. You may have typed a cell address that doesn't exist, one of the cells in the formula may have an error, the operator you are using may be incorrect—for example, back slash (\) instead of slash (/)—or you may be trying to perform an impossible calculation. Check your formula carefully, correct any mistakes, and try again.

5 **Select cell C5 and press** Del.

This deletes the contents of cell C5. To enter a new formula with the Formula palette, the active cell must be empty.

6 **Click the Edit Formula button on the formula bar.**

Excel inserts an equal sign into the formula bar and opens the Formula palette (see Figure 3.2). With the Formula palette, you can see the result of the formula as you create it. You can also select functions to include in the formula, as you learn in Project 4, "Calculating with Functions."

7 **Type c2.**

The cell address appears in the formula bar and in the active cell. In the Formula palette, you can see the result of the formula so far, which is simply the value of cell C2: $1,100 (see Figure 3.2).

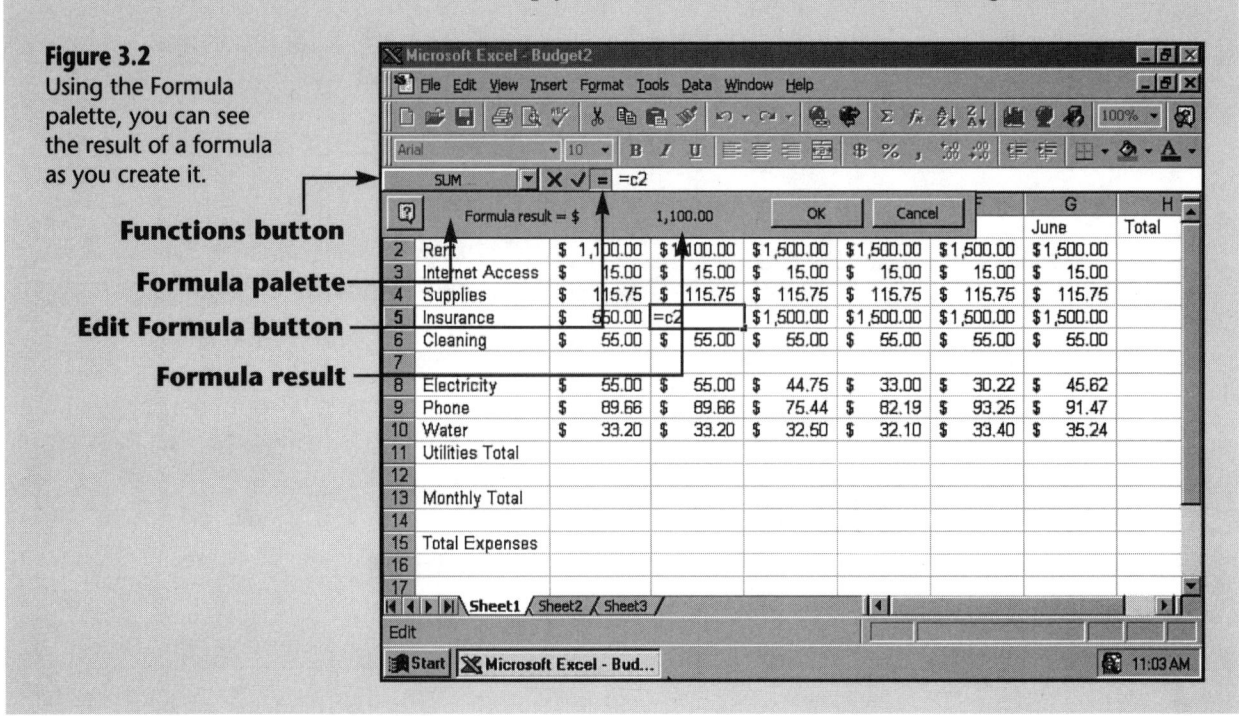

Figure 3.2
Using the Formula palette, you can see the result of a formula as you create it.

Functions button
Formula palette
Edit Formula button
Formula result

Lesson 2: Creating Formulas by Selecting Cells 71

Tip for Students

You can use the asterisk (*) on the numerical keypad instead of ⇧Shift+8 to save a keystroke.

❽ Type *.5.

This completes the formula for multiplying the value of cell C2 by one-half (0.5). The asterisk (*) is the operator for multiplication. (Press ⇧Shift+8 to enter the asterisk.) Notice that Excel updates the result of the formula in the Formula palette.

❾ Click OK in the Formula palette.

Excel closes the palette, enters the formula in cell C5, and displays the result. You can click the Enter button or press ↵Enter instead of clicking OK. Save the changes you have made to the Budget2 worksheet and keep it open. In the next lesson, you learn how to create formulas by selecting cells.

The parentheses in a formula tell Excel which order to use when performing calculations. For example, if you want to add two numbers and then divide them by 2, you use the formula =(A12+B12)/2. The part of the formula in parentheses takes precedence over the other parts of the formula.

If you don't use parentheses in a formula, Excel sets precedence in the following way: exponential calculations first, multiplication and division second, and addition and subtraction third. Therefore, with such a formula as =B12+C12/A10, Excel first divides C12 by A10, then adds the resulting number to B12. If you want to add the first two cells and then divide, use the formula =(B12+C12)/A10.

You can use Excel's AutoCalculate feature to find out the result of a calculation without actually entering a formula. Simply select the cell or range of cells you want to total, and look at the AutoCalculate button on the status bar. By default, Excel uses the SUM function. To select a different function, right-click the AutoCalculate button and choose the function you want to use.

Lesson 2: Creating Formulas by Selecting Cells

On Your Mark

What other ways can you reference cells in formulas other than typing their cell addresses?

You can also enter cell addresses into formulas by selecting the cell or range of cells in the worksheet. This simplifies the process of creating a formula, and also helps to ensure that you enter the correct cell address that you want to use.

In this lesson, you create a formula for totaling the monthly utility expenses by selecting the cells you want to include. You then create a formula that includes a function and a selected range of cells.

To Create Formulas by Selecting Cells

❶ In the Budget2 worksheet, select cell B11 and click the Edit Formula button.

You want the result of the formula displayed in cell B11. To calculate the total, add the values in cells B8, B9, and B10.

continues

To Create Formulas by Selecting Cells (continued)

2 **Click cell B8.**

Excel enters B8 into the formula. A flashing dotted line appears around the cell to remind you that it is the cell you selected for the formula. Also, the value of cell B8 appears in the Formula palette.

3 **Press + and click cell B9, then press + again and click cell B10.**

The formula appears in the formula bar and in cell B11. You can see the result of the formula in the Formula palette (see Figure 3.3).

> **Tip for Students**
> You can use the plus (+) on the numerical keypad instead of Shift+= to save a keystroke.

Figure 3.3
Click a cell to enter its address into the current formula.

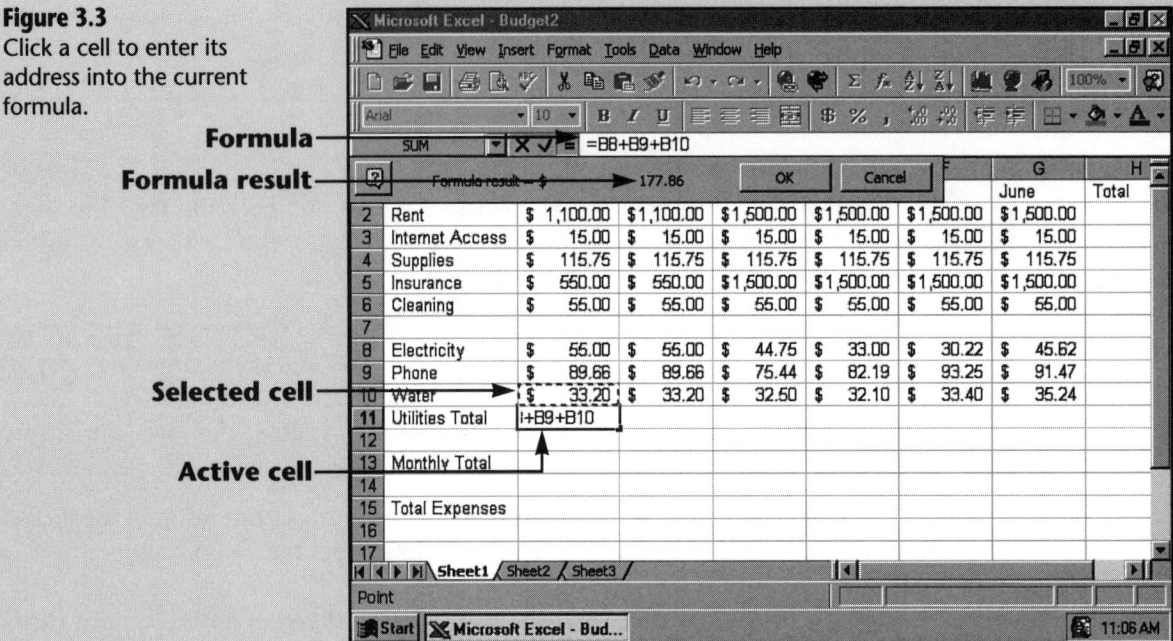

4 **Click OK in the Formula palette.**

Excel enters the formula in cell B11 and displays the results in that cell. Now, try creating a formula to calculate the total of January's expenses by clicking the AutoSum button and selecting a range of cells.

5 **Select cell B13 and click the AutoSum button on the Standard toolbar.**

Clicking the AutoSum button automatically enters a formula that uses the SUM function to calculate the total of the cells above or to the left of the active cell. In this case, the formula =SUM(B8:B12) appears in cell B13 and in the formula bar. SUM is the function; the address of the range to be added appears selected within the parentheses (see Figure 3.4). However, to correctly calculate January's expenses, you must add the values in cells B2:B10. Before you enter the formula into the active cell, change the range in the formula so that it includes cells B2:B10.

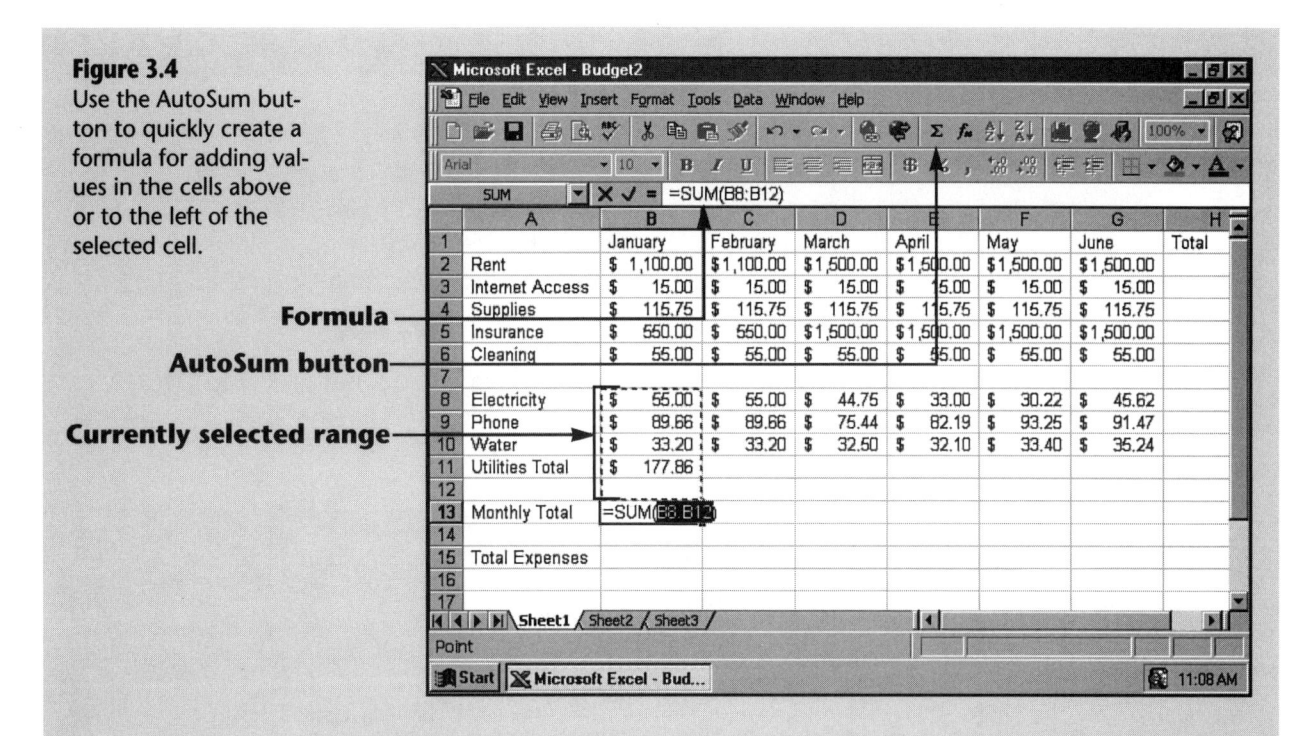

Lesson 2: Creating Formulas by Selecting Cells

Figure 3.4
Use the AutoSum button to quickly create a formula for adding values in the cells above or to the left of the selected cell.

6 **Click cell B2 and drag down to cell B10, then release the mouse button.**

Dragging across the cells selects them; they replace the range previously entered in the formula.

7 **Click the Enter button on the formula bar.**

The values in cells B2 to B10 are totaled, and the result, $2,013.61, appears in cell B13 (see Figure 3.5). Now use AutoSum to enter a formula totaling all the rent expenses in the worksheet.

Figure 3.5
You can quickly build a formula by selecting a range of cells.

continues

To Create Formulas by Selecting Cells (continued)

8 Select cell H2 and click the AutoSum button on the Standard toolbar.

This time, clicking the AutoSum button totals the cells to the left of the cell you selected. The formula =SUM(B2:G2) appears in the formula bar. This formula is correct for totaling all rent expenses.

9 Click the Enter button on the formula bar.

Excel enters the formula and displays the result $8,200 in cell H2, as shown in Figure 3.6. Save your changes and leave the Budget2 worksheet open. You learn to copy formulas in the next lesson.

Figure 3.6
The result of the formula in the formula bar appears in cell H2.

Formula
Result

You can change the cell addresses in a formula in a few different ways. You can simply click in the Formula bar to position the insertion point where you want to make a change, then delete the incorrect characters and type the correct ones.

Range Finder
A feature of Excel that helps you locate cells referenced in a formula by color coding them. The range in the formula is highlighted in the same color as the range in the worksheet.

When you click in the formula bar to edit a formula, Excel starts the *Range Finder*. You can use the Range Finder to replace cell addresses in the formula. When the Range Finder is active, Excel displays each cell address or range in the formula in a different color, and highlights the actual cells in the worksheet in corresponding colors.

To change an address in the formula, drag the corresponding colored cell border to the correct address in the worksheet. To add or remove cells from a range, drag the handle on the lower-right corner of the colored border to include more or fewer cells. When you finish making changes, click the Enter button on the formula bar. You can also start the Range Finder by double-clicking the cell that contains the formula you want to change.

Lesson 3: Copying Formulas

> **On Your Mark**
> In what situations would you be able to save time by copying a formula instead of re-entering it?

Relative cell reference
A reference to the contents of a cell that is adjusted by the program when you copy the formula to another cell or range of cells.

After you create a formula, you can copy it to other cells or worksheets to help speed up your work. You copy formulas in Excel using the same techniques you used in Project 2 to copy cells and data.

When you copy a formula from one cell to another, Excel automatically changes the formula so that it is *relative* to its new location. That means that it changes the cell addresses in the formula, thus making it correct in a new location. For example, if you copy a formula that adds the contents of cells A1:A9 from cell A10 to cell B10, Excel automatically changes the formula to add the contents of cells B1:B9.

Now copy formulas in the Budget2 worksheet.

To Copy Formulas

❶ Select cell C5 in the Budget2 worksheet.

Cell C5 contains the formula =C2*0.5, which is the formula you want to copy to the rest of the cells in the Insurance row.

❷ With the mouse pointer in cell C5, click the right mouse button.

A shortcut menu appears, which you can use to copy the formula.

> **Quicksand**
> Make sure that the cell pointer is directly over cell C5 before right-clicking; otherwise, the active cell will change when you right-click.

❸ Click the Copy command on the shortcut menu.

The shortcut menu disappears, and the formula is copied to the Clipboard. Remember, you are copying the formula, not the value in the cell.

❹ Select cells D5 through G5.

This is the range where you want to paste the copied formula.

❺ Move the mouse pointer to the active cell (D5), right-click to open the shortcut menu, then choose the Paste command.

Excel pastes the copied formula into the selected cells, as shown in Figure 3.7. Again, make sure that you move the mouse pointer to the active cell before you issue the **P**aste command. Notice that the formulas copied into each cell are *relative* to the new cells. For example, the formula in D5, =D2*0.5, refers to rent information for the month of March rather than the month of February. Because there was an increase in rent in March, there is also an increase in the insurance expense for March. The results of the new formulas are displayed in each cell.

continues

Project 3   Creating Formulas

To Copy Formulas (continued)

Figure 3.7
The formula calculates the Insurance amount and enters the result in the correct cells.

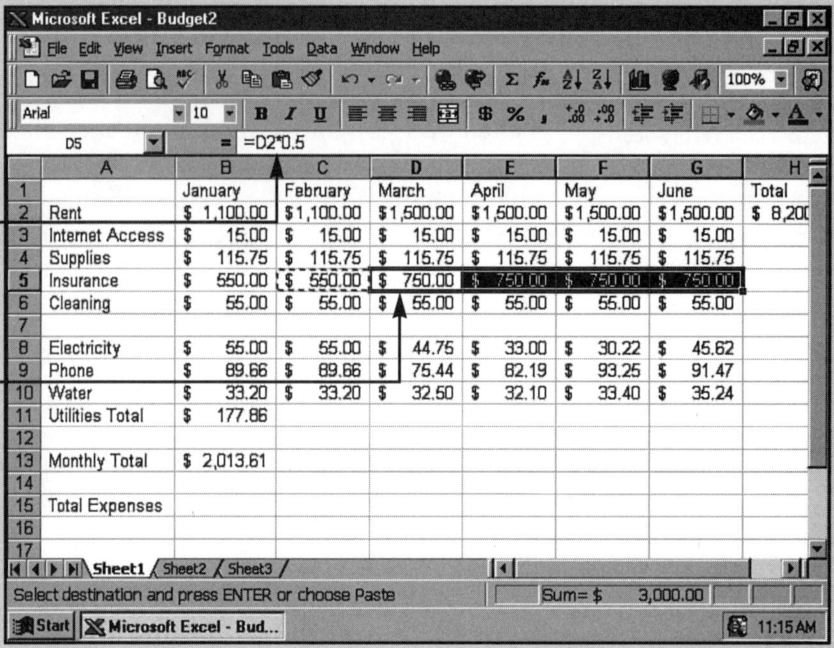

Pasted formula becomes relative to the new location

Active cell

	A	B	C	D	E	F	G	H
1		January	February	March	April	May	June	Total
2	Rent	$ 1,100.00	$1,100.00	$1,500.00	$1,500.00	$1,500.00	$1,500.00	$ 8,200
3	Internet Access	$ 15.00	$ 15.00	$ 15.00	$ 15.00	$ 15.00	$ 15.00	
4	Supplies	$ 115.75	$ 115.75	$ 115.75	$ 115.75	$ 115.75	$ 115.75	
5	Insurance	$ 550.00	$ 550.00	$ 750.00	$ 750.00	$ 750.00	$ 750.00	
6	Cleaning	$ 55.00	$ 55.00	$ 55.00	$ 55.00	$ 55.00	$ 55.00	
7								
8	Electricity	$ 55.00	$ 55.00	$ 44.75	$ 33.00	$ 30.22	$ 45.62	
9	Phone	$ 89.66	$ 89.66	$ 75.44	$ 82.19	$ 93.25	$ 91.47	
10	Water	$ 33.20	$ 33.20	$ 32.50	$ 32.10	$ 33.40	$ 35.24	
11	Utilities Total	$ 177.86						
12								
13	Monthly Total	$ 2,013.61						
14								
15	Total Expenses							

D5 = =D2*0.5

Now copy the formula for the Utilities total for the rest of the months using buttons on the Standard toolbar.

If you have problems...

The flashing dotted line remains around the cell you copied to the Clipboard until you copy or cut another selection. You can continue working as usual, but if you find the flashing dotted line distracting, simply press Esc to cancel it.

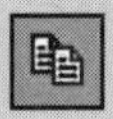

6 **Select cell B11 and click the Copy button on the Standard toolbar.**

You can use the toolbar buttons or menu commands to copy and paste formulas the same way you copy text or numbers.

7 **Select cells C11 through G11.**

You want to paste the formula into these cells.

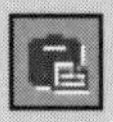

8 **Click the Paste button on the toolbar.**

Excel copies the formula to add the Utilities total in each month to the cells you selected. Again, notice that the cell references in the formulas refer to the appropriate month in each case.

Now use the fill handle to copy the formula, calculating the totals for each expense category.

Lesson 3: Copying Formulas

9 **Select cell H2 and move the mouse pointer to the lower-right corner of the cell so that the pointer changes to a thin black plus sign.**

You can use the fill handle to copy the contents of a cell to other cells, just as you used it to fill a range with a series of data in Project 2. You may have to scroll the worksheet to see all of column H.

10 **Click the left mouse button and drag down to select cells H3 to H11.**

This selects the range you want to fill. When you release the mouse button in cell H11, Excel fills the range with the formula and displays the results of the formula in each cell. Again, the formulas are relative to their locations. Finally, copy and paste the formula to calculate the monthly totals.

11 **Select cell B13, then drag the fill handle right to cell H13.**

Excel copies the formula from cell B13 to the other cells in the row. The results appear, as shown in Figure 3.8. Because you don't need the formula in cell H7, delete it now.

12 **Click cell H7 to make it active, press** Del**, then press** ↵Enter**.**

Excel deletes the contents of the cell. Save your changes. In the next lesson, you learn how to use absolute cell references in a formula.

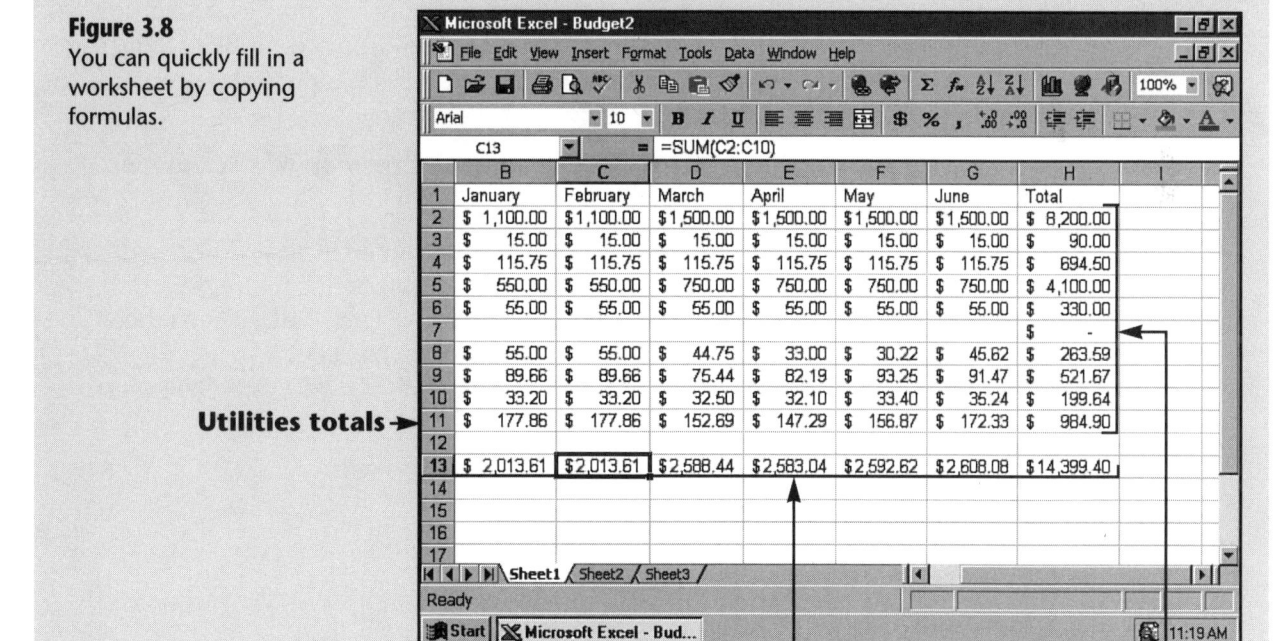

Figure 3.8
You can quickly fill in a worksheet by copying formulas.

Utilities totals →

Monthly totals

Expense totals

	B	C	D	E	F	G	H
1	January	February	March	April	May	June	Total
2	$ 1,100.00	$1,100.00	$1,500.00	$1,500.00	$1,500.00	$1,500.00	$ 8,200.00
3	$ 15.00	$ 15.00	$ 15.00	$ 15.00	$ 15.00	$ 15.00	$ 90.00
4	$ 115.75	$ 115.75	$ 115.75	$ 115.75	$ 115.75	$ 115.75	$ 694.50
5	$ 550.00	$ 550.00	$ 750.00	$ 750.00	$ 750.00	$ 750.00	$ 4,100.00
6	$ 55.00	$ 55.00	$ 55.00	$ 55.00	$ 55.00	$ 55.00	$ 330.00
7							$ -
8	$ 55.00	$ 55.00	$ 44.75	$ 33.00	$ 30.22	$ 45.62	$ 263.59
9	$ 89.66	$ 89.66	$ 75.44	$ 82.19	$ 93.25	$ 91.47	$ 521.67
10	$ 33.20	$ 33.20	$ 32.50	$ 32.10	$ 33.40	$ 35.24	$ 199.64
11	$ 177.86	$ 177.86	$ 152.69	$ 147.29	$ 156.87	$ 172.33	$ 984.90
12							
13	$ 2,013.61	$2,013.61	$2,588.44	$2,583.04	$2,592.62	$2,608.08	$14,399.40

Cell C13 = =SUM(C2:C10)

Project 3 Creating Formulas

> **On Your Mark**
>
> In what situations would you want your formulas to refer to the same cells, even if you move or copy your formulas? How do you ensure that your formulas refer to the same cells when you move or copy them?

Lesson 4: Using Absolute Cell References

As you learned in Lesson 3, when you copy a formula, Excel assumes that the formula is relative. If, for example, you copy the formula =SUM(A2:A9) from cell A10 to cell B10, the formula automatically changes to =SUM(B2:B9). No matter where you copy the formula, it updates to reflect the cells that are relative to it.

> **Absolute cell reference**
> Does not adjust when you copy or move a formula.

However, if you want to copy a formula to another cell and have it return exactly the same result as in the original location, you must specify *absolute cell references*. To do so, add a dollar sign ($) before the values specifying the cell address. In other words, you insert a dollar sign before each column and row indicator in the formula. For example, to copy =SUM(A2:A9) and make sure that the resulting value is the same no matter where in the worksheet the formula is pasted, change the formula to =SUM($A$2:$A$9).

In this lesson, you create a formula that uses absolute cell references, so you can copy the formula to a different location in the worksheet and obtain the same result.

To Use Absolute Cell References

> **Tip for Instructors**
>
> Because the concept of absolute cell references hasn't been practiced, this exercise should be done in class as a group.

① In the Budget2 worksheet, click cell H13 then click the Copy button on the Standard toolbar.

This copies the formula in H13 to the Clipboard. This formula calculates the total expenses for the six-month period included in the worksheet by adding each expense total. You would like to display this total in cell B15 as well. First, see what happens when you copy and paste the relative formula.

② Click cell B15, then click the Paste button on the Standard toolbar.

Excel pastes the formula into cell B15 and displays the results, as shown in Figure 3.9. Notice that the result is not the same as in cell H13 because Excel has automatically changed the cell references in the formula so they are relative to the new location.

Lesson 4: Using Absolute Cell References

Figure 3.9
When you copy and paste a relative formula, the result may not be the value you want.

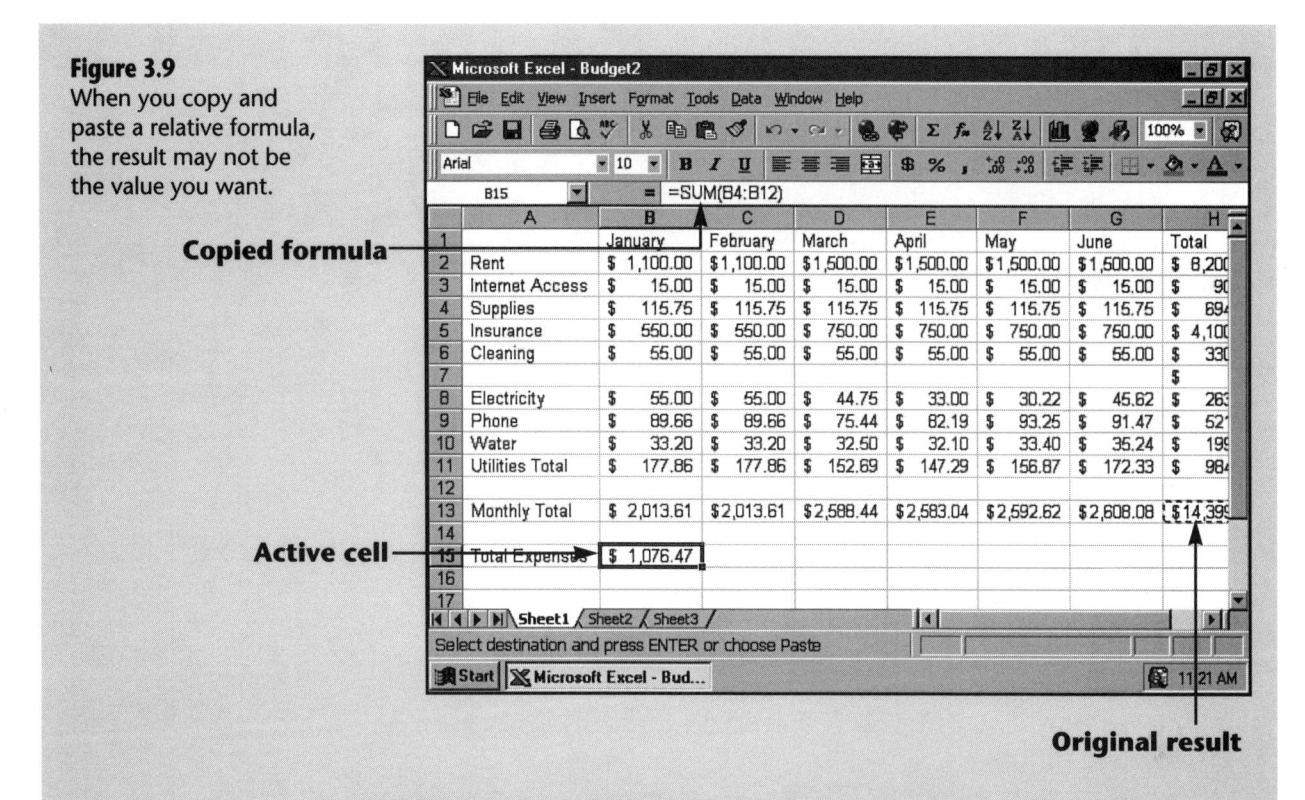

Copied formula

Active cell

Original result

❸ **Press** [Del] **to delete the formula from cell B15, and select cell H13 again.**

To be sure that Excel returns the actual total of all expenses, you must make the cell references in the formula absolute.

Tip for Students
Press [F4] to apply absolute references when creating or editing a formula.

❹ **Click in the formula bar, and position the insertion point between the open parentheses and the first column letter H.**

This places the insertion point in the formula where you want to make a change. You want to insert a $ in front of each column and row reference in the formula. When you click in the Formula bar, Excel assumes you want to change the cell addresses in the formula, so it activates the Range Finder. You can ignore the Range Finder; Excel will close it automatically.

❺ **Type $ and press** [→]; **type** [$] **and press** [→] **twice; type** [$] **and press** [→]; **type** [$].

You should now have a dollar sign in front of each column and row reference in the formula, as shown in Figure 3.10.

continues

Project 3 Creating Formulas

To Use Absolute Cell References (continued)

Figure 3.10
Dollar signs in a formula tell Excel to use absolute cell references.

Formula with absolute cell references

❻ Click the Enter button on the formula bar.

Excel enters the new formula in cell H13. The result of the formula is the same. Now see what happens when you copy and paste the formula with absolute cell references.

❼ With cell H13 still selected, click the Copy button on the Standard toolbar, select cell B15, then click the Paste button on the Standard toolbar.

Excel copies the formula exactly as it appears in cell H13 into cell B15 and displays the result, as shown in Figure 3.11.

You have now completed the lessons on creating basic formulas. Save the changes you have made to the Budget2 worksheet. If requested by your instructor, print two copies, then close the Budget2 file. If you have completed your session on the computer, exit Excel and Windows 95. Otherwise, continue with the "Checking Your Skills" section at the end of this project.

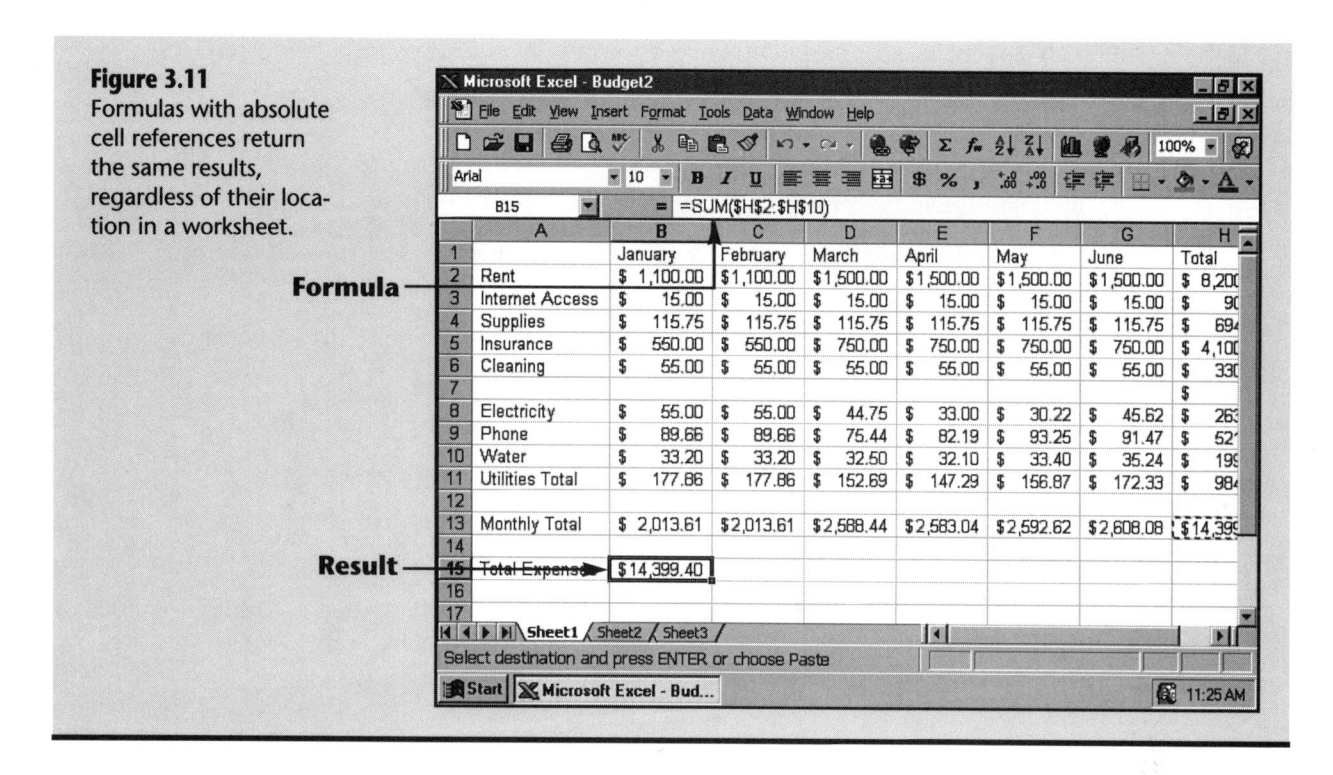

Figure 3.11
Formulas with absolute cell references return the same results, regardless of their location in a worksheet.

Project Summary

To	Do This
Enter a formula	Type an equal sign (=), then type the formula.
Open the Formula palette	Click the Edit Formula button on the Formula palette.
Automatically total a row or column of cells	Click the AutoSum button on the Standard toolbar.
Copy a formula	Select the cell containing the formula, click the Copy button, select the cell where you want to paste the formula, and click the Paste button.
Use absolute cell reference	Type a dollar sign ($) in front of the row number and column letter in the cell address in the formula.

Checking Your Skills

True/False

For each of the following, check *T* or *F* to indicate whether the statement is true or false.

__T ✔F **1.** Excel can use only mathematical operators for addition and subtraction.

✔T __F **2.** Excel automatically updates the result of a formula when you change a value referenced in the formula.

✔T __F **3.** To make a cell address absolute, you must type a dollar sign before each row and column reference in the formula.

Project 3 Creating Formulas

✓T __F **4.** You can use the fill handle to copy a formula from one cell to an adjacent cell.

__T ✓F **5.** You can reference only one cell address in each formula.

✓T __F **6.** To enter a new formula with the Formula palette, the active cell must be empty.

✓T __F **7.** By default, when you copy a formula it is relative to its new location.

__T ✓F **8.** If a formula is relative to its new location, this means that the cell address does not change when you copy it to a new location.

✓T __F **9.** An advantage to using the Formula palette is that you can see the result of the formula as you create it.

✓T __F **10.** When you click in the formula bar to edit a formula, Excel starts the Range Finder.

Multiple Choice

Circle the letter of the correct answer for each of the following questions.

1. Which of the following is a valid formula?

   a. B3+B4+B5

   b. (B3+B4+B5)

   c. =B3+B4+B5

   d. $B$3+$B$4+$B$5

2. Which of the following cannot be used to copy a formula?

   a. the Copy button on the Standard toolbar

   b. The Edit, Copy command

   c. The fill handle

   d. The Range Finder

3. Which of the following is a valid mathematical operator?

   a. ^ (caret)

   b. @ (*at* sign)

   c. $ (dollar sign)

   d. ? (question mark)

4. What appears in the active cell where you enter a formula?

   a. The formula

   b. The result of the formula

   c. The cell address

   d. An equal sign

5. What function is used to add the values in a range of cells?

   a. ADD

   b. PLUS

   c. SUM

   d. TOTAL

6. If you do not use parenthesis in a formula, which type of calculation takes precedence?

   a. exponential calculations

   b. multiplication

   c. division

   d. addition

7. What is the operator for multiplication?

   a. caret (^)

   b. asterisk (*)

   c. forward slash (/)

   d. back slash (\)

8. In the formula =(A12+B12)*C2^2/7, which calculation is performed first?

   a. adding A12 + B12

   b. multiplying B12 by C2

   c. squaring C2

   d. Dividing the square of C2 by 7

9. What is the resulting function when you copy the function =SUM(C2:C10) from cell C12 to cell E12?

   a. =SUM(C2:C10)
   b. =SUM(D2:D10)
   c. =SUM(E2:E10)
   d. =SUM(E4:E12)

10. When you copy the formula =$C$2+$C$3 from cell C4 to cell D4, what is the resulting formula?

    a. =$D$1+$D$2
    b. =$D$2+$D$3
    c. =$C$1+$C$2
    d. =$C$2+$C$3

Completion

In the blank provided, write the correct answer for each of the following statements.

1. Type a dollar sign in front of a cell address to make the reference _absolute_.
2. Click the Edit Formula button on the formula bar to open the _Formula Palette_.
3. Every formula must start with a(n) _equal_ sign.
4. To quickly create a formula to total a row or column of numbers, click the _AutoSum_ button.
5. To make sure Excel performs one calculation before another in a formula, enclose the first calculation in _parentheses_.
6. To find out the result of a calculation without actually entering a formula, use the _AutoCalculate_ feature.
7. Clicking the _AutoSum_ button automatically enters a formula that uses the SUM function to calculate the total of the cells above or to the left of the active cell.
8. To remove the flashing dotted line around the cell you copied to the Clipboard, press _Esc_.
9. When you click the Edit Formula button, Excel inserts a(n) _equal sign_ into the formula bar and opens the Formula palette.
10. You can start the Range Finder by _clicking_ the cell that contains the formula you want to change.

Matching

In the blank next to each of the following terms or phrases, write the letter of the corresponding term or phrase.

_i_ 1. A built-in formula that automatically performs calculations.
_e_ 2. A calculation that Excel performs on data entered in a worksheet.
_j_ 3. The mathematical operator for division
_g_ 4. The mathematical operator for exponents
_b_ 5. Helps you locate cells referenced in a formula by color coding them.
_a_ 6. A formula that is updated to reflect its new location.
_d_ 7. A formula that remains exactly the same, no matter where it is copied in the worksheet.
_h_ 8. The first calculation performed in a formula
_f_ 9. The second calculation performed in a formula
_c_ 10. The third calculation performed in a formula

Project 3 Creating Formulas

a. relative
b. Range Finder
c. addition and subtraction
d. absolute
e. formula
f. multiplication and division
g. ^ (caret)
h. exponential calculations
i. function
j. / (forward slash)

Screen ID

Label each element of the Excel screen shown in Figure 3.12.

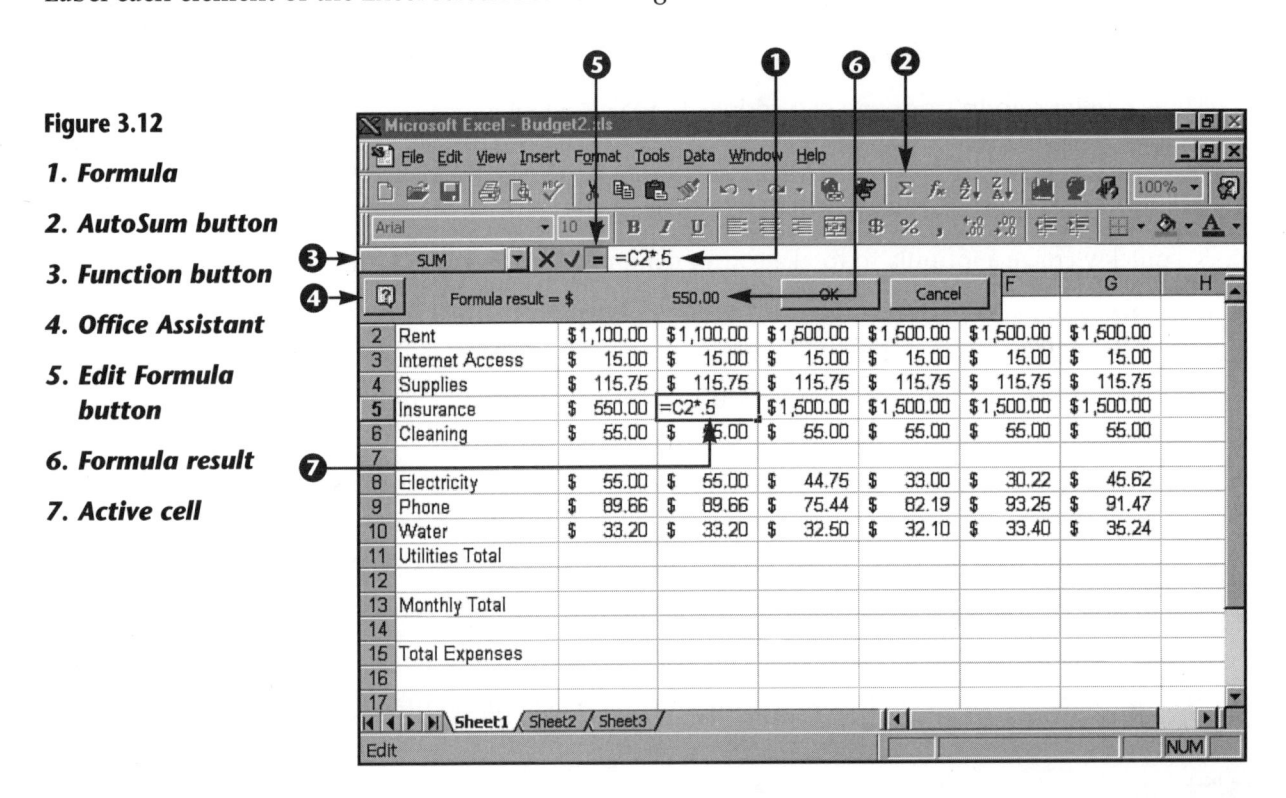

Figure 3.12

1. Formula
2. AutoSum button
3. Function button
4. Office Assistant
5. Edit Formula button
6. Formula result
7. Active cell

Applying Your Skills

Practice

The following exercises enable you to practice the skills you have learned in this project. Take a few minutes to work through these exercises now.

1. Estimating Attendance

Now that you are familiar with Excel formulas, you can make use of them to estimate how many people will attend the monthly coffee tastings you hold at the shop.

To Estimate Attendance

1. Open the file Proj0302 and save it as **Attendance**.
2. Assuming that ¾ of the number of invitees will actually attend a tasting, enter a formula in cell D3 to calculate the estimated number of attendees.
3. Copy the formula from cell D3 to cells D4:D8.

4. Use AutoSum to enter a formula calculating the total number of invitees and the total number of attendees.

5. Change the number of guests invited in October to 15 and in November to 20.

6. Save the changes to the worksheet. If requested by your instructor, print two copies of the worksheet, then close it.

> In this exercise, students enter a formula to indicate the number of attendees at a coffee tasting. The formula to use in cell D3 is =C4*0.75. Students then copy this formula to adjacent cell addresses. The AutoSum command is used to enter formulas for calculating the total number of invitees and the total number of attendees. A solution file is saved as **Attendance** on the Instructor's Resource disk.

2. Calculating Costs

Calculate the costs of ordering inventory for your coffee shop. Using the sample file Proj0303, complete the worksheet by creating formulas.

To Calculate Costs

1. Open the file Proj0303 and save it as March Orders.

2. In cell B7, create a formula that calculates the cost of ordering Arabica in March by multiplying the price per pound by the amount ordered.

3. Copy the formula to cells C7 and D7 to find the cost of ordering French Roast and Kona, respectively.

4. In cell B8, create a formula that calculates the total cost of ordering coffee in March.

5. Save your work. If requested by your instructor, print two copies. Close the March Orders file.

> In this exercise, students create and copy simple formulas. The formula to use in cell B7 is =B4*B5. The formula to use in cell B8 is =B7+C7+D7. A solution file is saved as **March Orders** on the Instructor's Resource disk.

3. Calculating Salaries

Use the information provided to complete a worksheet calculating the new salaries for your coffee shop employees.

To Calculate Salaries

1. Open the file Proj0304 and save it as Salary.

2. In cell D4, enter a formula that calculates the new salary for the buyer by multiplying the old salary by the percent of increase, then adding that total to the old salary.

3. Copy the formula from cell D4 to cells D5:D8.

4. In cell B10, use AutoSum to enter a formula to calculate the total of the old salaries.

5. Copy the formula from cell B10 into cell B11, then edit the range in the formula so it calculates the total of the new salaries. (*Hint:* You can type the new range, select the new range, or use the Range Finder to change the range.)

Project 3   Creating Formulas

6. In cell B13, enter a formula to calculate the increase in salary.

7. Save the changes to the worksheet. If requested by your instructor, print two copies of the worksheet, then close it.

> Students continue to enter formulas in this activity. The formula to use in cell D4 is =(B4*C4)+B4. The formula to use in cell B10 is =SUM(B4:B9). The formula to use in cell B11 is =SUM(D4:D9). The formula to use in cell B13 is =B11-B10. The solution file is saved as **Salary** on the Instructor's Resource disk.

4. Calculating Advertising Costs

Use the worksheet provided to calculate the costs of advertising your coffee shop and to determine which type of advertisement generates the most effect in terms of revenue and which generates the most profit.

To Calculate Advertising Costs

1. Open the file Proj0305 and save it as Ad Costs.

2. In cell F3, enter a formula to calculate the profit generated by the print ad by subtracting the cost from the effect.

3. Copy the formula from cell F3 to cells F4 and F5.

4. In cell B7, create a formula for totaling the cost of the three ads.

5. In cell B8, create a formula for totaling the effect of the three ads.

6. In cell B9, create a formula for totaling the profits generated by the three ads.

7. In cell G3, create a formula to calculate the print ad's percentage of the total effect.

8. Copy the formula from cell G3 to cells G4 and G5. Notice that Excel returns a result of 0 in both cells G4 and G5 because it changes the copied formula to keep it relative to the new locations.

9. Edit the formula in G3 so it always references cell B8, then copy it again to cells G4 and G5.

10. In cell H3, create a formula to calculate the print ad's percentage of the total profit using an absolute cell reference for cell B9, then copy the formula from cell H3 to cells H4 and H5.

11. Save the changes to the worksheet. If requested by your instructor, print two copies of the worksheet, then close it.

> In this activity, students continue to enter and copy formulas. Both relative and absolute cell references are used in the exercise. The formula to use in cell F3 is =E3-D3. The formula to use in cell B7 is =D3+D4+D5. The formula to use in cell B8 is =E3+E4+E5. The formula to use in cell B9 is =B8-B7. The formula to use in cell G3 is =F4/$B$8. The formula to use in cell H3 is =F3/$B$9. The solution file is saved as **Ad Costs** on the Instructor's Resource disk.

5. Creating a Formula Using Mathematical Operators

In this project, you learned to perform calculations using formulas with mathematical operators. In this exercise, you calculate the co-payment amount for each medical expense in the Medical Expenses worksheet.

Applying Your Skills

To Create a Formula

1. Open `Proj0306` and save it as `Medical Expenses 3`. Notice that this is the same worksheet you used in the previous project, with a column added for the co-payment amount.
2. Your co-payment is 20% of the charge. You need to enter a formula to calculate this amount. Activate cell F4.
3. Enter the formula `=E4*.2` into this cell. This calculates 20% of the amount in cell E4 and enters it into the cell.
4. Select cell F4 again, and copy it to the other cells by positioning the mouse pointer on the fill handle.
5. Hold down the left mouse button, and drag the mouse pointer down to cell F10. Release the mouse button, and the formula is copied to the remaining cells.
6. Save the file, and leave it open for the following exercise.

> In this activity students use and copy formulas and mathematical operators. The formula to use in cell F4 is =E4*.2. The solution file is saved as **Medical Expenses 3** on the Instructor's Resource disk.

Challenge

The following challenges enable you to use your problem-solving skills. Take time to work through these exercises now.

1. Entering the SUM Function

To total all of your medical expenses for the year, enter the SUM function into the `Medical Expenses 3` worksheet. Total the co-payments for the year and enter the word TOTAL in cell D12. Save the workbook. If requested by your instructor, print two copies of the worksheet before closing it.

> This activity requires students to use the SUM function to total co-payments in the Medical Expenses 3 file. The SUM function formula in cell F12 is =SUM(F4:F10). The solution file is saved as **Medical Expenses 3** on the Instructor's Resource disk.

2. Using a Formula to Calculate Sales Commission

As sales manager for your company, you want to calculate sales commission and gross profit for the year. You do so by using a formula. Open the file `Proj0307` and save it as `Profit Loss Stmt`. In cell B7, enter the formula `=B5*.025` to calculate sales commissions of 2.5% of the total sales. Enter the formula `=B5-B6-B7` into cell B9 to calculate the gross profit (sales minus expenses minus sales commissions). Save the workbook and leave it open for the following exercise.

> In this activity, students continue to enter and copy formulas. The formula to use in cell B7 is =B5*0.025. The formula to use in cell B9 is =B5-B6-B7. A solution file is saved as **Profit Loss Stmt** on the Instructor's Resource disk.

3. Using an Absolute Cell Reference

You now need to calculate taxes due for the year by multiplying the tax rate by the gross profit. To do so, you enter a formula into the Profit Loss Stmt workbook. Because you will be copying this formula to other cells, the reference to the cell containing the tax rate (cell B17) needs to be absolute.

In cell B11, enter the formula =B9*$B$17. Make sure you include the dollar signs in the cell address for the tax rate. Enter the formula =B9-B11 into cell B13 to calculate the net profit by subtracting the taxes from the gross profit. Save the workbook again, and leave it open for the following exercise.

> In this exercise, students use an absolute cell reference in cell B11. The formula to use in cell B11 is =B9*$B$17. The formula to use in cell B13 is =B9-B11. A solution file is saved as **Profit Loss Stmt** on the Instructor's Resource disk.

4. Copying Formulas

Now that you have the formulas entered into the Profit Loss Stmt workbook, you need to copy them to the columns for May and June.

Copy the sales commission formula (cell B7) to cells C7:D7. Copy the formula in cell B9 to cells C9:D9. Copy the remaining formulas using AutoFill. Select cells B11:B13. Notice that all of these formulas are copied with relative cell addresses, except the formula for the taxes. The cell address remained B17 when you copied it to the other cells, because you entered the cell address as an absolute address. Save the workbook and, if requested by your instructor, print two copies before closing it.

> In this activity, students continue to edit the Profit Loss Stmt worksheet by using the AutoFill command to copy formulas. A solution file is saved as **Profit Loss Stmt** on the Instructor's Resource disk.

5. Keeping a Running Balance

To keep a running balance of the total in your checkbook, you decide to use formulas. Open Proj0308 file and save it as Checking Account 3. Add a formula to cell F6 to calculate the total in the checking account after making the mortgage payment. Because you will be copying this formula to other cells, be sure to add any amounts in the Deposit column, and subtract any amounts in the Check Amount column. Copy this formula down the column. Save the workbook and, if requested by your instructor, print two copies before closing it.

> This activity requires students to insert and copy formulas. The formula to use in cell F6 is =F5+D6-E6. A solution file is saved as **Checking Account 3** on the Instructor's Resource disk.

Project 4

Calculating with Functions

Projecting Office Expenses

In this project, you learn how to:
- Name Ranges
- Use Named Ranges
- Use Functions
- Build Formulas with Functions
- Use Conditional Statements

Why Would I Do This?

In Project 3, "Creating Formulas," you learned to devise formulas to calculate values in your worksheet and use cell addresses to refer to specific cells. You also learned how to use simple functions to help speed up your work with formulas. In this project, you expand your knowledge of formulas and functions so that you can easily perform more complex calculations. You learn to automate data input using such functions as TODAY (which inserts the current date in a worksheet). You also learn how to use conditional functions, such as IF, to provide different answers depending on the results of your calculations.

Another useful feature of Excel that can help you simplify the process of creating formulas is the range name. You can assign a descriptive name to a value or a formula in a single cell or a range of cells, then use the assigned name rather than the cell addresses when specifying cells that you want to use.

In this project, you use range names and functions to project the costs of rent, paper, and other supplies for your office for the coming months.

Lesson 1: Naming Ranges

When you create a worksheet and plan to use a cell or range of cells many times, you may want to name the range. For example, you can name the range containing the total income to make the income range easy to use in formulas. Rather than look up the address of the range, simply name the range *income*, and use the range name in the formula in place of the range address. You can also use range names in other Excel commands and to move around the worksheet.

Range names can be up to 255 characters long, but you should keep them short so that you can easily remember them and have more room to enter the formula. Range names of up to 15 characters can be displayed in most scrolling list boxes. Additionally, observe the following rules when naming ranges:

- Both upper- and lowercase letters can be used
- Range names cannot contain spaces
- Range names must begin with a letter or underscore
- Any characters except math operators and hyphens can be used
- Range names can contain numbers, but cannot start with a number

Avoid combinations of letters and numbers that look like a cell address (such as a34) because that can be confusing. Choose names that describe the contents or the use of the range, such as *expenses*, *income*, and *average*.

Try naming ranges using the sample office expenses worksheet supplied for this project.

✓ On Your Mark

Why should you name ranges? Under what circumstances would you want to name a range?

Tip for Students

A named range can be one cell or several cells. All cells in a range must be adjacent, and the range must be rectangular.

**Project Time
75 minutes**

Lesson 1: Naming Ranges   91

To Name Ranges

❶ **Open the file Proj0401 and save it as Office.**

❷ **Click cell B3 and drag to cell C4 to select the range B3:C4.**

This is the first range you want to name. (You learned the different methods for selecting cells and ranges in Project 2, "Building a Spreadsheet.")

❸ **Open the Insert menu, move the mouse pointer to the Name command, then choose Define from the submenu that appears.**

The Define Name dialog box appears (see Figure 4.1). By default, Excel assumes that the label text from the row in which the active cell is located will be the range name, and enters it in the Names in **w**orkbook text box. The selected range address is entered in the **R**efers to text box, including the current worksheet name, Sheet1, and absolute references.

Figure 4.1
Use the Define Name dialog box to name ranges.

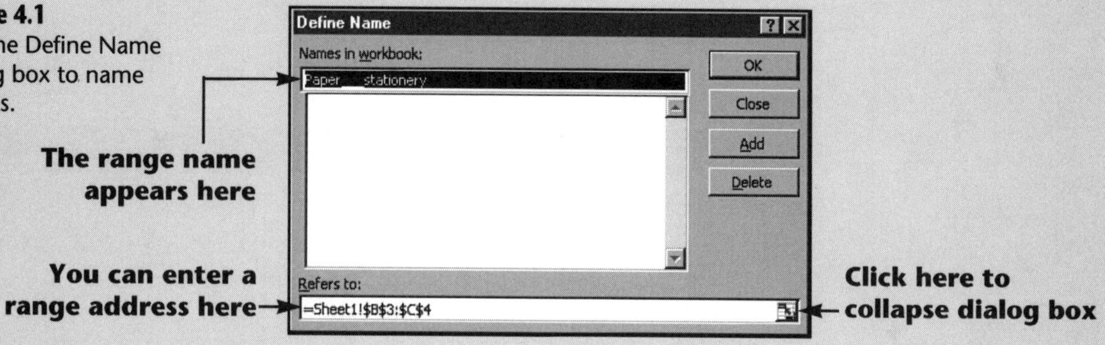

The range name appears here

You can enter a range address here

Click here to collapse dialog box

❹ **Replace the default name Paper_stationery (in the Names in workbook text box) with paper97.**

This name describes the cells in the range, which includes all your paper expenses for 1997.

❺ **Click OK.**

The dialog box closes, and the selected range is now named paper97. Notice that the range name appears in the Name box in the Formula bar because the range is still selected. Now name another range.

❻ **Select cells F3 through G4 in the worksheet.**

This selects the next range you want to name.

❼ **Open the Insert menu, move the mouse pointer to the Name command, then choose Define from the submenu that appears.**

This opens the Define Name dialog box again. Notice that the paper97 range name now appears in the Names in **w**orkbook list.

continues

To Name Ranges (continued)

Tip for Students

Clicking **A**dd in the Define Name dialog box adds the name to the list and keeps the dialog box open so you can add more names.

8 **In the Names in Workbook text box, type** `paper98`, **then click the Add button.**

The new range name appears in the Names in workbook list. Now try naming a range without closing the Define Names dialog box.

9 **In the Define Name dialog box, click the collapse button at the right end of the Refers to text box (refer to Figure 4.1).**

This collapses the dialog box so that you can select the range you want to name in the worksheet. Only the **R**efers to text box is still visible on the screen with the absolute reference to the current range entered: $F$3:$G$4. Now, select the new range you want to name.

10 **Select cells B5 through C6 in the worksheet.**

A flashing dotted line appears around the selected cells, and the **R**efers to text box displays the new range address, as shown in Figure 4.2. The flashing dotted line indicates the cells that you have selected to include in the named range. Cells F3:G4 are still selected and highlighted in the worksheet, and cell F3 is still the active cell.

If you have problems...

If the collapsed dialog box covers the cells you want to select, simply drag it out of the way. To drag it, point at the title bar, press and hold the left mouse button, and drag. Release the mouse button when the box is where you want it.

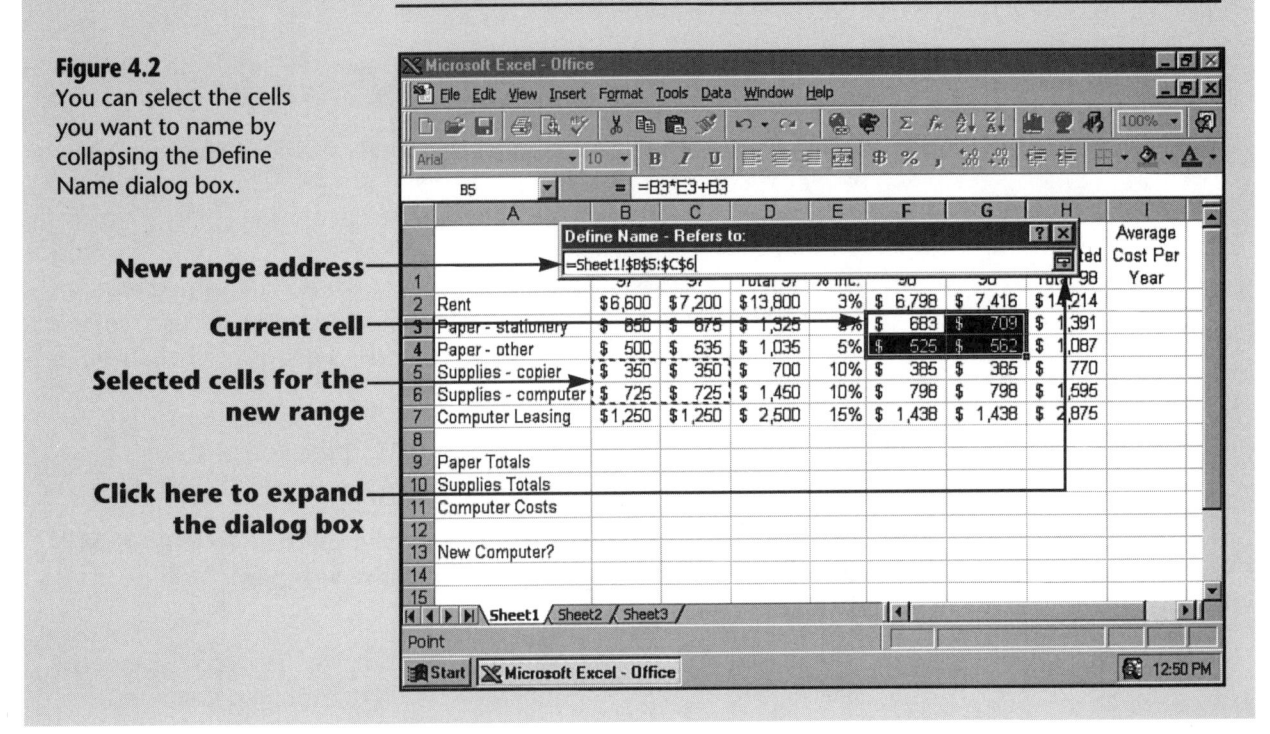

Figure 4.2
You can select the cells you want to name by collapsing the Define Name dialog box.

New range address

Current cell

Selected cells for the new range

Click here to expand the dialog box

Lesson 2: Using Named Ranges

⑪ Click the expand button at the right end of the Refers to text box.

Excel expands the Define Name dialog box. The new range now appears in the **R**efers to text box, but you must still enter a name for the new range.

⑫ In the Names in workbook text box, replace paper98 **with** supplies97**, and then click Add.**

The supplies97 range includes all your expenses for supplies for 1997. Now name one more range.

⑬ Click the button to collapse the Define Name dialog box, then select cells F5 through G6 in the worksheet.

⑭ Click the button to expand the Define Name dialog box, name the new range supplies98**, then click Add.**

You have now named four ranges that you can use later to build formulas and move around the worksheet. All four are listed in the Define Name dialog box.

⑮ Click OK to close the dialog box.

Click anywhere outside the selected cells to better see your worksheet. Save your work and keep the Office worksheet open to use in the next lesson.

To quickly name a range, select the range, type the name in the Name box on the Formula bar, and press ↵Enter. If you add or delete cells, rows, or columns to a named range, you may have to redefine the range to be sure it includes all of the cells you want.

You can delete the name of a range by choosing **I**nsert, **N**ame, **D**efine to open the Define Name dialog box. Select the name in the Names in **w**orkbook list, and click **D**elete. Click OK to close the dialog box. If you delete the definition of a named range in a cell with a formula that uses it, then #NAME? appears in the cell. You must edit the formula to include the correct range, cell, or value so that the formula can compute the result. Alternatively, delete the formula.

Lesson 2: Using Named Ranges

On Your Mark

What can you do with a named range? How do named ranges speed up your worksheet tasks?

You can use a named range in any formula to quickly and easily refer to a specific cell or range of cells. You can also use the Name box in the formula bar to quickly move to and select a named range. Now practice using named ranges to move around the Office worksheet.

To Use Named Ranges

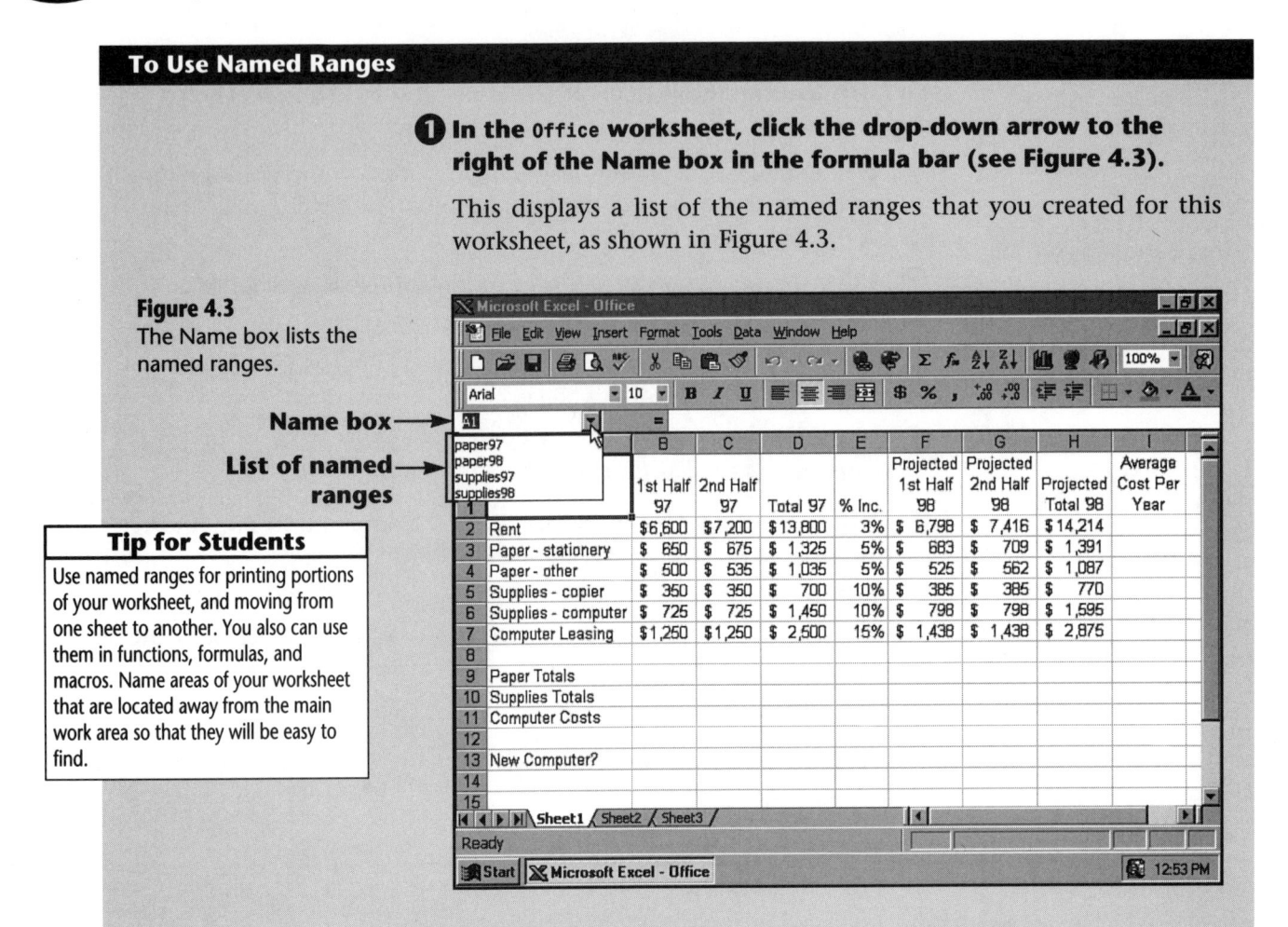

① In the `Office` **worksheet, click the drop-down arrow to the right of the Name box in the formula bar (see Figure 4.3).**

This displays a list of the named ranges that you created for this worksheet, as shown in Figure 4.3.

Figure 4.3
The Name box lists the named ranges.

Name box →
List of named ranges →

> **Tip for Students**
>
> Use named ranges for printing portions of your worksheet, and moving from one sheet to another. You also can use them in functions, formulas, and macros. Name areas of your worksheet that are located away from the main work area so that they will be easy to find.

② From the Name box drop-down list, select `paper98`.

This selects the range `paper98`, as shown in Figure 4.4. You can now edit, copy, move, or otherwise modify the named range. This shortcut for moving to named ranges is especially useful when you create workbooks that contain multiple worksheets. Now try moving to another named range.

> **Tip for Students**
>
> You can also press F5 to invoke the Go To dialog box for navigating to a named range. This function is used by many software programs.

> **Concept Note**
>
> When you move to a named range, either from the Name box or by pressing F5, the entire range is selected, and the upper-left cell in the range is active.

Lesson 2: Using Named Ranges 95

Figure 4.4
Selecting the name of the range in the Name box list selects the entire range of cells.

Range name
Selected range

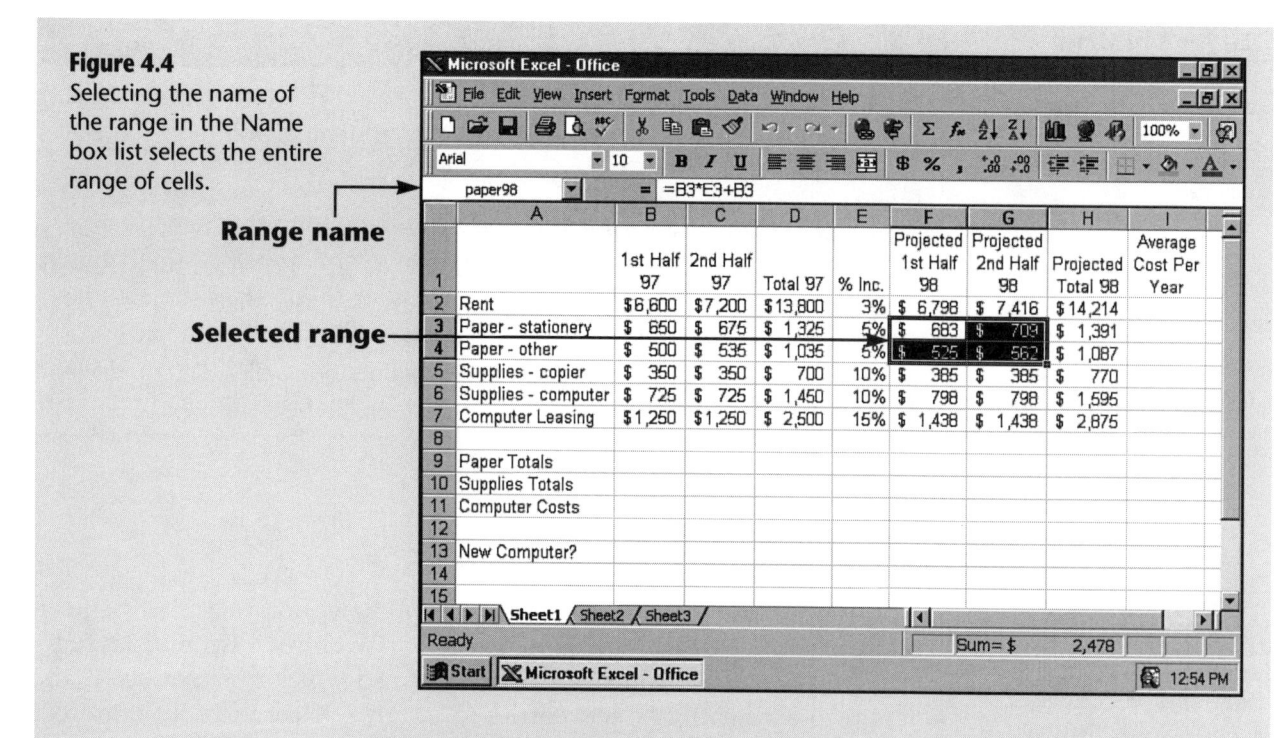

	A	B	C	D	E	F	G	H	I
1		1st Half 97	2nd Half 97	Total 97	% Inc.	Projected 1st Half 98	Projected 2nd Half 98	Projected Total 98	Average Cost Per Year
2	Rent	$6,600	$7,200	$13,800	3%	$ 6,798	$ 7,416	$14,214	
3	Paper - stationery	$ 650	$ 675	$ 1,325	5%	$ 683	$ 709	$ 1,391	
4	Paper - other	$ 500	$ 535	$ 1,035	5%	$ 525	$ 562	$ 1,087	
5	Supplies - copier	$ 350	$ 350	$ 700	10%	$ 385	$ 385	$ 770	
6	Supplies - computer	$ 725	$ 725	$ 1,450	10%	$ 798	$ 798	$ 1,595	
7	Computer Leasing	$1,250	$1,250	$ 2,500	15%	$ 1,438	$ 1,438	$ 2,875	
8									
9	Paper Totals								
10	Supplies Totals								
11	Computer Costs								
12									
13	New Computer?								

Tip for Students
In a workbook that uses multiple sheets, the named ranges from all sheets appear in the Name box.

Tip for Instructors
Clarify that the range name is visible in the Name box whenever the entire named range is selected. If only a portion of the range is selected (one cell, for example), then the active cell coordinates appear in the Name box.

❸ **Click the Name box drop-down arrow, and select** `supplies97`.

The `supplies97` range is now selected in the worksheet. Notice that the name of the range appears in the Name box. Save your work and keep the `Office` worksheet open. You use range names and functions to continue creating the worksheet in the next lesson.

To use a range in a formula, simply type the name in the formula in place of the range address. You learn more about using range names in formulas in Lesson 3.

In Excel, you can also name your worksheets and reference them in formulas. (As you learned in Project 1, "Getting Started with Excel," each Excel file is called a *workbook*, and each workbook is made up of one or more *worksheets*.) At the bottom of each worksheet is a sheet tab with the default sheet name on it. The first sheet is called `Sheet1`, the second sheet is called `Sheet2`, and so on. To view a different sheet, click the sheet tab. To change a sheet name, double-click the sheet tab, and type the new name.

To reference a worksheet, type the worksheet name followed by an exclamation point and the cell address, range address, or range name. For example, if you have a workbook for a five-year forecast with each year's data on a different worksheet, you can reference the different worksheets to create formulas to total, average, or in other ways work with the data from each worksheet. You saw an example of this in the **R**efers to text box in the Define Name dialog box while you were naming ranges in Lesson 1.

Project 4 Calculating with Functions

> **Tip for Students**
> If you use a range name in a formula before assigning the name (generating the error message #NAME?), the formula automatically corrects itself when you assign the name to a range.

> **If you have problems...**
> If you use a range name in a formula before you assign the name, Excel returns the error message #NAME?. Name the range first, and then you can use it in a formula.
>
> If you receive an error message dialog box when using the named range in a formula, check for spaces, math operators, or numbers at the beginning of the name. If the name contains any of these, then remove the offending characters and try your formula again. Before you can make changes, you must first respond to the dialog box: click OK to make changes to your name, or choose **H**elp to get online help from Excel.

> **✓ On Your Mark**
> Can you think of some advantages to using functions instead of creating your own equivalent formulas? Describe some of the functions for which you may anticipate such a need.

Lesson 3: Using Functions

As you learned in Project 3, functions are shortened formulas that perform specific operations on a group of values. You have already used the SUM function to total columns and rows of numbers, so you know that SUM is the function to automatically add entries in a range. Excel provides hundreds of functions that fit into 10 categories to help you with tasks, such as determining loan payments and calculating interest on your savings. Table 4.1 describes some common functions used in Excel.

Table 4.1 Common Functions

Function	Category	Description
AVERAGE	Statistical	Displays the average of a list of values.
AVERAGEA	Statistical	Displays the average of a list of arguments, including numbers, text, and logical values.
CELL	Information	Returns information about a cell or its contents.
DATE	Date & Time	Lists the date according to the computer's clock.
ERROR.TYPE	Information	Displays a number corresponding to one of Excel's error values. Used to debug macros and worksheets.
EVEN	Math & Trig	Rounds a value up to the nearest even integer.
MAX	Statistical	Finds the largest value in a list of numbers.
MAXA	Statistical	Finds the largest value in a list of arguments, including text, numbers, and logical values.
MIN	Statistical	Finds the smallest value in a list of numbers.
MINA	Statistical	Finds the smallest value in a list of arguments, including text, numbers, and logical values.
NOW	Date & Time	Calculates the current date and time on the computer's clock.
ODD	Math & Trig	Rounds a value up to the nearest odd integer.
PMT	Financial	Calculates the periodic payment amount needed to repay a loan.

Lesson 3: Using Functions

Function	Category	Description
PRODUCT	Math & Trig	Calculates the product of a list of values by multiplying each value in turn.
ROUND	Math & Trig	Rounds a value to a specific number of decimal places.
SUM	Math & Trig	Adds a list of values.
TIME	Date & Time	Lists the time according to the computer's clock.
TODAY	Date & Time	Calculates the serial number for the current date and displays it in date format. It is used for date and time calculations.

You can enter functions into Excel formulas in many ways. If you know the name of the function you want to use, you can type it into the cell where you want the result to appear, or you can type it into the Formula bar. You can also use the Formula palette or the Paste Function dialog box to select from a list of functions.

In this lesson, you learn to include functions in formulas using the different methods described previously. You also learn how to include range names in formulas and how to use the TODAY function, which displays the current system date. Try using functions to build the Office worksheet now.

To Use Functions

Tip for Students

All Excel functions are structured in the same manner: an equal, the function name, an open parenthesis, information necessary to perform the function, and a close parenthesis. Some functions, such as =TODAY( ), don't require additional information, so there is nothing between the parentheses.

Arguments

The values on which the function performs its calculations. An argument can be a single cell, a range of cells, or any value you enter.

❶ Click cell D2 in the Office worksheet.

Cell D2 already contains a formula that uses the SUM function to calculate the total rent for 1997. You can see the formula in the formula bar and the result of the formula in cell D2. Now, try using the TODAY function to enter today's date in a cell in the worksheet.

❷ Select cell A1 in the Office worksheet.

This is where you want the result of the formula—today's date—to appear. To create a formula using a function, you can type the formula in the cell or the formula bar.

❸ Type =today( ) and click the Enter button (the green check mark) on the formula bar.

This is the formula that uses the TODAY function to calculate today's date. Excel enters the system date in cell A1. Like all formulas, functions begin with an equal sign. You then type the function name in upper- or lowercase letters without leaving any spaces. The function name is followed by the function *arguments*, which are enclosed in parentheses and separated by commas. With the TODAY function, you do not need to include any arguments. Now use the Formula palette to enter a function to find the total amount you will spend on paper in 1997.

continues

98 Project 4 Calculating with Functions

To Use Functions (continued)

④ Select cell D9 and click the Edit Formula button on the formula bar.

Excel opens the Formula palette. With the Formula palette, you can select a function and enter the arguments you want to use.

⑤ Click the drop-down arrow to the right of the Function button.

A list of functions appears, as shown in Figure 4.5. The most recently used functions appear at the top of the list. You can click More Functions to open the Paste Function dialog box and display additional functions.

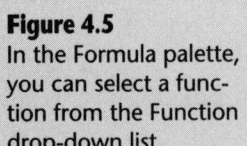

> **Tip for Students**
> The Formula palette helps you learn the structure of functions, and helps you include all the information necessary to perform a function. If you are comfortable with the function, you can simply type it.

Figure 4.5
In the Formula palette, you can select a function from the Function drop-down list.

- Function button
- Function list
- Click here to display additional functions
- Edit Formula button
- Formula palette

> **Tip for Students**
> You can check to see the answer that the function will return while in the Formula palette.

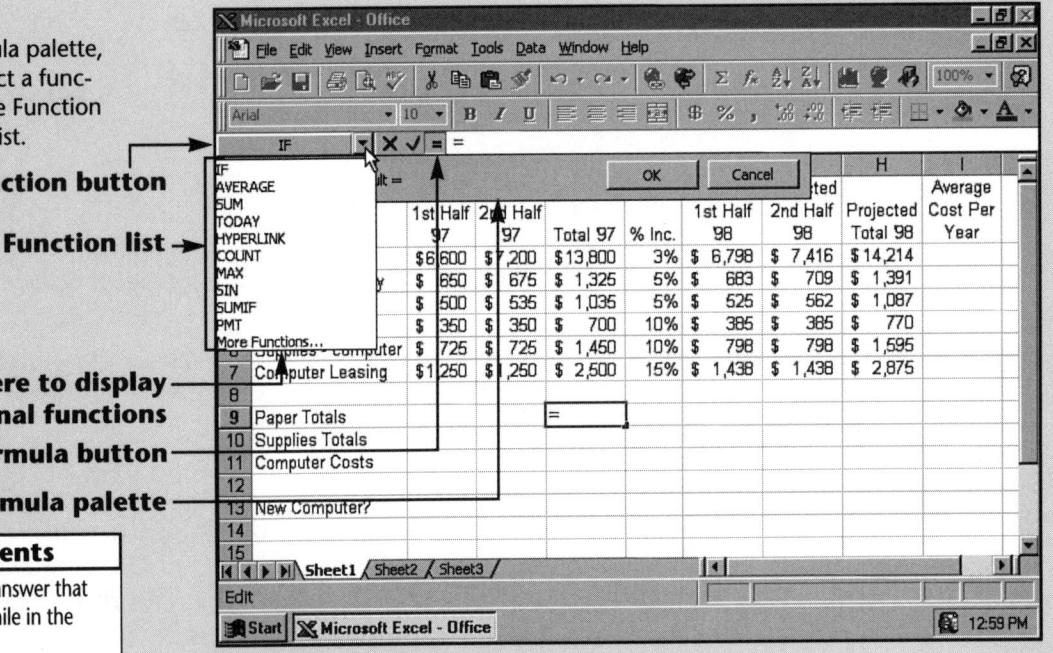

⑥ Select SUM.

Excel inserts the SUM function into the formula and expands the Formula palette, as shown in Figure 4.6. In the expanded palette, you can enter arguments, read a description of the function, and preview the result of the formula. Excel guesses which cells you want to total and displays the range address in the Number 1 text box. In this case, however, it guesses wrong. To correct the formula, you must enter the correct arguments or range of cells that you want to total.

> **If you have problems...**
> If the SUM function does not appear in the drop-down list of functions, select More Functions to open the Paste Function dialog box. In the Function **C**ategory list, select All, then scroll down in the Function **N**ame list, and select SUM. Choose OK to enter the SUM function in the formula.

Lesson 3: Using Functions   99

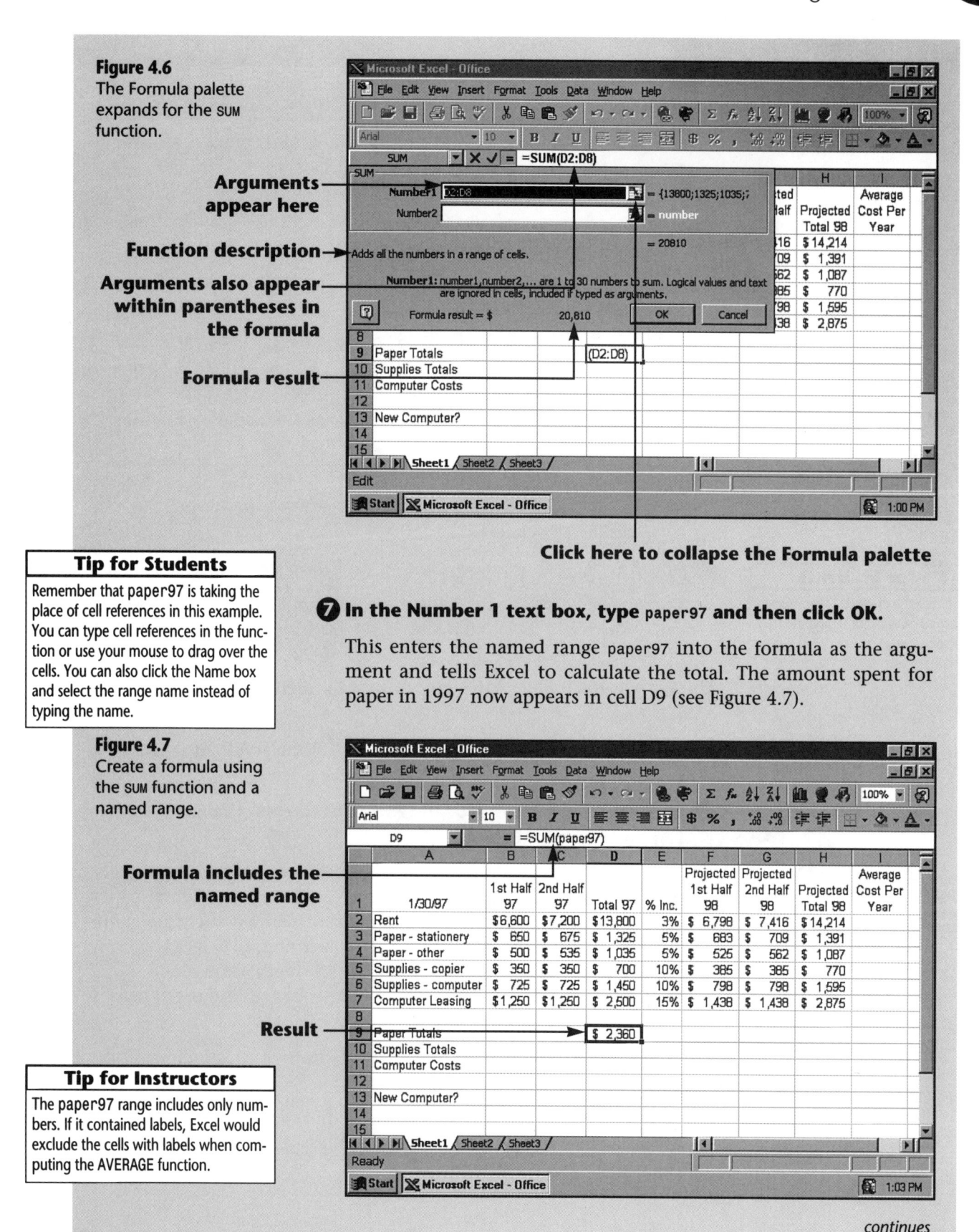

Figure 4.6
The Formula palette expands for the SUM function.

- Arguments appear here
- Function description
- Arguments also appear within parentheses in the formula
- Formula result

Click here to collapse the Formula palette

Tip for Students
Remember that paper97 is taking the place of cell references in this example. You can type cell references in the function or use your mouse to drag over the cells. You can also click the Name box and select the range name instead of typing the name.

7 **In the Number 1 text box, type paper97 and then click OK.**

This enters the named range paper97 into the formula as the argument and tells Excel to calculate the total. The amount spent for paper in 1997 now appears in cell D9 (see Figure 4.7).

Figure 4.7
Create a formula using the SUM function and a named range.

- Formula includes the named range
- Result

Tip for Instructors
The paper97 range includes only numbers. If it contained labels, Excel would exclude the cells with labels when computing the AVERAGE function.

continues

To Use Functions (continued)

> **If you have problems...**
>
> If you enter a function with a mistake in it, Excel displays an error message in the cell, such as #NAME? or #VALUE?. If Excel thinks it knows the problem, it displays a message box asking if it is okay to go ahead and correct it. Choose **Y**es to have Excel automatically correct the formula, or **N**o to try to fix it on your own.
>
> When troubleshooting formulas, first make sure that you used an existing named range and then check for typos in the range name. Study the formula and check the range name for invalid characters, such as punctuation marks and mathematical operators. The error message #NAME? will appear if your range name contains any of these symbols. Remove the offending symbol or number and try again.

Now enter functions to total the rest of your paper and supply expenses for 1997 and 1998.

8 In cell D10, type =sum(supplies97), **and then press** ⏎Enter.

> **Tip for Students**
> You can click the Name box and select supplies97 instead of typing the range name.

The sum showing the total spent for supplies in 1997 appears in the cell. You could also click the Enter button on the formula bar instead of pressing ⏎Enter.

9 Select cell H9, then click the AutoSum button on the Standard toolbar.

The SUM function with the *incorrect* range as the argument appears in cell H9.

10 In the worksheet, select cells F3:G4, then click the Enter button on the formula bar.

> **Tip for Students**
> With most functions, you can skip typing the close parenthesis. When you press Enter, Excel will insert the close parenthesis for you.

This replaces the incorrect range in the formula with the correct range—paper98—and enters the formula. The projected total paper expenses for 1998 appears in cell H9. As you can see, there are many ways to enter functions and arguments into formulas in Excel. You can decide for yourself which is the easiest method or which is the most appropriate. Enter one more formula for totaling the expenses for supplies for 1998.

11 Select cell H10, click the Edit Formula button, then choose SUM from the Function drop-down list.

Excel opens the Formula palette with the wrong range entered as the argument. Try selecting the correct range to insert it into the formula.

Lesson 3: Using Functions

12 Click the collapse button at the right end of the Number 1 text box (refer to Figure 4.6).

Excel collapses the Formula palette so you can select the cells you want to use in the worksheet. Only the Number 1 text box appears on the screen.

13 Select cells F5:G6 to enter the `supplies98` range, then click the expand button at the right end of the Number 1 text box.

Excel expands the Formula palette with the correct range entered in the formula.

> **If you have problems...**
>
> If the collapsed palette covers the column or row labels, you should still be able to select the correct range by counting the rows and columns or by referring to the numbers and letters that are visible. If the palette covers the range that you want to select, you must move it out of the way while it is full-size. To move it, expand it, point anywhere within the palette area, then click and drag to move it out of the way. When it is out of the way, try collapsing it and selecting the cells again.

14 Click OK in the Formula palette.

The projected total expense for supplies in 1998 appears in cell H10. Your worksheet should now look similar to the one shown in Figure 4.8. Save your work and keep the `Office` worksheet open for the next lesson, in which you create more complex formulas with functions.

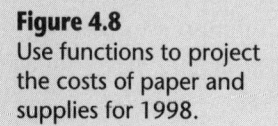

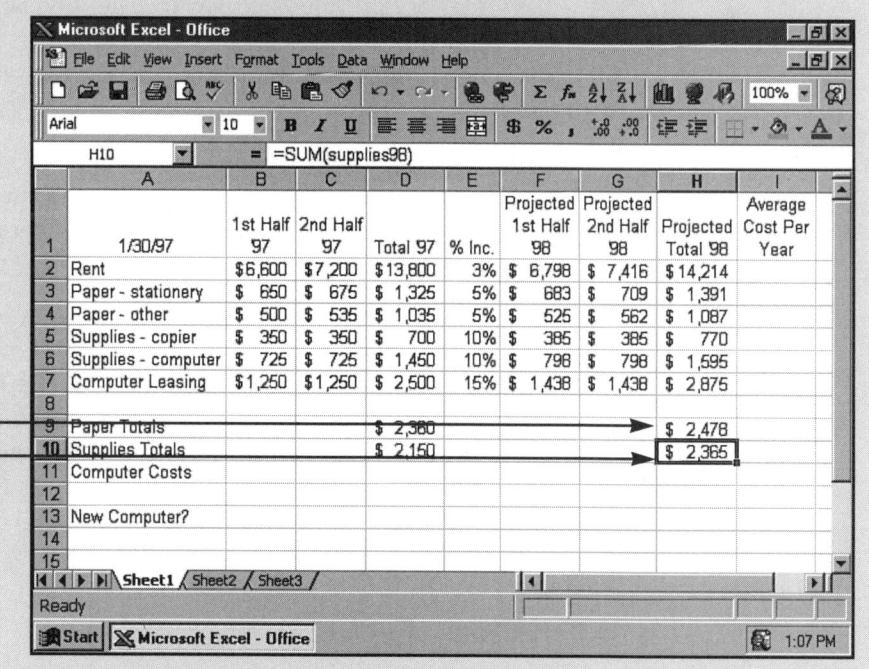

Figure 4.8
Use functions to project the costs of paper and supplies for 1998.

Projected paper total for 1998
Projected supplies total for 1998

	A	B	C	D	E	F	G	H	I
1	1/30/97	1st Half 97	2nd Half 97	Total 97	% Inc.	Projected 1st Half 98	Projected 2nd Half 98	Projected Total 98	Average Cost Per Year
2	Rent	$6,600	$7,200	$13,800	3%	$ 6,798	$ 7,416	$14,214	
3	Paper - stationery	$ 650	$ 675	$ 1,325	5%	$ 683	$ 709	$ 1,391	
4	Paper - other	$ 500	$ 535	$ 1,035	5%	$ 525	$ 562	$ 1,087	
5	Supplies - copier	$ 350	$ 350	$ 700	10%	$ 385	$ 385	$ 770	
6	Supplies - computer	$ 725	$ 725	$ 1,450	10%	$ 798	$ 798	$ 1,595	
7	Computer Leasing	$1,250	$1,250	$ 2,500	15%	$ 1,438	$ 1,438	$ 2,875	
8									
9	Paper Totals			$ 2,360				$ 2,478	
10	Supplies Totals			$ 2,150				$ 2,365	
11	Computer Costs								
12									
13	New Computer?								

H10 = =SUM(supplies98)

Project 4   Calculating with Functions

> **If you have problems...**
>
> If you think a function that uses a range is not returning the correct answer, make sure that the range is entered correctly. Ensure that all cells you need are included and that no extra cells containing data are included.

Jargon Watch

Several differences exist between regular formulas and **functions**. One difference is that you can customize regular formulas more to your liking. You use functions as shortcuts to tell Excel how to calculate values.

As demonstrated in Project 3, entering a function, such as **=SUM(B2:B9)**, is quicker and easier than entering its corresponding formula: **=B2+B3+B4+B5+B6+B7+B8+B9**. In a regular formula, you must specify every operation to be performed. That's why there are so many plus signs in the preceding formula. In a function, however, the operations are programmed in, so you need only supply the necessary information in the form of **arguments**. In the function =SUM(B2:B9), B2:B9 is the argument. Functions can include multiple arguments, as you learn in Lesson 4.

When you add arguments to a function, you must use the proper **syntax**, which is simply the exact and correct way to type commands and functions. In general, computer programs are inflexible about even one wrong keystroke, such as a missing comma.

If your formula returns an error message, use the Excel Help feature to find out more about the syntax for the specific function you are trying to use.

Tip for Students

You will see the correct syntax for functions when you use the Formula palette. Excel will help you get it right if you use this feature. If you're unsure of the syntax, take advantage of the Formula palette.

You can also use the Paste Function dialog box to select a function. Click the Paste Function button on the Standard toolbar to open the dialog box. It displays a list of functions grouped by category. Select the category and the function you want to use, then click OK. Excel inserts the function into the formula and opens the Formula palette, so you can enter the arguments you want to use.

Instead of typing a range into a function, you can use the mouse to select the range. For example, you can type **=SUM(** and then drag the mouse to select the range. Excel enters the range in the formula bar as you drag, as well as the closing parenthesis. End the function by pressing (↵Enter) to calculate the formula.

Another way to enter the name of a range in a function or formula is to use the Paste Name dialog box. When you reach the place in the formula where you want to insert the named range, press (F3). The Paste Name dialog box appears with a list of named ranges. Choose the name of the range from the Paste **N**ame list box. Click OK to close the dialog box, then continue creating the formula.

Lesson 4: Building Formulas with Functions

Also, don't forget that you can quickly check the result of a calculation without actually entering the formula by using the AutoCalculate button on the status bar.

> **✓ On Your Mark**
>
> Can you think of some typical formulas you use in worksheets that incorporate functions? Can you think of instances in which a function alone is not sufficient to produce a calculation you need?
>
> **Nest**
> To place one function within another.

Lesson 4: Building Formulas with Functions

Functions are easy to use in building complex formulas. For example, you can add two SUM functions together (as you do in this lesson using the Office worksheet). You can also *nest* functions by using them as arguments for other functions.

This lesson shows you how to create complex formulas by combining and nesting functions.

To Build Formulas with Functions

> **Tip for Students**
>
> You can use your mouse to drag over the cells. Press Ctrl while selecting non-adjacent cells.

❶ In cell I2 of the Office worksheet, enter the formula `=average(b2+c2,f2+g2)`.

This enters the formula and calculates the average cost of rent per year. When you use two arguments in a function, you separate them with a comma. Don't forget to click the Enter button on the formula bar.

Note that you can get the same result from the simple formula `=average(d2,h2)`. In general, it's best to use the simplest formula possible in your worksheets. You are asked to build more complex formulas in this lesson to learn how functions can be used together.

> **If you have problems...**
>
> If the average doesn't appear to be correct, make sure that the ranges you used don't include any extra cells with values or labels. When using the AVERAGE function, be sure to use only the specific cells with the contents you want to average.

> **? Q&A**
>
> What are four other ways to copy your formula from cell I2 to cells I3 through I7? *Answers*: Toolbar buttons, Edit menu options, AutoFill, and keyboard shortcuts.

❷ Select cell I2 again, click the right mouse button to open the shortcut menu, then choose Copy.

This copies the formula in cell I2 to the Windows Clipboard.

❸ Select cells I3 through I7, open the shortcut menu, then choose Paste.

This copies the formula to cells I3 through I7 where the results are displayed, as shown in Figure 4.9. Because no decimal places are displayed, Excel rounds the totals to the nearest whole number; however, the actual value is used in all calculations. The formulas in the cells are relative. In Project 3, you learned that *relative* means that the formula conforms to its current address, no matter where it was first entered. In this example, the formula is always relative to the numbers in the cells to the left of the formula's current cell address.

continues

To Build Formulas with Functions (continued)

Figure 4.9
The function averages the values relative to its current cell address.

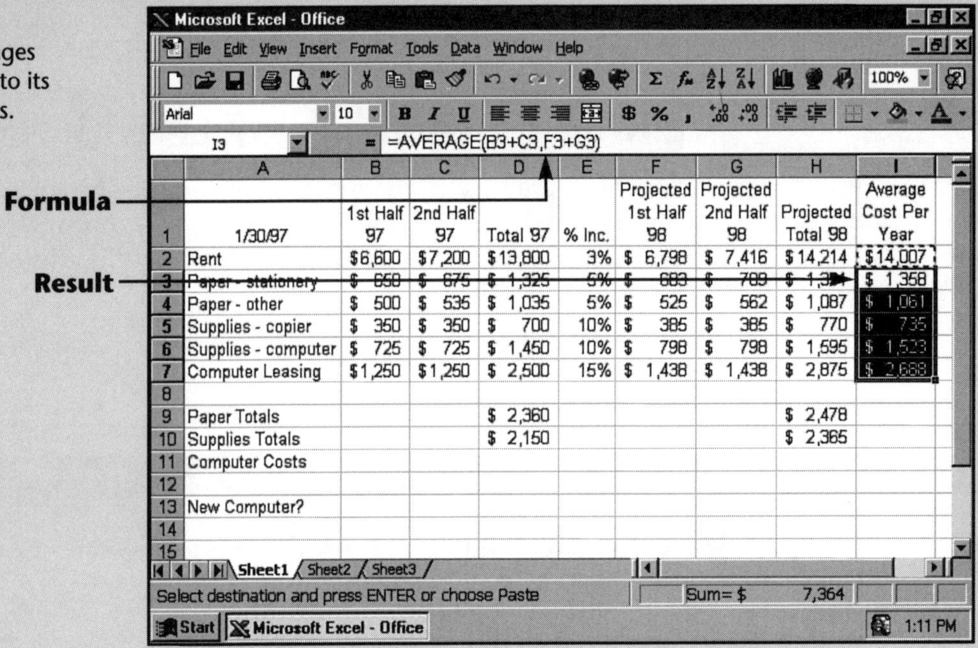

Formula
Result

④ **In cell D11, enter the formula** =sum(b6:c6)+sum(b7:c7).

This calculates the total computer costs for 1997 by adding the total costs of computer supplies and the total costs of computer leasing. You built the formula by combining two functions with the plus sign operator.

Once again, you are using more complex formulas than are necessary, so you can learn the different methods of entering functions. You can get the same result with the simple formula =D6+D7, which adds the total computer supplies and computer leasing expenses for the year.

Now use the Formula palette to enter a formula to calculate the total computer costs for 1998.

⑤ **Select cell H11, click the Edit Formula button, and choose the SUM function.**

Instead of combining two SUM functions to complete the formula, try using two arguments within one function.

⑥ **In the Number 1 text box, type the range** f6:g6, **and press** Tab. **Then, in the Number 2 text box, type the range** f7:g7, **and click OK.**

Excel sets up the formula by enclosing the arguments in parentheses and separating them with a comma. The projected total computer cost for 1998 appears in cell H11, as shown in Figure 4.10.

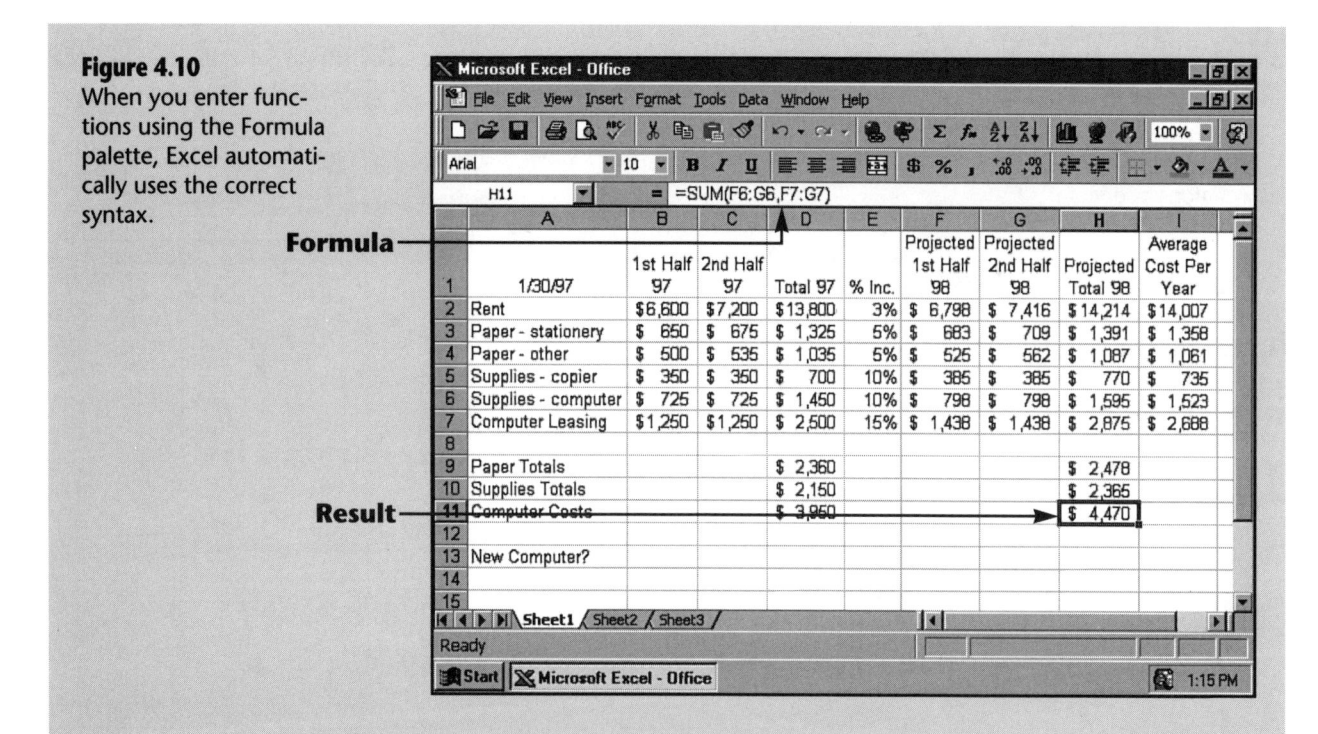

Figure 4.10
When you enter functions using the Formula palette, Excel automatically uses the correct syntax.

Formula — (pointing to formula bar showing `=SUM(F6:G6,F7:G7)`)

Result — (pointing to cell H11 showing `$ 4,470`)

Now create a complex formula to calculate the average total computer cost per year. Use your choice of methods to enter the formula.

☑ **❼ In cell I11, enter the formula** =average(sum(b6:c7),sum(f6:g7)).

In this formula, the SUM functions are nested as arguments for the AVERAGE function. Excel calculates the sum of B6:C7 and the sum of F6:G7, then finds the average of the two resulting values. By combining several functions, you have created a formula that calculates the average total computer cost per year, as shown in Figure 4.11. Note the placement of the parentheses, which specify the arguments that are used for each function.

Again, note that you can also achieve the same result with the simpler formula =**AVERAGE**(D11,H11), which adds the total costs for 1997 and 1998, then finds the average of the two. Note also that D11 equals SUM(D6:D7) and that H11 equals SUM(H6:H7). In creating the more complex formula, you have simply replaced the SUM functions for cells D11 and H11.

continues

106 Project 4 Calculating with Functions

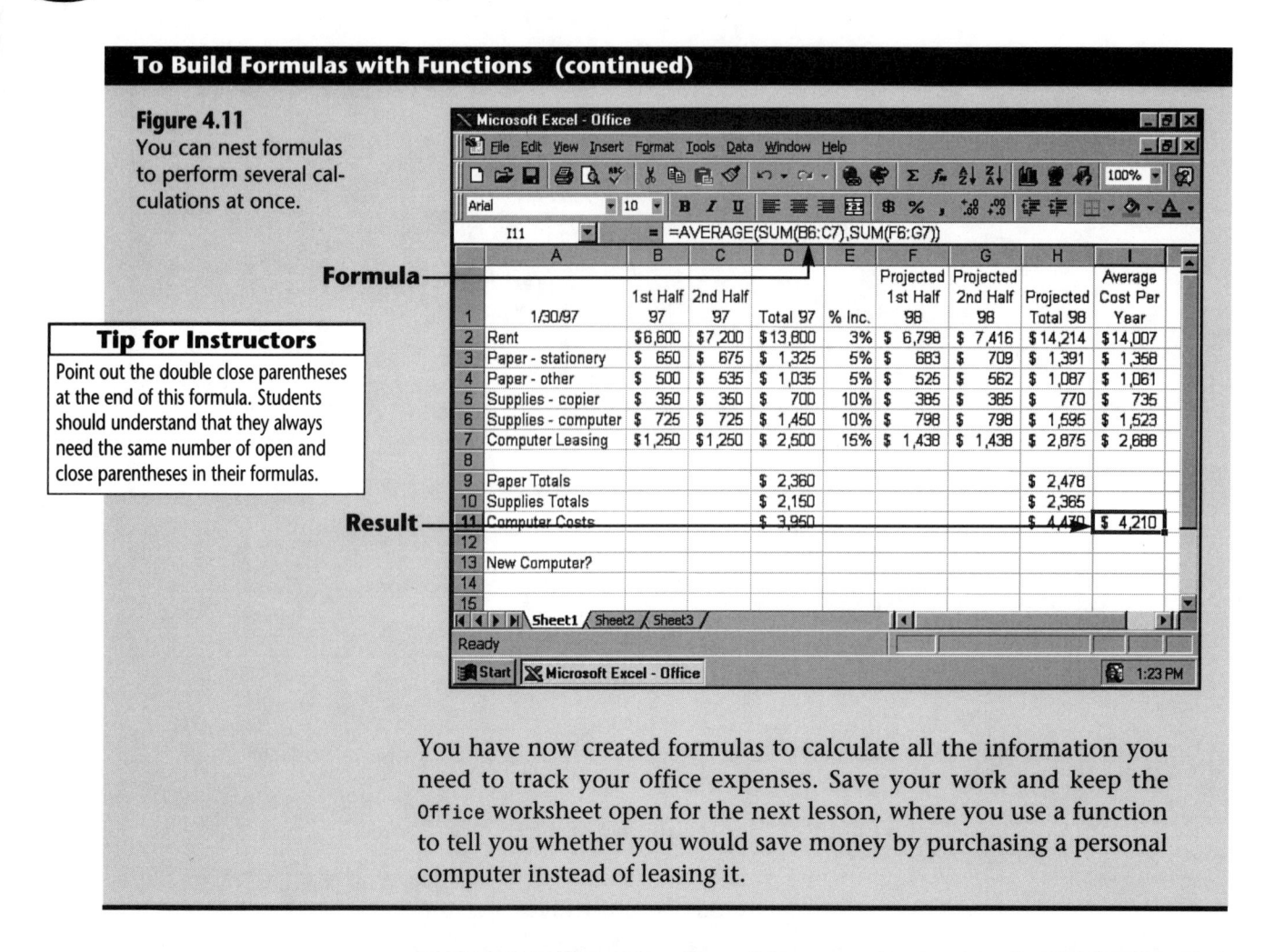

To Build Formulas with Functions (continued)

Figure 4.11
You can nest formulas to perform several calculations at once.

Formula — =AVERAGE(SUM(B6:C7),SUM(F6:G7))

	A	B	C	D	E	F	G	H	I
1	1/30/97	1st Half 97	2nd Half 97	Total 97	% Inc.	Projected 1st Half 98	Projected 2nd Half 98	Projected Total 98	Average Cost Per Year
2	Rent	$6,600	$7,200	$13,800	3%	$ 6,798	$ 7,416	$14,214	$14,007
3	Paper - stationery	$ 650	$ 675	$ 1,325	5%	$ 683	$ 709	$ 1,391	$ 1,358
4	Paper - other	$ 500	$ 535	$ 1,035	5%	$ 525	$ 562	$ 1,087	$ 1,061
5	Supplies - copier	$ 350	$ 350	$ 700	10%	$ 385	$ 385	$ 770	$ 735
6	Supplies - computer	$ 725	$ 725	$ 1,450	10%	$ 798	$ 798	$ 1,595	$ 1,523
7	Computer Leasing	$1,250	$1,250	$ 2,500	15%	$ 1,438	$ 1,438	$ 2,875	$ 2,688
8									
9	Paper Totals			$ 2,360				$ 2,478	
10	Supplies Totals			$ 2,150				$ 2,365	
11	Computer Costs			$ 3,950				$ 4,470	$ 4,210
12									
13	New Computer?								

Result — (points to $4,210 in I11)

Tip for Instructors
Point out the double close parentheses at the end of this formula. Students should understand that they always need the same number of open and close parentheses in their formulas.

You have now created formulas to calculate all the information you need to track your office expenses. Save your work and keep the Office worksheet open for the next lesson, where you use a function to tell you whether you would save money by purchasing a personal computer instead of leasing it.

If you have problems...

A common mistake in complex functions involves parentheses. Be sure that for every open parenthesis, there is a corresponding close parenthesis. All parentheses must be placed in the correct location to avoid a syntax error.

Another fairly common mistake is substituting a plus sign for the colon in a SUM formula. The formula =SUM(D10:I10) is much different than =SUM(D10+I10). In the latter formula, only the first and last cells are added, whereas in the first formula, all cells from D10 to I10, including D10 and I10, are added.

If Excel responds with the error message #NAME?, don't worry. Simply check your formula carefully to make sure that all parentheses are present and all addresses are correct. If you still can't find the problem, check the values and formulas in the referenced cells for typos. One typographical error can affect formulas in many parts of the worksheet if the formulas refer to the cell containing the error.

Tip for Instructors
Point out Excel's method of highlighting paired parentheses as you edit a formula. This is an excellent debugging tool.

Tip for Instructors
When explaining formula construction, encourage students to work through a formula by saying it out loud. Talking through the formula helps students place the parts of the formula in logical order.

Tip for Students
If you use range names in a formula, the range has a relative reference.

A colon between the cell addresses in a range argument (such as F6:G7) is simply the standard method that Excel uses to show the range. A comma is used to separate arguments in a function.

To nest one function within another using the Formula palette, simply make sure the insertion point is in the location where you want the nested function to appear in the formula, then select the function from the Function drop-down list. The insertion point can be in an argument text box in the Formula palette or in the Formula bar. Excel will open the Formula palette for the nested function. When you have entered all of the arguments for the nested function, click in the Formula bar to display the Formula palette for the original function.

Remember, when you paste a formula from one cell into another, each cell reference in the original formula is converted to a relative reference.

Lesson 5: Using Conditional Statements

Your Office worksheet now contains information and formulas that you need to track the cost of running an office over two years. Now look at how you can have the worksheet calculate whether you should purchase computer equipment instead of continuing to lease it.

Using *conditional statements*, you can implement different actions, depending on whether a condition is true or false. The simplest conditional function in Excel is the IF function: If the condition is true, then Excel displays one result; if the condition is false, then Excel displays a different result.

Try using the IF function to see whether your computer costs are sufficiently high to warrant purchasing a personal computer.

> **On Your Mark**
>
> Can you think of situations in a worksheet when the contents of a cell depend on circumstances in another part of the worksheet? (*One example*: The percentage of income tax you pay increases as your income increases.)
>
> **Conditional statement**
> A function that returns different results depending on whether a specified condition is true or false.

To Use Conditional Statements

❶ Select cell B13 of the Office worksheet.

❷ Click the Paste Function button on the Standard toolbar.

The Paste Function dialog box opens.

❸ Choose Logical in the Function Category list, and then choose IF in the Function Name list.

Excel displays the function syntax—=IF(logical_test,value_if_true, value_if_false)—at the bottom of the dialog box, along with a description of the function (see Figure 4.12).

> **Tip for Instructors**
>
> You can display the Paste Function dialog box by clicking the Paste Function button on the toolbar, or by choosing **I**nsert, **F**unction from the menu bar.

continues

To Use Conditional Statements (continued)

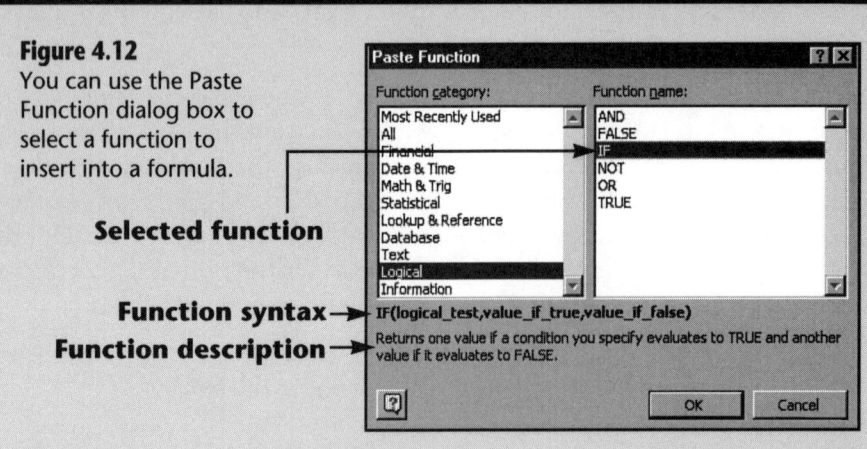

Figure 4.12
You can use the Paste Function dialog box to select a function to insert into a formula.

- Selected function
- Function syntax
- Function description

For this example, the logical test is whether or not your yearly computer costs are greater than $4,000. *If* they are, *then* it makes sense to purchase a computer. *If* they are not, *then* it makes sense to continue leasing.

❹ Click OK.

Excel pastes the selected function into the formula and opens the Formula palette, so you can enter the arguments (see Figure 4.13).

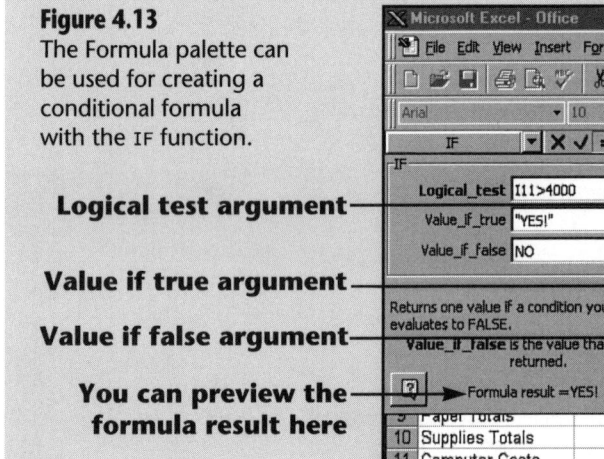

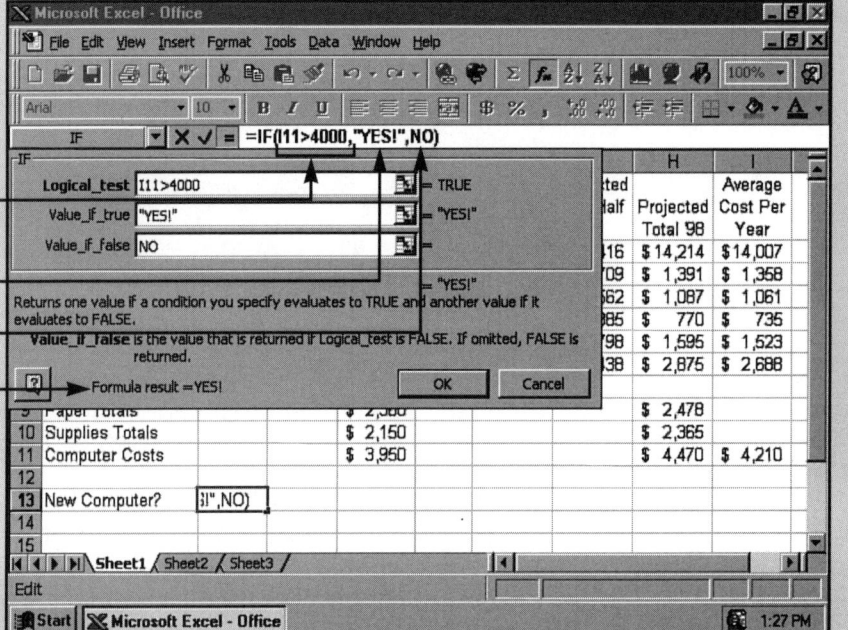

Figure 4.13
The Formula palette can be used for creating a conditional formula with the IF function.

- Logical test argument
- Value if true argument
- Value if false argument
- You can preview the formula result here

❺ In the Logical_Test text box, type I11>4000 and press Tab.

This enters the logical test argument, and moves the insertion point to the next text box. I11 refers to the cell where the average total computer costs are calculated, the > sign is the mathematical operator that means *greater than*, and 4000 is the value you want to use for comparison.

Tip for Students

Move from one text box to the next in the Formula palette with Tab (forward) or Shift+Tab (backward). Also, you can move by clicking in a different text box. Don't press Enter until you are finished entering all the information in the Formula palette.

Lesson 5: Using Conditional Statements

❻ In the Value_if_true text box, type YES!, including the exclamation mark, and press Tab.

This enters the `value_if_true` argument of the function. It tells Excel what value to display in the cell if the condition is true. In other words, if the total average cost per year is greater than $4,000, Excel will enter YES! in the current cell.

❼ In the Value_if_false box, type NO.

This enters the `value_if_false` argument. It tells Excel the value to display if the condition is false—that is, if the value in cell I11 is less than $4,000. The Formula palette should now look like the one in Figure 4.13.

❽ Click OK.

Excel performs the calculation, and the word YES! should now appear in cell B13, as shown in Figure 4.14. When you use the IF function, Excel tells you that you should purchase the computer based on the information currently in the worksheet. If the projected expenses were to decrease so that the average total was less than $4,000, Excel would return NO as the response.

> **Tip for Students**
> Excel has already calculated the formula result, which appears at the bottom of the Formula palette.

> **Tip for Students**
> The easiest way to figure out the structure of an IF function is to verbalize it. Go ahead and actually say out loud what you want the formula to calculate.

> **Tip for Students**
> Notice the actual structure of the IF statement when it appears in your worksheet. Text strings belong in quotation marks, so if you were typing this statement yourself, you would type "YES!". Omitting the quotation marks generates the Error in formula message.

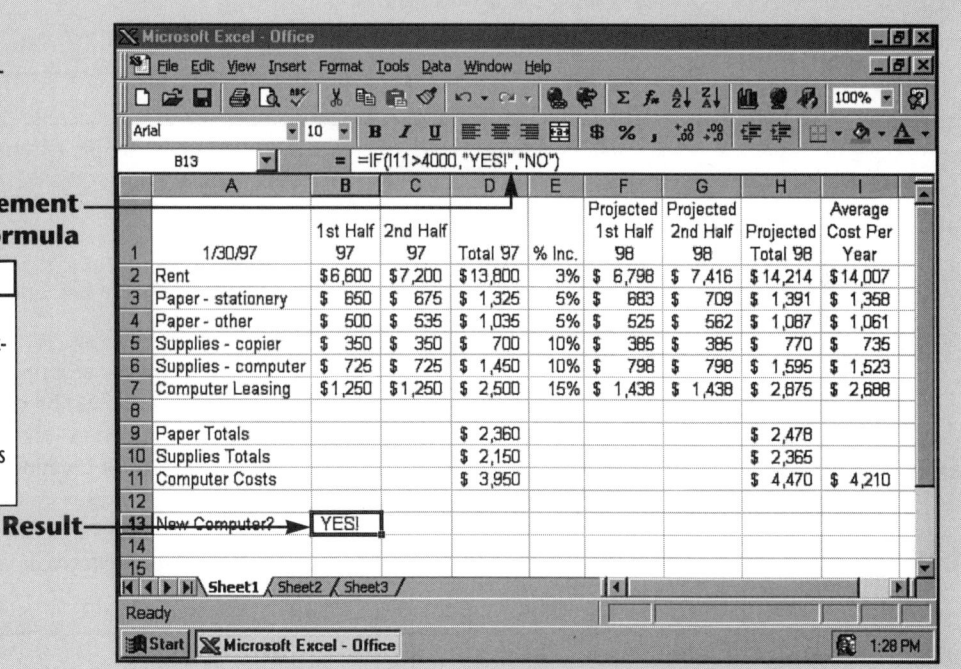

Figure 4.14
The result of the conditional statement is Yes!

Conditional statement formula

Result

Save your work. If requested by your instructor, print two copies, then close the worksheet. If you have completed your session on the computer, exit Excel and Windows 95 before turning off the computer. Otherwise, continue with the "Checking Your Skills" section at the end of this project.

Jargon Watch

Conditional statements use many mathematical terms that can be confusing. In most cases, however, a conditional statement takes the form of a simple if/then sentence: *if* this happens, *then* that happens.

Conditional statements or arguments, such as the one in this lesson, typically use a **logical operator**. Logical operators include the following:

Operator	Meaning
=	Equal
<	Less than
>	Greater than
<=	Less than or equal to
>=	Greater than or equal to

Think of these operators simply as replacements for the words in the "Meaning" column above.

Project Summary

To	Do This
Name a range	Select the range, choose **I**nsert, **N**ame, **D**efine, type a name in the Names in **w**orkbook text box, and click OK.
Select a named range	Click the drop-down arrow in the Name box in the formula bar, and select the range name.
Enter a function in a formula	Type an equal sign followed by the function name and the arguments enclosed in parentheses (separated by commas). Or, click the Paste Function button on the Standard toolbar, select the function, then click OK. Or, open the Formula palette, and select the function from the Function drop-down list. Complete the formula and then click OK.
Perform *what-if* analyses on data	Use the logical IF function.

Checking Your Skills

True/False

For each of the following, check *T* or *F* to indicate whether the statement is true or false.

__T ✔F **1.** You can name a range, but not an individual cell.

✔T __F **2.** Range names can consist of up to 255 characters.

__T ✔F **3.** If Excel displays the error message #NAME? when using a named range in a formula, check to make sure you have the equal sign in the name.

✔T __F **4.** An IF function includes a condition and two arguments.

__T ✔F **5.** Use the CALENDAR function to display the current system date.

✔T __F **6.** You can use both upper- and lowercase letters in a range name.

__T ✔F **7.** Range names must begin with a letter, underscore, or number.

__T ✔F **8.** To display a list of named ranges in the worksheet, right-click the formula bar.

✔T __F **9.** You cannot use spaces in a function name.

__T ✔F **10.** You cannot delete the name of a defined range.

Multiple Choice

Circle the letter of the correct answer for each of the following questions.

1. Which of the following is a collection of cells that you can use in a formula?

  a. B2...B2

  b. B2:G2

  c. B2:G2,B6

  d. B4+C4,C6

2. Which of the following is a valid formula?

  a. =AVERAGE(B2;C2;D4;G4)

  b. SUM(B2:B8)-AVG(D2:D4)

  c. =SUM(AVG(C3;C4),(AVG F6:F9

  d. =SUM:AVG(SUM,(C3:C9,SUM,(D3:D9))

3. Which of the following is a valid range name?

  a. tuitionandfees96

  b. tuition 1996

  c. tuition+fees

  d. 96tuitionandfees

4. When using the IF conditional statement, you can do what?

  a. Set a condition and get one answer if the condition is true and a second answer if the condition is false.

  b. Set one condition and one argument to analyze a formula.

  c. Enter a condition that performs a calculation on a formula.

  d. List between two and six arguments that apply to the IF condition.

5. Which of the following could cause the error message #NAME? to be returned as a result?

  a. Using too many functions

  b. Using a nonexistent range name

  c. Using too many parentheses

  d. Using the wrong symbols for operators

Project 4 Calculating with Functions

6. The command used to name a range is located on which menu?

   a. Edit

   b. Insert

   c. Format

   d. Tools

7. To quickly name a range, you select the range and then type the name in the Name box in which location?

   a. formula bar

   b. Formatting toolbar

   c. Standard toolbar

   d. status bar

8. To calculate a loan payment, you use which function?

   a. SUM

   b. MAX

   c. MIN

   d. PMT

9. Which cells are totaled in the function =SUM(D10:I10)?

   a. Cell D10 and cell I10

   b. All cells from D10 through I10

   c. All the cells between D10 and I10

   d. none of the above

10. An argument in a function can be which of the following?

    a. A single cell

    b. A range of cells

    c. Any entered value

    d. all the above

Completion

In the blank provided, write the correct answer for each of the following statements.

1. The _Name box_ in the formula bar lists named ranges.

2. When you use a named range in a formula before you assign the name, Excel returns a(n) _#Name?_ in the cell.

3. You can combine or _nest_ functions within a formula so that you can perform complex calculations at one time.

4. The _argument_ is always placed within parentheses to indicate which data the function will use to perform its calculation.

5. Click the _Paste Functions_ button on the Standard toolbar to select a function.

6. Functions must begin with a(n) _equal sign_.

7. You can use the _Paste Function_ dialog box to select a function.

8. When you use two arguments in a function, separate them with a(n) _comma_.

9. To change the name of a worksheet, _double-click_ the sheet tab, then type the new name.

10. To use the Paste Name dialog box to insert the name of a range in a function or formula, press _F3_.

Checking Your Skills

Matching

In the blank next to each of the following terms or phrases, write the letter of the corresponding term or phrase.

_j_ **1.** The exact and correct way to type commands and functions.

_i_ **2.** The values on which the function performs its calculations.

_h_ **3.** To place one function within another

_d_ **4.** A function that returns different results depending on whether a specified condition is true or false.

_a_ **5.** Greater than or equal to

_f_ **6.** Less than or equal to

_b_ **7.** A name given to a cell or range of cells

_e_ **8.** Function arguments are enclosed in these

_g_ **9.** Function that finds the largest value in a list of numbers

_c_ **10.** Function that finds the smallest value in a list of numbers

a. >=

b. range name

c. MIN

d. conditional statement

e. parentheses

f. <=

g. MAX

h. nest

i. arguments

j. syntax

Screen ID

Label each element of the Excel screen shown in Figure 4.15.

Figure 4.15

1. *Function button*
2. *Function list*
3. *Display additional functions*
4. *Cancel button*
5. *Paste Function button*

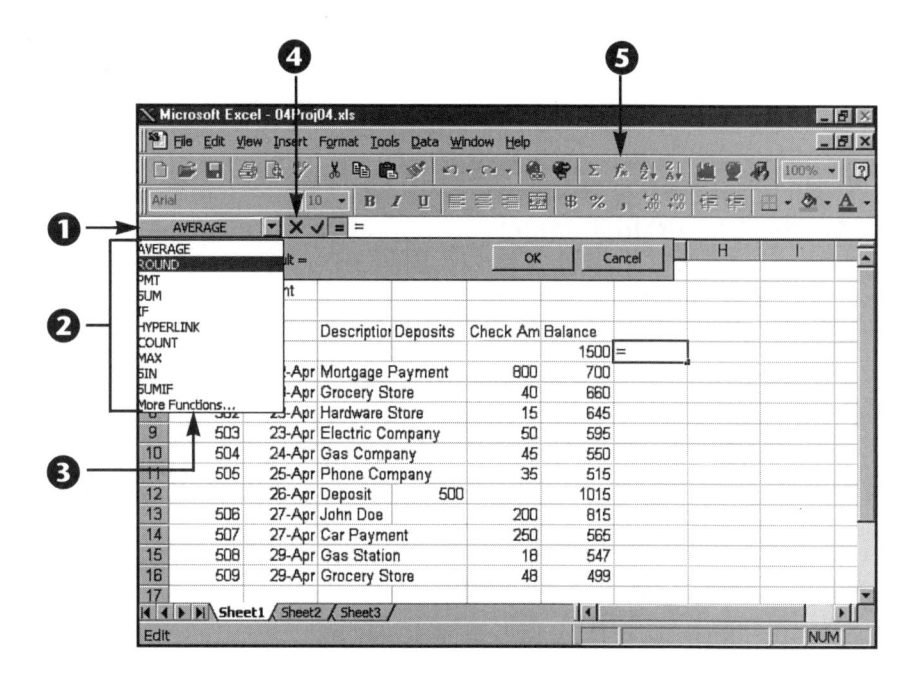

Project 4 Calculating with Functions

Applying Your Skills

Practice

The following exercises enable you to practice the skills you have learned in this project. Take a few minutes to work through these exercises now.

1. Checking Sales Figures

As the owner and business manager of a small coffee shop, you need to evaluate the performance of the merchandise you stock in your store. You want to know if you are buying the right mix of coffees to satisfy your customers.

To find out if you are buying the right coffee, use the sample sales figures provided in Proj0402 to calculate total sales for the first quarter for each type of coffee. Devise a formula using conditional statements that will alert you if sales of any type fall below a certain level. If necessary, use the Excel Help feature to find out more about the function you use.

NOTE: You can force Excel to round a number by reducing the number of decimal places. In fact, you can cause some calculations to look incorrect when you decrease decimal places. For example, 33.3 + 33.3 = 66.6. Remove decimal places, and your worksheet reads 33 + 33 = 67.

To Check Sales Figures

1. Open the file Proj0402 and save it as **Sales Figures**.

2. In the Total column, create a formula to calculate the total sales for January, February, and March for each type of coffee. Have the formula round the totals to whole numbers (no decimal places). (*Hint:* Use more than one function.)

3. In the Check column, use functions to return a message that either warns of sales below a minimum level of $500 or reports that sales are OK. Include this check for each type of coffee you sell.

4. Save your work. If requested by your instructor, print two copies of the completed worksheet, then close it.

> In this exercise, students create a formula to calculate the total sales for January, February, and March. In addition, the formula must round the totals to whole numbers. The formula to use is =ROUND(SUM(B4:D4),0). The conditional statement used in the Check column to return messages is =IF(E4<500, "Sales are below minimum", "Sales are OK"). A solution file is saved as **Sales Figures** on the Instructor's Resource disk.

2. Calculating Future Salary Requirements

You can use functions and formulas to determine whether your business can support increasing salaries. Use the data provided to calculate the amount of money spent on current salaries and to forecast projected salaries.

To Calculate Future Salary Requirements

1. Open the file Proj0403 and save it as **Salary Forecast**.

2. Calculate the projected salaries for each employee.

Applying Your Skills

3. Calculate the average current salary in cell C8 and the average projected salary in cell E8.

4. Calculate the total amount of all current salaries in cell C10 and of all projected salaries in cell E10.

5. In cell B12, use a conditional statement to determine whether you will be able to increase salaries as proposed. To make the decision, assume that if the average projected salary is less that $21,500, you can afford increases.

6. Change all of the increase percentages to five percent to see how the conditional statement is affected.

7. Save your work. If requested by your instructor, print two copies before closing the document.

> In this activity, students use formulas to calculate sums. The sum formula in cell E3 is =C3*D3+C3. This formula is then copied to cell addresses E4:E7. The average formula used in cell C8 is =AVERAGE(C3:C7). The average formula used in cell E8 is =AVERAGE(E3:E7). The sum function used in cell B10 is =SUM(C3:C7). The sum function used in cell E10 is =SUM(E3:E7). A conditional statement is used to return messages. The conditional statement used in B12 is =IF(E8<21500, "Yes", "No"). A solution file is saved as **Salary Forecast** on the Instructor's Resource disk.

3. Creating a Worksheet to Calculate the Benefits of Advertising

Create a worksheet that calculates the average amount you spend on each type of advertising each month and how much revenue the advertising generates. Use a conditional statement that will tell you which ad campaigns are worth continuing and which you should cancel.

To Create the Advertising Worksheet

1. Open the file Proj0404 and save it as Ad Revenues.

2. In column F, calculate the revenues derived from each type of advertising.

3. In cell B8, calculate the average cost of advertising, rounded to two decimal places. (*Hint:* Nest the AVERAGE function within the ROUND function.)

4. In cell B9, calculate the average ad revenue, rounded to two decimal places.

5. In cell G4, create a conditional statement that tells you whether you should continue to use print advertising. For this study, assume that if you generate more revenue than the ad costs, you should continue.

6. Copy the formula to cells G5 and G6.

7. Save the worksheet. If requested by your instructor, print two copies, then close it.

> In this exercise, students create a formula to calculate the average cost of advertising. In addition, the formula must round the totals to two decimal places. The formula to use in cell B8 is =ROUND(AVERAGE(D4:D6),2). Students create a formula to calculate the average revenues for each type of advertising. Also, the formula must round the totals to two decimal places. The formula to use in cell B9 is =ROUND(AVERAGE(F4:F6),2). A conditional statement used in G4 to return messages is =IF(F4>D4, "Yes", "No"). The formula is copied to cells G5 and G6. A solution file is saved as **Ad Revenues** on the Instructor's Resource disk.

Project 4 Calculating with Functions

4. Calculating Utility Expenses

Create a worksheet to calculate the utility expenses for the coffee shop and to see if you can afford air conditioning for the shop.

To Calculate Utility Expenses

1. Open the file Proj0405 and save it as Utility Expenses.

2. In column I, calculate the average cost per month of each of the three utilities.

3. In row 7, calculate the average total cost of all utilities for each month.

4. In cell B9, use a conditional statement to determine whether or not you can afford air conditioning. For this example, the average monthly cost of electricity must be less than $40, or the average monthly phone bill must be less than $30 for you to be able to afford air conditioning. (*Hint:* Nest an OR function within an IF function.)

5. Save the worksheet. If requested by your instructor, print two copies before closing it.

> In this exercise, students create a formula to calculate the average cost per month of each of the three utilities. The formula to use in I3 is =AVERAGE(B3:G3). The formula is copied to cells I4:I5. In row 7, students calculate the average total cost of all utilities for each month. The formula to use is B7 is =AVERAGE(B3:B5). The formula is then copied to cells C7:G7. In cell B9, the conditional formula used to return messages is =IF(OR(I3<40,I4<30), "Yes", "No"). A solution file is saved as **Utility Expenses** on the Instructor's Resource disk.

5. Naming Ranges in a Worksheet

In this project, you learned to use named ranges to make it easier to use ranges in formulas and to quickly access certain areas of the worksheet. In this exercise, you name ranges in the Profit Loss worksheet.

To Name Ranges in a Worksheet

1. Open Proj0406 file and save it as Profit Loss 2.

2. Select the range of cells B5:B13.

3. Choose **I**nsert, **N**ame, **D**efine to display the Define Name dialog box.

4. Make sure April displays in the Names in **w**orkbook text box, then click OK. The range B5:B13 is now named April.

5. Now name the columns for May and June.

6. Save the workbook again and leave it open for the following exercise.

> Students create named ranges in this activity by selecting a data range, then choosing the **I**nsert, **N**ame, **D**efine command. The solution file is saved as **Profit Loss 2** on the Instructor's Resource disk.

Challenge

The following challenges enable you to use your problem-solving skills. Take time to work through these exercises now.

1. Selecting a Named Range

Now that you have named ranges, you can use them in formulas or to quickly select a named range. Select the April range that you named in the Profit Loss 2 worksheet and then copy the range to the Sheet2 worksheet. Select the May range and copy it to Sheet3. Save the workbook and leave it open for the next exercise.

> Students continue working with the range names they created in Exercise 5. Students select the April range (using the Name Box). Once the range is selected, students use copy and paste procedures to copy the range to the Sheet2 worksheet. Students select the May range (using the Name Box). Once the range is selected, students use copy and paste procedures to copy the range to the Sheet3 worksheet. The solution file is saved as **Profit Loss 2** on the Instructor's Resource disk.

2. Using Functions to Calculate Quarterly Profits

Your boss has asked that you calculate quarterly profits in the Profit Loss 2 workbook. Because functions make it much easier to perform various calculations in Excel, you decide to use them.

In cell F4, type Quarterly Profit. Move to cell F5 and click the AutoSum button on the Standard toolbar. When the range for the argument displays, drag across cells B13:D13. Click the Enter button on the formula bar. The net profit for April, May, and June is calculated and entered into this cell.

Move to cell G4 and type Quarterly Average. Activate cell G5 and click the Edit Formula button on the formula bar. Use the AVERAGE function to average the net profit for this quarter.

If requested by your instructor, print one copy of all the worksheets in the workbook. Save and close the workbook when you have finished.

> Students continue to use the Profit Loss 2 workbook as they use functions to calculate quarterly profits. In cell F5, students use the AutoSum button as they change the argument range to B13:D13. The formula in cell F5 is =SUM(B13:D13). In cell G5, students use the average function to average the profit for the quarter. The formula in cell G5 is =AVERAGE(B13:D13). The solution file is saved as Profit Loss 2 on the Instructor's Resource disk.

3. Using Conditional Statements

As manager of a hardware store, you need to use conditional statements to determine if a customer has earned a discount by paying a bill promptly. If a customer pays their bill within 10 days of the billing date, they receive a 2% discount. To calculate whether the customer receives a discount, you must determine if the payment was received in 10 days or less. If it was, the customer receives a 2% discount. If not, the customer does not receive a discount.

Project 4   Calculating with Functions

Open `Proj0407` and save it as `Billing`. Activate cell E4 and enter the following function:

    =IF(D4-A4<=10,-C4*.02,0)

Copy this function down the column. Next, you need to calculate the amount due. Activate cell F4 and enter the formula `=C4+E4`. Copy this formula down the column. Save the workbook and leave it open for the following exercise.

> Students create a conditional statement in cell E4 to determine if customers are entitled to a discount. The conditional statement used in E4 is =IF(D4–A4<=10,-C4*0.02,0). The formula is then copied to cells E5:E9. A solution file is saved as **Billing** on the Instructor's Resource disk.

4. Editing the Function

You now want to determine if customers are entitled to a discount or if they owe a penalty for paying a bill past 30 days.

Select cell E4 in the `Billings` worksheet and double-click the cell to edit the function so that it reads as follows:

    =IF(D4-A4<=10,-C4*.02,IF(D4-A4>30,C4*.015,0))

This complex formula now determines if the bill was paid within 10 days, the company gets a 2% discount, if the bill was paid in more than 30 days, the company is charged 1.5%, if the payment does not meet either condition, a 0 is entered into the cell.

Copy the formula down the column.

Next, you need to determine the balance owed for each company. In cell H4, enter the formula `=F4-G4`. Copy this formula down the column. Save the file again and, if requested by your instructor, print a copy. Close the workbook when you have finished.

> Students continue to edit the Billing workbook they created in the previous challenge as they edit the formula in cell E4. The revised conditional statement used in E4 is =IF(D4–A4<=10, –C4*0.02,IF(D4–A4>30,C4*0.015,0)). The formula is then copied to cells E5:E9. In cell H4, students enter the formula =F4–G4, then copy the formula to cells H5:H9. A solution file is saved as **Billing** on the Instructor's Resource disk.

5. Copying the Function

You have decided that you no longer want to pay your bank service fees. You use an Excel function to identify when your checking account goes below the minimum balance.

Open `Proj0408` and save it as `Checking Account 4`. In cell G4, type **Below Min?** Add a function to cell G5 to determine if the balance is below the minimum of $500. If the balance is below $500, you want to enter **Yes** into the cell. If it is not below $500, **No** should be entered into the cell. Copy the function down the column. If requested by your instructor, print two copies. Save and close the file when you have finished.

> In this activity, students create a function in cell G5 to determine if the checking account balance is below the minimum of $500. The conditional statement to use in G5 is =IF(F5<500, "Yes", "No"). The formula is then copied to cells G6:G16. A solution file is saved as **Checking Account 4** on the Instructor's Resource disk.

Project 5

Improving the Appearance of a Worksheet

Formatting a Budget

In this project, you learn how to:
- Use Fonts and Their Attributes
- Change Column Width
- Align Text and Numbers
- Format Numbers
- Add Borders and Patterns
- Use Conditional Formatting
- Use the AutoFormat Feature
- Check the Spelling in a Worksheet

Project 5 Improving the Appearance of a Worksheet

Why Would I Do This?

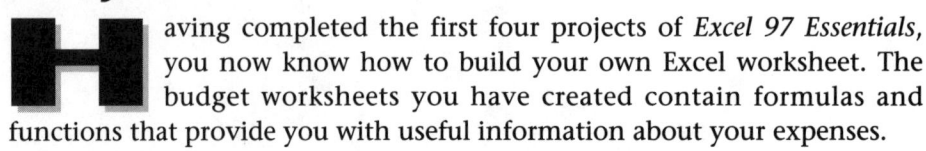

Having completed the first four projects of *Excel 97 Essentials*, you now know how to build your own Excel worksheet. The budget worksheets you have created contain formulas and functions that provide you with useful information about your expenses.

Formatting
Applying attributes to text and data to change the appearance of a worksheet or to call attention to certain information.

After you create a basic worksheet, however, you may want to improve its appearance by *formatting* it so that it is more readable and attractive. In this project, you learn how to improve the appearance of worksheets by using many of Excel's formatting features. You also learn how to check for spelling errors in a worksheet.

Lesson 1: Using Fonts and Their Attributes

Font
The typeface, type size, and type attributes of text or numbers.

You can dramatically improve the appearance of your worksheet by using different fonts. A *font* is the typeface, type size, and type attributes that you apply to text and numbers. Excel 97 and Windows 95 supply a variety of typefaces and sizes that you can use.

> **On Your Mark**
> What can you do to change and enhance the appearance of your worksheet?

In this lesson, you use toolbar buttons and the Font dialog box to format with fonts and font attributes. Toolbar buttons let you quickly apply a single formatting characteristic, such as a different font, while the dialog box enables you to preview and apply many formatting characteristics at one time. Try using some different fonts and type attributes in a worksheet now.

To Use Fonts and Font Attributes

Tip for Students
You can click the Select All button (the gray button just above the row numbers) to make a global change to your worksheet.

❶ Open the Proj0501 worksheet and save it as Expenses.

❷ Select cells B3 through H3 in the Expenses worksheet.

This selects the column headings in the Expenses worksheet—the first text you want to change. In Excel, you can change the formatting of a single selected cell or a range of selected cells.

Tip for Students
You can also right-click the selected area and choose **F**ormat Cells from the shortcut menu.

❸ Choose Format, Cells.

Excel displays the Format Cells dialog box, in which you can change a number of formatting settings for the selected cells.

❹ Click the Font tab.

The Font options appear, as shown in Figure 5.1.

**Project Time
60 minutes**

Lesson 1: Using Fonts and Their Attributes

Figure 5.1
The Font tab of the Format Cells dialog box enables you to choose font attributes.

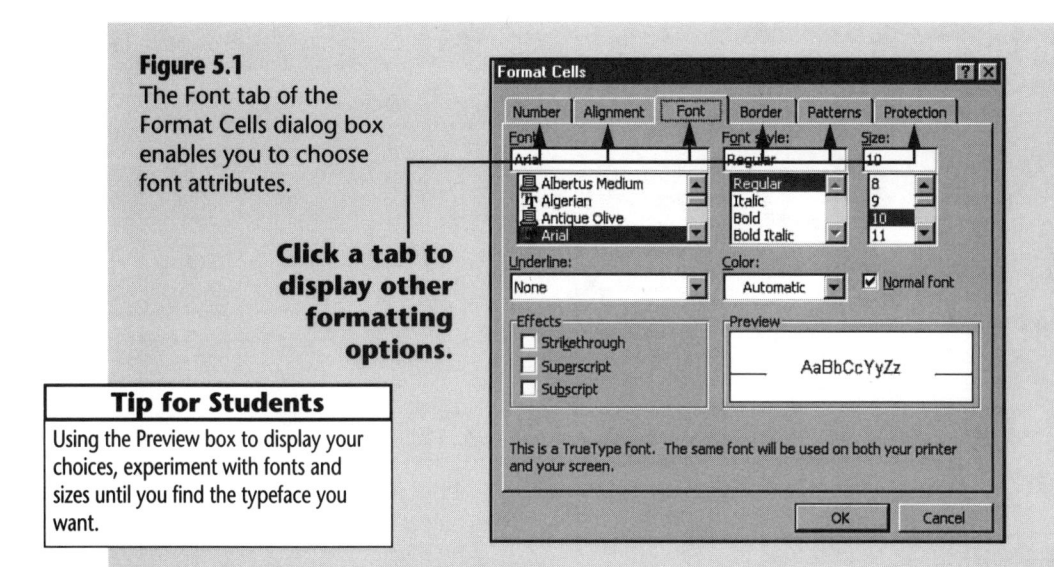

Click a tab to display other formatting options.

Tip for Students
Using the Preview box to display your choices, experiment with fonts and sizes until you find the typeface you want.

Tip for Students
Your computer may display a different selection of fonts, depending on your printer and software.

Point
A unit of measurement used in printing and publishing to designate the height of type. There are roughly 72 points in an inch.

Tip for Students
You can always choose Cancel if you change your mind about making a font selection.

❺ In the Font list box, select Times New Roman.

This selects the typeface you want to apply to the selected cells in this example. You may have to use the scroll arrows to scroll down through the list of fonts to get to Times New Roman. Excel displays a sample of the typeface in the Preview box.

❻ In the Size list box, select 12.

Again, you may need to scroll down the list to find 12. The numbers in the Size list refer to *point* size, which is the unit of measurement of font characters. The default type size is 10 points, so changing the size to 12 increases the size of the type. Excel shows how the new type will look in the Preview box.

❼ In the Font style box, select Bold.

The text in the Preview box now appears bold.

❽ Choose OK.

The dialog box closes, and all the formatting changes are applied to the selected cells. All the month headings now appear in the new font and font attributes. Deselect the cells to get a better look at the formatting, as shown in Figure 5.2. Notice that the row height automatically adjusts to accommodate the new type size, although the column widths do not.

Next, format the worksheet's title—Expenses—so that it is obviously the main title. In the following steps, you use the Formatting toolbar's buttons to apply fonts and their attributes.

continues

Project 5 Improving the Appearance of a Worksheet

To Use Fonts and Font Attributes (continued)

Figure 5.2
The month headings appear in a new typeface and type size.

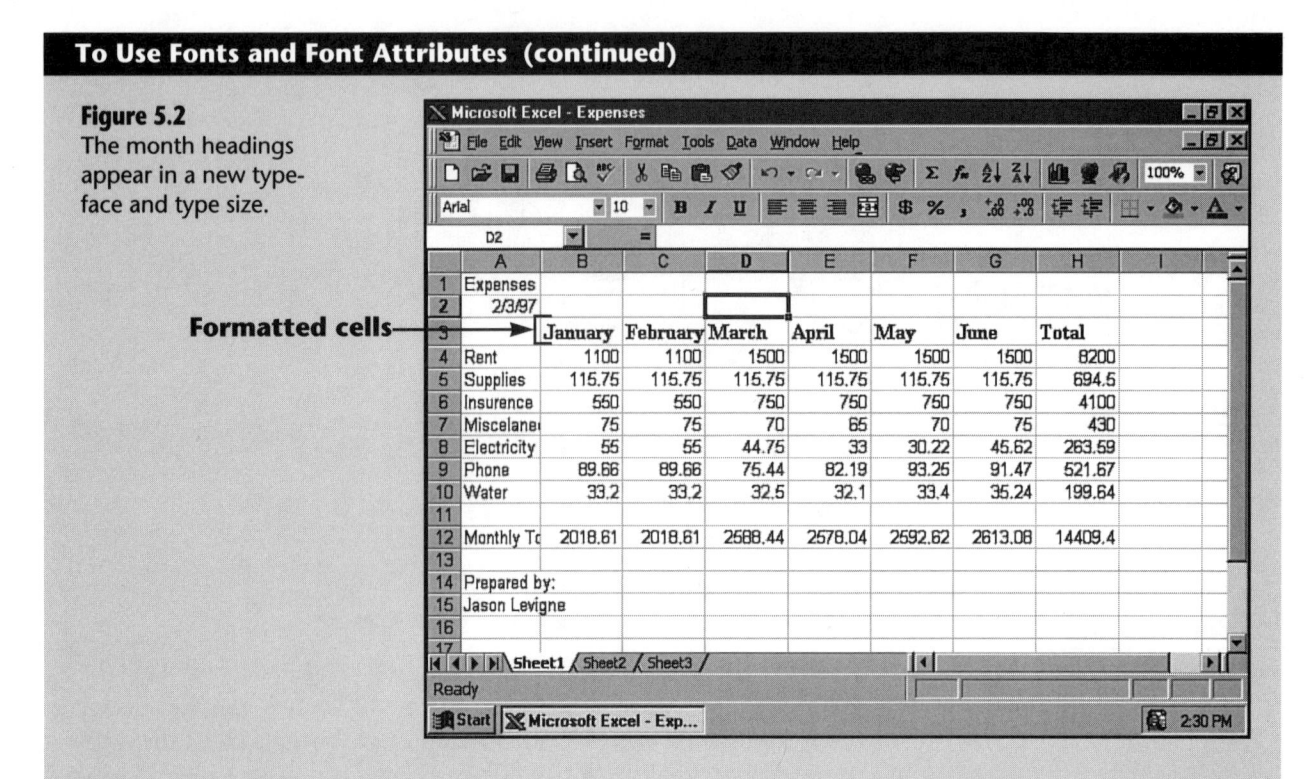

Formatted cells

⑨ **Select cell A1, then click the Font drop-down arrow on the Formatting toolbar.**

A list of fonts appears, as shown in Figure 5.3.

Figure 5.3
You can easily apply fonts and font attributes using the Formatting toolbar.

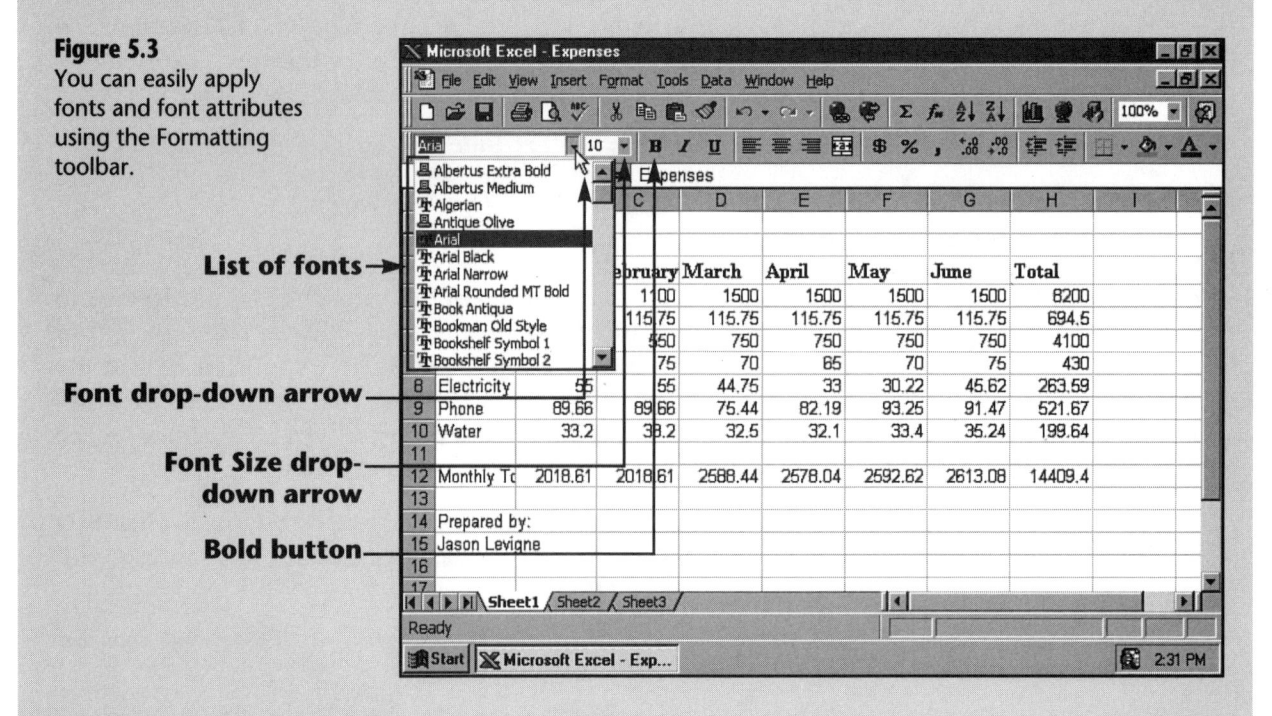

List of fonts

Font drop-down arrow

Font Size drop-down arrow

Bold button

⑩ **Select Times New Roman from the list.**

Excel changes the font in the selected cell.

Lesson 1: Using Fonts and Their Attributes

Tip for Instructors
Point out to students that Excel automatically adjusts the height of the row to accommodate the larger font size.

⑪ **Click the Font size drop-down arrow on the Formatting toolbar and select 18.**

Excel increases the font size in the selected cell.

⑫ **Click the Bold button on the Formatting toolbar.**

Excel applies the bold attribute to the selected cell.

When you have formatted a cell the way you like, you can use the Format Painter button to copy that formatting to one or more other cells. This tool is extremely handy because it enables you to format cells quickly without opening dialog boxes or making multiple selections from toolbars. Next, use the Format Painter button to copy the type style used for the column headings to the expense labels in column A.

⑬ **Select cell B3, then click the Format Painter button on the Standard toolbar.**

A flashing dotted line appears around cell B3, and the Format Painter button appears pressed in. Note that you only need to select one cell to copy formatting. Just choose one of the cells that already contains the desired formatting, then click the Format Painter.

Tip for Instructors
Remind students that the Format Painter button works across worksheets in a workbook, but it doesn't work across workbooks.

⑭ **Select cells A4 to A12, then release the mouse button.**

When you release the mouse button, the formatting from cell B3 is applied to the range you selected. When you deselect the range, your worksheet should look similar to the one shown in Figure 5.4.

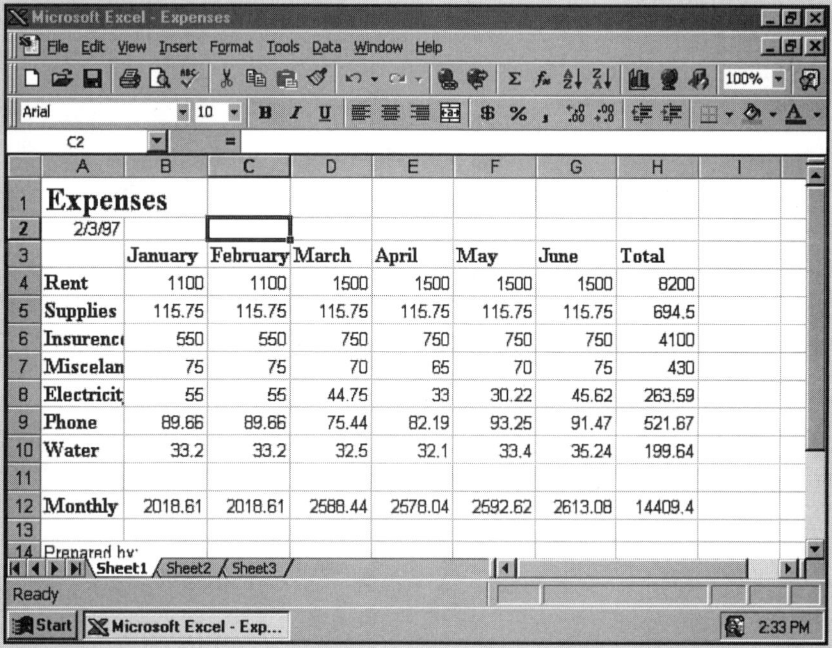

Figure 5.4
Fonts and their attributes can be applied to a range of cells, using the Format Painter button.

Tip for Students
Clicking the Format Painter button enables you to copy the format once. To copy the formatting to multiple ranges, double-click the Format Painter button, then select as many ranges as you like. Press Esc when you are finished.

Save your work and leave the Expenses workbook open for the next lesson, where you learn how to change the widths of columns in your worksheet.

Project 5   Improving the Appearance of a Worksheet

In Excel, you can use the buttons on the Formatting toolbar to italicize and underline characters as well as apply boldface. To change attributes, simply select the cells that you want to format, then click the relevant button on the formatting toolbar, or use the following keyboard shortcuts: Bold is Ctrl+B, italic is Ctrl+I, and underline is Ctrl+U. To remove an attribute, click its button again.

To quickly open the Format Cells dialog box, press Ctrl+1, or right-click the active cell and choose Format Cells from the shortcut menu.

To quickly scroll through the Font drop-down list, start typing the name of the font you want to apply. Excel locates the fonts alphabetically.

Tip for Students
The downside of using the Font button on the toolbar is that you can't preview the fonts before you make a selection. You have to know the typeface you are choosing.

Quicksand
When choosing attributes, such as bold, italic, or underline, be sure to first select the cells to which these attributes will apply, then click the attribute.

On Your Mark
How can you tell when column widths need to be changed?

Lesson 2: Changing Column Width

As you may have noticed, several of the column and row labels of the Expenses worksheet don't fit in the default column width. Although row heights adjust automatically when you change fonts, column widths do not. As a result, data entered in one column may be hidden by the data in the column to its right. To make your information fit, you can increase or decrease column widths; you can also change row height, if necessary.

To Change Column Width

Tip for Instructors
Explain that you can change column widths from the Format menu, but it's much quicker to change widths on-screen with the mouse.

❶ In the Expenses worksheet frame, move the mouse pointer to the line to the right of column letter A.

The mouse pointer changes to a double-headed black arrow, as shown in Figure 5.5. Column A is the first column you want to change. Notice that several of the expense labels in column A are covered by information in column B. Notice also that when there is no data in column B, Excel simply extends the data in column A across the cell border.

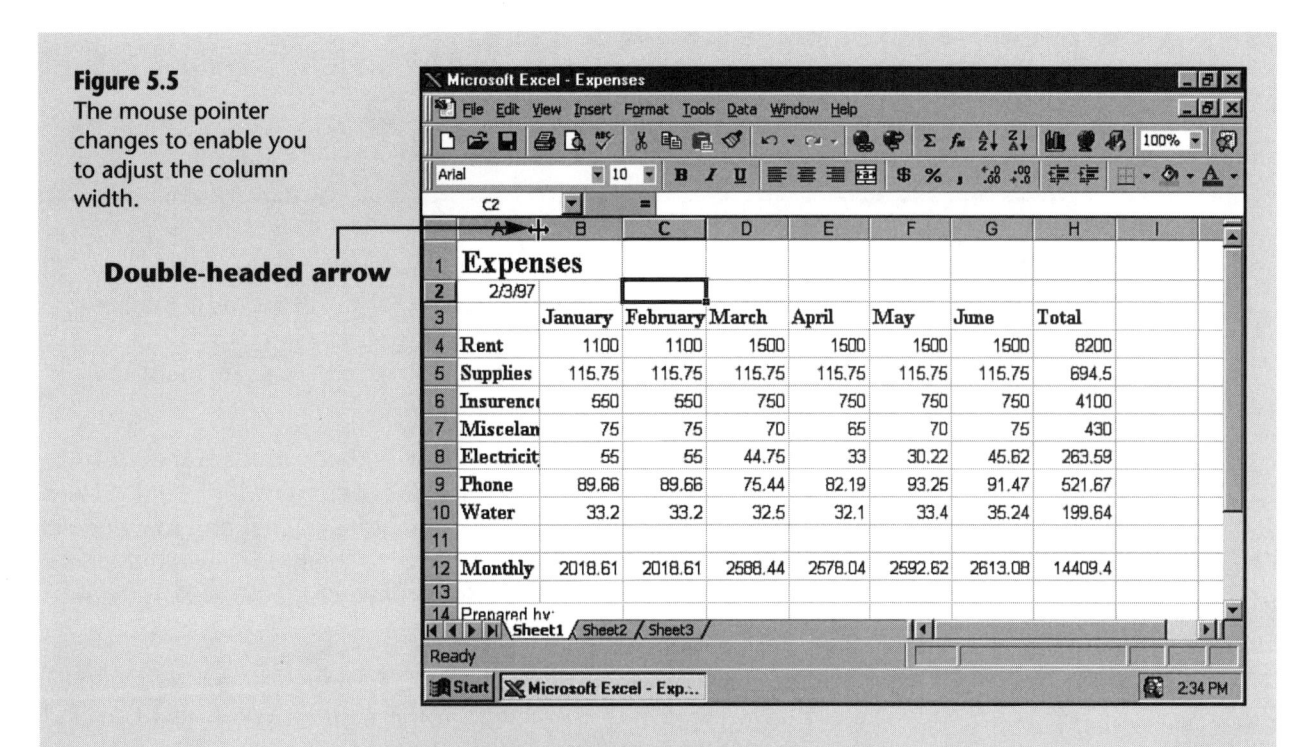

Lesson 2: Changing Column Width   125

Figure 5.5
The mouse pointer changes to enable you to adjust the column width.

Double-headed arrow

Tip for Students
Instead of double-clicking, you can drag the line between the column letters to expand or contract the column width. Notice the measurement of the column in the Name box as you drag.

❷ **Double-click the left mouse button.**

When you double-click the column border between column letters A and B, the width of column A automatically adjusts to fit the longest entry. Now adjust the widths of columns B and C.

❸ **Double-click the column border to the right of column B, then double-click the column border to the right of column C.**

These actions adjust the widths of columns B and C to fit the longest entry. Your worksheet should now look like Figure 5.6.

Figure 5.6
The adjusted column width fits the longest entry in the column.

Tip for Students
The Best Fit option (double-clicking, as opposed to dragging on the line between the column letters) is especially useful if the longest entry in that column is not displayed on screen.

continues

To Change Column Width (continued)

Save your work and keep the Expenses worksheet open. In the next lesson, you learn how to change the alignment of data in a cell.

When text doesn't fit in the width of a column, the label appears to be cut off or hidden by the next cell. If a number doesn't fit in the width of a column, a series of pound signs (######) appears in the cell. In either case, the data is stored in the worksheet; it just might not be displayed. You can adjust the column width to display the entire cell contents.

Rather than double-clicking the column or row border to force Excel to automatically reset the width or height, you can experiment with widths and heights by using the double-arrow pointer to drag the column and row borders in the worksheet frame. Move the mouse pointer to the border; when the double arrow appears, click and drag the border until you're satisfied with the new width or height.

To enter a precise column width, choose F**o**rmat, **C**olumn, Column **W**idth, then enter the width (in number of characters) in the Column Width text box and choose OK. To enter a precise row height, choose F**o**rmat, **R**ow, Row H**e**ight, then enter the height (in points) in the Row Height text box and choose OK. The default row height is 12.75 points.

If you want to reset the column width to the original setting, choose F**o**rmat, **C**olumn, **S**tandard Width; make sure that 8.43 is entered in the Standard Column Width box, and then choose OK.

To undo the most recent formatting changes, click the Undo button, or choose **E**dit, **U**ndo.

You can select several cells, columns, or rows simultaneously to apply any formatting changes to all the selected parts of the worksheet.

Tip for Students
When entering a precise column width, click any cell in the column that you want to adjust. You don't need to select the entire column.

Q&A
What happens if you decrease the column width to zero? *Answer:* The column becomes hidden.

How do you display the contents of a column again after you've changed the width to zero? *Answer:* Choose **E**dit, **U**ndo if it was the last operation you performed. Otherwise, select the columns on either side of the hidden column, right-click inside the selected columns, and choose **U**nhide from the shortcut menu.

Tip for Students
You can resize multiple columns (or rows) simultaneously by using the Best Fit option, or by setting all selected columns or rows to a fixed width.

On Your Mark
How are text and numbers typically aligned when you use Excel? (*Answer:* Text is left-justified; numbers are right-justified.)

Lesson 3: Aligning Text and Numbers

When you enter information into a cell, text aligns with the left side of the cell, and numbers, dates, and times automatically align with the right side of the cell. You can change the alignment of information at any time. For instance, you may want to fine-tune the appearance of column headings by centering all the information in the column. You can also align data across several columns in one step, wrap data onto multiple lines, and rotate text within the cell.

To Align Text and Numbers

Tip for Instructors
Remind the students how to select cells from the keyboard using ⇧Shift with the arrow keys.

❶ Select cells A1 through H1 in the Expenses worksheet.

You want this title centered over the width of the worksheet.

Lesson 3: Aligning Text and Numbers

Tip for Students
Experiment also with the Center and Align Left buttons on the toolbar.

Quicksand
The title to be centered must always reside in the left-most column of the area where the text is to be centered.

Quicksand
Be sure that the students click the Merge and Center button—not just the Center button.

Figure 5.7
The contents of the selected cells are now centered.

❷ **Click the Merge and Center button on the Formatting toolbar.**

Excel merges the selected cells into one cell, and centers the text across the width of the worksheet. Even though the worksheet title is centered across the worksheet, it is still located in cell A1. If you want to select the text for further formatting or editing, you must select cell A1. Now, try aligning the column labels.

❸ **Select cells B3 through H3.**

This selects all the cells you want to align. Notice that the column labels are left-aligned. You can improve the appearance of the worksheet by centering the data in the selected cells.

❹ **Click the Center button on the Formatting toolbar.**

Excel centers the data in each cell, as shown in Figure 5.7. However, the column labels might look even better if the text appeared vertical or at an angle in the cells. Try rotating the text now.

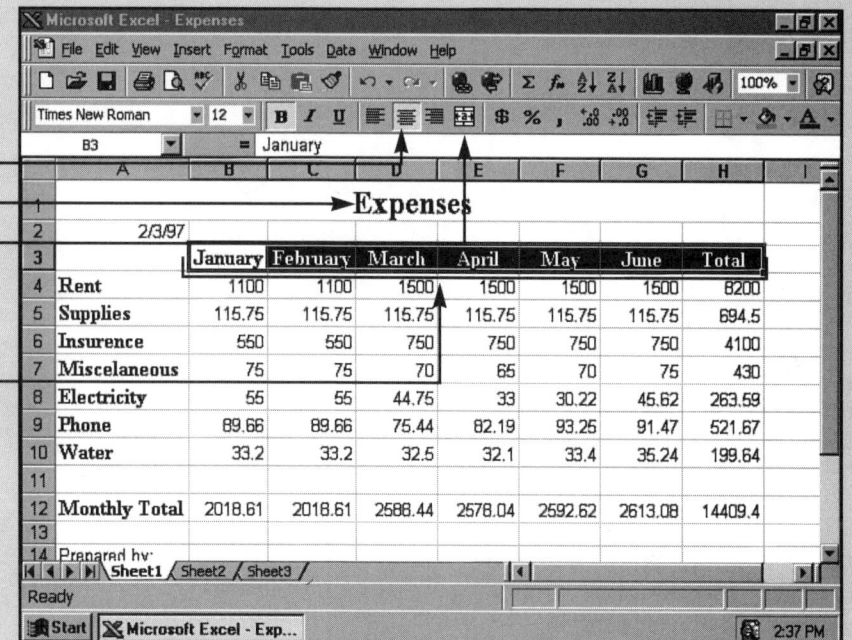

Center button
Centered title
Center Across Columns button
Centered labels

❺ **Right-click anywhere along the selected range of cells, and choose Format Cells from the shortcut menu.**

The Format Cells dialog box is displayed.

❻ **Click the Alignment tab.**

The Alignment options are displayed, as shown in Figure 5.8.

continues

128 Project 5 Improving the Appearance of a Worksheet

To Align Text and Numbers (continued)

Figure 5.8
The Alignment tab of the Format Cells dialog box enables you to choose from a variety of text-alignment options.

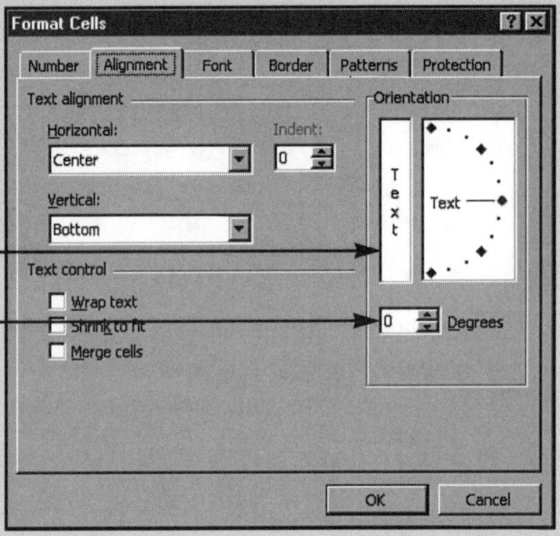

Click here to rotate the text vertically

Enter the degrees of rotation here

❼ In the Orientation area, type 45 in the Degrees text box.

This tells Excel to rotate the text in the selected cells 45 degrees up. To rotate the text down, enter a negative number.

❽ Choose OK.

Excel rotates the text. Deselect the cells so you can see the formatting clearly. Your worksheet should look similar to the one in Figure 5.9.

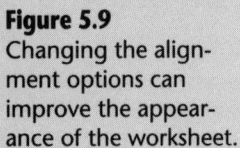

Figure 5.9
Changing the alignment options can improve the appearance of the worksheet.

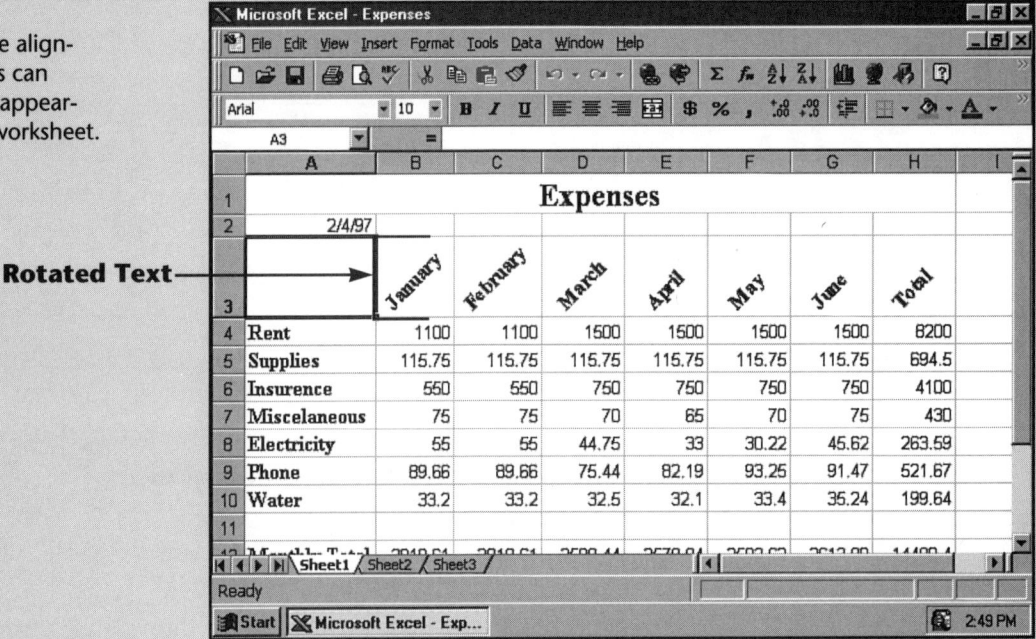

Rotated Text

Save your work and keep Expenses open for the next lesson, where you learn how to apply different number formats to cells.

Lesson 4: Formatting Numbers 129

If you want text to appear vertically—one character above the next—click the Vertical orientation box on the Alignment page of the Format Cells dialog box.

On the Alignment page of the Format Cells dialog box, you can also select a **W**rap Text option, a Shrin**k** to Fit option, and a Merge cells options. Choose **W**rap Text when you want to enter more than one line of text within a cell. As you type, the text automatically wraps to the next line in the cell. Choose Shrin**k** to Fit when you want to reduce the appearance of the data so it fits within the displayed column width. Choose **M**erge Cells when you want to combine two or more selected adjacent cells into one larger cell.

If you want to indent characters from the left edge of the cell, select Left alignment, then enter an increment in the **I**ndent text box on the Alignment page of the Format Cells dialog box. Each increment you enter in the text box is equal to the width of one character.

Lesson 4: Formatting Numbers

On Your Mark
What number formats do you use in worksheets and reports that you create?

When you enter a number or a formula into a cell, the entry may not appear as you hoped it would. You might type 5, for example, but want it to look like $5.00. You could type the dollar sign, decimal point, and zeros, or you can have Excel automatically format the number for you. When you want to apply a standard format to a number, you format the cell in which the number is displayed.

In Excel, you can format numbers in many ways. You will usually format numbers as currency, percentages, dates, or times of day. Remember that when you apply any kind of formatting, you apply it to the worksheet cell, not to the information itself. This means that if you change the information, the formatting still applies. You can even format empty cells so that when data is entered, it automatically appears with the correct format.

To Format Numbers

1 Select cells B4 through H12 in the Expenses worksheet.

You want to format these cells as currency.

2 Click the Currency Style button on the Formatting toolbar.

This changes the selected cells to display the default currency format, as shown in Figure 5.10. Note that the blank cells within the selection are formatted as well, even though the formatting doesn't show; if you enter data in those cells, it will appear in the currency style.

continues

Project 5 Improving the Appearance of a Worksheet

To Format Numbers (continued)

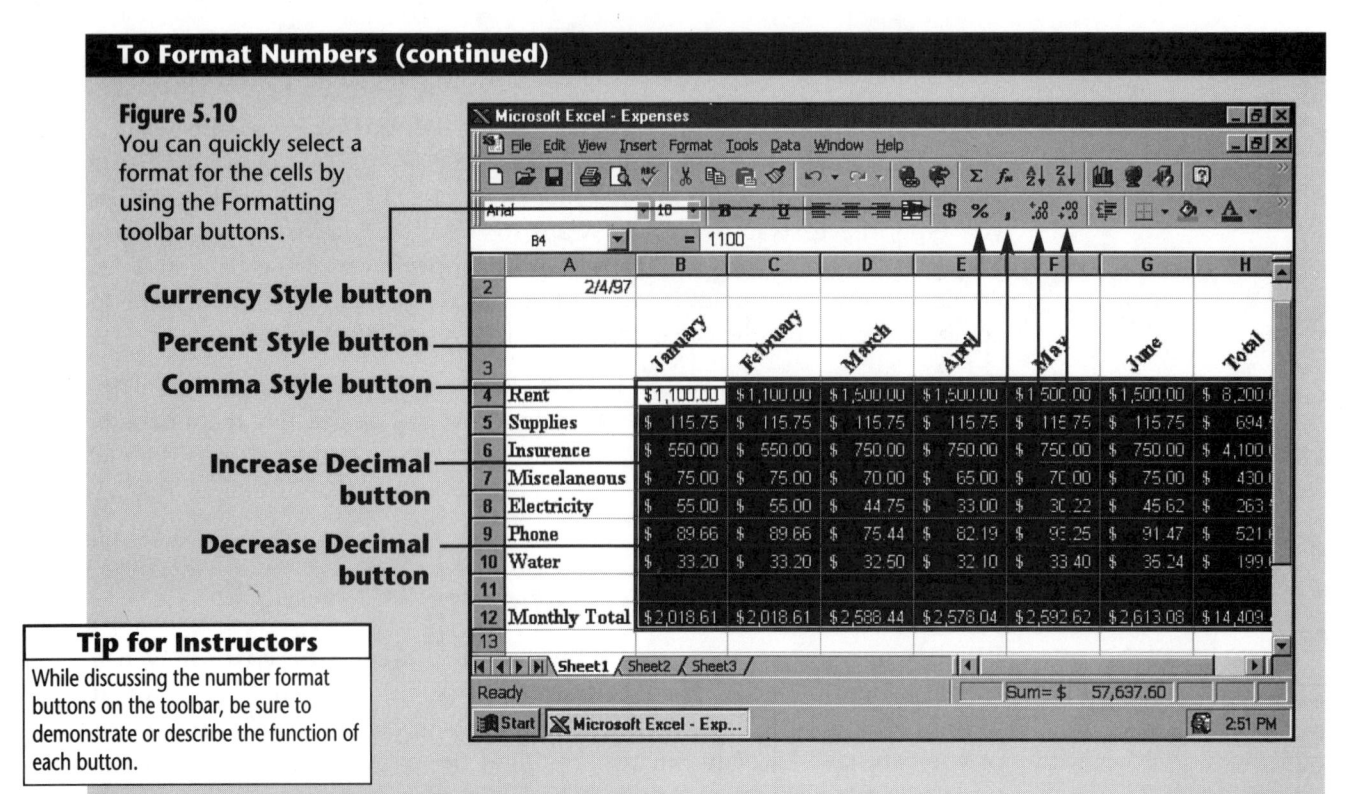

Figure 5.10
You can quickly select a format for the cells by using the Formatting toolbar buttons.

- Currency Style button
- Percent Style button
- Comma Style button
- Increase Decimal button
- Decrease Decimal button

Tip for Instructors
While discussing the number format buttons on the toolbar, be sure to demonstrate or describe the function of each button.

Quicksand
Note the potential problem in choosing zero decimal places; sometimes the results appear incorrect. For example, 44.3+42.3 is rounded down to 44+42. The sum is also rounded—but to 87, not 86! (Excel calculates the decimal places, even though they aren't displayed.)

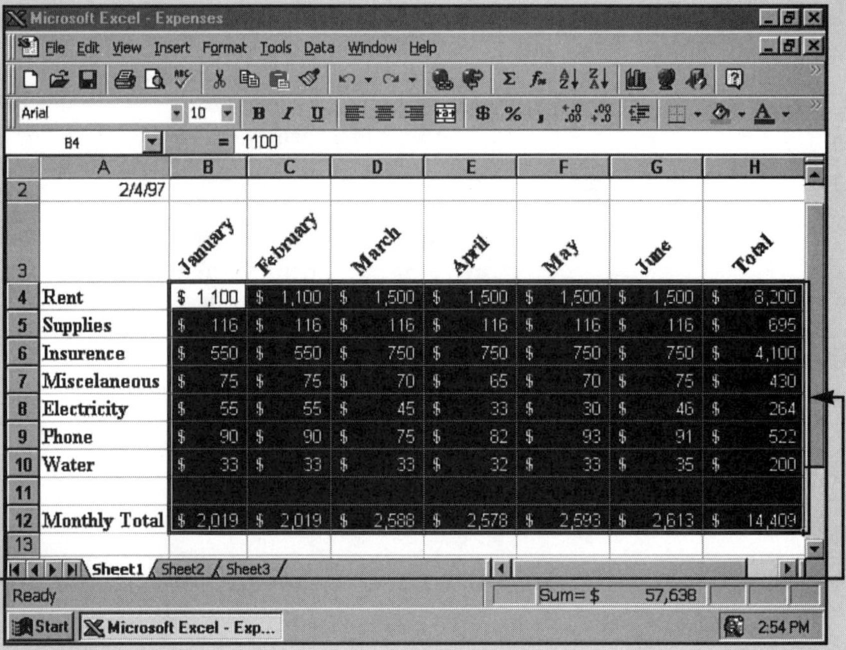

Figure 5.11
Use the Decrease Decimal button to decrease the number of decimal places displayed.

Speedy Class
After you've formatted numbers from the toolbar as currency or with commas, you may want to return to a general, plain style. There isn't a button with which to accomplish this. If you change your mind right after you make the change, you can choose Edit, Undo. Otherwise, you have to select the cells, choose Format, Cells, and select a number format that fits your needs.

Rounded numbers with zero decimal places

3 With cells B4:H12 still selected, click the Decrease Decimal button twice.

Each time you click the button, Excel removes one decimal place. Because no decimal places are displayed, Excel rounds the values that are displayed to fit this format (see Figure 5.11). However, the actual values will be used in any calculations. You can adjust column widths again to fit the worksheet within the document window.

Now, change the way the date is displayed in the worksheet.

Lesson 5: Adding Borders and Patterns

❹ Move the mouse pointer to cell A2, click the right mouse button, and choose Format Cells from the shortcut menu.

Excel opens the Format Cells dialog box.

❺ Click the Number tab in the Format Cells dialog box.

Excel displays the Number options (see Figure 5.12). Since the selected cell contains a date, the Date category is already selected. You can choose the general type of formatting you want from the **C**ategory list, then select the specific format from the **T**ype list.

❻ Select the 4-Mar-97 format from the Type list box.

Notice that the Sample line shows the date in cell A2 in the format you selected.

Tip for Students
Excel recognizes common date formats when you type them, so it doesn't try to use the slashes to divide.

Figure 5.12
You can format numbers in a wide variety of categories and styles.

Select the category of number here →

Preview the formatting here

Select the number format here

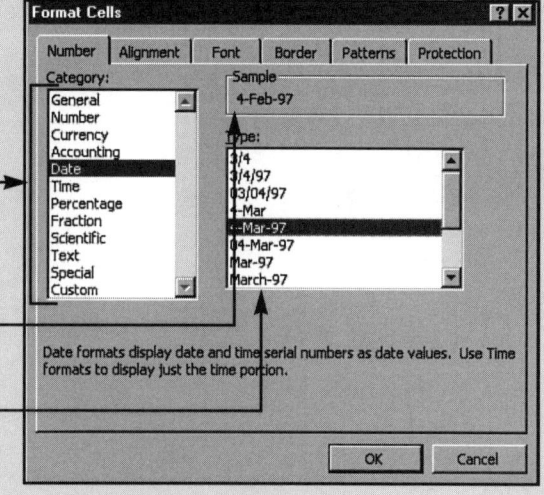

❼ Choose OK.

Excel displays the date in the new format. Save your changes to the Expenses worksheet and leave it open to use in the next lesson.

Lesson 5: Adding Borders and Patterns

✓ On Your Mark
What types of elements in a worksheet might you want to emphasize with borders and shading?

To call attention to specific cells in a worksheet, you can accent them with formatting. You can make them stand out by changing the font or font attributes of the numbers, as you learned in Lesson 1, or you can change the appearance of the cell itself.

You can add patterns to a cell or range of cells to emphasize important information. For example, you may want to call attention to the highest sales for a month and the grand total. In addition, when you print a worksheet, the grid between columns and rows does not appear. If you want to include lines between cells, you must add borders.

Project 5 Improving the Appearance of a Worksheet

To Add Borders and Patterns

1 Select cell G12 in the Expenses worksheet.

The monthly expenses for June are the highest in the worksheet. In this example, you decide to emphasize this cell with a pattern and a border.

Tip for Students
The Borders and Fill Color buttons on the Standard and Formatting toolbars, respectively, are alternatives to the menu items for borders and shading.

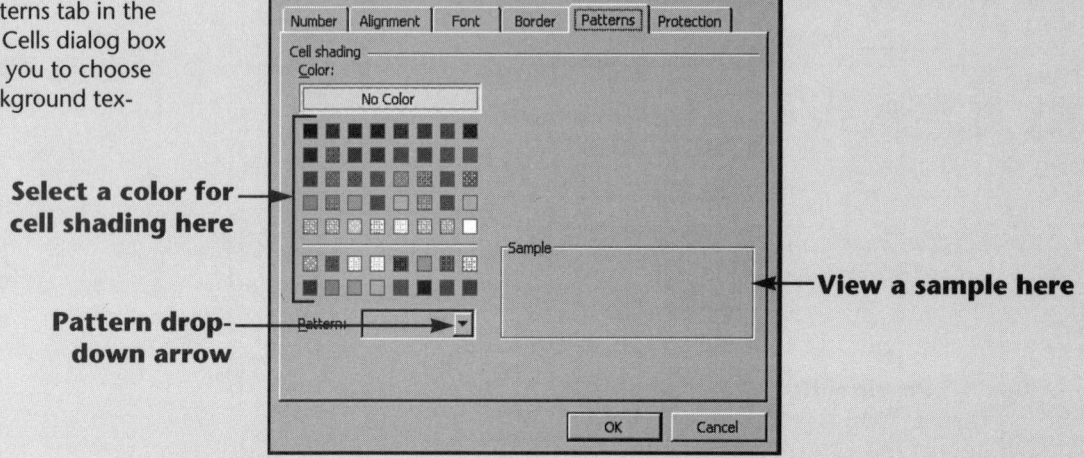

2 Choose Format, Cells, then click the Patterns tab in the Format cells dialog box.

Excel displays the Patterns options in the Format Cells dialog box, as shown in Figure 5.13.

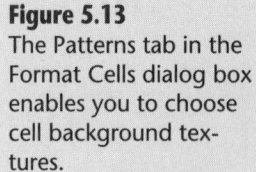

Figure 5.13
The Patterns tab in the Format Cells dialog box enables you to choose cell background textures.

Select a color for cell shading here

Pattern drop-down arrow

View a sample here

3 Click the Pattern drop-down arrow.

A palette of shading patterns appears, as shown in Figure 5.14. You can choose a color or a geometric pattern, then preview a sample in the Format Cells dialog box.

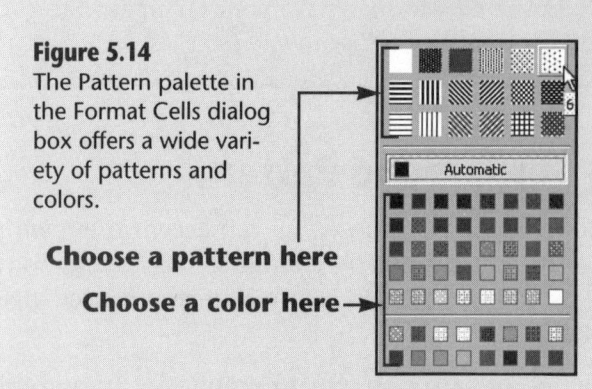

Figure 5.14
The Pattern palette in the Format Cells dialog box offers a wide variety of patterns and colors.

Choose a pattern here

Choose a color here

Lesson 5: Adding Borders and Patterns 133

④ Click the 6.25% Gray pattern at the far right in the first row of the palette.

This selects a light, dotted pattern, which is displayed in the sample box. This simple pattern will not obscure data entered in the formatted cell.

⑤ Choose OK.

This confirms the change. You see the shading in cell G12 on-screen (see Figure 5.15). Next, add a border to outline the cell.

⑥ Click the Borders drop-down arrow on the Formatting toolbar.

A palette of border options is displayed, as shown in Figure 5.15.

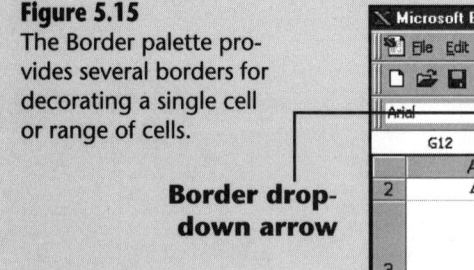

> **Tip for Students**
> You can also use the toolbar to remove borders or shading by selecting the range in question, clicking the appropriate toolbar button, and choosing the option that indicates *none* (such as No Fill from the Fill Color button).

Figure 5.15
The Border palette provides several borders for decorating a single cell or range of cells.

Border drop-down arrow

Bold, four-sided border

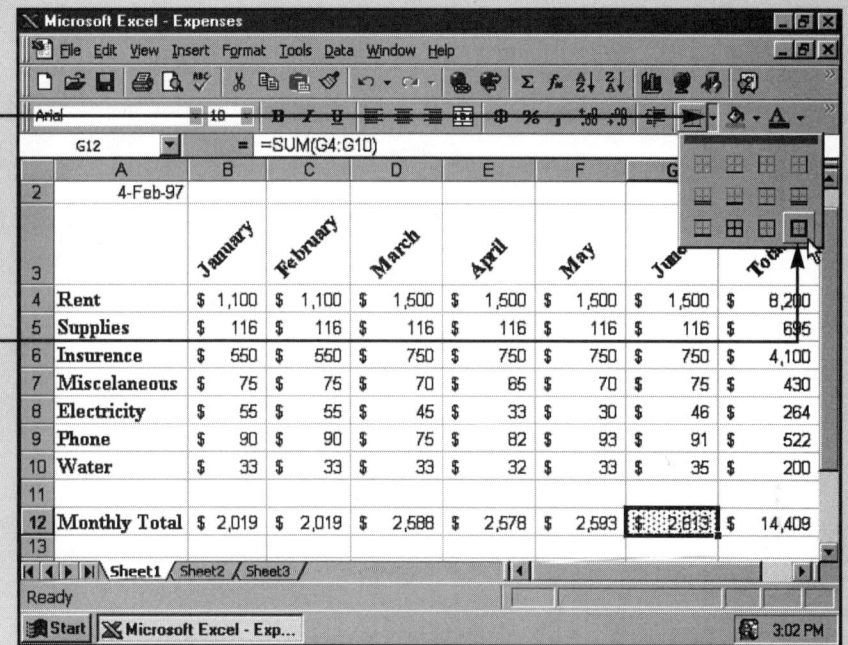

⑦ Click the bold, four-sided border on the bottom row.

Excel applies the border to the selected cell. Deselect the cell to get a good look at the formatting. Your worksheet should now look like the one shown in Figure 5.16.

continues

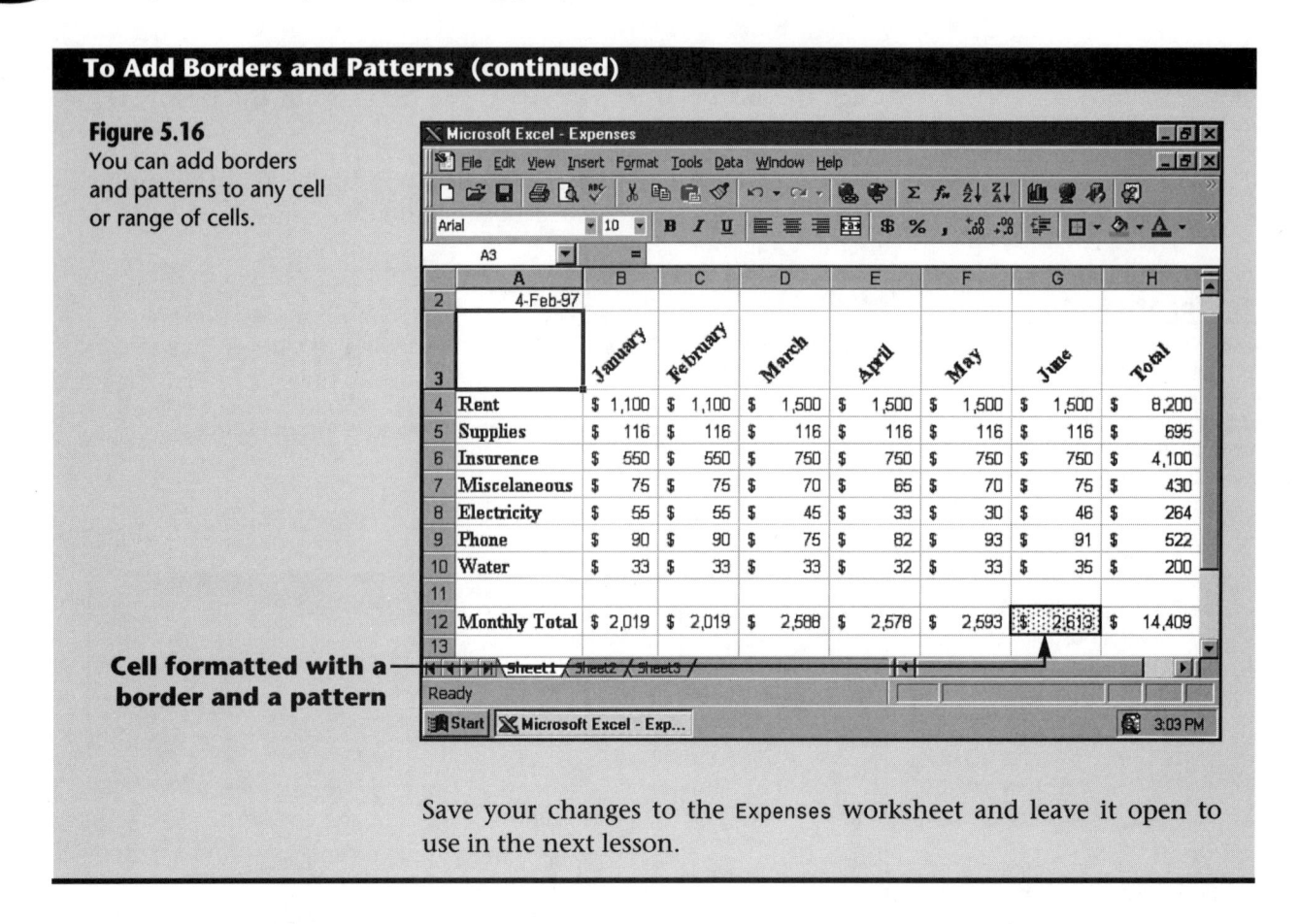

To Add Borders and Patterns (continued)

Figure 5.16
You can add borders and patterns to any cell or range of cells.

Cell formatted with a border and a pattern

Save your changes to the Expenses worksheet and leave it open to use in the next lesson.

Speedy Class

Discuss the differences among underline options using borders, regular underline, or the accounting underline.

You can customize borders and lines on the Border tab of the Format Cells dialog box. You can select border placement as well as the type of line you want to use. Simply open the Format Cells dialog box, click the Border tab, make your selections, then choose OK.

One of the most entertaining things about working with Windows 95 applications is being able to use a variety of colors. Excel enables you to personalize your work with color through the Format Cells dialog box. To quickly apply a color to fill a selected cell or range, click the Fill Color drop-down arrow on the Formatting toolbar, and select a color from the palette. To quickly apply a color to the data in a selected cell or range, click the Font color drop-down arrow on the Formatting toolbar, and select a color from the palette.

Unfortunately, colored letters on a colored background may be clear and attractive on-screen, but hard to read in printed form. Keep in mind that you need to be connected to a color printer to be able to print color worksheets. Without a color printer, colors may turn out to be muddy gray on paper, and all but the simplest patterns can make information on the worksheet hard to read.

Have fun experimenting with the colors and patterns in the Format Cells dialog box, but keep the formatting simple on worksheets that you need to print.

Lesson 6: Using Conditional Formatting

On Your Mark
In what situations would you want to base a cell's format on its value or the result of a formula?

Using formats to emphasize cells in a worksheet can call attention to specific data. When you format a cell, however, the formatting remains in effect even if the data changes. If you want to accent a cell depending on the value of the cell, you can use conditional formatting.

Like the conditional statements you used in formulas in Project 4, "Calculating with Functions," conditional formats return a result based on whether or not the value in the cell meets a specified criteria. For example, in a worksheet tracking monthly sales, you may want to accent a monthly total only if it is less than the previous month's total or if it is greater than the target sales figure you have set.

To Use Conditional Formatting

1 In the Expenses worksheet, select cells B9 to G9.

This selects the row containing phone expenses. For this example, you want to emphasize any monthly phone expenses that exceed $90.

Tip for Students
Like other Excel cell formats, conditional formats can be copied using the Format Painter.

2 Choose Format, Conditional Formatting.

The Conditional Formatting dialog box appears, as shown in Figure 5.17.

Figure 5.17
The Conditional Formatting dialog box enables you to format a cell based on the value in the cell.

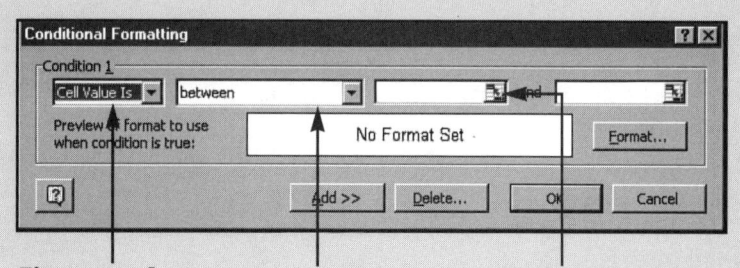

First text box   Comparison text box   Value text box

If you have problems...

If the Office Assistant opens, click the No, Don't Provide Help Now button to close it and continue.

3 Make sure Cell Value Is appears in the first text box, then press Tab.

This tells Excel that the condition you are going to specify depends on the constant value entered in the selected cells, then moves the insertion point to the comparison text box. You can also choose to use the value of the formula in the selected cells.

continues

To Use Conditional Formatting (continued)

4 **From the comparison drop-down list (the second drop-down list in the dialog box), select greater than, then press Tab.**

This identifies the type of comparison you want to use, and moves the insertion point to the value text box.

5 **In the value text box, type 90.**

The conditional statement now tells Excel that if the cell value is greater then 90, it should apply the specified formatting. Now, set the formatting.

> **Tip for Students**
>
> Choose formatting that is consistent with your organization's standards so that the reason for formatting is easily understood. For example, you might want to use the same font type and attributes for your worksheet titles as your company's name.

6 **Click the Format button.**

The Format Cells dialog box is displayed. You can set font style, color, underline, and strikethrough on the Font page, and you can choose border and patterns formatting as well.

7 **Click Bold in the Font style list, click the Color drop-down arrow, click the red square in the color palette, then choose OK.**

This tells Excel to format the data in the cell in red bold type if the condition is met. In this case, if the monthly phone expense is more than $90, it appears in red. In the Conditional Formatting dialog box, you see a sample of the formatting, as shown in Figure 5.18.

Figure 5.18
The conditional statement determines whether a cell is formatted or not.

Comparison phrase

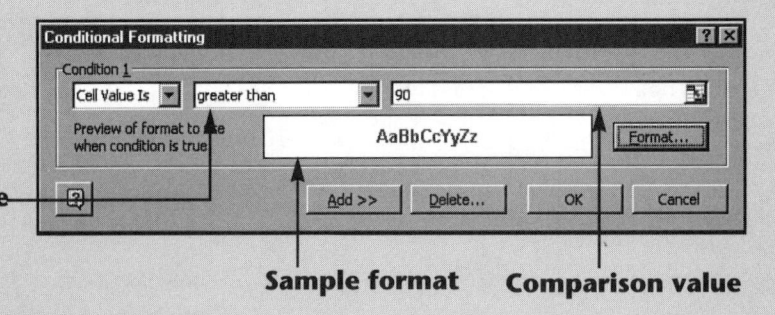

Sample format **Comparison value**

8 **Choose OK.**

Excel applies the formatting to any of the selected cells that meet the specified criteria, in this case, cells F9 and G9. Deselect the cells so you can get a better look at the result. Your worksheet should look similar to the one in Figure 5.19.

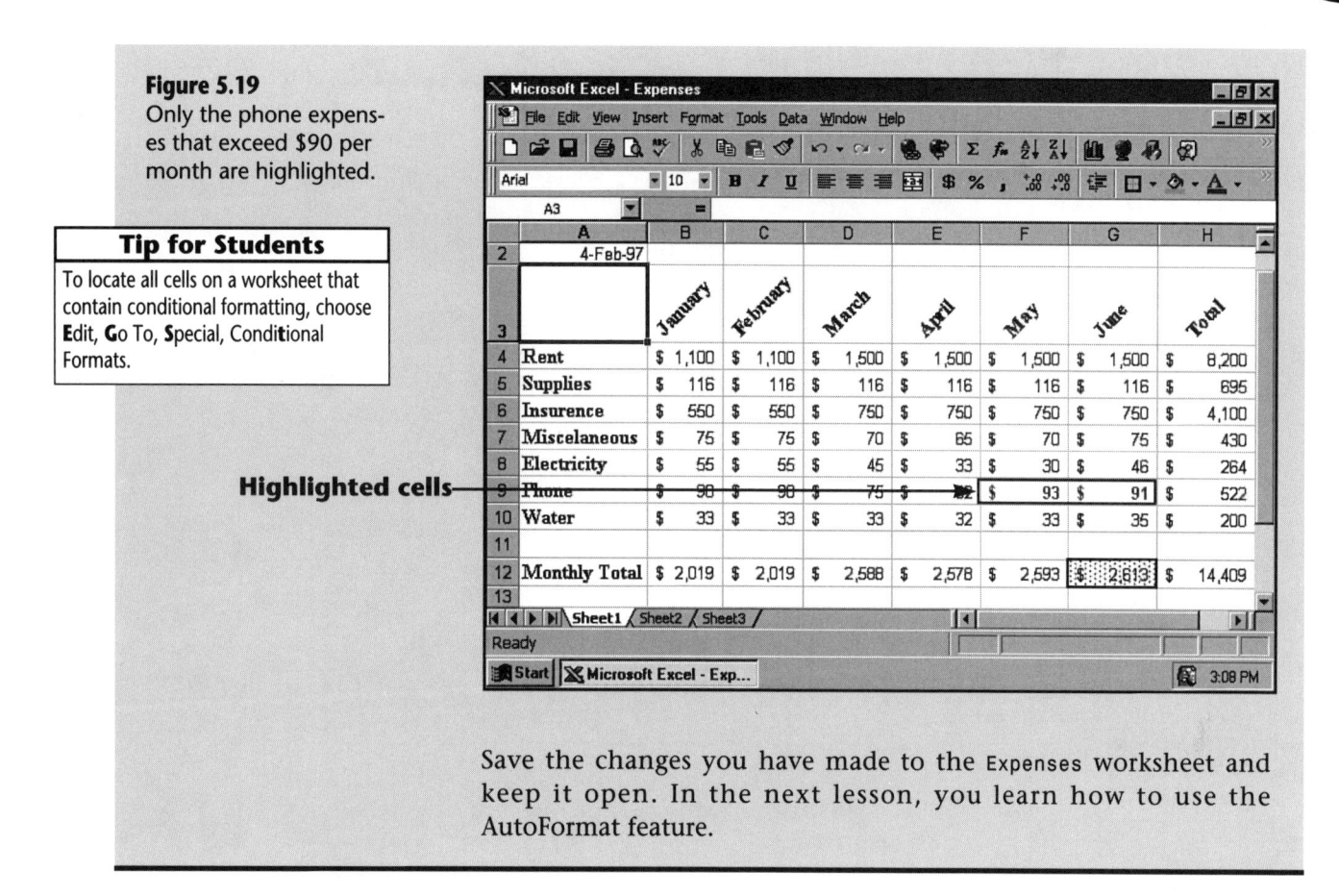

Figure 5.19
Only the phone expenses that exceed $90 per month are highlighted.

Tip for Students

To locate all cells on a worksheet that contain conditional formatting, choose **E**dit, **G**o To, **S**pecial, Cond**i**tional Formats.

Highlighted cells

Save the changes you have made to the Expenses worksheet and keep it open. In the next lesson, you learn how to use the AutoFormat feature.

You can set up to three conditions that must be met in order for the formatting to be applied. Simply click **A**dd in the Conditional Formatting dialog box to display another set of Condition text boxes. Use the **D**elete button to remove one or more conditions.

Lesson 7: Using AutoFormat

On Your Mark

What types of designs would you like to be able to create using the borders and shading options?

If you don't want to spend a lot of time formatting a worksheet, or if you want to rely on someone else's flair for design, you can use Excel's AutoFormat feature. The AutoFormat feature contains several pre-defined table formats that you can apply to selected cells in your worksheet.

Each format contains various alignment, number format, color, and pattern settings to help you create professional-looking worksheets. Generally, you apply one format at a time to a selected cell or range of cells. With a table format, however, you can apply a collection of formats supplied by Excel all at once.

Project 5 Improving the Appearance of a Worksheet

To Use AutoFormat

Tip for Students

Be sure to select the range *before* implementing AutoFormat because it doesn't apply to your entire worksheet—only to the selected range.

① Select cells A1 through H15 in the Expenses worksheet.

This highlights the entire worksheet. Now apply a new format to this range.

② Choose Format, AutoFormat.

Excel displays the AutoFormat dialog box (see Figure 5.20). A list of table formats and a Sample area appear in the dialog box. The Simple table format is currently selected. You can click other table formats to see what they look like in the Sample area.

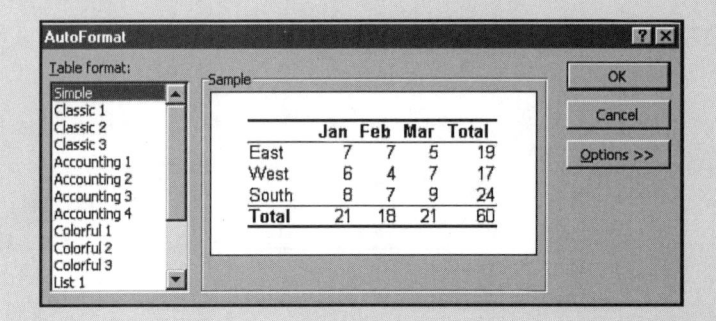

Figure 5.20
The AutoFormat dialog box enables you to format a range of cells by choosing from a list of standard table styles.

Quicksand

AutoFormat will override changes made to the worksheet, such as borders, shading, and justification. It may also affect number formats.

Tip for Students

As you scroll down the list of available formats in AutoFormat, you can click any table format to see a preview.

③ Scroll down the Table format list box and select the 3D Effects 1 format.

This selects the 3D Effects 1 table format and displays the formatting in the sample area.

④ Choose OK.

Excel changes the selected cells to the new format. Click any cell to deselect the range so that you can see the formatting clearly, as shown in Figure 5.21. Notice that the previous formatting in the Expenses worksheet has been replaced by the new format. Only the conditional formatting is still in effect. If you plan to use the AutoFormat feature, apply AutoFormat before adding other formatting.

Tip for Students

If you change your mind about AutoFormat, Undo can remove it if you catch it in time. Alternatively, you can go back to AutoFormat and choose None.

Quicksand

If you decide to remove AutoFormat by choosing None as the AutoFormat option, the enhancements that you previously made to your worksheet, such as centering and bold, will be gone. The exception to this is changes to column widths.

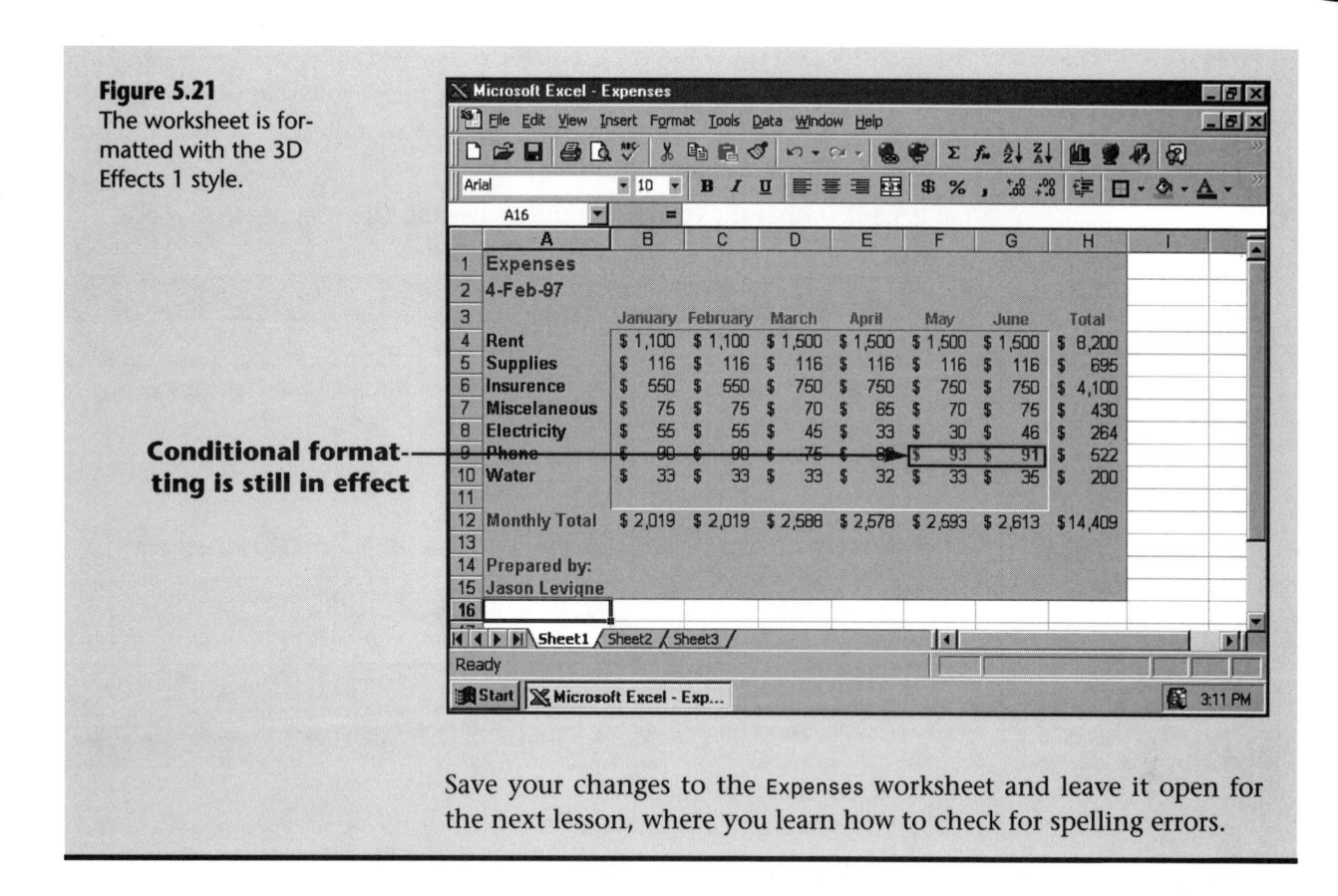

Lesson 8: Checking the Spelling in a Worksheet

Figure 5.21
The worksheet is formatted with the 3D Effects 1 style.

Conditional formatting is still in effect

Save your changes to the Expenses worksheet and leave it open for the next lesson, where you learn how to check for spelling errors.

> **If you have problems...**
>
> The table formats in the AutoFormat dialog box can drastically change the appearance of your worksheet. If you don't like the results after closing the AutoFormat dialog box, choose the **E**dit, **U**ndo command before you take any other action. Alternatively, you can continue making formatting changes to the worksheet.

Lesson 8: Checking the Spelling in a Worksheet

✓ **On Your Mark**
When should you check spelling in a worksheet?

When presenting a worksheet, you should make sure that no misspelled words are in the document. You can use the Excel spelling checker feature to rapidly find and highlight any misspelled words in a worksheet.

The spelling checker highlights words that it doesn't recognize—which, in addition to misspelled words, may be proper nouns, abbreviations, technical terms, and so on—that actually are spelled correctly, but aren't in Excel's spelling dictionary. You have the option of correcting or bypassing words that the spelling checker highlights. To personalize the program, you can add proper names, cities, and technical terms to a spelling dictionary file called CUSTOM.DIC.

Project 5 Improving the Appearance of a Worksheet

The spelling checker won't alert you to a word that is spelled correctly, but used incorrectly, such as *principle* when you mean *principal.* You still need to be watchful when creating a document, and not rely on the spelling checker to catch every possible mistake.

Table 5.1 describes the common options used in the Spelling dialog box.

Table 5.1	Spelling Button Options
Option	Description
Change **A**ll	Substitutes all occurrences of the questionable word with the word in the Change To text box.
Change	Substitutes only one occurrence of the questionable word with the word in the Change To text box.
Ignore All	Ignores all occurrences of the questionable word in a worksheet.
Ignore	Ignores only one occurrence of the questionable word.
Add	Adds the word to the dictionary (CUSTOM.DIC file).

To Check the Spelling in a Worksheet

❶ Select cell A1.

This makes A1 the current cell so that Excel will begin checking the spelling at the top of the worksheet.

❷ Choose Tools, Spelling.

Excel starts to search the worksheet for spelling errors. When it finds a word it doesn't recognize, it stops, highlights the word in the text, and opens the Spelling dialog box in which it offers suggestions for correcting the word.

In this example, Excel stops on the word Insurence and displays the Spelling dialog box. "Insurence" is misspelled, so it does not appear in the spelling dictionary. Excel makes a guess as to what word you really meant to type, and suggests a list of alternative spellings. The correct spelling—Insurance—is highlighted at the top of the list. You can select a different alternative, or, if the correct spelling isn't listed, you can type it in the Change **t**o text box.

Lesson 8: Checking the Spelling in a Worksheet

❸ Choose Change.

Excel replaces the incorrect spelling with the correct spelling and continues to check the spelling of the rest of the worksheet. The spelling checker stops at `Miscelaneous`, which is also misspelled, and offers a list of alternatives. The correct spelling is highlighted.

❹ Choose Change.

Excel replaces the word and continues checking the spelling. It stops at `Levigne`, which is a proper noun that is not in the main spelling dictionary, but it is spelled correctly. If you think you will include the name in many workbooks, you should add it to the custom dictionary. Then if you use the word in the future, Excel won't stop and highlight it if it is spelled correctly, and will suggest a correction if it is misspelled.

❺ Choose Add.

Excel adds the name to the `CUSTOM.DIC` dictionary and moves on. Excel doesn't find any more misspelled words, so it displays the message `The spell check is complete for the entire sheet.`

❻ Choose OK.

This confirms that the spelling check is complete. The words `Insurance` and `Miscellaneous` are now spelled correctly in the `Expenses` worksheet, and the name `Levigne` has been added to the `CUSTOM.DIC` dictionary.

Save your work and close the worksheet. If you have completed your session on the computer, exit Excel and Windows 95 before turning off the computer. Otherwise, continue with the "Checking Your Skills" section at the end of this project.

> **Tip for Students**
> Add proper nouns and other commonly used words to the dictionary. In this manner, they won't show up as being misspelled in the future.

If you have problems...

If the Spelling dialog box doesn't suggest alternatives to a misspelled word, you need to select the Always suggest check box in the Spelling dialog box. Conversely, if you don't want it to suggest alternatives, make sure the Always suggest check box is not selected.

To quickly start the spelling checker, click the Spelling button on the Standard toolbar or press F7.

If you start the spelling checker in the middle of the worksheet, when Excel reaches the end of the worksheet, it asks if you want to continue checking from the beginning. Choose Yes to check the spelling from the beginning of the worksheet. Choose No to close the spelling checker.

Excel comes with an AutoCorrect feature that automatically corrects common spelling errors. For example, if you type **adn**, Excel will automatically replace it with and. To see the list of words that Excel automatically corrects, choose Tools, AutoCorrect. To add your own spelling bugaboos to AutoCorrect, enter

> **Speedy Class**
> Select AutoCorrect while in the spelling checker to correct misspelled words as you type them.

the incorrect spelling in the **R**eplace text box and the correct spelling in the **W**ith text box, choose **A**dd, then choose OK. Alternatively, when the spelling checker stops on a misspelled word, you can choose AutoCo**r**rect in the Spelling dialog box to add it to the AutoCorrect spelling list.

Project Summary

> **Tip for Students**
> Double-click the column border for the Best Fit.

To	Do This
Change fonts, font sizes, or font attributes	Select the cells to format, and choose F**o**rmat, C**e**lls. Click the Font tab, make selections, and choose OK.
Align data	Select the cells and click the appropriate alignment button on the toolbar or open the Format Cells dialog box. Click the Alignment tab, make selections, and choose OK.
Change column width	Drag the column border to the desired width.
Automatically adjust column width	Double-click the border between columns.
Format numbers as currency	Select the cells and click the Currency button on the toolbar.
Change the format of numbers	Select the cells and choose F**o**rmat, C**e**lls. Click the Numbers tab, select the number type, select the number format, and choose OK.
Add borders to cells	Select the cells and choose F**o**rmat, Ce**l**ls. Click the Borders tab, select the border location, select the border style, and choose OK.
Add patterns or shading to cells	Select the cells and choose F**o**rmat, C**e**lls. Click the Patterns tab, choose the pattern or shading options, and choose OK.
Apply conditional formatting	Select the cell and choose F**o**rmat, Con**d**itional Formatting. Select the type of comparison, enter the value to compare, click Format, select the formatting, choose OK, then choose OK again.
Automatically format a range	Select the cells and choose F**o**rmat, **A**utoFormat. Select the table format and choose OK.
Check spelling in a worksheet	Click the Spelling Checker button on the toolbar, and follow the prompts.
Copy formatting	Select the formatted cell, click the Format Painter button, and select the cells to format.

Checking Your Skills

True/False

For each of the following, check T or F to indicate whether the statement is true or false.

__T ✔F **1.** You can quickly adjust the column width to fit the column contents by right-clicking the line between two columns.

__T ✔F **2.** AutoFormat overrides conditional formatting already in the worksheet.

✔T __F **3.** By default, numbers are right-aligned in a cell.

__T ✔F **4.** You can add a border to one cell or to a group of cells, but you cannot add shading to more than one cell at a time.

✔T __F **5.** You can add the name of the city you live in to the spelling Checker dictionary so that it doesn't question you every time it comes across that name.

✔T __F **6.** When you use the Merge and Center button to center a heading, the heading text remains in cell A1.

__T ✔F **7.** The column width adjusts automatically when you change the type size.

✔T __F **8.** When text doesn't fit in the width of the column, a series of pound signs (######) appears in the cell.

✔T __F **9.** When you apply formatting, it applies to the worksheet cell, not to the number itself.

__T ✔F **10.** You should use a lot of different colors for the letters and the background to improve the appearance of your spreadsheets.

Multiple Choice

Circle the letter of the correct answer for each of the following questions.

1. Which of the following options enables you to skip a word that Excel identifies as misspelled?

  a. Ignore
  b. Change
  c. Add
  d. Alternatives

2. Which of the following is *not* a method of adjusting column width?

  a. Format, Column, Width command
  b. Edit, Column, Width command
  c. double-clicking the right column border on the worksheet frame
  d. dragging the column border on the worksheet frame

3. Which of the following *cannot* be formatted using the Formatting toolbar?

  a. Fonts
  b. Type size
  c. Column width
  d. Numerical formatting

4. How many conditions can you apply to each conditional format?

  a. One
  b. Two
  c. Three
  d. Four

144 Project 5 Improving the Appearance of a Worksheet

5. If pound signs (######) fill a cell, it means what?
   a. The cell is not active.
   b. The formula is impossible.
   c. The column is not wide enough.
   d. You must recalculate the formula.

6. To copy formatting from one cell to another, you use which of the following?
   a. Formatting toolbar
   b. Font dialog box
   c. Format Painter button
   d. shortcut menu

7. What is the keyboard shortcut to bold selected text?
   a. Ctrl + B
   b. Ctrl + O
   c. Ctrl + L
   d. Ctrl + 1

8. When you enter the column width in the Column Width text box, you enter the width in which of the following?
   a. points
   b. number of characters
   c. inches
   d. centimeters

9. To rotate text 90 degrees down, you enter what in the Degrees text box?
   a. 90 d
   b. 90
   c. 90 down
   d. -90

10. You can set up to how many conditions that must be met for formatting to be applied?
    a. three
    b. four
    c. two
    d. five

Completion

In the blank provided, write the correct answer for each of the following statements.

1. _double-click_ the left mouse button to quickly adjust column width to fit the longest entry.
2. To customize the spelling checker, add words to the _custom dictionary_.
3. When formatting a number as currency, you can use the _Increase Decimal_ tool to add decimal places.
4. _Row_ height adjusts automatically to accommodate changes in font size.
5. When aligning data in a cell, use _negative_ numbers to rotate text down.
6. The numbers in the Font Size list box refer to the _point_ size.
7. To enter more than one line of text within a cell, choose the _Wrap Text_ option on the Alignment page of the Format Cells dialog box.
8. To accent a cell depending on the value of the cell, use _conditional formatting_.
9. To quickly start the spelling check, press the _F7_ function key.
10. The _AutoCorrect_ feature automatically corrects common spelling errors.

Checking Your Skills

Matching

In the blank next to each of the following terms or phrases, write the letter of the corresponding term or phrase.

_g_ **1.** The typeface, type size, and type attributes of text or numbers.

_i_ **2.** A unit of measurement used to designate the height of type.

_a_ **3.** Keyboard shortcut to italicize text.

_h_ **4.** Keyboard shortcut to underline text.

_c_ **5.** To set a precise column width, use an option on this menu.

_j_ **6.** Aligns with the left side of a cell.

_e_ **7.** Aligns with the right side of a cell.

_d_ **8.** Centers text across columns.

_b_ **9.** Centers text in a cell.

_f_ **10.** You can add words to this spelling dictionary.

a. Ctrl+I
b. Center button
c. Format
d. Merge and Center button
e. numbers
f. custom
g. font
h. Ctrl+U
i. point
j. text

Screen ID

Label each element of the Excel screen shown in Figure 5.22.

Figure 5.22

1. **List of fonts**
2. **Font drop-down arrow**
3. **Font size drop-down arrow**
4. **Bold button**
5. **Format Painter button**
6. **Italic button**
7. **Underline button**
8. **Center button**
9. **Merge & Center button**

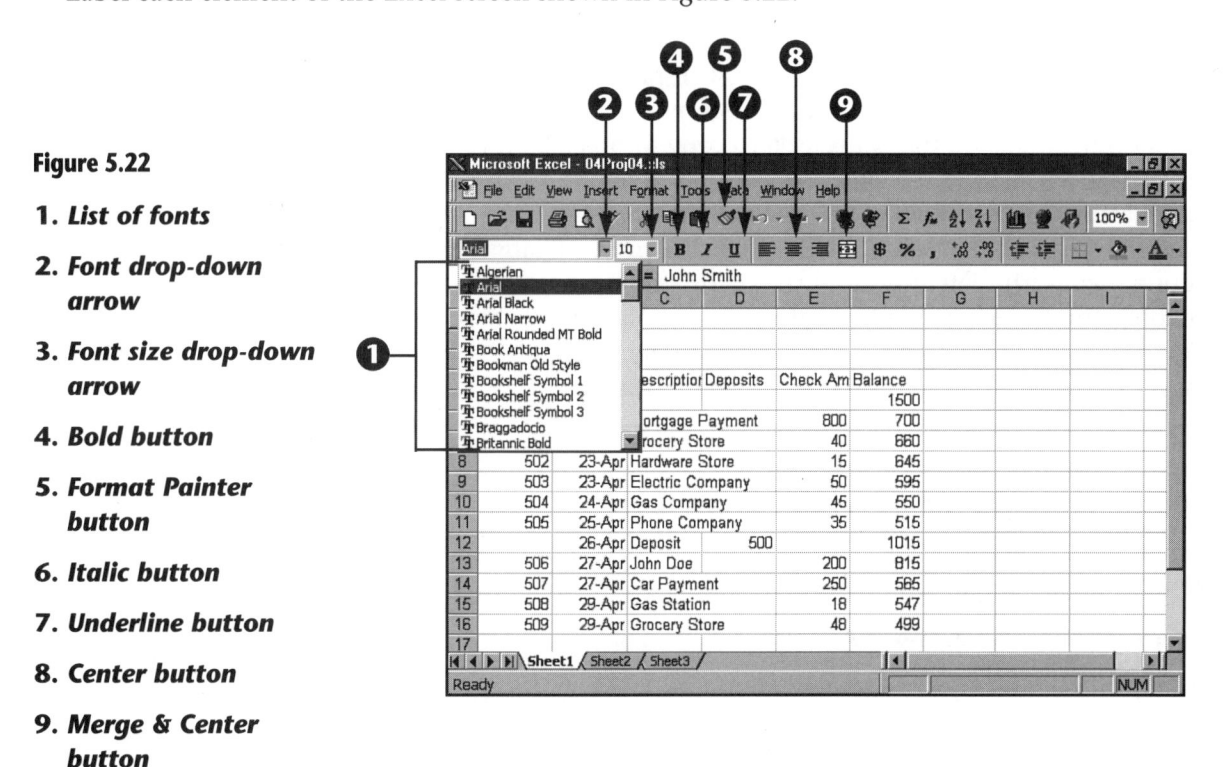

Applying Your Skills

Practice

The following exercises enable you to practice the skills you have learned in this project. Take a few minutes to work through these exercises now.

1. Formatting the Sales Worksheet

Practice using different formatting techniques to improve the appearance of the worksheet detailing monthly sales figures. Center the title, change the font and font size of the headings, adjust column widths, add borders or patterns, and check the spelling in the worksheet.

To Format the Sales Worksheet

1. Open the file Proj0502 and save it as Sales 2.
2. Center the title across the worksheet.
3. Make the column headings stand out by changing the font, font size, and other attributes.
4. Copy the formatting from the column headings to the row headings.
5. Adjust column widths to fit all the data.
6. Format all dollar values as currency with two decimal places.
7. Add borders or patterns to highlight the monthly totals.
8. Check and correct the spelling, and add proper names to your personal dictionary if you want.
9. Save the worksheet. If requested by your instructor, print two copies, then close the file.

> In this exercise, students apply formatting techniques to improve the appearance of a worksheet. Students center the title using the Merge and Center button. Students format the columns by using the Format, Cells command, then choosing the Font tab. The Paintbrush tool on the Standard toolbar is used to copy formats. To format dollar values as currency with two decimal places, students use the Currency Style and Decrease Decimal tools on the Formatting toolbar. To increase column width, they move the mouse pointer to the line to the right of a column letter, then when the mouse changes to a double-headed black arrow, double-click the left mouse button. Students can use the Format, Cells command, then choose the Border tab and/or Patterns tab to add borders or patterns to the worksheet. The Tools, Spelling command is used to check the spelling of the worksheet. The solution file is saved as **Sales 2** on the Instructor's Resource disk.

2. Formatting the Ad Revenues Analysis

Format the Ad Revenues worksheet to improve its appearance. Use conditional formatting to draw attention the most profitable ad campaign. Use AutoFormat to quickly apply formatting.

To Format the Ad Revenues Analysis

1. Open the file Proj0503 and save it as Ad Revenues 2.
2. Change the number formatting so that dollar values appear as currency with zero decimal places.

3. Change the date formatting to 9/27/97.

4. Set up conditional formatting to highlight ad revenues that fall between $200 and $300.

5. Use the AutoFormat feature to apply an appropriate table format.

6. Check the spelling.

7. Save the worksheet. If requested by your instructor, print two copies, then close it.

In this exercise, students apply formatting techniques to improve the appearance of a worksheet. To format dollar values as currency with zero decimal places, use the Currency Style and Decrease Decimal tools on the Formatting toolbar. The F**o**rmat, Con**d**itional Formatting command is used to create a conditional format in cells F4:F6. The F**o**rmat, **A**utoFormat command is used to apply formatting to the worksheet. Students use the **T**ools, **S**pelling command to check the spelling of the worksheet. The solution file is saved as **Ad Revenues 2** on the Instructor's Resource disk.

---

3. Formatting the Salary Forecast

Format the salary forecast worksheet using conditional formatting, number formatting, and alignment.

To Format the Salary Forecast

1. Open the file `Proj0504` and save it as `Salary 2`.

2. Adjust the column widths.

3. Increase the font size of the title to 14 points, then center the title across the worksheet.

4. Use number formats to display all dollar values as currency with zero decimal places, and to display the percent increase values as percentages with percent signs.

5. Use conditional formatting to highlight projected salaries that exceed $20,000.

6. Rotate the text in the column headings 45 degrees.

7. Save the worksheet. If requested by your instructor, print two copies, then close it.

In this activity, students apply formatting techniques to improve the appearance of a worksheet. Students center and bold the title using the Merge and Center tool and the Bold tool on the Formatting toolbar. To format dollar values as currency with zero decimal places, they use the Currency Style and Decrease Decimal tools on the Formatting toolbar. To display the percent increase values as percentages with percent signs, students use the Percent Style tool on the Formatting toolbar. The F**o**rmat, Con**d**itional Formatting command is used to create a conditional format in cells E3:E7. Students use the F**o**rmat, C**e**lls command, then choose the Alignment tab to rotate the text in the column headings 45 degrees. The solution file is saved as **Salary 2** on the Instructor's Resource disk.

Project 5   Improving the Appearance of a Worksheet

4. Formatting the Utility Expense Worksheet

Practice formatting techniques to improve the appearance of the utility expense worksheet. Apply the proper number format where needed, make the headings stand out, and change the text font to add interest. Adjust column widths. You can also add borders and shading to emphasize important cells. Use conditional formatting and change alignment within cells. If you want, use AutoFormat to quickly format the worksheet, then fine-tune it manually. Don't forget to check your spelling.

To Format the Utility Expense Worksheet

1. Open the file Proj0505 and save it as Utilities 2.

2. Make formatting changes as suggested. Be creative, but also try to keep the formatting clean and simple so that the worksheet will look professional.

3. Check the spelling in the worksheet.

4. Save your changes to the worksheet. If requested by your instructor, print two copies, then close it.

> In this activity, students apply a variety of formatting techniques to an existing worksheet. Students are to use their own discretion as they apply number formats, text fonts, adjust column widths, insert borders and shading, apply conditional formatting, and align text within cells. Although student solutions will vary, a solution file is saved as **Utilities 2** on the Instructor's Resource disk.

5. Using Fonts and Their Attributes

You have learned to change the font and the appearance of text in your worksheets. In this exercise, you improve the appearance of the Profit Loss workbook by changing fonts and font attributes.

To Use Fonts and Their Attributes

1. Open the file Proj0506 and save it as Profit Loss 3.

2. Select cells A1:A2 and choose Format, Cells.

3. Click the Font tab.

4. Change the font style to bold and the font size to 14.

5. Click OK to return to the worksheet.

6. Select cells B4:D4.

7. Click the Bold button on the Formatting toolbar to boldface these cells.

8. Save the file again, then leave it open for the following exercise.

> In this exercise, students use the Format, Cells command, then select the Font tab to change font size and font style. In addition, the Bold tool on the Formatting toolbar is used to bold cells B4:D4. A solution file is saved as **Profit Loss 3** on the Instructor's Resource disk.

Applying Your Skills

Challenge

The following challenges enable you to use your problem-solving skills. Take time to work through these exercises now.

1. Formatting a Worksheet

Your boss has asked you to format your department's profit and loss statement. Make sure that the `Profit Loss 3` workbook is open and then change the width of column A to 18. Widen column F so that the longest entry fits in the cell. Merge and center the first heading across the width of the worksheet. Center the headings in cells B4:D4. Save the file and leave it open for the next exercise.

> In this activity, students continue to format the Profit Loss 3 worksheet. To increase column width, they move the mouse pointer to the line to the right of a column letter, then when the mouse changes to a double-headed black arrow, double-click the left mouse button. Students center the title using the Merge and Center tool on the Formatting toolbar. The headings in cells B4:D4 are centered by clicking the Center tool on the Formatting toolbar. The solution file is saved as **Profit Loss 3** on the Instructor's Resource disk.

2. Changing the Format of Numbers

Your boss has now decided that he would like you to format the profit and loss workbook further. Make sure that the `Profit Loss 3` workbook is open. Change the format of the numbers in cells B5:G13 to include a 1000 separator (,) and two decimal places. Add a light gray shading to the monthly numbers (cells B4:D13). Save the worksheet. If requested by your instructor, print two copies of the worksheet before closing it.

> Students continue to format the Profit Loss 3 worksheet in this exercise. To format values in cells B5:G13 to include a 1000 separator and two decimal places, students use the Comma Style tool on the Formatting toolbar; and, if necessary, use the Increase Decimal tool to display two decimal places in the values. To add a light gray shading to the monthly numbers, students use the F**o**rmat, C**e**lls command, then choose the Patterns tab to select a cell shading color. The solution file is saved as **Profit Loss 3** on the Instructor's Resource disk.

3. Using Conditional Formatting

You have been asked by your demanding boss to quickly identify those customers that owe your company money and those that have overpaid the company. He would also like you to format the information before you present it. He wants you to have the information ready for him within the hour. You decide to use Conditional formatting and the AutoFormat feature to accomplish these tasks quickly.

Open `Proj0507` and save it as `Billing 2`. Select cells H4:H9 and set up condition 1 so that if the cell value is greater than 0, the value displays in red. Set up condition 2 so that if the cell value is less than 0, the value displays in blue.

Merge and center the headings in cells A1:H1. Use the AutoFormat feature to change to List 3 format. Make sure the columns are wide enough for the data to fit. Save the workbook and leave it open for the following exercise.

Project 5 Improving the Appearance of a Worksheet

> In adding to applying conditional formatting to cells, students merge and center headings, adjust column widths, and apply the AutoFormat feature to a worksheet in this activity. The F**o**rmat, Con**d**itional Formatting command is used to create a conditional format in cells H4:H9. The F**o**rmat, **A**utoFormat command is used to apply formatting to the worksheet. To increase column width, students move the mouse pointer to the line to the right of a column letter, then when the mouse changes to a double-headed black arrow, double-click the left mouse button. Students center the title using the Merge and Center tool on the Formatting toolbar. The solution file is saved as **Billing 2** on the Instructor's Resource disk.

4. Using the Spelling Checker

You decide to use the Spelling Checker before you present the worksheet to your boss. Make sure the `Billing 2` worksheet is open and then check the spelling in the entire worksheet. Correct any misspelled words. Save the worksheet. If requested by your instructor, print two copies before closing it.

> In this activity, students use the **T**ools, **S**pelling command to check the spelling of the Billing 2 worksheet. The solution file is saved as **Billing 2** on the Instructor's Resource disk.

5. Improving the Appearance of a Worksheet

You have decided that you are ready to practice your formatting techniques to improve the appearance of your checking account worksheet.

Open `Proj0508` and save it as `Checking Account 5`. Center the headings in the top two rows across the worksheet columns, and boldface the text. Increase the font size of these headings. Format the numbers in columns D, E, and F so that they use commas as the thousands separator and display with two decimal places. Boldface the headings in row 4. Adjust the column widths so that they are wide enough to fit all the entries. Use Conditional Formatting so that if the balance goes below 500, the amount displays in red. Spell check the worksheet before saving the file. If requested by your instructor, print two copies. Close the file when you have finished.

> Students continue to format worksheets in this activity. Students center and bold the headings in the first two rows using the Merge and Center tool and the Bold tool on the Formatting toolbar. The Font size tool is used to increase the font size of these two headings. To format values in columns D, E, and F to include a 1000 separator and two decimal places, students use the Comma Style tool on the Formatting toolbar; and, if necessary, use the Increase Decimal tool to display two decimal places in the values. Students bold the headings in row 4 by clicking the Bold tool on the Formatting toolbar. To increase column width, they move the mouse pointer to the line to the right of a column letter, then when the mouse changes to a double-headed black arrow, double-click the left mouse button. The F**o**rmat, Con**d**itional Formatting command is used to create a conditional format in cells F5:F16. Finally, students use the **T**ools, **S**pelling command to check the spelling of the worksheet. The solution file is saved as **Checking Account 5** on the Instructor's Resource disk.

Project 6

Using Charts and Maps

Objectives

In this project, you learn how to:
- Create a Chart
- Format Text in a Chart
- Change the Chart Type
- Enhance a Chart
- Print a Chart
- Create a Map

Project 6 Using Charts and Maps

Why Would I Do This?

> **On Your Mark**
> In what types of situations would a visual display of your numbers enhance the message the numbers should convey?

After you create a worksheet, you may want to show the information to someone else. You can simply print the worksheet if you need only numerical detail, or you can transform the information in the worksheet into a chart. With Excel, you can also chart geographical information with maps. Charts and maps are great for visually representing relationships between numerical values while improving the appearance of a presentation.

This project shows you how to use sample data to create and enhance various types of charts. You also learn how to add a map to a worksheet.

Lesson 1: Creating a Chart

> **Embedded chart**
> A graphical representation of worksheet data created within the worksheet rather than as a separate worksheet.

In Excel, you can create an embedded chart directly on the worksheet. An *embedded chart* is a graphic object—a picture of the data—that appears on the worksheet along with your worksheet data. You can also add a chart of the data on a separate worksheet.

> **Tip for Students**
> An embedded chart resides on the same worksheet as your numbers, and can be printed on the same page with the numbers. When choosing a spot in your worksheet to place the chart, consider where the chart will print.

To create a chart, you select the data you want to use in the chart; then choose **I**nsert, **C**hart or click the Chart Wizard button on the Standard toolbar. The Chart Wizard provides step-by-step assistance through a series of dialog boxes to choose a chart type and specify chart options; then automatically creates the chart from the selected data and places it in a box (frame). You can then change or enhance the chart. Now try creating a chart to help you analyze your monthly office expenses.

To Create a Chart

❶ Open the file Proj0601 and save it as Expenses.

This is the workbook file you use in this project.

> **Tip for Instructors**
> Explain the importance of considering the numbers being charted before choosing a chart design. Refer students to Table 2.1.

❷ Select cells A2 through G7.

This is the data you will use to create the chart. You can create a chart using any of the information in the worksheet. The range you selected here lets you see how your expense costs change over the course of six months.

❸ Click the Chart Wizard button on the Standard toolbar.

Excel displays the Chart Wizard - Step 1 of 4 - Chart Type dialog box, as shown in Figure 6.1. This dialog box contains two tabs, Standard Types and Custom Types, which contain chart types from which to make your selection.

> **Speedy Class**
> You can select nonadjacent sets of numbers to be charted by holding down Ctrl while dragging over numbers in various areas of the worksheet. Make sure that the sets of numbers selected represent the same data series.

**Project Time
60 minutes**

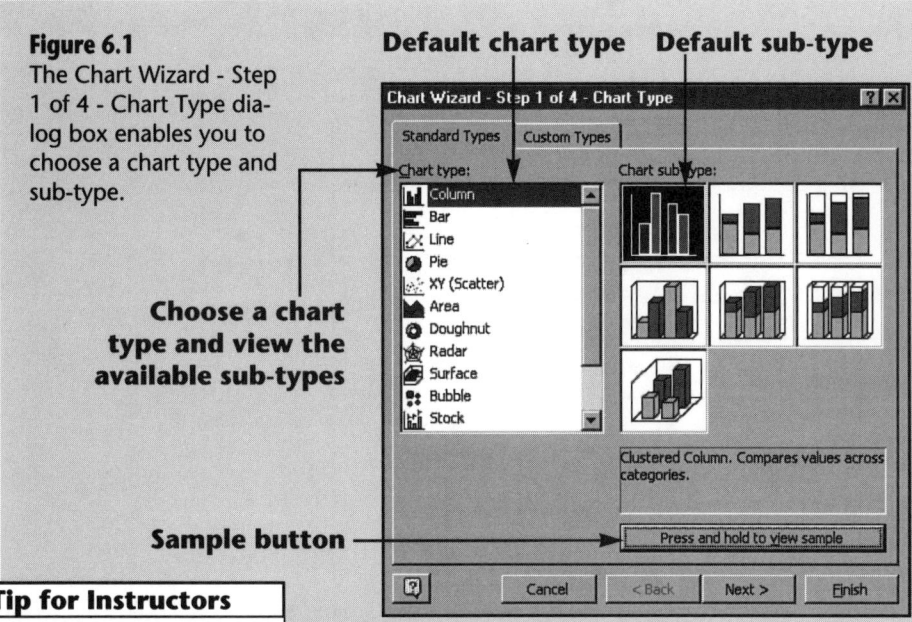

Lesson 1: Creating a Chart

Figure 6.1
The Chart Wizard - Step 1 of 4 - Chart Type dialog box enables you to choose a chart type and sub-type.

- Default chart type
- Default sub-type
- Choose a chart type and view the available sub-types
- Sample button

Tip for Instructors
In Excel 97, the Chart Wizard - Step 1 of 4 - Chart Type dialog box opens before the student specifies the location of the chart. The location of the chart (embedded object or separate sheet) won't be selected until Step 4 of the Chart Wizard.

Tip for Students
When you select a chart type from the list, the appropriate chart sub-types are displayed.

Tip for Students
When you click a Chart sub-type, its description appears below the grouping of pictures in the lower-right corner of the dialog box.

Tip for Students
Step 2 of the Chart Wizard gives you an opportunity to change the range you originally chose for the numbers that are being charted. Simply drag over a new range of numbers to rewrite the range. You can click the Collapse Dialog button next to the **D**ata Range text box to reduce the size of the dialog box. In this way you can select the range on the worksheet.

4 **In the Chart Type list, click Column, if it is not already selected.**

For this example, the default chart type, Column, is acceptable. Otherwise, you could select a different chart type. Now you can choose a chart sub-type. In this case, you will use the default clustered column sub-type for the column chart.

5 **Make sure the Clustered Column sub-type from the Chart sub-type list is selected.**

6 **Point to the Press and hold to view sample button; then click and hold down the left mouse button.**

A sample of your chart is displayed in the Sample box.

7 **Release the mouse button; then click the Next button.**

The chart type and sub-type are accepted and the Chart Wizard - Step 2 of 4 - Chart Source Data dialog box appears, as shown in Figure 6.2. A sample of the chart you are creating is displayed in the Data Range tab of the dialog box. If necessary, you can change the way the *data series* is displayed from rows to columns, but for this example the default settings are fine. The Series tab enables you to add or remove a series or change the ranges being used for the names and values of each chart series.

continues

154 Project 6 Using Charts and Maps

To Create a Chart (continued)

Figure 6.2
The Chart Wizard - Step 2 of 4 - Chart Source Data dialog box enables you to change the display of the data series.

Value (Y) axis labels list dollar amounts

Data series

Legend

Category (X) axis labels list months

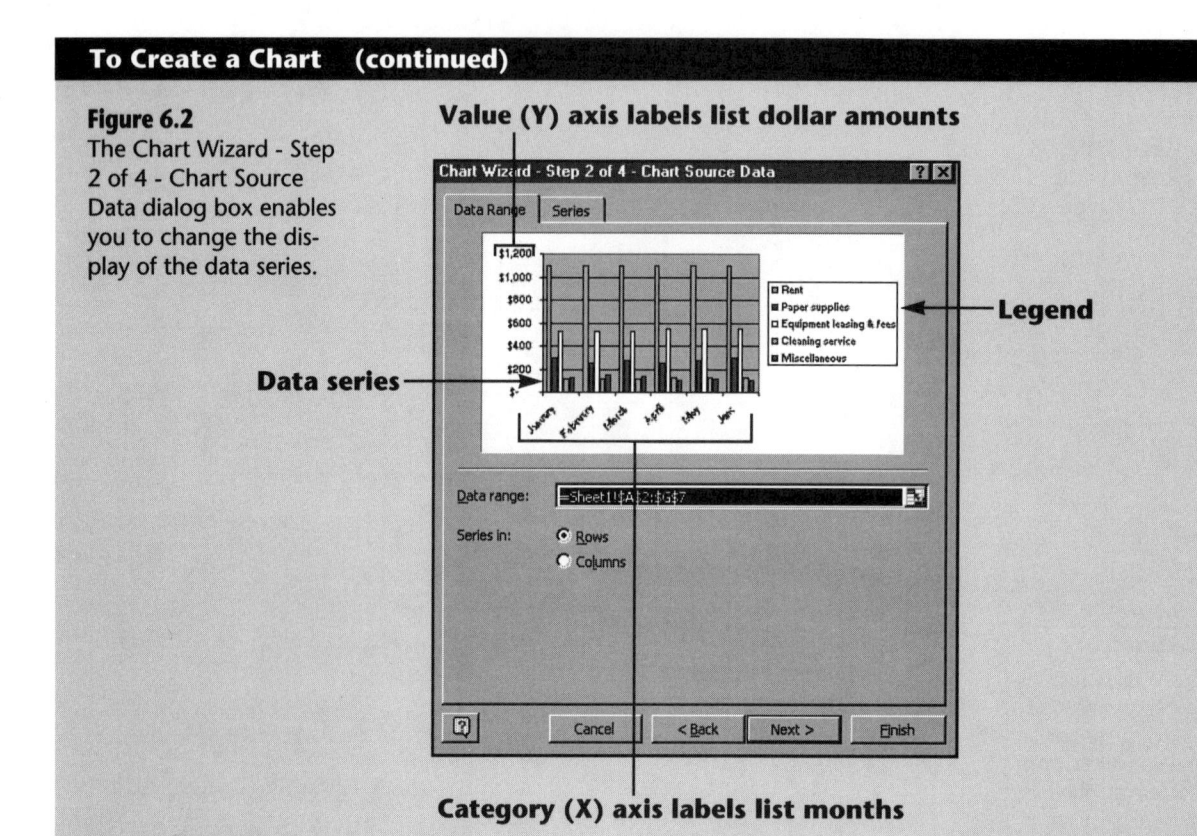

8 **Click the Next button.**

The defaults are accepted and the Chart Wizard - Step 3 of 4 - Chart Options dialog box appears. Here, the tabs are displayed so that you can choose to add chart *titles*, label the *axes*, add *gridlines*, hide or change the placement of the *legend*, add *data labels*, or show the *Data table*.

Tip for Students
Remember, you can always click the **B**ack button in the Chart Wizard dialog box to return to a previous step.

9 **Click the Titles tab; then click the Chart title text box. Type** Office Expenses **and then press** Tab.

Excel adds the title to the chart and moves the insertion point to the **C**ategory (X) Axis text box.

10 **Type** Months **in the Category (X) axis text box, press** Tab, **and then type** Dollars **in the Value (Y) axis text box.**

Excel labels the axes on the chart. The Chart Wizard - Step 3 of 4 - Chart Options dialog box should now look like the one shown in Figure 6.3.

Lesson 1: Creating a Chart 155

Figure 6.3
In the Chart Wizard - Step 3 of 4 - Chart Options dialog box, you can change the standard options for the selected chart type.

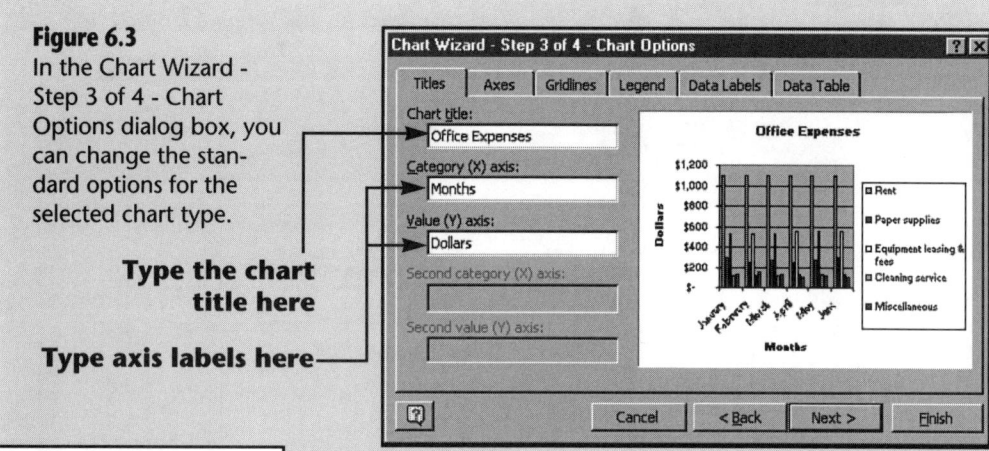

Type the chart title here

Type axis labels here

Tip for Instructors
In Excel 97, there is no opportunity in the Chart Wizard, - Step 4 of 4 - Chart Location dialog box to specify where on the worksheet an embedded chart should be placed. When the student clicks the **F**inish button, Excel places the chart on the worksheet data. The student then needs to drag the chart to the desired location.

Figure 6.4
The Chart Wizard - Step 4 of 4 - Chart Location dialog box enables you to specify the location of your chart.

Handles
The small, black squares around a selected object. You use these squares to drag, size, or scale the object.

⓫ Click the Next button.

The Chart Wizard - Step 4 of 4 - Chart Location dialog box appears, as shown in Figure 6.4. If you want to see the chart displayed next to its source data, you can embed it as an object on the worksheet. If you prefer to work with the chart separately, place it on its own sheet and Excel will automatically size it to fill an entire page.

Click here to place the chart on its own sheet

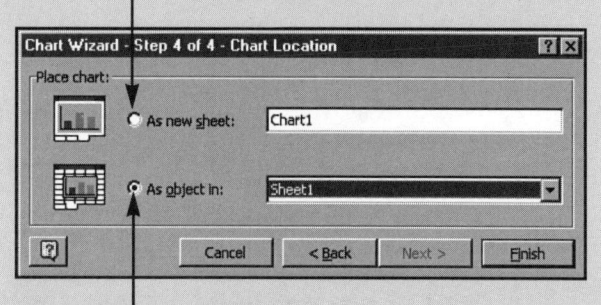

Click here to embed the chart on the worksheet of your choice

⓬ Click Finish.

Excel creates the chart and displays it with eight black squares called *handles* surrounding the box, as shown in Figure 6.5. The Chart toolbar, which you can use to edit the chart, should automatically appear. If it does not, choose **V**iew, **T**oolbars, Chart to display it.

With the chart selected, selection handles are displayed, and you can drag the chart to a new position below the worksheet.

continues

To Create a Chart (continued)

Figure 6.5
Excel creates the chart and embeds it as an object in the current worksheet.

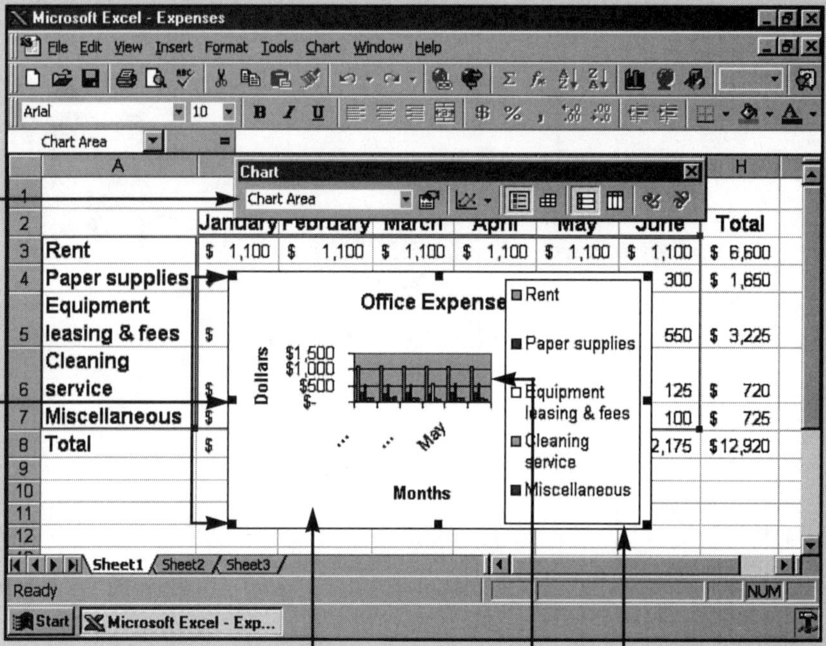

Callouts: The Chart toolbar; Selection handles; Chart area; Plot area; Legend

13 **Click inside the chart area (in any blank area) and drag the chart so that the upper-left corner is positioned in cell A10.**

As you drag the chart, the pointer changes to a four-headed arrow. The chart is repositioned, but it needs resizing. It is important to resize the chart before you format it. If you do not resize first, the formatting and added enhancements will be out of proportion with the chart.

14 **Point to the selection handle in the lower-right corner of the chart.**

The pointer changes to a two-headed diagonal arrow.

15 **Drag this selection handle down and to the right until the chart expands through cell G25.**

The chart now fills cells A10:G25.

Save your work and keep the Expenses worksheet open for the next lesson, where you learn how to format and enhance the appearance of the chart.

Tip for Students

To maintain the original proportions of the chart as you resize it, press and hold down ⇧Shift and then drag a corner handle.

Quicksand

Students may have trouble resizing the chart by using the selection handles. Point out how to drag the handles in any direction.

Tip for Instructors

Students may be concerned about the appearance of the individual components of the chart (such as the legend and axes labels). Tell them that the chart components will be formatted in the next lesson.

Lesson 2: Formatting Text in a Chart

Jargon Watch

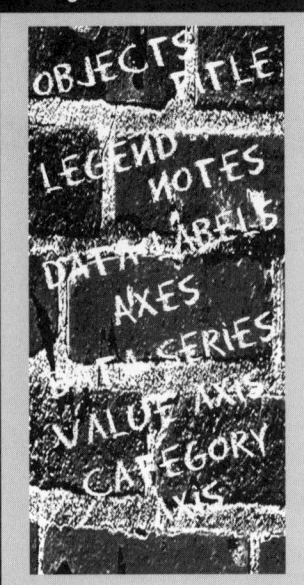

Charts and maps are considered to be **objects** in Excel. An object is an item that has its own frame or box and that can be selected, moved, copied, sized, and formatted independently of the worksheet cells behind it. Other objects in Excel include text boxes and clip art.

Charts consist of a number of elements, most of which you can modify or delete. A chart's **title**, for example, is simply the chart's name.

Charts can also include other text such as a **legend**, **notes**, and **data labels**. A legend tells what each color or symbol in the chart's data series represents. Notes are brief descriptions or explanations of the data in the chart. Data labels are names such as "Months" or "Dollars" that appear along the vertical and horizontal **axes** to describe the data in the chart. The **data series** is a range of values in a worksheet, such as the expense information you used to create the chart in Lesson 1.

The axes provide the scale used to measure the data in the chart. The **Value axis** (Y-axis) is the vertical line of the chart and the **Category axis** (X-axis) is the horizontal line. On a 3-D chart, a second **Value axis** (Z-axis) is included.

Speedy Class
The scale of the axes can be changed by selecting an axis, choosing S**e**lected Axis from the F**o**rmat menu, and then clicking the Scale tab.

You can move a selected chart or its elements (such as the legend and titles) on the chart by dragging them to a new location. You can also resize a selected chart or element by positioning the mouse pointer over any one of the chart box handles until the pointer changes to a two-headed arrow. Drag the handle away from the center of the chart box to enlarge the box and toward the center of the box to reduce it.

When you drag a handle on the middle of one side of the box, you change the size horizontally or vertically. When you drag a corner handle, you change the vertical and horizontal dimensions at the same time. If you hold down (Shift) while dragging a corner handle, you maintain the original proportions of the chart.

Be careful when increasing the size of a chart, as data series proportions can be misleading. For example, if you stretch the height of a chart without maintaining the original proportions, you visually exaggerate the numerical differences in the data, which can change the impact of the information.

If you want to delete a chart, simply select the chart and press (Del).

You can create a chart on its own sheet in the default (2-D column) chart type by selecting the data and pressing (F11) or the (Alt) + (F1) key combination. You can then modify the chart by using the chart commands.

Lesson 2: Formatting Text in a Chart

On Your Mark
What types of circumstances warrant changing the appearance of the text in the chart's titles, axes labels, or a legend?

After you create a chart, you can format chart text to enhance the chart's title, axes labels, or legend. You can even change the emphasis of the chart's details. You can change text in a chart simply by clicking the text area you want to modify and then making the change, or by formatting the text in the entire chart area at the same time.

Project 6 Using Charts and Maps

> **Tip for Instructors**
> In Excel 97, you don't have to double-click an embedded chart to work on it. Just click a chart component to select it in order to make a change.

You change the format of the text in Excel charts using the same methods you use to format text in worksheet cells. Now try formatting text in the chart you created in Lesson 1.

To Format Text in a Chart

> **Tip for Students**
> When you click an embedded chart to select it, the ranges on the worksheet are outlined in blue, green, and purple. These outlines designate which worksheet cells make up the chart components.

❶ In the Expenses worksheet, scroll up until you can see the top of the chart. If the handles are not displayed, click anywhere in the chart area.

The selected chart can be edited and formatted. The Chart Objects text box in the Chart toolbar shows that the chart area is selected.

If you cannot see the Chart toolbar on your screen, choose **V**iew, **T**oolbars, and then click the Chart option.

❷ Click the Format Chart Area button on the Chart toolbar.

The Format Chart Area dialog box is displayed.

> **Tip for Students**
> With the chart selected, you can point to a chart object with the mouse, and a ScreenTip appears.

❸ Click the Font tab.

This displays the Font options used to change the appearance of text in a chart, as shown in Figure 6.6.

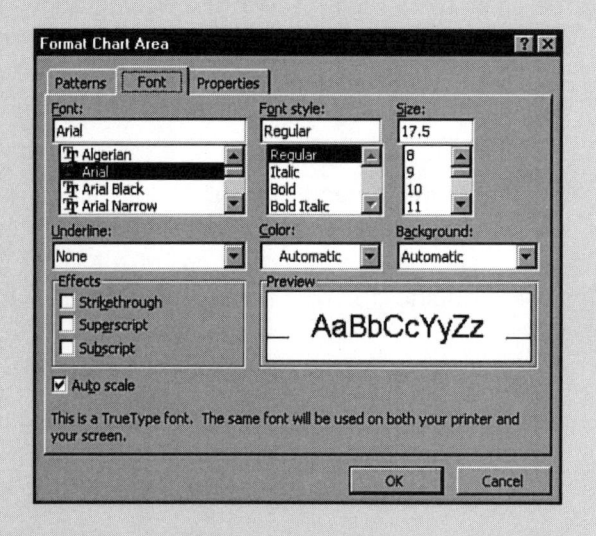

Figure 6.6
The Font tab of the Format Chart Area dialog box enables you to change the appearance of the chart text.

> **Tip for Students**
> Note that you can preview font changes before making a final selection.

❹ In the Font list, select Times New Roman. In the Font style list, select Bold. In the Size list, select 8. Then click OK.

This changes all of the text in the chart to the Times New Roman font with bold style, and reduces the font size to 8 points.

❺ Double-click the chart's title.

A selection box appears around the chart's title and the Format Chart Title dialog box appears.

> **Quicksand**
> If students double-click the chart title and get an insertion point instead of the Format Chart Title dialog box, just have them click elsewhere on the worksheet and try again.

❻ Click the Font tab if it is not displayed.

Lesson 2: Formatting Text in a Chart   159

> **Speedy Class**
> Discuss the use of the text box button on the Drawing toolbar for adding text beyond the chart title and axes titles.

7 In the Size list box, select 24; then click OK.

This increases the size of the chart's title to 24 points and closes the dialog box.

8 Scroll down the worksheet until the bottom of the chart appears; then double-click a Category (X) axis label.

The Format Axis dialog box appears. Now you will change the orientation (direction) of the text for the Category (X) axis. From the Chart toolbar, you can rotate text up or down 45 degrees; however, if you want the text to be rotated 90 degrees, you need to use the Alignment tab in this dialog box.

9 Click the Alignment tab of the Format Axis dialog box.

The alignment options are displayed, as shown in Figure 6.7.

Figure 6.7
The orientation of the text for the chart's titles, except for the legend, can be rotated upward or downward.

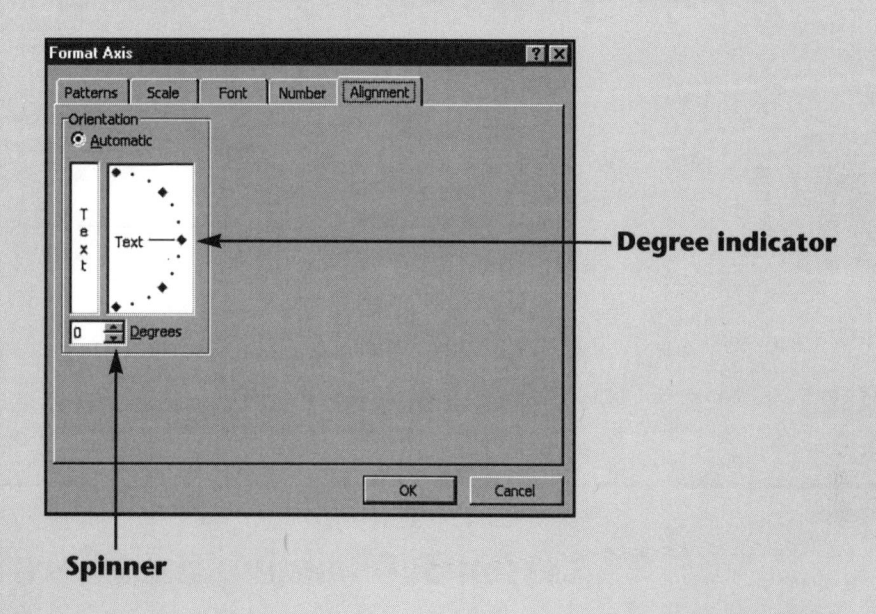

— Degree indicator

Spinner

> **Tip for Students**
> Users can also use the spinner buttons to change the degree of text orientation.

> **Speedy Class**
> While on the Alignment tab, experiment with various alignment options, discussing situations in which you might want an alternative alignment.

10 Drag the degree indicator up until 90 degrees is displayed; then click OK.

The Format Axis dialog box closes. Now view the completed chart in its own window. This eliminates scrolling through the worksheet to view a chart, and chart editing can be done while the chart is open in the window.

11 Choose View, Chart Window.

The entire chart appears in a chart window that is the same size as the chart on your worksheet, as shown in Figure 6.8.

continues

Project 6 Using Charts and Maps

To Format Text in a Chart (continued)

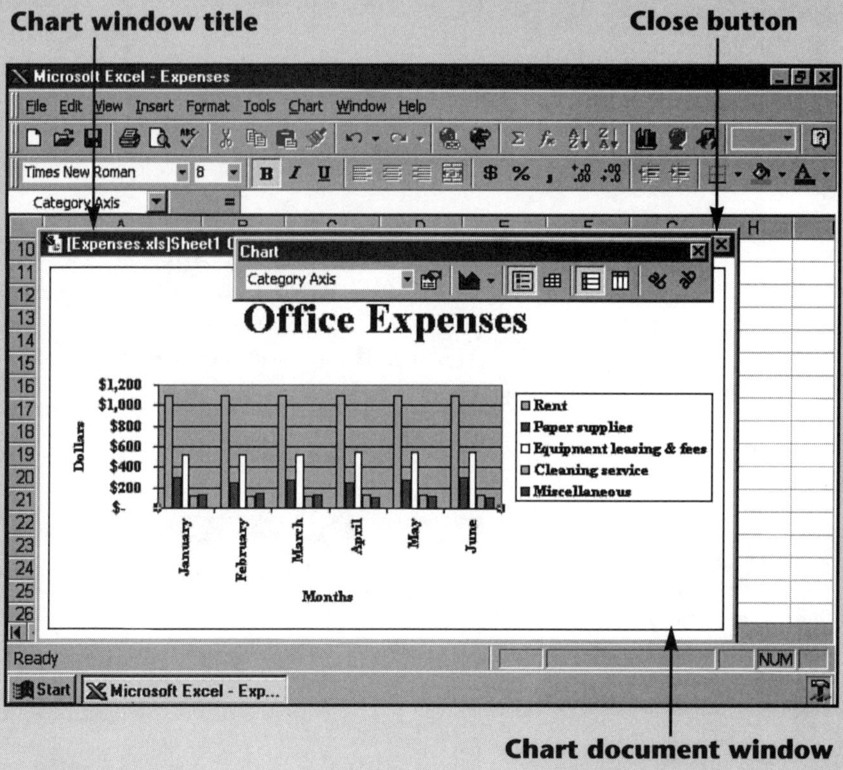

Figure 6.8
The chart title now appears in 24-point Times New Roman. The legend, Value (Y) axis, and Category (X) axis appear in 8-point Times New Roman. The Category axis is rotated 90 degrees.

Chart window title — *Close button* — *Chart document window*

12 Click the Close button on the chart window.

The chart window is closed. Save your work and keep the Expenses worksheet open. In Lesson 3, you learn how to change chart types.

Lesson 3: Changing the Chart Type

On Your Mark

The type of chart you use can enhance the message you want your numbers to give. Consider the following groups of numbers and the types of charts that would best display meaningful results: one group of data pieces that make up a whole, a trend over a period of time, or comparisons of items.

After you create a chart, you may decide that you do not like the type of chart you have selected. Because Excel has a wide variety of chart types, you can display information in a way that best conveys its meaning.

Certain chart types are best for certain situations. It is important to select a chart type that can help you display the information in the most dramatic, appropriate, and meaningful manner possible. For example, you can usually spot trends more easily with a line chart, while a pie chart is best for showing parts of a whole.

Now try changing the Expenses chart to a different type of chart.

Lesson 3: Changing the Chart Type   161

To Change the Chart Type

> **Quicksand**
> The Chart toolbar may not appear (or may not be obvious) on all screens, depending on whether it was used and where it was used last. Show students how to display the Chart toolbar if it's not visible on-screen.

❶ In the Expenses **worksheet, make sure the chart is selected and the Chart toolbar is displayed.**

Eight selection handles appear on the chart box frame to show that the chart is selected, as shown in Figure 6.9. When you select the chart, the Chart toolbar automatically appears so that the tools associated with charting are available for your use.

Figure 6.9
The selected chart has a border and selection handles.

❷ Click the drop-down arrow next to the Chart Type button on the Chart toolbar.

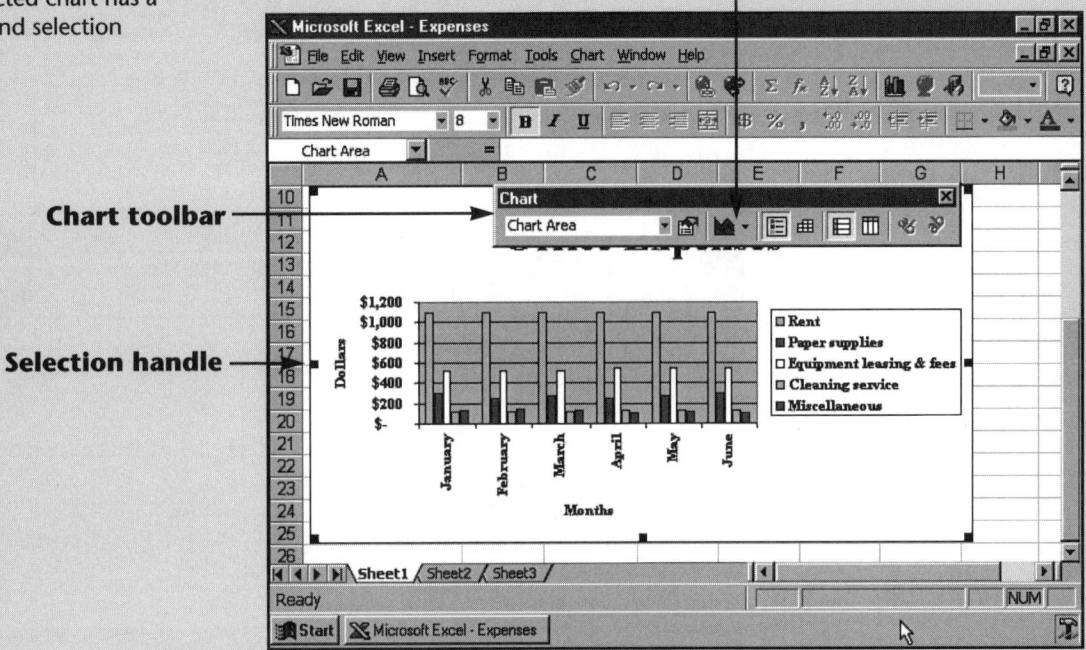

The various chart types are displayed in a three-column, drop-down list, as shown in Figure 6.10. If you cannot see the Chart toolbar on your screen, choose **V**iew, **T**oolbars, and then click the Chart option.

continues

Project 6 Using Charts and Maps

To Change the Chart Type (continued)

Figure 6.10
Select a chart type from the drop-down list.

Line Chart button

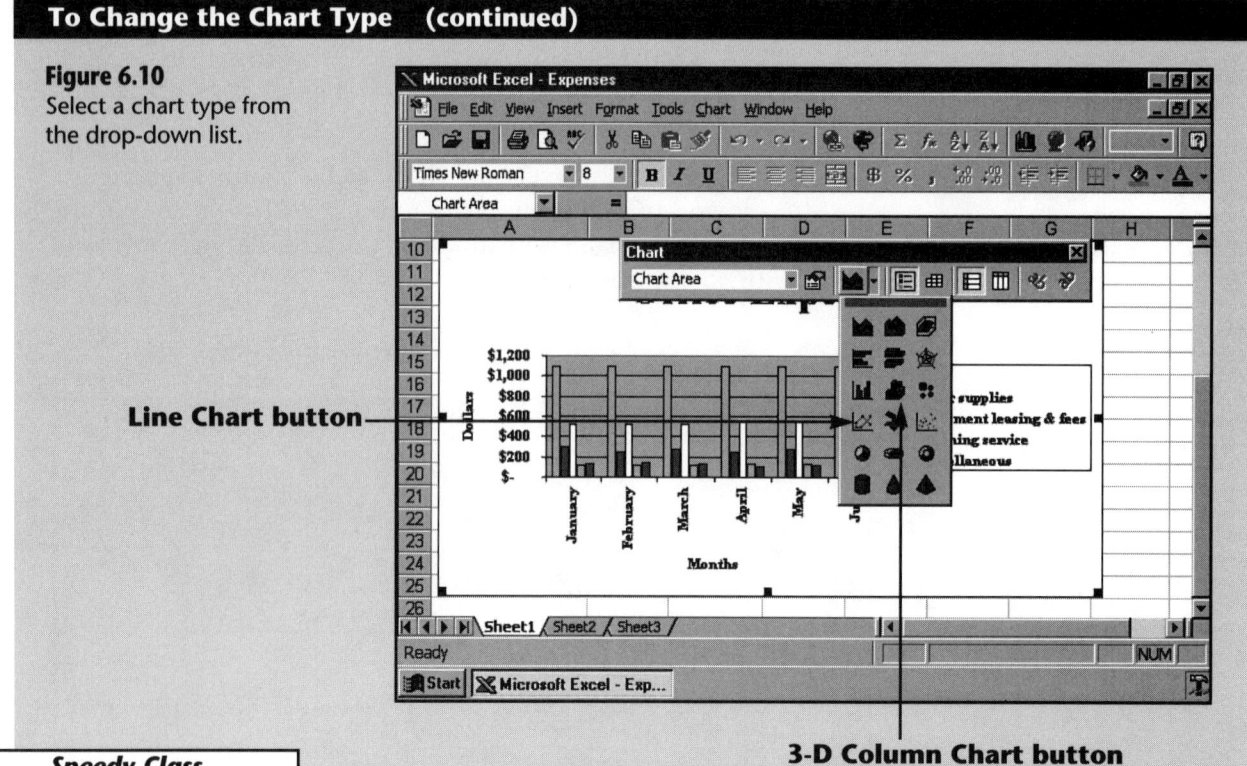

3-D Column Chart button

Speedy Class
Sometimes the chart type you have chosen is right for the job, but your chart is disproportionate. Try resizing the chart, stretching it horizontally or vertically, or making it more compact before giving up on a chart type.

3 Click the 3-D Column Chart button (the third button down in the second column).

Excel changes the chart type to the 3-D column format, as shown in Figure 6.11.

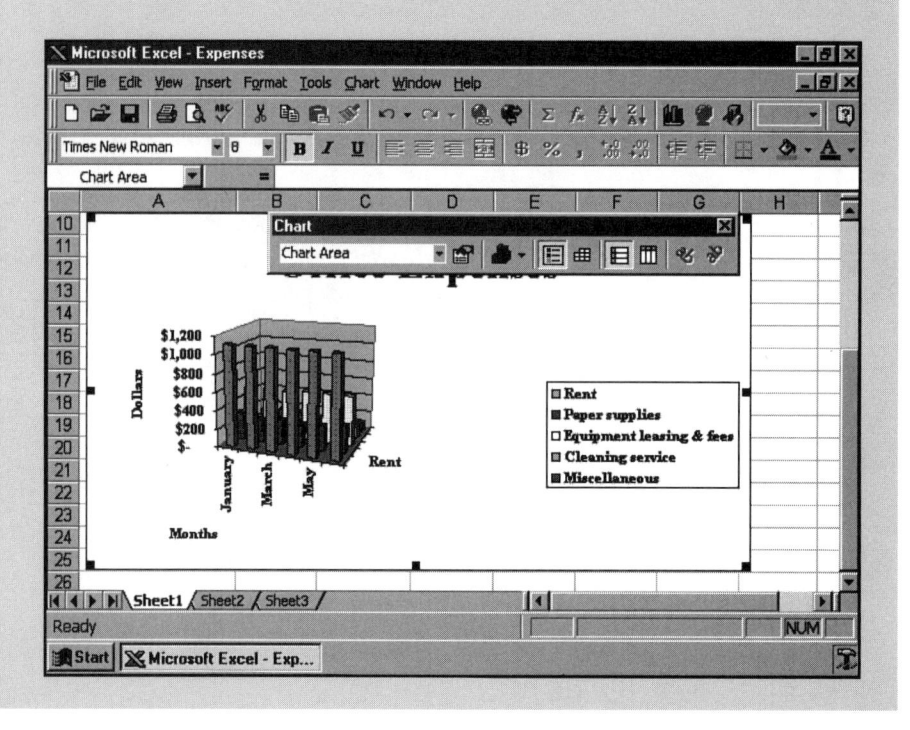

Figure 6.11
The Expenses data appears as a 3-D column chart.

Lesson 3: Changing the Chart Type

The 3-D column chart does not provide a very good representation of your data. If you want to examine the trends of the source of your income over time, there may be better chart types to use. Consult Table 6.1 to learn more about the different chart types and how they represent your data. Now you will select another type of chart that can more clearly illustrate the trend.

❹ In the Chart Type drop-down list, click the Line Chart button (the fourth button down in the first column).

The chart type changes to a line chart, as shown in Figure 6.12.

Figure 6.12
In a line chart, you can easily examine trends over time.

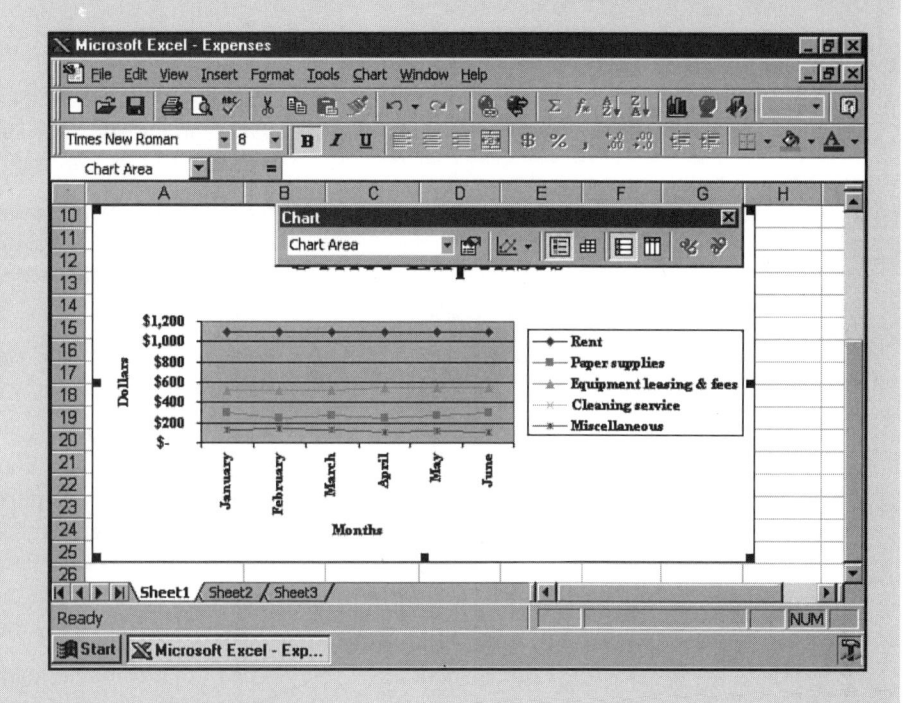

Save your work and keep the Expenses worksheet open. In Lesson 4, you learn how to enhance your chart's appearance.

If you have problems...

If you are not sure which chart type to select for a specific job, select one chart type and study the results. Check to see whether the data is accurately represented and conveys the appropriate meaning. Try various chart types until you find the one that best suits your needs.

Table 6.1 describes the various chart types available in Excel.

Table 6.1 Common Chart Types

Chart Type	Description
Area	A line chart that shows the area below the line filled with a color or pattern. Use an area chart to compare several sets of data.
Bar or Column	A chart that represents data by the height of the vertical columns or length of the horizontal bars. Use a bar chart to compare one item to another or to compare different items over a period of time.
Line	A chart consisting of a series of data at various points along the axis. The points are connected by a line. Use a line chart to indicate a trend over a period of time.
Pie	A circular chart in which each piece (wedge) shows a data segment and its relationship to the whole. Use a pie chart to sort data and compare parts of the whole.
Doughnut	A circular ring-shaped chart that compares the sizes of pieces in a whole. It is similar to a pie chart but can include multiple data series, appearing in concentric rings.
Radar	A line or area chart enclosed around a central point. Use a radar chart to show the uniformity of data.
XY or Bubble (Scatter)	A chart in which data points are placed along the Value (Y) axis and a numeric X-axis, similar to a line chart. Use an XY chart to compare trends over uneven time or measurement intervals (scientific data). Use a Bubble chart to plot two variables against the Category (X) and Value (Y) axis, similar to the XY chart, adding a third variable represented by the size of the bubble.
Combination	A chart that combines parts from a line, bar, or area chart so that you can plot data in two forms on the same chart. Use a combination chart to show a correlation between two data series.
Surface	A chart that represents optimum combinations between two sets of data. Patterns and colors are added to indicate sections that are in the same range of values.
Stock	A chart to plot stock prices; the data must be organized in the correct order. It can also be used for scientific data.
3-D (Area, Bar, Line, Pie)	A chart that represents data in the same way as its two-dimensional counterpart. Besides displaying height and width, however, a 3-D chart adds depth to the appearance of the chart.
Cone, Cylinder, Pyramid	A chart that enhances the data markers on 3-D column and bar charts.

Lesson 4: Enhancing a Chart

> **✓ On Your Mark**
> Have you done enough to make your chart express the idea you want to get across? Can you think of other ways in which to enhance your chart and make it more useful?

After you have decided which type of chart best conveys the information in your worksheet, you can enhance the chart's appearance in several ways. The most common enhancements include changing chart colors, adding a grid, and formatting the chart labels.

The easiest way to change any part of a chart is to select the chart, move the mouse pointer over the part you want to change, click the right mouse button, and then choose a command from the shortcut menu.

Now try using this easy method to enhance the Expenses chart.

To Enhance a Chart

> **Quicksand**
> Make sure that students have either selected the area they intend to enhance or have carefully positioned the mouse over the appropriate area. Also make certain they don't move the mouse to another part of the chart before clicking.

❶ In the Expenses worksheet, make sure that the chart is selected.

With the chart selected, the selection handles are displayed and individual elements of the chart can be edited.

❷ Right-click one of the points of the line representing Rent in the chart.

A shortcut menu appears and the Rent line is selected, as shown in Figure 6.13.

Figure 6.13
Each element of a chart has its own shortcut menu for editing.

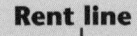

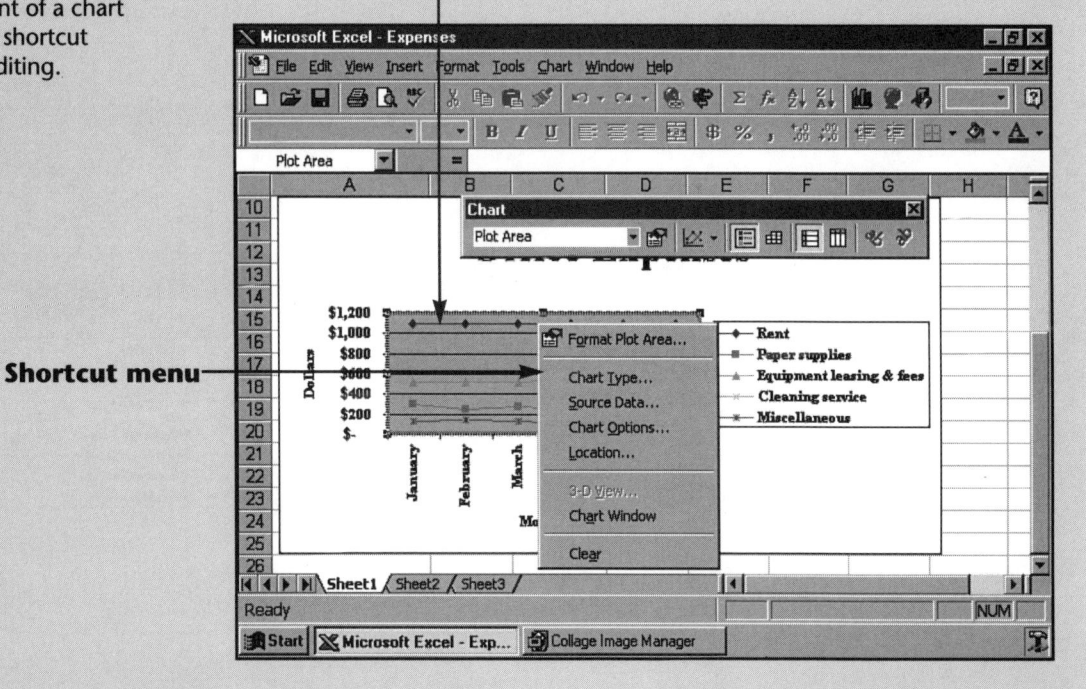

❸ Choose Chart Type from the shortcut menu.

The Chart Type dialog box appears, as shown in Figure 6.14.

continues

Project 6 Using Charts and Maps

To Enhance a Chart (continued)

Figure 6.14
The Chart Type dialog box enables you to change the chart type and subtype.

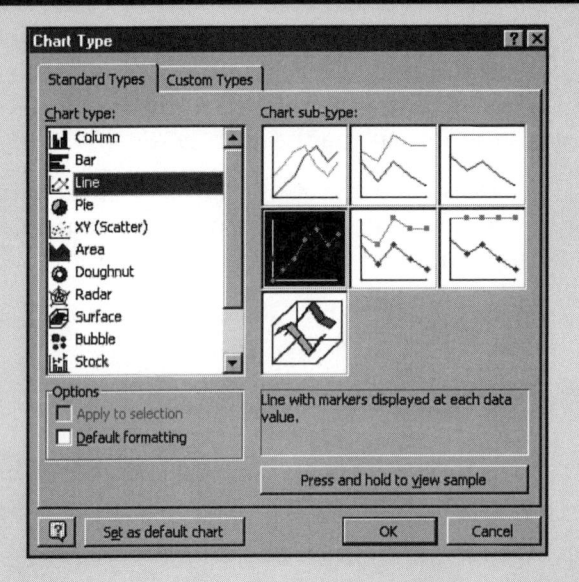

❹ **Click Area in the Chart type list; then click the first chart (Area) in the Chart sub-type list and click OK.**

The chart is now a combination area and line chart, as shown in Figure 6.15. Rent, the element you selected to edit, is represented by the large area from $- to the straight black line at $1100 on the Value (Y) axis, while the rest of the chart remains unchanged. Now change the color of the total area.

Figure 6.15
This is an example of a combination area and line chart.

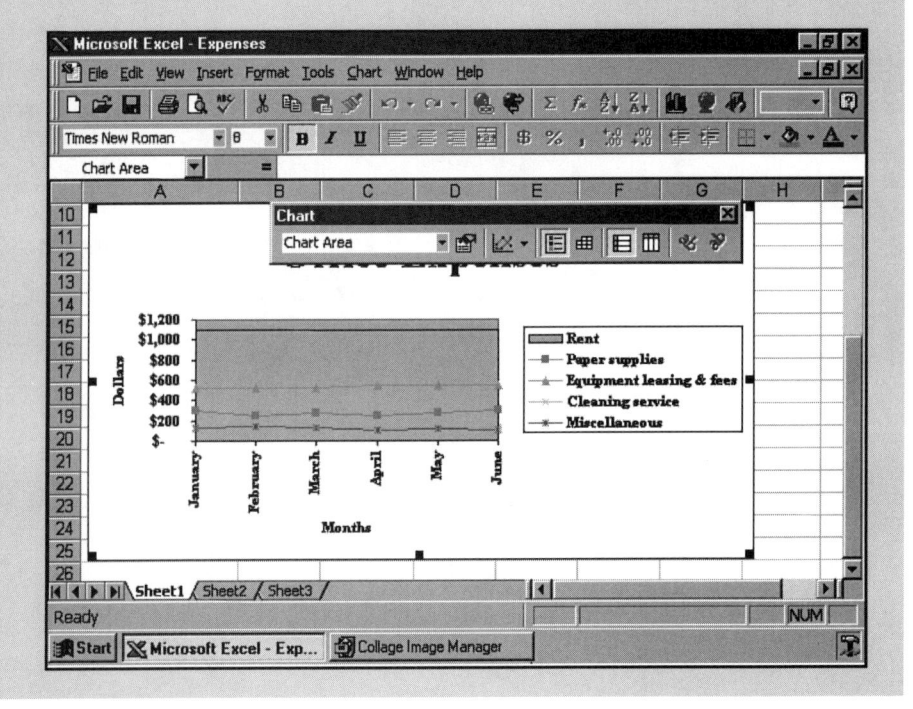

Lesson 4: Enhancing a Chart   167

5 **Right-click the Rent area and choose Format Data Series from the shortcut menu.**

The Format Data Series dialog box opens with the Patterns tab selected. In the Area section of the dialog box, a palette of colors is displayed. The current color for the Rent area is shown in the Sample box in the lower-left corner.

6 **Select gray, the third color down in the last column.**

The new color appears in the Sample box, as shown in Figure 6.16.

Figure 6.16
The Format Data Series dialog box enables you to choose a new color for the selected data series.

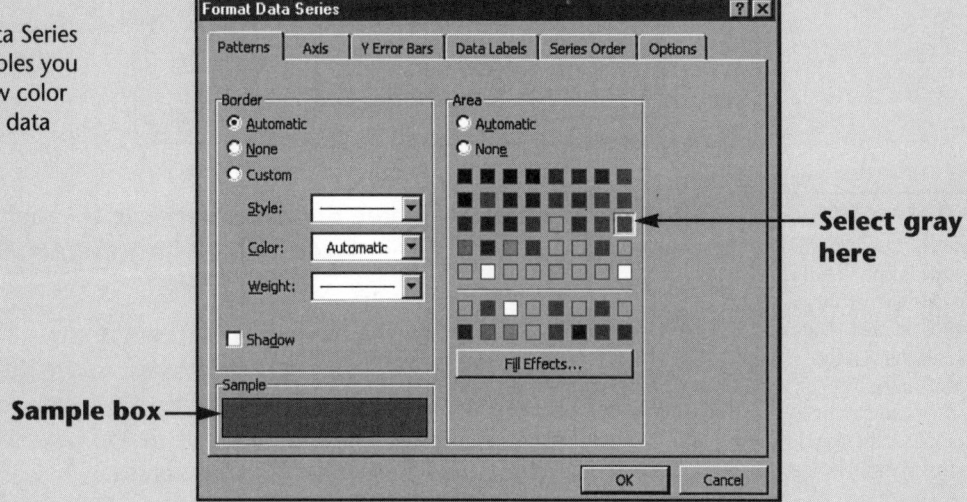

Sample box

Select gray here

7 **Click OK.**

The dialog box closes and the new color appears in the chart. Now you will change the number format of the labels on the Value (Y) axis to show dollars with two decimal places.

8 **Right-click any of the dollar amounts on the Value (Y) axis of the chart and choose Format Axis from the shortcut menu.**

The Format Axis dialog box appears.

9 **Select the Number tab.**

The Number tab and its options appear with the Custom category selected, as shown in Figure 6.17.

continues

Project 6 Using Charts and Maps

To Enhance a Chart (continued)

Figure 6.17
On the Number tab of the Format Axis dialog box, you can specify a different number format.

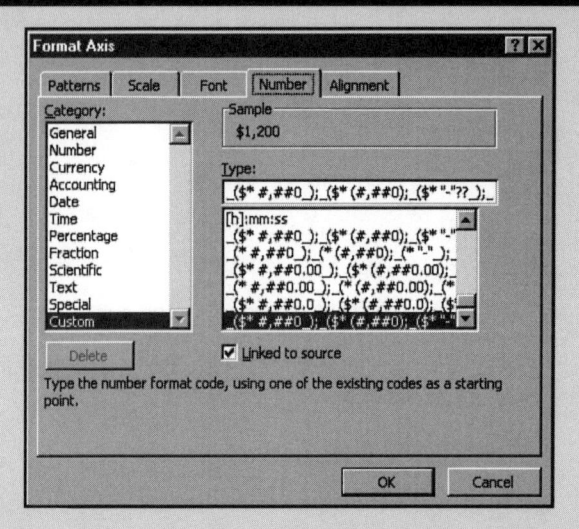

> **Tip for Instructors**
> Chart enhancement is an area in which students love to experiment. Give them the general guidelines such as the following: how to select an object and then right-click to see the available menu options, mention the types of objects they can alter, and give some specific suggestions for enhancing their chart. Make sure that you also let them be creative.

⑩ Scroll through the Type list and select the type with a dollar sign and two decimal places, $#,##0.00_);($#,##0.00); then click OK.

Excel applies this format, which includes a $ sign, a comma as a thousands separator, and two decimal places, to the dollar values on the Value (Y) axis, as shown in Figure 6.18. Save your work and keep the Expenses workbook open. You use it in the next lesson to learn how to print a worksheet that includes a chart.

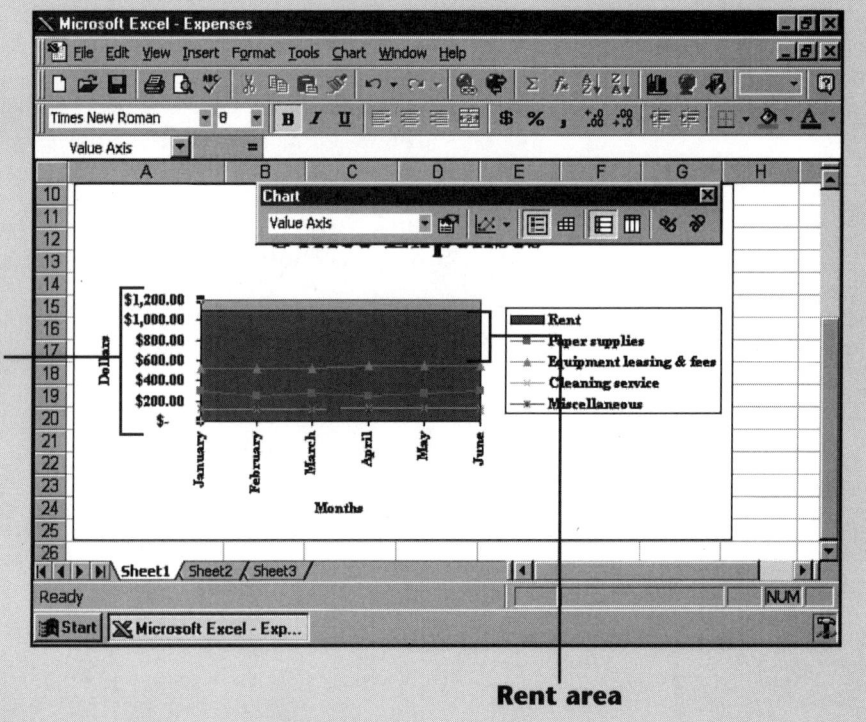

Figure 6.18
The enhanced chart is easier to read.

Dollar values have two decimal places

> **Speedy Class**
> Ask students to share ideas with the class. Try to keep them focused on making a chart that will serve to illuminate certain features about the numbers being charted. Remind students of the Undo button if they find they're disappointed with the results of enhancement attempts.

Rent area

Lesson 5: Printing a Chart

> **On Your Mark**
> What are the advantages of printing a chart instead of viewing it on-screen?

Unless you want to carry around a laptop computer to show your work on-screen, you need to be able to print your worksheets.

Printing lets you view the worksheets you have created, even when you are away from your computer. A printed copy of a chart combined with the worksheet data makes a very effective presentation. Now try printing the entire Expenses workbook file, including the chart.

To Print a Chart

> **Tip for Students**
> Before printing, be sure to view your chart on-screen with the Print Preview feature.

> **Tip for Students**
> You can also access the Page Setup dialog box directly from the Print Preview window by clicking the **S**etup button.

1 In the Expenses **worksheet, click anywhere outside the chart.**

This makes sure that no range in the worksheet is selected, not even the chart. The Chart toolbar is removed from the screen.

2 Choose File, Page Setup.

The Page Setup dialog box appears, as shown in Figure 6.19. Use this dialog box to adjust the page setup before you print your worksheet. This dialog box provides a wide range of options from which you can choose to customize your printed worksheet. For this example, you will change the margins, header, and footer for the printed worksheet.

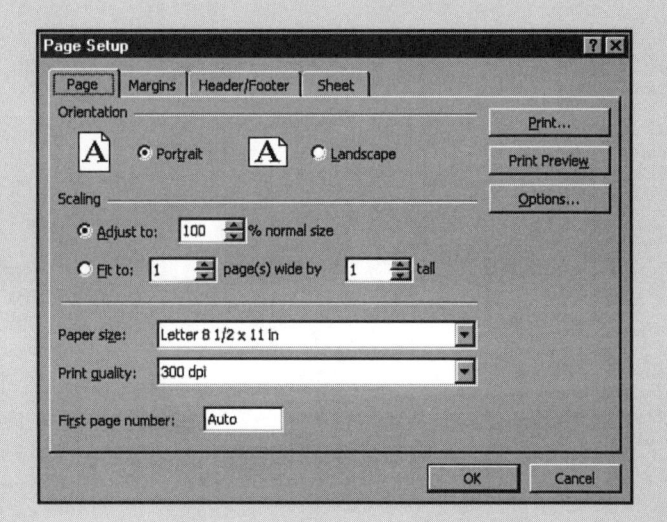

Figure 6.19
The Page Setup dialog box.

3 In the Page Setup dialog box, click the Header/Footer tab.

The Header and Footer options let you specify information to print in the header and footer area of each page. You can choose from predefined headers and footers, or you can create your own.

4 Click the drop-down arrow next to the Header text box, scroll up, and select (none).

This removes the default header text, and nothing will print in the header area.

continues

Project 6 Using Charts and Maps

To Print a Chart (continued)

5 **Click the drop-down arrow next to the Footer text box and select Expenses.**

This footer prints the current file name in the center of the footer area.

6 **Click the Margins tab in the Page Setup dialog box.**

This displays the Margins options.

7 **In the Top text box, click the up arrow twice.**

This changes the top margin from 1 to 1.5.

8 **In the Bottom text box, click the down arrow once.**

This changes the bottom margin from 1 to 0.75. You have now finished setting up the worksheet page for printing. Now preview the page to make sure it is the way you want it to print.

9 **Click the Print Preview button in the Page Setup dialog box.**

Excel closes the Page Setup dialog box, makes the changes you requested to the page setup, and displays the Print Preview window, as shown in Figure 6.20. In Print Preview, you can see the worksheet as it will look when you print it. (You can also open the Print Preview window by clicking the Print Preview button on the Standard toolbar when the Page Setup dialog box is not open.) Everything looks right, so you are ready to print.

> **Tip for Students**
>
> If the chart is selected before opening the Page Setup dialog box, Excel assumes that you want to print the chart on a page by itself. You can get Page Setup options that relate specifically to the chart.

Figure 6.20
Print Preview shows you the page as it will print, including the chart.

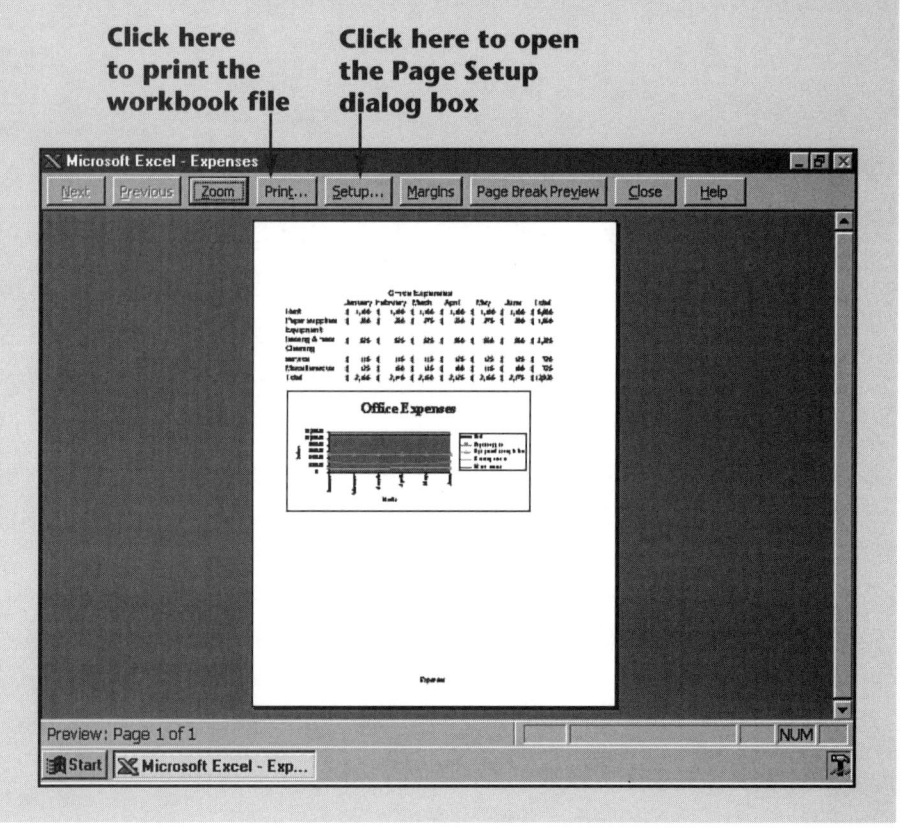

Click here to print the workbook file

Click here to open the Page Setup dialog box

Lesson 6: Creating a Map

Tip for Instructors
Discuss returning to the main worksheet screen from the Print Preview screen for editing changes.

10 **Click the Print button on the Print Preview toolbar.**

The Print Preview window closes and the Print dialog box appears.

11 **In the Number of Copies text box, change the number of copies to 2 and then click OK.**

Excel prints two copies of the worksheet, including the chart. When you are done printing, save and close the Expenses workbook. In Lesson 7, you learn how to create a map by using data in a different workbook file.

> **INSIDE**
>
> You can print just a chart in Excel without printing the entire worksheet. Select the chart; then choose **F**ile, **P**rint to open the Print dialog box. Click the Selected Chart option button in the Print What area, and then click OK.
>
> If you want to leave additional space between the chart and the worksheet data, simply select the chart and drag it down a few rows. Remember to deselect the chart before printing.

Lesson 6: Creating a Map

On Your Mark
Can you think of situations in which a geographic mapping of business locations or events might be useful? How would it be helpful to see a map where your company sales offices are geographically located? How would a map showing where company sales are the highest be helpful?

Maps are useful for charting information that is defined by state, country, or province. Maps are not one of Excel's built-in chart types; rather, they are a separate feature of Excel. Maps can help you visualize your worksheet information geographically. In this lesson, you compare how many company offices are located in different states in the U.S. By creating a map, you can see where most of the offices are located.

Try creating a map now, using the sample worksheet provided.

To Create a Map

Quicksand
Make sure that Microsoft Data Map software has been installed in the training room machines before class begins. Suggest to students that they may need to go back to Excel setup if this feature is unavailable on their home computers.

1 **Open the file Proj0602 on this book's companion disk and save it as SiteMap.**

2 **Select cell A3. Hold down ⇧Shift and press Ctrl+End.**

This selects all the data in the worksheet so that the information can be used to create your map.

3 **Click the Map button on the Standard toolbar.**

The mouse pointer changes to a crosshair, which you can use to specify where in the worksheet Excel should create the map.

continues

Project 6 Using Charts and Maps

To Create a Map (continued)

Tip for Students
Dragging through the designated map cells is optional. You can click the worksheet at the place where the upper-left corner of the map should appear, and Excel will fill in the map.

❹ Click cell A21 and hold down the left mouse button; then drag the mouse to cell G35.

When you release the mouse button, Excel begins creating the map in the range A21:G35. This may take a few seconds. Excel looks to see which map the data belongs in, based on the geographical data included in the selected data range. If the data could fit in more than one map (which is the case in this example), the Multiple Maps Available dialog box appears, as shown in Figure 6.21.

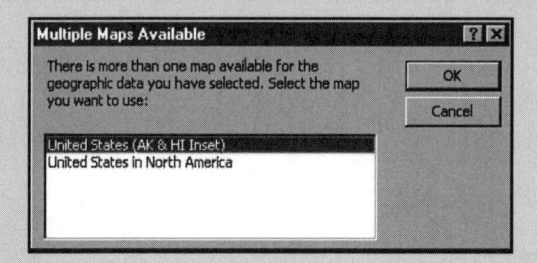

Figure 6.21
The Multiple Maps Available dialog box.

Tip for Students
To move the Data Map Control dialog box (if it blocks worksheet data), drag the title bar of the dialog box.

❺ Select United States in North America; then click OK.

You may have to wait for several seconds while Excel composes the map. The map appears in the selected cells along with the Microsoft Map Control dialog box, as shown in Figure 6.22. The map is inserted into a frame, which you can use to resize and move the map. You can use the Microsoft Map Control dialog box to change some formatting characteristics of the map. Currently, the # of Offices column is displayed in the map. Because the shading values in the map are not easy to discern, try changing the colors of the map now.

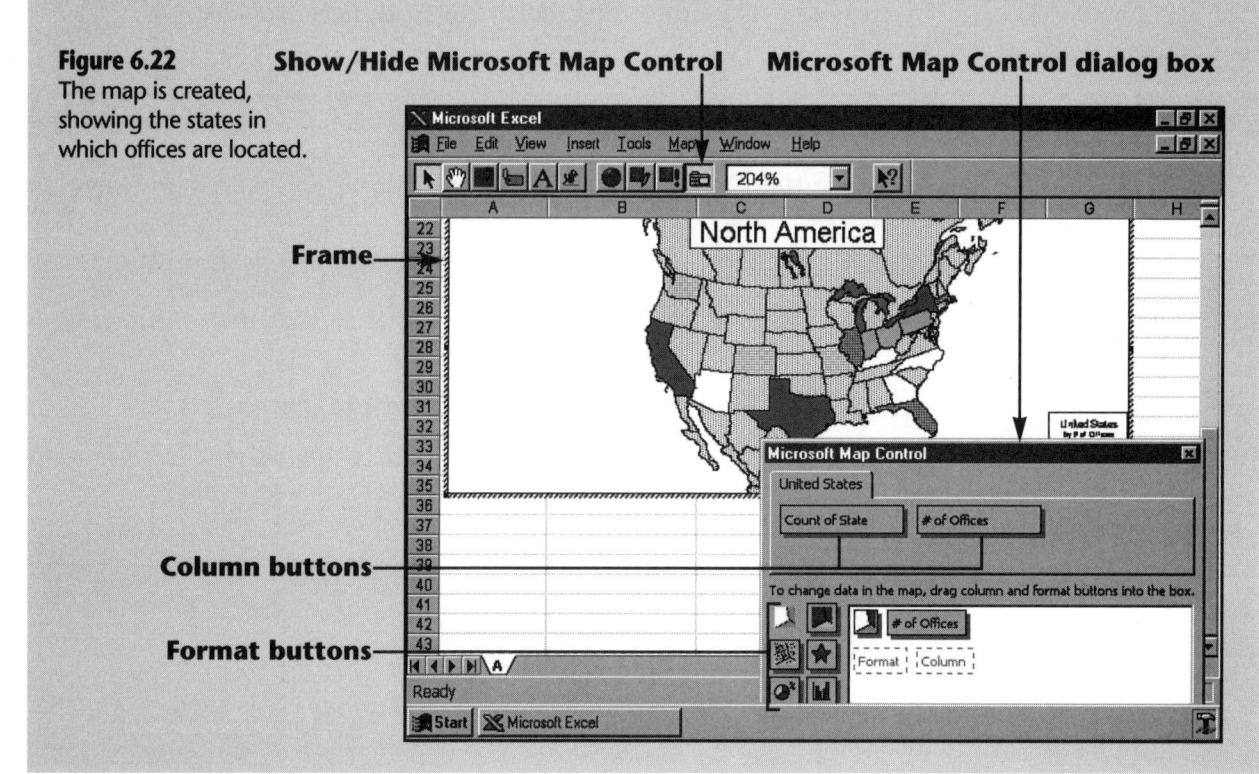

Figure 6.22
The map is created, showing the states in which offices are located.

Lesson 6: Creating a Map

> **If you have problems...**
>
> If the Microsoft Map Control dialog box is covering the map so you cannot see it, simply drag the dialog box out of the way. You can open and close the dialog box by using the Show/Hide Microsoft Map Control button on the toolbar.

6 In the Microsoft Map Control dialog box, drag the Category Shading button onto the # of Offices button, as shown in Figure 6.23.

Figure 6.23
Use the Microsoft Map Control dialog box to change the format of the map.

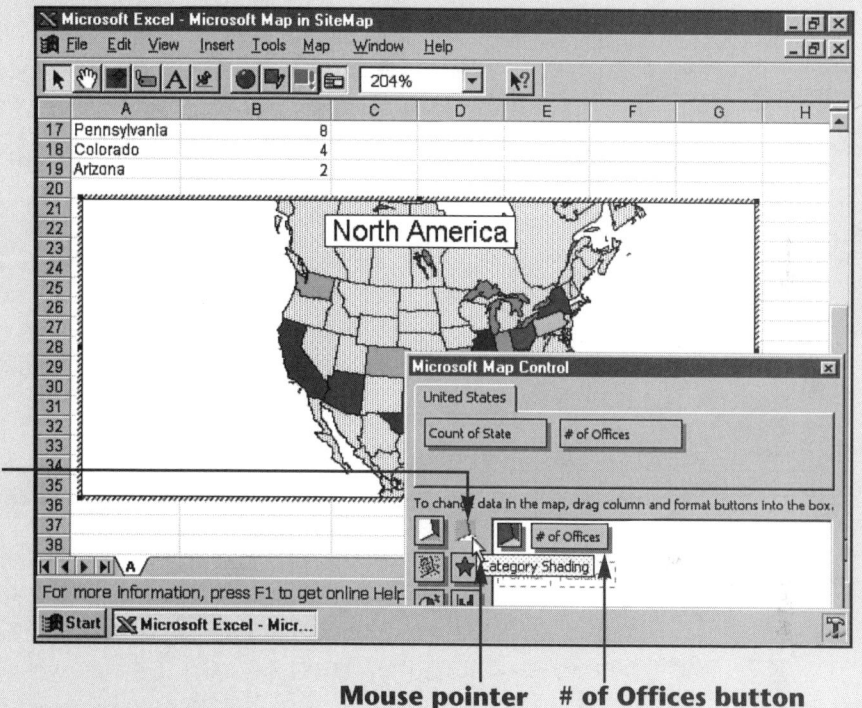

Category Shading button

Mouse pointer   **# of Offices button**

When you release the mouse button, Excel redraws the map, adding color to indicate the number of offices in each state.

7 Close the Microsoft Map Control dialog box.

The map is complete, as shown in Figure 6.24. The location of offices is now clearly indicated by different colors. The expanded legend is partially hidden in the map frame and is difficult to read.

continues

Project 6 Using Charts and Maps

To Create a Map (continued)

Figure 6.24
The map with an expanded legend.

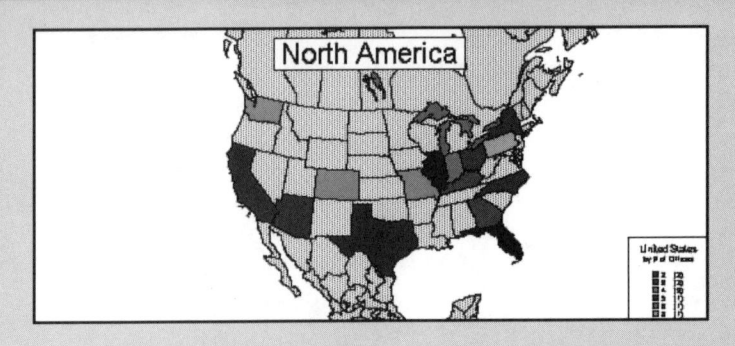

> **Quicksand**
>
> When you click a map to select it, eight selection handles appear around the border for moving or resizing. When you double-click a map to activate it, a thick border surrounds the map. Now you can format objects such as the legend and title.

> **Tip for Students**
>
> An expanded legend is the default format for a map legend. If you right-click the legend, you can choose **C**ompact Legend from the shortcut menu, or even hide the legend.

> **Q&A**
>
> What other types of changes can be made to the text? (Answer: Changes to font, type size, and attributes.)

8 Drag the legend up to display the entire box.

9 Drag the upper-left corner of the legend box up and to the left (approximately even with row 24); then click inside the map to deselect the box.

You can now see the colors and the numbers in the legend to identify which part of the country has the greatest number of offices (the number identifies the number of offices in each state by color; the number in parentheses identifies how many states have that number of offices). You decide to focus your research on the states surrounding Ohio. Try zooming in on the map now.

10 Click the Zoom Percentage of Map drop-down arrow; then select 400%.

Excel redraws the map, increasing its magnification. Now change the title of the map.

> **If you have problems...**
>
> If you are unhappy with the view, use the Zoom Percentage of Map button to change the view percentage. You can return to the previous view by opening the **V**iew menu and choosing **P**revious. To view the entire map, choose **V**iew, **E**ntire Map.

11 Double-click the Map title.

This selects the map's title and positions an insertion point in the text so that you can enter and edit the title text. You can change the text as well as the text attributes, including font, font size, and font style.

12 Change the text to Office Locations; then press ⏎Enter.

This changes the map's title. You can drag it to a new location on the map or resize it so that it does not cover any of the target states.

13 Drag the map title to the upper-left corner of the map.

The map title is moved. You can also reposition the map within its frame.

Lesson 6: Creating a Map

Speedy Class

Students can try changing the Zoom percentage and repositioning the map inside the frame by using the Grabber button.

Figure 6.25
The completed map appears below the worksheet data.

Q&A

What types of information might you include in a map of state names? (Answer: Sales by state, number of employees by state, number of office locations in each state, and so on.)

⑭ Click the Grabber button on the Microsoft Map toolbar; then click the map and drag it around in the frame until it is positioned to the left of the legend.

Click anywhere outside the map frame to deselect it. The map is complete, as shown in Figure 6.25. Save your work. If requested by your instructor, print two copies of the worksheet with the map. Then close the workbook.

If you have completed your session on the computer, exit Excel and Windows 95 before turning off your computer. Otherwise, continue with "Checking Your Skills" at the end of this project.

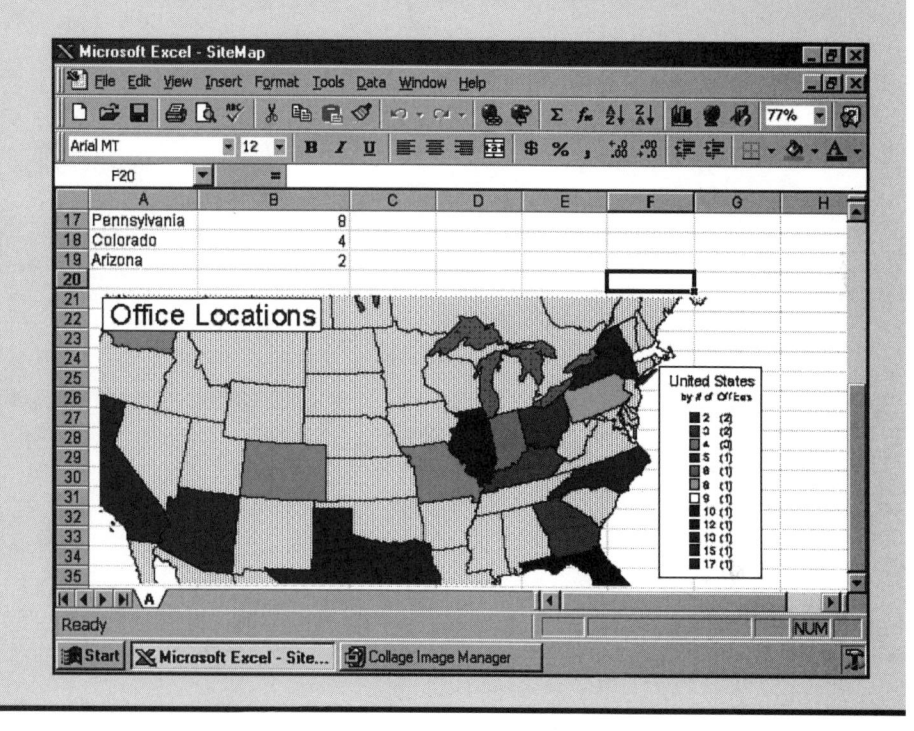

When creating a map, you need to have two columns of data. The first column contains the name of the region, state, or country. You can use abbreviations—such as WV, TN, NC, and so on—or you can use the state's full name. The second column contains the worksheet information. The data in the second column is represented on the map by colors and/or patterns.

As with the elements in a chart, you can right-click elements in a map to open a shortcut menu. You can use the commands on the shortcut menus to quickly edit or enhance the parts of the map.

To print the worksheet with the map, choose **F**ile, **P**rint, select the options you want in the Print dialog box, and then click OK. To print the map without printing the entire worksheet, select the worksheet cells surrounding the map, click the Selectio**n** option button in the Print dialog box, and then click OK. You can change options such as the header, footer, and margins by using the Page Setup dialog box, just as you do for all worksheets.

Project 6 Using Charts and Maps

Project Summary

To	Do This
Start the Chart Wizard	Select the range to be charted; then click the Chart Wizard button on the Standard toolbar or choose **I**nsert, **Ch**art.
Select a chart	Click the chart.
Format a chart element	Click the chart element and click the right mouse button. From the shortcut menu, choose the **Fo**rmat option.
Change a chart type	Select the chart; then choose a chart type from the Chart Type drop-down list on the Chart toolbar.
Print a chart	Select the chart; then click the Print button on the Standard toolbar.
Create a map	Select the range to be mapped; then click the Map button on the Standard toolbar and click in the worksheet where you want the upper-left corner of the map to appear.

Checking Your Skills

True/False

For each of the following, check *T* or *F* to indicate whether the statement is true or false.

__T ✔F 1. A chart can only be placed on the worksheet with the data.

✔T __F 2. Charts and maps are objects on the worksheet.

__T ✔F 3. An embedded chart must be viewed in a chart window before the elements can be selected, moved, copied, sized, or formatted.

__T ✔F 4. The Category (X) axis provides the scale used to measure the data in the chart.

✔T __F 5. After a chart is created, you can choose another chart type if you are not satisfied with the representation of your data.

✔T __F 6. An object has its own frame.

✔T __F 7. When creating a map, the first column of data should contain the names of regions, states, or countries.

__T ✔F 8. Three ways to create a chart from selected data in Excel are by pressing (F1), pressing (Alt)+(F1), and using the Chart Wizard.

__T ✔F 9. Excel cannot create three-dimensional charts.

✔T __F 10. You should resize a chart before formatting it.

Multiple Choice

Circle the letter of the correct answer for each of the following questions.

1. Which type of chart usually helps you spot trends easily?
   a. area
   b. column
   c. line
   d. pie

2. Which type of chart is best for showing parts of a whole?
   a. area
   b. column
   c. line
   d. pie

3. What is the element of a chart that identifies colors or patterns assigned to a data series or chart categories?
   a. chart area
   b. chart title
   c. legend
   d. value (Y) axis

4. What are some common enhancements that are often made to a chart to improve its appearance?
   a. add a grid
   b. change colors
   c. format the chart labels
   d. all the above

5. How many columns of data are needed in your worksheet to create a map?
   a. one
   b. two
   c. three
   d. as many as you want

6. The default chart type is what?
   a. column
   b. bar
   c. pie
   d. line

7. The mouse pointer changes to which of the following when you drag a chart?
   a. 2-headed arrow
   b. 4-headed arrow
   c. hand
   d. pointing finger

8. Three-dimensional charts have a third axis, called what?
   a. x-axis
   b. y-axis
   c. z-axis
   d. d-axis

9. Which of the following is used to identify the data in a chart?
   a. legend
   b. gallery
   c. Chart Wizard
   d. none of the above

10. Use which type of chart to show a correlation between two data series?
    a. column
    b. combination
    c. pie
    d. line

Project 6 Using Charts and Maps

Completion
In the blank provided, write the correct answer for each of the following statements.
1. The _Chart Wizard_ button on the Standard toolbar assists you in creating a chart.
2. Excel creates a chart from a(n) _data range_ you specify on the worksheet.
3. Click the _right_ mouse button on a chart or chart element to display a shortcut menu.
4. Select a chart or chart element; then drag a(n) _selection handle_ to resize it.
5. Create a(n) _map_ to chart information that is defined by state, country, or province.
6. A(n) _data series_ is a range of values in a worksheet.
7. The labels along the bottom of a chart are the _x-axis_ labels.
8. The labels along the left side of a chart are the _y-axis_ labels.
9. To delete an embedded chart, click it to select it, and press _Del_.
10. The mouse pointer should be shaped like a(n) _cross-hair_ on the worksheet cell where you want the upper-left corner of a map to start.

Matching
In the blank next to each of the following terms or phrases, write the letter of the corresponding term or phrase.

_b_ 1. A range of values in a worksheet
_g_ 2. Identifies data series
_d_ 3. Black squares surrounding a chart
_j_ 4. Vertical axis of a chart
_a_ 5. Horizontal axis of a chart
_c_ 6. A chart that appears on the worksheet along with the worksheet data
_e_ 7. Brief descriptions of the data in a chart
_i_ 8. A chart type in which each segment shows a data segment and its relationship to the whole
_f_ 9. A chart type consisting of a series of data at various points along the axis
_h_ 10. An item that has its own frame or box

a. category axis
b. data series
c. embedded
d. handles
e. legend
f. line
g. notes
h. object
i. pie
j. value axis

Applying Your Skills

Screen ID

Label each element of the Excel screen shown in Figure 6.26.

1. *Chart toolbar*
2. *Selection handles*
3. *Chart area*
4. *Plot area*
5. *Legend*

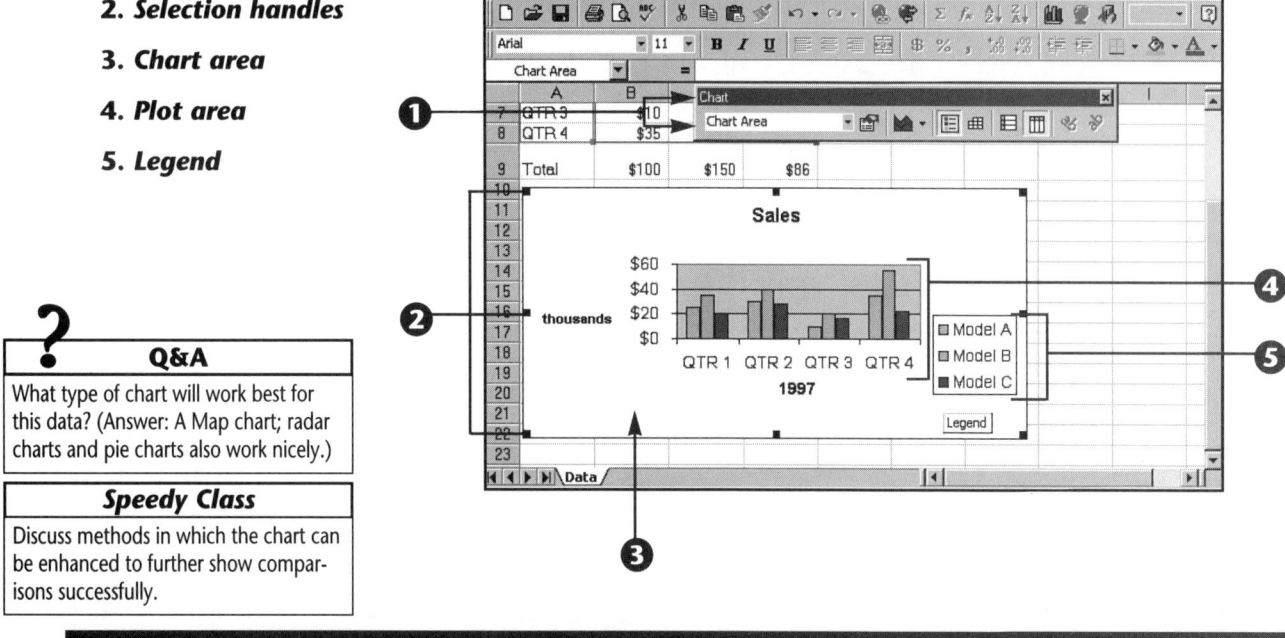

❓ Q&A
What type of chart will work best for this data? (Answer: A Map chart; radar charts and pie charts also work nicely.)

Speedy Class
Discuss methods in which the chart can be enhanced to further show comparisons successfully.

Applying Your Skills

Practice

The following exercises enable you to practice the skills you have learned in this project. Take a few minutes to work through these exercises now.

1. Creating a Chart and Map Showing Mail Order Sales

In the past six months, you have tried to expand your business by adding a mail order catalog that you send to potential customers in the western United States. Create a chart and a map to show the sales for a mail order catalog business in the first quarter of 1997.

To Create a Chart and Map Showing Mail Order Sales

1. Open the file Proj0603 and save it as MOSChart.

2. Select the data for both columns and create a chart embedded in the worksheet. Think about which type of chart will best show a comparison of the states in the mail order channel. Do not forget to add a title to the chart.

3. Move the chart below the worksheet, starting in cell A20. Increase the size of the chart so that it fills the range A20:G35.

4. Format the chart area, changing the font to a 10-point size.

5. Select the data for both columns and create a map, starting in cell A37 through cell G50 of the worksheet.

6. Experiment with some of the map features to enhance the map. For example, change the colors on the map. Change the zoom percentage to draw attention to the states where the sales are concentrated. Move the legend so that it is displayed inside the map frame.

7. Change the map title to `Mail Order Sales`. Try editing the font and font size in the title text.

8. Save your work. If requested by your instructor, print two copies of the worksheet with the chart and map before closing the file.

> Students gain practice creating and formatting an embedded chart and a map in this exercise. After creating the chart, students format the chart area by using a chart shortcut menu option, Format Chart Area command, to change the font size of chart text. Remind students that unlike charts, when creating maps, they must select the worksheet area where they want the map to be displayed before the map can appear. After creating a map, students double-click the map title to change the title text to Mail Order Sales. While selected, students change the font size and font style of the title. Also, students select, then drag, the map legend to a new location. The solution file is saved as **Mail Order Sales** on the Instructor's Resource disk.

2. Comparing Expenses Using a Chart

Using `Proj0604`, create a pie chart that compares how much you spend on various types of school expenses. Your tuition each semester is determined by the university, but you can try to manage other costs. Use the chart to see how changes in how much you spend on the Books—Additional category affects the makeup of the total amount.

To Compare Expenses Using a Chart

1. Open the file `Proj0604` and save it as `Charting Expenses`.

2. Create a pie chart, using the expense data for only the Spring 1997 semester for the following expense headings:

   `Books – Main subjects`

   `Books – Additional`

   `Supplies – General`

   `Supplies – Lab`

   `Lab Fees`

   Move the chart below the worksheet data.

3. Now change the chart type so that you can compare how the various types of expenses contribute to your total expenses for the semester. (*Tip:* Refer to Table 2.1.) Resize the chart and reduce the size of the font for the chart area to make sure that the Category (X) axis displays all the expense labels.

4. What happens to the worksheet and the chart when you decrease the amount in the worksheet for Books–Additional from $85 to $25?

5. What happens to the worksheet and the chart when you drastically increase the amount in the worksheet for Books–Additional to $475?

6. Save your work. If requested by your instructor, print two copies of the worksheet with the increased expense for Books–Additional.

Applying Your Skills 181

> In this exercise, students create a pie chart, then change the chart type to column. The chart is resized so that the Category (X) axis displays all the expense labels. The answer to the question, "What happens to the worksheet and the chart when you decrease the amount in the worksheet for Books-Additional from $85 to $25?" is that the columns representing the Books-Additional on the chart are shorter. On the worksheet, totals recalculate to reflect the change in the Books-Additional cell.
>
> The answer to the question, "What happens to the worksheet and the chart when you increase the amount in the worksheet for Books-Additional to $475?" is that the columns representing the Books-Additional on the chart are longer. On the worksheet, totals recalculate to reflect the change in the Books-Additional cell. The solution file is saved as **Charting Expenses** on the Instructor's Resource disk.

3. Creating a Map of the Home States of Rollerblading Club Members

In an effort to show prospective club members how diverse the rollerblading club is, you decide to create a map showing the home states of all current members.

To Create the Map

1. Open `Proj0605` and save it as `Membership Map`.
2. Use the data provided to create a map.
3. Zoom in on the target area.
4. Format the map to clearly show from which states most club members come. For example, make use of the legend, show the states in color, and use titles and text.
5. Save the worksheet. If requested by your instructor, print two copies. Then close the worksheet.

> In this exercise, students create a map, zoom in on the target area, then format the map to indicate from which states most club members come. Students use the Microsoft Map Control feature to display the states in color. The solution file is saved as **Membership Map** on the Instructor's Resource disk.

4. Creating an Embedded Area Chart

In this exercise, you create an area chart for the first quarter sales expenses of Midwestern Enterprises.

To Create an Embedded Area Chart

1. Open `Proj0606` and save it as `Quarterly Expenses`.
2. Create an embedded area chart using the data range of A4:D9.
3. Position the chart below the data area (rows 13 through 24).
4. Use the **C**hart, Chart **O**ptions command to insert a chart title, an x-axis title, and a y-axis title. The chart title is `1st Quarter Expenses`. The x-axis title is `Office Expenses`, and the y-axis title is in dollars.

Project 6 Using Charts and Maps

5. Adjust the size of the chart so that the category x labels are displayed.

6. If requested by your instructor, print two copies of the worksheet and chart.

7. Save and then close the workbook.

> This exercise provides students an additional opportunity to create an embedded chart. Students use the **C**hart, Chart **O**ptions command to insert a chart, x-axis, and y-axis title to the chart. Also, the chart size is adjusted so that all information is displayed. The solution file is saved as **1st Quarter Expenses** on the Instructor's Resource disk.

5. Creating a Line Chart on a Chart Sheet

In this exercise, you have the opportunity to create a chart on a separate chart sheet; then change the chart type and add titles.

To Create a Line Chart on a Chart Sheet

1. Open `Proj0607` and save it as `Beverages`.

2. Select the data range of A4:D7, then press `F11` to create a chart on its own sheet.

3. When the chart sheet appears, right-click to display a chart shortcut menu.

4. Choose the Chart **T**ype command to change the column chart to a line chart.

5. Right-click to display a chart shortcut menu, then select the Chart **O**ptions command to insert a chart title and an x-axis title. The chart title is `1st Quarter Sales`. The x-axis title is `Beverage Sales`.

6. If requested by your instructor, print two copies of the worksheet and chart.

7. Save and then close the workbook.

> Students create a line chart on a chart sheet by selecting the data range, then pressing `F11`. After creating the chart, students change the chart type to column, using a chart shortcut menu option, Chart **T**ype command. Students also use the chart shortcut menu to add chart and x-axis titles. The solution file is saved as **Beverages** on the Instructor's Resource disk.

Challenge

The following challenges enable you to use your problem-solving skills. Take time to work through these exercises now.

1. Creating an Embedded Pie Chart

To show your employees the sales results for July, you create an embedded pie chart. Open `Proj0608` and save it as `July Sales`. Use the data range A5:B11 to create the chart. Position the chart in rows 14 through 25 below the data area. Insert the chart title `July Sales`. If requested by your instructor, print two copies of the worksheet and chart. Save and then close the workbook.

In this activity, students create an embedded pie chart. Students use the **Chart, Chart O**ptions command to insert a chart title. The solution file is saved as **July Sales** on the Instructor's Resource disk.

2. Formatting a Chart

Your boss has asked you to format a columnar sales chart that he will be using in a meeting. Open Proj0609 and save it as `Formatted Chart`. Position the chart below the data area (rows 10 through 22). Insert the chart title `Sales`. Label the x-axis as `1997` and the y-axis title as `in thousands`. Change the Model B data series to the color yellow. Change the Model C data series to red. Change the chart type to bar. If requested by your instructor, print two copies of the worksheet and chart. Save and then close the workbook.

In this exercise, students format an existing chart by moving the chart, and using the **Chart, Chart O**ptions command to insert a chart and an x-axis title. Students also select a data series, right-click to choose F**o**rmat Data Series from the shortcut menu to change series color. Note: students may also want to change the font size of chart text so to display all text in the chart area. The solution file is saved as **Formatted Chart** on the Instructor's Resource disk.

3. Creating a Map

Open Proj0610 and save it as `Company Agents`. Create a map using the State and Agents data columns. Add the map title, `Agents by State`. Apply Category Shading to the Count of State column. Finally, if requested by your instructor, print two copies of the worksheet and map; then save and close the workbook.

In this activity, students create a map. After creating a map, students double-click the map title to change the title text to Agents by State. Students use the Microsoft Map Control feature to display the states in color. Students may desire to further format the map. A solution file is saved as **Company Agents** on the Instructor's Resource disk.

4. Changing Chart Type

Open the Proj0611 and save it as `Garnet & Gold`. Create a column chart using the data in columns A and B. Move the chart to the range A15:E30. Add a chart title, `Garnet & Gold Industries`. Adjust the size of the chart so that all x-axis labels display. Also, delete the legend by selecting it and pressing [Del]. If requested by your instructor, print two copies of this chart. Change the chart type to a clustered column with a 3-D visual effect. If requested by your instructor print two copies of the worksheet; save and then close the workbook.

In this exercise, students create a column chart. Use the **Chart, Chart O**ptions command to insert a chart title. Students also adjust the size of the chart so that all x-axis titles are displayed. The legend is deleted by selecting it and pressing [Del]. After creating the chart, students change the chart type to a clustered column with a 3-D visual effect, using a chart shortcut menu option, Chart **T**ype command. The solution file is saved as **Garnet & Gold** on the Instructor's Resource disk.

5. Creating Embedded Charts

Open `Proj0612` and save the workbook with the name `Motor Pool`. Create six embedded column charts, one for each car in the motor pool. Include appropriate chart titles. If requested by your instructor, print two copies of the worksheet. Save and then close the workbook.

> This activity requires students to create and format six embedded column charts, one for each car in the motor pool. The solution file is saved as **Motor Pool** on the Instructor's Resource disk.

Project 7

Managing Data

Creating an Address Database

In this project, you learn how to:
- Name a List
- Add Records
- Sort Records
- Find and Delete Records
- Extract Records Using AutoFilter

Why Would I Do This?

The purpose of creating a *database* (called a *list* in Excel) is to organize information and view selected parts of the information. A good example of a database is a phone book, which organizes information by city and then by name. To see only a portion of the phone book, you turn pages and scan columns of names arranged alphabetically. To see only part of a list in Excel, you use commands.

Computer databases provide you with a powerful way to organize and search for information. In this project, you learn to use a sample database of names, company names, addresses, and phone numbers. A simple Excel list, such as the one in this project, can make staying in contact with business associates easy.

Lesson 1: Naming a List

> **On Your Mark**
> What types of data lend themselves to listing, sorting, and searching techniques?

A list in Excel is a special kind of worksheet in which column headings are *fields,* and each row of worksheet data is a *record*. To continue with the phone book example, *last name* is one field, *first name* is another field, *address* is yet another field, and so on. A record consists of the set of information for one person: the person's first name, last name, address, and telephone number. (See the Jargon Watch that follows this lesson for more information about the database terminology used in this lesson.)

Each workbook file can contain more than one list, just as it can contain more than one worksheet; or you can create one workbook for each list. Each list can be on a separate worksheet or in separate ranges in a single worksheet.

Before you start to create a list, give some thought to the structure you want. Think about what you want to do with the information in the list; planning can keep you from having to move and insert columns later.

Follow these rules when creating a list in Excel:

- ➤ The field names (column headings) must be in a single row.
- ➤ A field name can contain letters, numbers, and spaces, but it should not start with a number.
- ➤ The field names must be unique.
- ➤ Don't leave a blank row between the row of field names and the first data record.
- ➤ A list should not contain blank columns; it's best not to have blank rows either.
- ➤ Every record must have the same fields, but you don't have to enter data into all the fields for every record. If the information is not available, you can leave some of the cells in a record empty.

**Project Time
45 minutes**

Lesson 1: Naming a List

Now that you know a little about how lists are created in Excel, try opening a worksheet file that already contains information suitable for a list, then naming the list in the file. As a list grows, referring to the collection of data by name is much easier than trying to remember the first and last cells of the list.

To Name a List

❶ Open the file Proj0701 and save it as Address Book.

This is a sample database of business associates that you will use throughout this project (see Figure 7.1). Notice that no empty rows or columns are within the worksheet. The column headings in row 1, such as First Name and Last Name, are the field names for the list.

Figure 7.1
In Excel, a list of names and addresses can be used as an address database.

Row 1 contains field names

Records

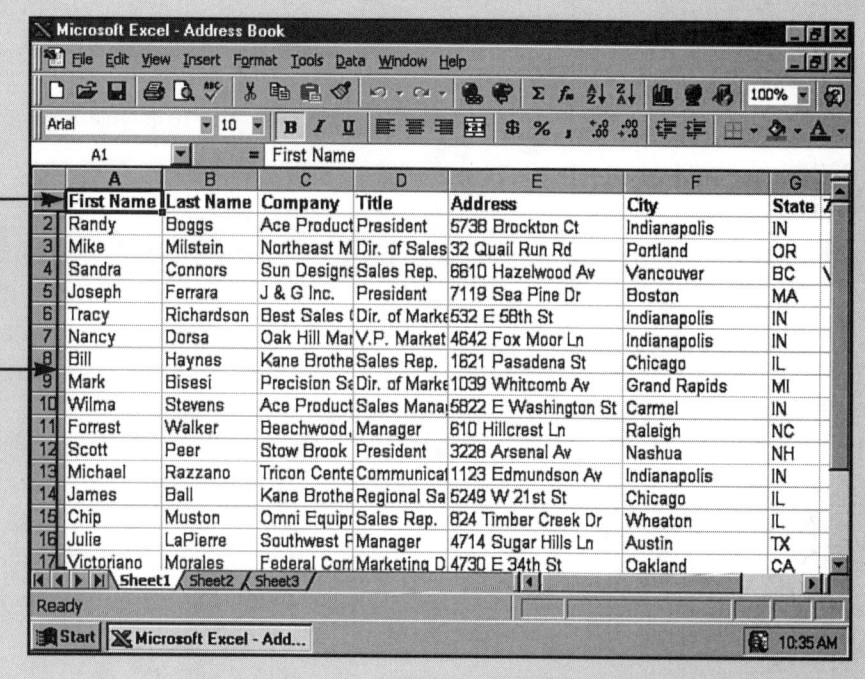

❷ Select the entire list, including the field names (cells A1:I21).

Naming a list is similar to naming any range of cells. You must first select the range you want to name—in this case, the entire list.

❸ Open the Insert menu, move the mouse pointer to the Name command, then choose Define from the submenu that appears.

The Define Name dialog box appears, as shown in Figure 7.2. By default, Excel lists the data from the active cell in the Names in workbook text box.

continues

Tip for Students

To quickly select the entire list, press Ctrl+Home to move the cell pointer to cell A1, then press ◆Shift+Ctrl+End to move the cell pointer to the lower-right corner of the list.

Tip for Students

You can name the range, including the column header row, as part of the database name. Including the column headings in the database range identifies each column by the heading at the top of the column.

Project 7 Managing Data

To Name a List (continued)

Figure 7.2
Use the Define Name dialog box to name a list.

List name
Selected range

Tip for Students
You can also name the list by selecting the list, clicking the drop-down arrow next to the cell address on the Formula bar, typing the name, and pressing ↵Enter.

4 In the Names in workbook text box, type Address, and then choose OK.

You have now named the database list so that you can easily refer to it in your work. You can deselect the list, then save the Address Book file and keep it open to use in the next lesson.

Jargon Watch

You may already know that the term **database** can also refer to a separate type of application software for personal computers. Applications such as Access, Paradox, and dBASE are powerful database programs used by all types of organizations and businesses. Many databases used in business and scientific research are so large and complex that they must run on mainframe computers.

In general terms, however, you can think of a database as an organized collection of related information—whether the information takes the form of a phone book, a recipe card file, or a disk file in a computer program.

Many database programs use what's called a **table** to organize the information contained in a database file. In Excel, this concept is referred to as a **list**, which is simply a worksheet of columns and rows.

Each collection of related information in a database is called a **record**. For example, in your Address Book database from Lesson 1, each name and its accompanying address, city, state, Zip code, and phone number is considered a record. A single database list can contain thousands of records; the only real limitation is the amount of memory of the computer holding the information.

Each record in a database contains several parts, or **fields**. For example, in the Personal Address database, the first name is a field, the last name is a field, the address is a field, the city is a field, and so on. Each field must have a designated field name so that it is easy to identify when used in the program. A field name can consist of up to 255 characters, but as a rule, you should keep field names brief and descriptive of the field's contents.

Lesson 2: Adding Records

Data form
A dialog box that displays only one row of your list—in other words, one record. Column headings appear as field labels. You can enter data or work with existing data using a data form.

After the initial database list is created, you may decide to add records to the list. You can simply type the new data into the rows at the end of the list, or you can use Excel's data form feature to add a number of records all at once.

A *data form* is a dialog box that shows all the fields in one data record. The data form presents an organized view of the data and makes data entry easier and more accurate. The data form is especially useful with much larger databases than the sample Address Book database used in this project.

✓ On Your Mark
Under what circumstances would you add data to a database list?

Try adding records to the Address Book database now.

To Add Records

Tip for Students
When adding to a list on-screen, you have the following options. You can insert rows to add data at particular places in the list (alphabetically, for example), or you can simply add the data to the end of the list and later sort the list by the information in any of the fields of the database.

① In the Address Book worksheet, select any cell in the list, then open the Data menu and choose Form.

A data form dialog box opens, displaying the contents of the first record in the Address list, as shown in Figure 7.3. The field names correspond to the column headings in the list. Notice that in the upper-right corner of the data form, Excel displays the record number and the total number of records in the list.

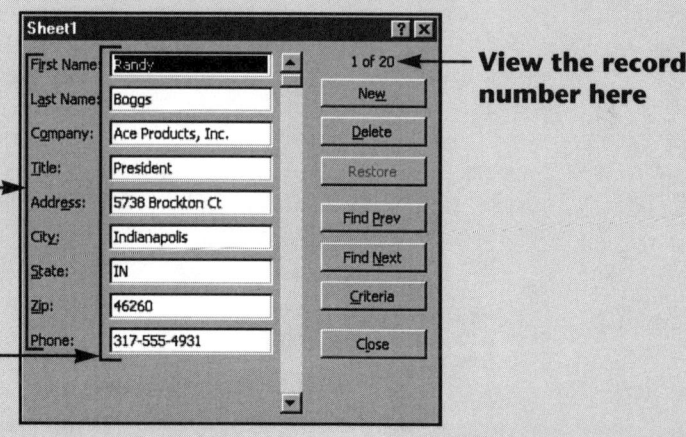

Figure 7.3
A data form is another way to display data from records in the list.

Field names →
Record data →

[Dialog box: Sheet1 — First Name: Randy, Last Name: Boggs, Company: Ace Products, Inc., Title: President, Address: 5738 Brockton Ct, City: Indianapolis, State: IN, Zip: 46260, Phone: 317-555-4931. Buttons: New, Delete, Restore, Find Prev, Find Next, Criteria, Close. 1 of 20]

← View the record number here

Speedy Class
When discussing entering data by using the data forms, mention that you can search for a particular record in the data form, then edit that record. Experiment with this technique if you have time and if the skills of the students are appropriate.

② Click the New button in the data form dialog box.

A new, blank form appears. You enter data for new records in the blank form.

③ Type Mohammed in the First Name field text box, then press Tab.

This enters the data into the First Name field of a new data record. Pressing Tab moves the insertion point to the next field text box.

④ Type Khalili in the Last Name field text box, then press Tab.

This enters the data into the Last Name field of the data record.

Tip for Students
In addition to pressing Tab to move from field to field, you can use the mouse to click the field to which you want to move.

continues

Project 7 Managing Data

To Add Records (continued)

> **If you have problems...**
>
> If you press [←Enter] or [↓] instead of [Tab⇥], Excel adds the new record to the list and displays a new, blank data form. If you had not completed filling out the data form, click the Find **P**rev button in the data form dialog box to display it. You can press [Tab⇥] to move forward through the data fields, or [⇧Shift]+[Tab⇥] to move backward. Alternatively, click in the field you want to edit. If you make a mistake when typing in a field, simply use the [←Backspace] or [Del] key to delete the error, then type the data correctly.

❺ Continue entering the record using the following data:

    Company: Gadgets, Inc.

    Title: Sales Manager

    Address: 526 Lynn St.

    City: Ithaca

    State: NY

    Zip: 14850

    Phone: 607-555-3421

Don't forget to press [Tab⇥] to move from one field to the next. When you are done, the record should look similar to the one in Figure 7.4.

> **Tip for Instructors**
> There is no capability to wrap text within a field, therefore producing a two-line field.

Figure 7.4
A new record is entered in the data form.

❻ Press [←Enter] after typing all the field information.

This enters the new data record into the list and displays a new blank form, which you can use to continue adding records. You can also click the Ne**w** button in the data form dialog box. Now add three more records to Address Book.

> **Tip for Students**
> You can either press [←Enter] or click the Ne**w** button to add a completed record to your database. From there you can continue adding new records.

Lesson 3: Adding Records   191

7 Enter the following record data:

    Natalie, Burnett, Style Systems, V.P. Marketing, 21
    Magnolia St, Battle Creek, MI, 49017, 616-555-2394

    Wendell, Feldman, Baker Computing, Dir. Sales, 270 West
    Limestone St, Orem, UT, 84057, 801-555-3002

    Eve, Shaw, Baker Computing, Sales Rep., 1170 North 17th
    St, Orem, UT, 84057, 801-555-8202

Remember to press Tab to move from field to field, and press ↵Enter to display a new, blank data form.

8 Click the Close button in the data form dialog box.

This clears the dialog box from the screen and displays the address list. Scroll down the list to see the new records in rows 22 through 25, as shown in Figure 7.5. Now you need to extend the range name for your list to include the new records.

Figure 7.5
The new records are added to the bottom of the list.

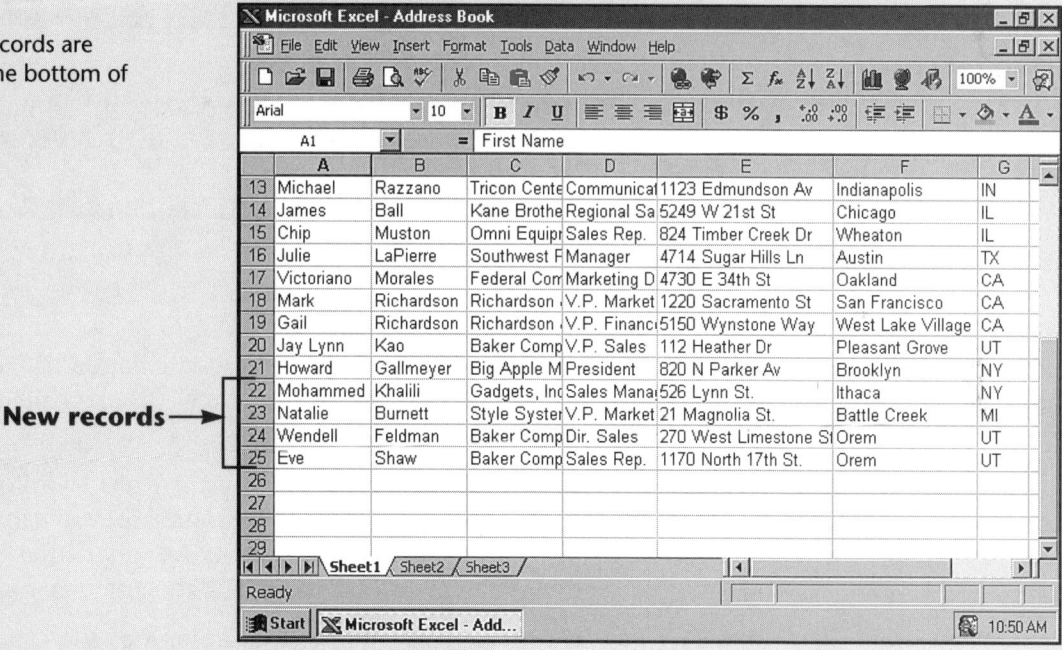

New records →

9 Select the entire list, including field names (cells A1:I25).

You must redefine the list name to include the new records.

10 Open the Insert menu, move the mouse pointer to the Name command, and choose Define.

The Define Name dialog box appears.

continues

Speedy Class

You can also insert records in your database on the regular Excel worksheet. If you add records at the end of your database, however, you still must redefine the list name to include the new records. If you insert blank rows in the body of your database and add new records, the boundaries of the previously defined name will expand to include the inserted rows.

To Add Records (continued)

⑪ **Select the list name Address in the Names in workbook list box.**

The list name (Address) appears in the Names in workbook text box (see Figure 7.6).

Figure 7.6
Redefine the Address list to include the new records.

Change the cell address here →

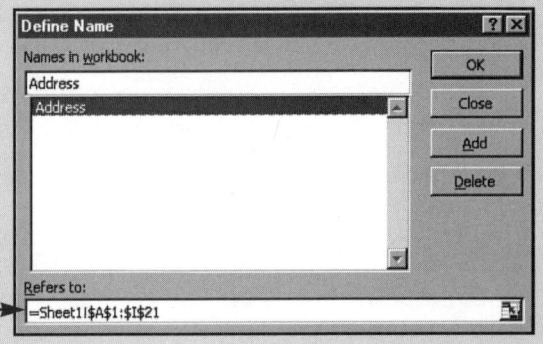

⑫ **In the Refers to text box, change the last cell reference from row 21 to row 25, then choose OK.**

This redefines the Address list to include the records you just added. Deselect the list, save your work, and keep the Address Book worksheet open to use in the next lesson.

Quicksand
Students should understand that even if they select the entire list on-screen before opening the Define Name dialog box, the range definition must be updated if they select the list's name (in this case, Address). As an alternative, select the new range, open this dialog box, and retype the list name. Excel names the new range with your original name.

Sort
A function that rearranges the data in a list so that it appears in alphabetical or numerical order.

Sort fields
The fields used to determine the order in which a list is sorted.

✓ On Your Mark
What are the advantages of sorting data? When would you want to sort this type of information?

Lesson 3: Sorting Records

To *sort* a list means to rearrange the list in a particular order. The sort order is determined by the *sort fields* you set for Excel. The sort fields are simply the fields you want Excel to use in sorting.

You can also choose the kind of order you want Excel to follow in sorting the field. For example, in your Address Book database, you can tell Excel to sort the Company field in ascending alphabetical order (that is, from *A* to *Z*), or in descending alphabetical order (from *Z* to *A*).

What if you have more than one person working at the same company? You can use additional sort fields to break ties; in this case, you can use the last name as a second field to sort, or perhaps the title field.

Try sorting records in your list now.

To Sort Records

Tip for Students
This step is optional. If you place the cell pointer anywhere in the data list and choose **D**ata, **S**ort, Excel automatically selects the entire data list for you.

❶ **In the Address Book worksheet, open the Name box drop-down list and choose Address.**

This selects the records that you want to sort: the entire list. (Remember, you used the Name box drop-down list to select named ranges in Project 4, "Calculating with Functions.")

Lesson 3: Sorting Records

2 **Open the Data menu and choose Sort.**

The Sort dialog box appears, as shown in Figure 7.7. The Sort by text box is selected with the name of the first field displayed. By default, the sort order is **A**scending, meaning *A* to *Z* or *0* to *9*. You can change the sort order to **D**escending, meaning *Z* to *A* or *9* to *0*.

Figure 7.7
Use the Sort dialog box to specify how you want the rows in the list arranged.

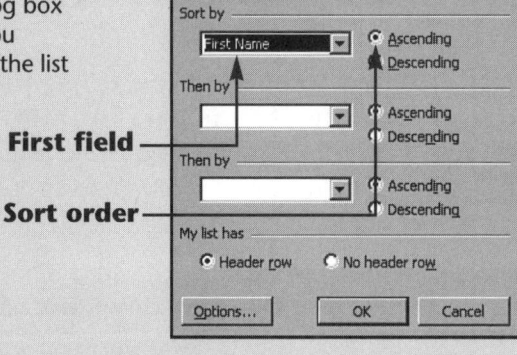

— First field
— Sort order

Q&A

What happens if you don't mark the Header **R**ow option in the My List Has box at the bottom of the Sort dialog box? *Answer:* The header row gets sorted with the rest of the database. Note also that the Sort By options refer to column letters rather than column names if there is no header row identified.

3 **In the My list has box at the bottom of the Sort dialog box, make sure that the Header row option button is selected.**

This confirms that you have included the field names in the first row in the sorting range. Excel will not sort the data in the header row.

4 **Type City in the Sort by text box, then choose OK.**

Excel sorts the records by city in ascending alphabetical order, as shown in Figure 7.8. Notice that the list records remain selected after the sort is performed. Now try resorting the list by more than one field at a time.

Figure 7.8
Records are sorted alphabetically according to the data in the City field.

— Sort by field

Tip for Instructors

Be sure to point out that sorting a list doesn't affect the file saved on disk. If you want to keep the file in its sorted form, you need to save it after sorting.

continues

To Sort Records (continued)

> **Speedy Class**
>
> To reliably recall the original entry order of a data list that is going to be sorted and saved regularly, add a column of numbers (1, 2, 3, and so on) that correspond chronologically to the order in which the items were added. Next, sort the list by this column. *Remember to always include the column of numbers in the sort range.*

❺ With the entire list still selected, open the Data menu and choose Sort.

The Sort dialog box appears again. Notice that City still appears in the Sort by text box.

❻ Click the drop-down arrow next to the Sort by text box, and select Company from the drop-down list of field names that appears.

This enters Company in the Sort by text box, telling Excel you want to sort the records according to the data in the Company field. However, because you know some of your records have the same data in the Company field, you also want to sort the list by Last Name.

❼ Click the drop-down arrow next to the first Then by text box, and select Last Name from the drop-down list of field names.

Now you have added a second sort field: Last Name (see Figure 7.9). Excel will first sort by Company and then by Last Name.

Figure 7.9
You can sort a list using up to three sort fields.

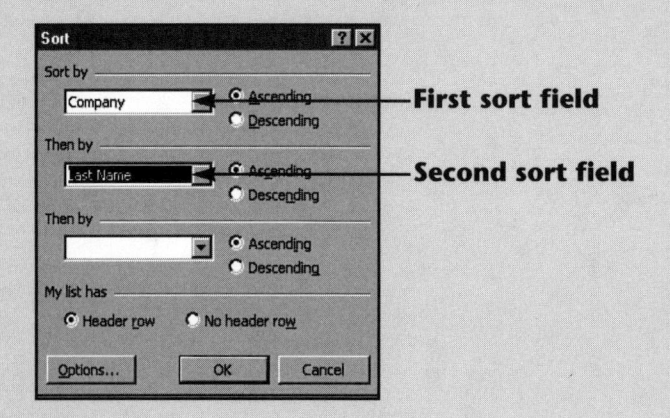

❽ Choose OK.

Excel closes the dialog box and sorts the records. You may want to deselect the list to get a better look at it. Notice that the records have been alphabetized by company name; in cases where there is more than one record per company, the records are further alphabetized by last name, as shown in Figure 7.10.

Lesson 3: Sorting Records

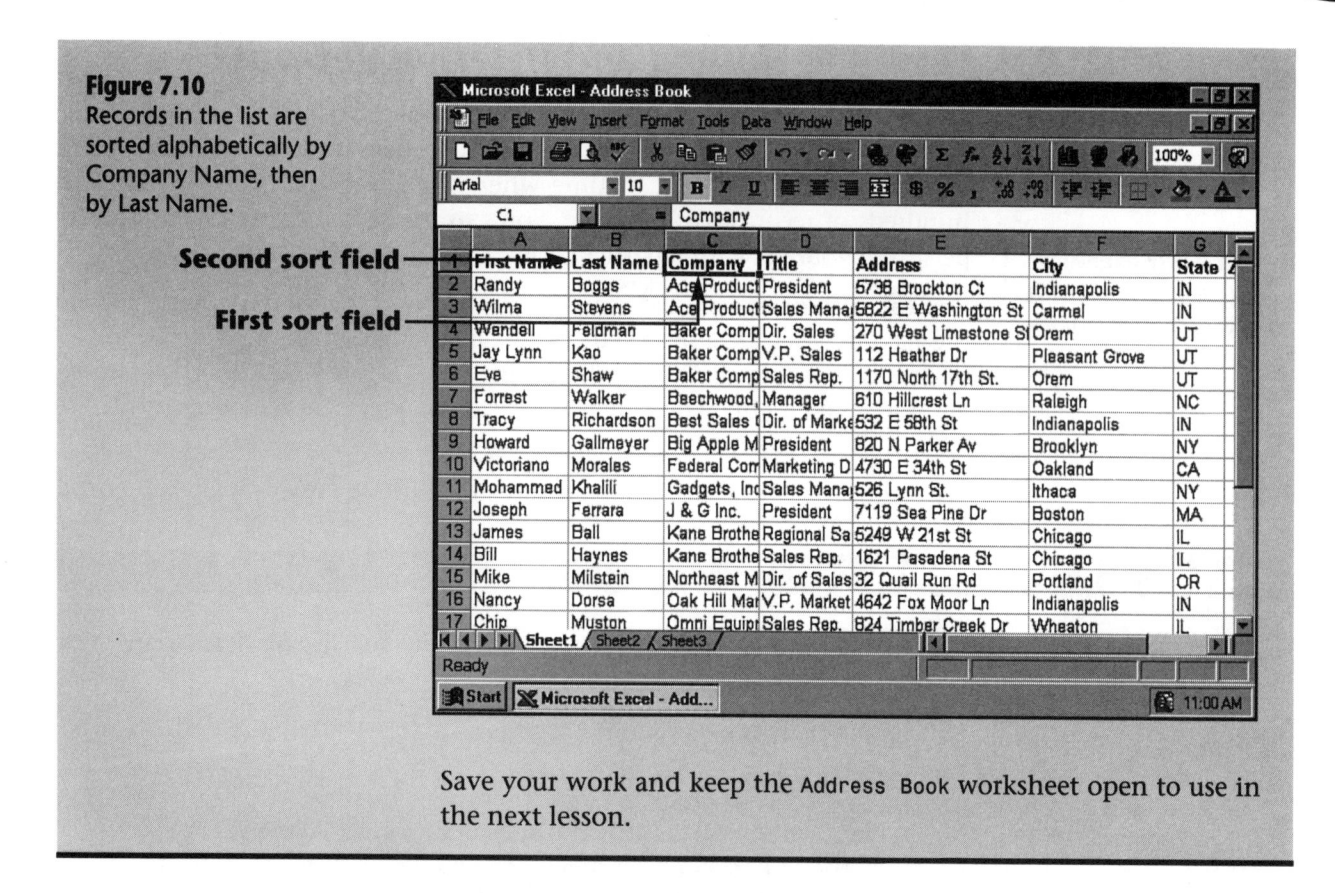

Figure 7.10
Records in the list are sorted alphabetically by Company Name, then by Last Name.

Second sort field
First sort field

Save your work and keep the Address Book worksheet open to use in the next lesson.

If you have problems...

Be careful when selecting the data to sort. If you select only a column or two of data, Excel sorts only the selected data. Therefore, columns that aren't selected are not included in the sort. For example, if you selected only the Company Name and Last Name fields when sorting, you may find addresses and phone numbers paired with the wrong names. To reverse the sort, click the Undo button before performing any other action.

It's always a good idea to save your file before you perform a sort. If you make an error in sorting, you can close the file without saving, open the original file, and try again.

To quickly sort a list by the data in the current field, click the Sort Ascending or Sort Descending buttons on the Standard toolbar.

Lesson 4: Finding and Deleting Records

Search criteria
A defined pattern or detail used to find matching records.

✓ **On Your Mark**
What types of things would you search for in a data list (such as one that contains employee information)?

One of the most useful functions of working with lists is using *search criteria* to find specific records. Using the Excel criteria data form to find specific records saves a great deal of time when you are working with dozens or hundreds of records. For example, you can use search criteria to find every person in your list with a particular job title.

You can also delete specific records in a list by using search criteria to find the records, then deleting them. For example, you can choose to delete all records containing a particular last name or all records containing a particular state. Be careful when deleting records: you can accidentally delete records that you need.

Try finding and deleting specific records in your list now.

To Find and Delete Records

❶ In the Address Book worksheet, click any cell in the list. Open the Data menu and choose Form.

A data form appears containing the data from the first record.

❷ Click the Criteria button in the data form dialog box.

A blank criteria data form appears, as shown in Figure 7.11. You use the criteria data form to specify the records you want to find. Now specify criteria to find and then delete all the records for people working at Baker Computing.

Figure 7.11
Use the blank criteria data form to find records that contain certain data.

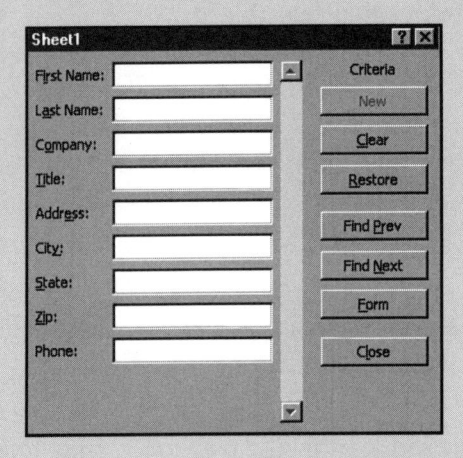

❸ Click in the Company text box and type Baker Computing.

This tells Excel to look through the Company field in every record to find the data Baker Computing.

❹ Click the Find Next button.

Excel begins the search and displays the data form for the next record in the list that matches the specified criterion—which is the next record from the company Baker Computing, as shown in Figure 7.12.

Lesson 4: Finding and Deleting Records

Figure 7.12
Excel displays a record that matches the criteria you entered.

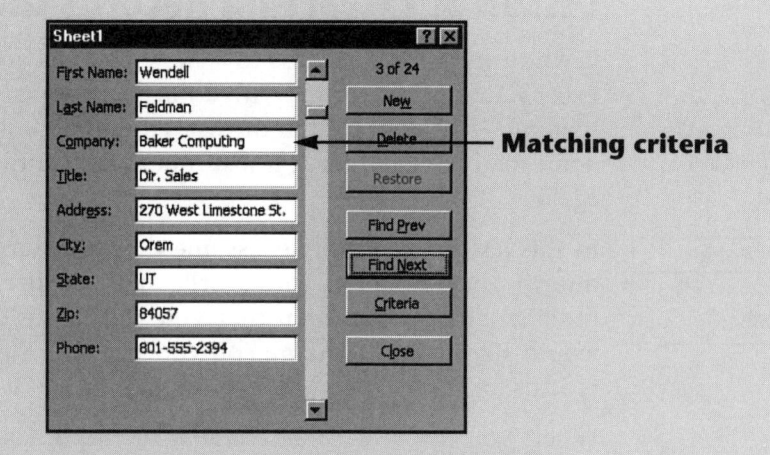

*(Data form dialog showing: First Name: Wendell, Last Name: Feldman, Company: Baker Computing ← **Matching criteria**, Title: Dir. Sales, Address: 270 West Limestone St., City: Orem, State: UT, Zip: 84057, Phone: 801-555-2394, record 3 of 24)*

❺ Click the Delete button.

Excel displays a dialog box warning you that the record will be permanently deleted.

> **If you have problems...**
>
> Be careful when deleting records from your database. Once you choose OK in the warning dialog box, Excel deletes the record permanently. You can't retrieve the deleted record using the **U**ndo command.

❻ Choose OK.

Excel deletes the record and displays the data form for the next record in the database, whether or not it matches the search criteria. (In this case, it does match because the records are sorted by company name.) Now continue your search using the criteria data form to delete the rest of the records from Baker Computing.

❼ Click the Find Next button.

Again, Excel displays the next record that matches the specified criteria.

❽ Click the Delete button, then choose OK in the warning box.

Excel deletes the record. Repeat the steps to find and delete any additional records from Baker Computing. When no further records in the list match the criteria, Excel beeps.

❾ Click the Close button in the data form dialog box.

This clears the dialog box and displays the Address Book worksheet. Save your work and keep the worksheet open. In the next lesson, you use Excel's AutoFilter feature to extract records from the database.

Quicksand

When you delete a record while in the Criteria dialog box, Excel automatically displays the next record that meets the criteria. Clicking the Find **N**ext button skips the second record that meets the criteria and takes you to the third matching record. Either skip step 7, or make sure students realize they have skipped a record by performing this step.

Filter
A method for controlling which records are extracted from the database and displayed in the worksheet.

> ✓ **On Your Mark**
> What's the difference between sorting records and filtering records?

Lesson 5: Extracting Records Using AutoFilter

If you want to find records that match more complex criteria, you can use Excel's AutoFilter feature. With a *filter*, you set criteria to specify the records that you want displayed in the list. Filtering does not delete the records that don't match your criteria; it just hides them until you want to display them again.

In this lesson, for example, assume that you want to send a letter to everyone in your database who works at a specific company in Chicago or Indianapolis, telling them that you will be visiting those cities soon and would like to meet them. You can use the AutoFilter to extract all the records for those cities from the original list.

When you use a large database with hundreds of records, filtering data enables you to work with a more manageable set of records and fields. Always save your file before you filter data. If you have a problem extracting the records, you can close the file and revert to the saved version of the original data. Try extracting records using AutoFilter and your Address Book database now.

To Extract Records Using AutoFilter

❶ In the Address Book worksheet, click in any cell in the list, then open the Data menu. Move the mouse pointer to the Filter command, and choose AutoFilter from the submenu.

Filter arrows appear next to each of the field names in the list, as shown in Figure 7.13. You specify the field that you want to use for filtering by using the filter arrow in that field. In this case, you want to filter records based on the City field.

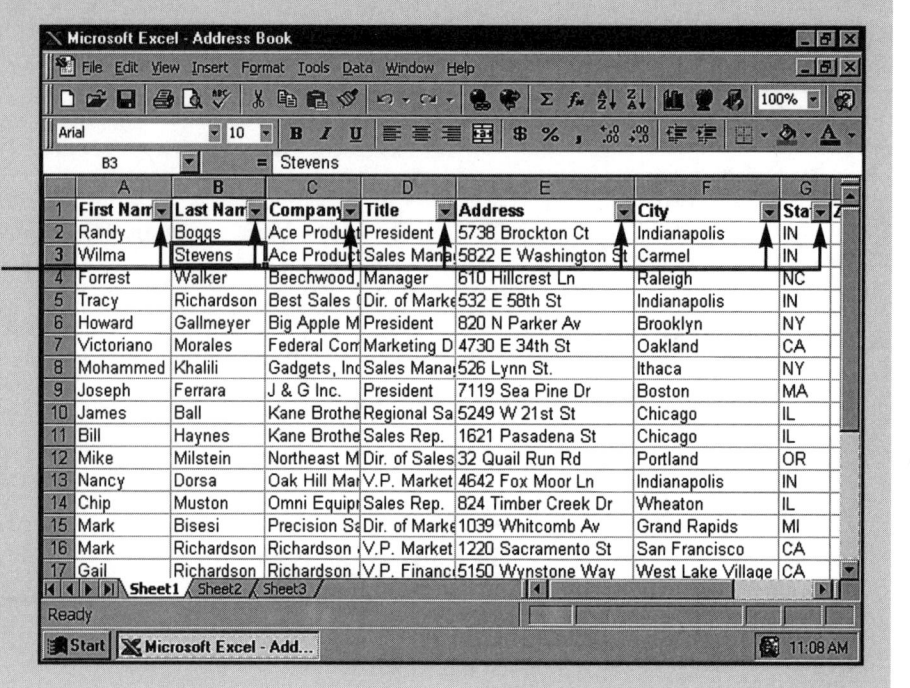

Figure 7.13
Use AutoFilter to hide the records you don't want to work with.

Filter arrows

Lesson 5: Extracting Records Using AutoFilter

❷ Click the filter arrow in cell F1.

A drop-down list of filtering criteria appears under the arrow. Some pre-defined filters, including (All), (Top 10...), and (Custom...), are displayed at the top of the list. (All), the default, shows all the records without using the field as a filter. Choose (All) when you want to remove any filtering criteria already in use for a field.

Choose (Top 10...) when you want to filter records according to the highest or lowest values in the list. For example, in a text field, such as Product Names, you would be able to filter the records by the letters *A* through *J* or *Q* through *Z*. In a numeric field, such as Price, you can filter the records by the ten highest values or the ten lowest values.

Choose (Custom...) to specify multiple selection criteria to use for filtering the field. To filter by a single criteria (such as a specific city name), simply select it from the list.

Speedy Class
Before using the Custom Filter feature, have students practice with filters based on data displayed in the AutoFilter lists that appear in each column.

Tip for Instructors
Point out to students that when using this custom filtering technique, they can choose two criteria, but only from the chosen field.

❸ From the drop-down list, select (Custom...).

The Custom AutoFilter dialog box appears (see Figure 7.14). This is where you specify the criteria that Excel uses to extract records from the database. You can specify two criteria, using two operators. *Operators* tell Excel the type of comparison you want to use. For example, *equals* means to match the criteria exactly, and *is less than* means to find records in which the data is less than the specified criteria. Notice that equals appears in the first operator text box by default.

Figure 7.14
The Custom AutoFilter dialog box enables you to specify the criteria for deciding which records to hide and which to display.

Second operator text box **First operator text box** **Second criteria text box** **First criteria text box**

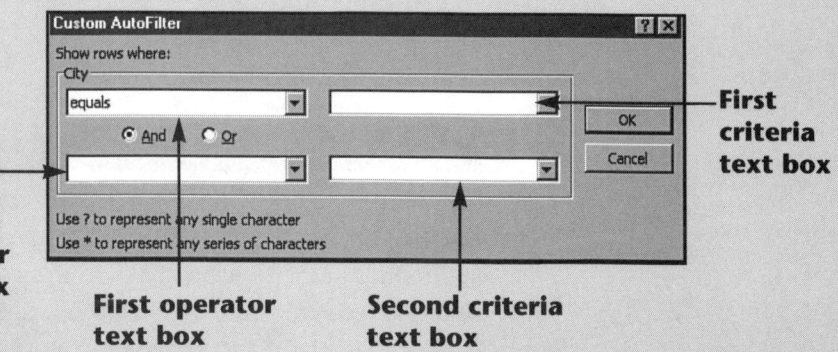

❹ Click the drop-down arrow next to the first criteria text box, and select Chicago.

This establishes "City equals Chicago" as the first filter criterion. Remember that you want to include records either from Chicago *or* from Indianapolis.

❺ Click the Or option button in the Custom AutoFilter dialog box.

Next, you want to include Indianapolis in the criteria statement.

continues

200 Project 7 Managing Data

To Extract Records Using AutoFilter (continued)

6 **Click the drop-down arrow next to the second operator text box.**

This displays a list of relational operators, as shown in Figure 7.15.

Figure 7.15
Specify the type of comparison by selecting an operator from the drop-down list.

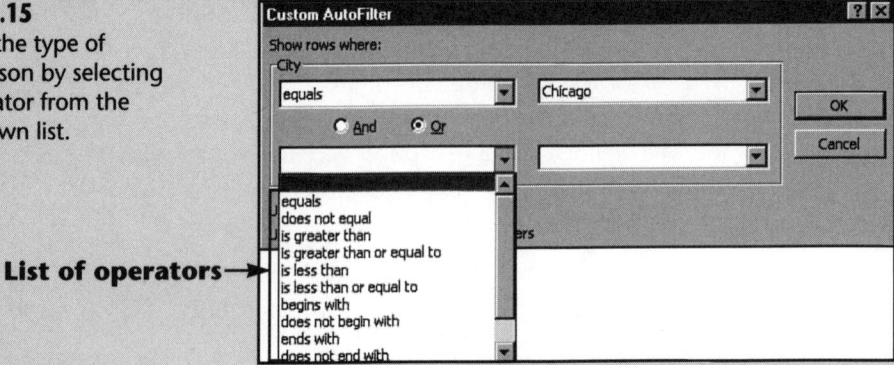

List of operators →

7 **Select `equals` from the drop-down list.**

This tells Excel you want to find all records that match the specified criteria exactly.

8 **Click the drop-down arrow next to the second criteria text box, and select Indianapolis from the list of data entries that appears.**

Your dialog box should now resemble Figure 7.16. Make sure that `equals` appears in both operator text boxes and the **Or** option is selected.

If you have problems...

Choosing the correct option button is critical. You would use the **And** option button if you wanted to display records that contain *both* values in the specified field. In this case, if you specified **And**, all of the records would be filtered out because none of them contains both Chicago and Indianapolis in the City field. On the other hand, **Or** tells Excel to find records that contain either Chicago *or* Indianapolis.

Figure 7.16
The completed Custom AutoFilter dialog box is ready to filter out records that don't meet the specified criteria.

Lesson 5: Extracting Records Using AutoFilter

Tip for Instructors

To change the custom filter in a previously filtered column, students don't have to reinstate the entire data list. They can choose new criteria from the AutoFilter list for that column, and the entire data list will be utilized. If students choose, however, an AutoFilter option from a column other than the original, Excel will filter data only from the records visible on-screen (the filtered records).

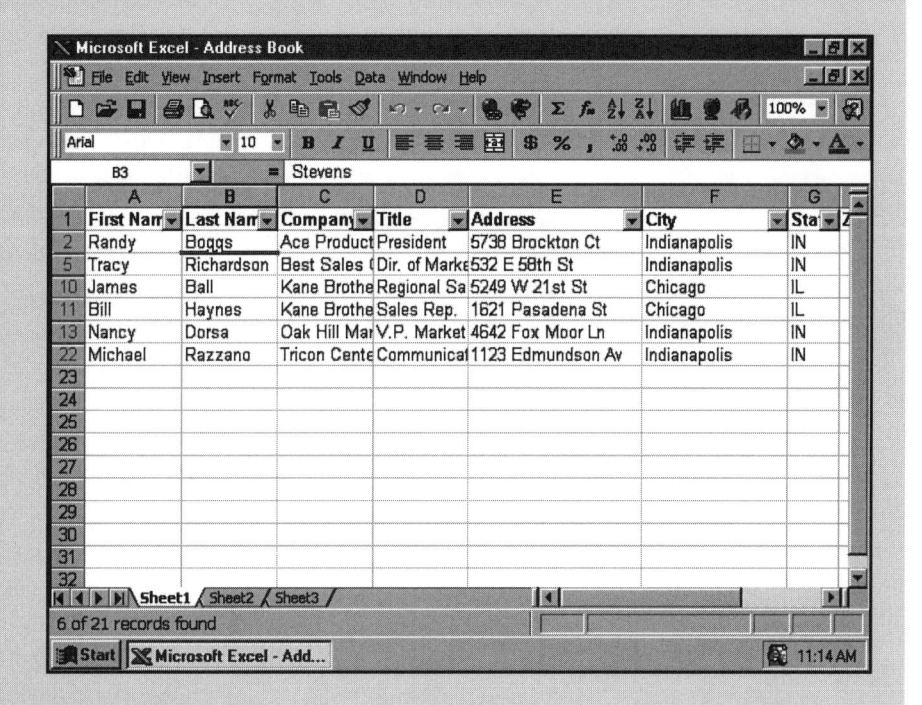

Figure 7.17
The extracted records for Chicago and Indianapolis are displayed.

Speedy Class

Discuss the concept of extracting records that meet multiple requirements, such as all the records from Indianapolis with a ZIP code of 46260, or names with a title of President. Set up criteria and output ranges in your worksheet, then choose **D**ata, **F**ilter, **A**dvanced Filter to extract the records that meet the multiple requirements.

❾ Choose OK in the Custom AutoFilter dialog box.

Excel extracts all records that match the specified criteria and displays them in the list, as shown in Figure 7.17. In this case, only records where the City field contains the data `Chicago` or `Indianapolis` are displayed. All other records are temporarily hidden. Notice that the filter arrow for the City field is colored blue to indicate that the City field has been used to filter data. Also, notice that the row numbers are blue, indicating that not all rows are displayed.

❿ Open the Data menu, move the mouse pointer to the Filter command, and choose AutoFilter from the submenu that appears.

This turns off the AutoFilter feature, and all records in the list are again displayed. Notice that the filter arrows disappear. Save your work. If requested by your instructor, print two copies, then close the worksheet.

If you have completed your session on the computer, exit Excel 97 and Windows 95 before turning off the computer. Otherwise, continue with the "Checking Your Skills" section at the end of this project.

Removing all old filtering conditions before you set new filtering conditions is always a good idea. Otherwise, you may forget that you have previously set a filtering condition that is still affecting a more recent search. Choose **D**ata, **F**ilter, **S**how All to clear the preceding filters.

You can clear a filter from a single column by clicking the filter button for that column and choosing **All** from the list. To turn off AutoFilter completely, simply choose **D**ata, **F**ilter, AutoFilter.

Project Summary

To	Do This
Name a list	Select the list, and choose **I**nsert, **N**ame, **D**efine. Type the name in the Names in workbook text box in the Define Name dialog box, then choose OK.
Add records	Choose **D**ata, Form, and click Ne**w**. Type data in the fields, pressing Tab to move from one field to the next.
Sort records by the current field	Click the Sort Ascending or Sort Descending buttons on the Standard toolbar.
Find records	Choose **D**ata, **F**orm, and click **C**riteria. Type the data to find in the appropriate field, and click Find **N**ext.
Delete records	Find the record you want to delete, and click **D**elete in the data form dialog box. Click OK in the warning dialog box.
Filter the list of records	Choose **D**ata, **F**ilter, then choose AutoFilter to create your own filter. Drop down the filtering criteria list in the field you want to filter, and choose the criteria you want to use, or choose Custom to specify your own filtering criteria.
Display all records	Choose **D**ata, **F**ilter, AutoFilter.

Checking Your Skills

True/False

For each of the following, check *T* or *F* to indicate whether the statement is true or false.

✔T __F   **1.** Naming a list is especially useful when you are working with a large amount of data.

✔T __F   **2.** Each collection of information in a list is divided into fields.

__T ✔F   **3.** The field name identifies each record in a database table.

__T ✔F   **4.** Excel can sort data using up to two fields.

__T ✔F   **5.** An Excel list can be sorted only in ascending order.

__T ✔F   **6.** You cannot leave any cells in a list empty.

✔T __F   **7.** A field name cannot start with a number.

__T ✔F   **8.** You can retrieve a deleted record using the Undo command.

__T ✓F **9.** If you filter records, those that do not match the criteria are deleted from the database.

✓T __F **10.** If you choose equals as an operator to filter records, data must match the criteria exactly.

Multiple Choice

Circle the letter of the correct answer for each of the following questions.

1. To view the data for one record at a time, what should you display?
   a. criteria
   b. filter
   c. Data form
   d. list

2. Which of the following is another name for a list?
   a. table
   b. worksheet
   c. field
   d. record

3. What feature do you use to display only selected records in a list?
   a. Sort
   b. AutoFilter
   c. Name
   d. Find

4. Which option in the criteria list, displayed when you click a filter arrow, removes any filters for that field?
   a. (Blank)
   b. <>
   c. (All)
   d. none of the above

5. To find the records that match a search condition in the list, you click which button in the data form?
   a. Search
   b. Seek
   c. Criteria
   d. none of the above

6. To move to the previous field text box in the Data Form, press which of the following keys?
   a. Tab
   b. Enter
   c. ↓
   d. Shift+Tab

7. To display records that match both criteria entered into the Custom AutoFilter dialog box, you click which option button?
   a. Or
   b. And
   c. And/Or
   d. Either

8. Which of the following is *not* a rule for creating a list in Excel?
   a. The field names must be in a single row.
   b. The field names must be unique.
   c. A field name can contain letters, numbers, and spaces.
   d. Leave a blank row between the row of field names and the first data record.

Project 7 Managing Data

9. Which of the following shows all the fields in one data record?
   a. Data form
   b. data list
   c. AutoFilter form
   d. custom list

10. How do you know when records have been filtered in the database?
    a. The word *filter* displays in the title bar.
    b. The column letters in the list are blue.
    c. The row numbers in the list are blue.
    d. all the above

Completion

In the blank provided, write the correct answer for each of the following statements.

1. The best way to add records to an existing list is by using the Data _form_.
2. By default, Excel sorts in _ascending_ order.
3. Each individual collection of related information in a database is called a(n) _record_.
4. To find records in a list where one criterion *or* the other is met, you use the _Custom AutoFilter_.
5. The _field_ names indicate the information contained in each record.
6. If you choose to sort a list in ascending alphabetical order, Excel will sort the list from _A to Z_.
7. Last name is an example of a(n) _field name_ in an Excel list.
8. When using the data form to find records, click the _Find Next_ button to locate the next record matching the criteria.
9. When you _filter_ records, they are hidden until you display them again.
10. To remove all filtering criteria being used in a field, choose _ALL_ from the drop-down list of filtering criteria.

Matching

In the blank next to each of the following terms or phrases, write the letter of the corresponding term or phrase.

_g_ 1. Column headings in a list
_j_ 2. Each row of worksheet data
_i_ 3. A dialog box that displays only one row of your list.
_h_ 4. A function that rearranges data in a list so it appears in alphabetical or numerical order.
_d_ 5. A defined pattern or detail used to find matching records.
_f_ 6. A method for controlling which records are extracted from the database.
_e_ 7. A dialog box that lets you specify criteria for which records to display.
_a_ 8. Limits the number of records in a list
_c_ 9. When using the data form, press this key to add the record to the list.
_b_ 10. When using the data form, press this key to move to the next field.

a. memory
b. `Tab`
c. `Enter`
d. search criteria
e. Custom AutoFilter

f. filter
g. fields
h. sort
i. Data form
j. record

Screen ID

Label each element of the Excel screen shown in Figure 7.18.

Figure 7.18

1. *First operator text box*
2. *First criteria text box*
3. *Second operator text box*
4. *Second criteria text box*
5. *List of operators*

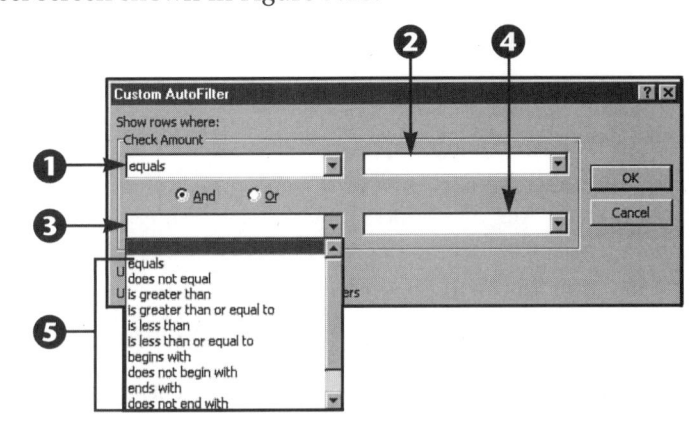

Applying Your Skills

Practice

The following exercises enable you to practice the skills you have learned in this project. Take a few minutes to work through these exercises now.

1. Creating an Inventory List

You can use Excel's database list feature to keep track of product inventory. You can store the product names, prices, and ordering information; then work with the data using the list features, such as sorting and filtering.

To Create the Inventory List

Use the product information provided to create an inventory list for keeping track of products.

1. Open the file `Proj0702` and save it as `Products`.
2. Insert a row at the top of the list, then change the worksheet into a list by adding field names to the top of each column, as follows:

    Column A: `Product Name`

    Column B: `Product Number`

    Column C: `Unit Cost`

    Column D: `In Stock?`

3. Sort the list alphabetically by product name so that you can easily find any product.

4. Extract a list of all products that are not in stock so that you know what needs to be reordered.

5. Save your list. If requested by your instructor, print two copies, then close the file.

> In this exercise, students create an inventory list by adding column field names to an existing worksheet. Students sort the list alphabetically by product, using the **D**ata, **S**ort command. The **D**ata, **F**ilter, AutoFilter command is used to extract a list of products that are not in stock. The solution file is saved as **Products** on the Instructor's Resource disk.

2. Creating a Telephone List

Create a telephone list that you can use for notifying customers of upcoming events.

To Create the Telephone List

1. Open the file Proj0703 and save it as Phone List.
2. Name the list Customers.
3. Sort the list alphabetically by customer last name.
4. Sort the list alphabetically by last name, then by first name.
5. Extract a list of customers who last attended a tasting in September.
6. Save the list. If requested by your instructor, print two copies, then close the file.

> In this activity, students create a data list by selecting all the worksheet data, then choosing the **I**nsert, **N**ame, **D**efine command. Students sort the list alphabetically by customer last name, using the **D**ata, **S**ort command. Then, students sort the list by last name, then by first name. The **D**ata, **F**ilter, AutoFilter command is used to extract a list of customers who last attended a tasting in September. The solution file is saved as **Phone List** on the Instructor's Resource disk.

3. Using an Employee Database

With Excel's list feature, you can create an employee database that can help you track vital information about staff members. You use this database to organize the work schedule and to analyze your staffing needs. In this example, use the sort and AutoFilter features of Excel to organize the employee data and evaluate salaried, hourly, and commissioned staff.

To Use an Employee Database

1. Open the file Proj0704 and save it as Employees.
2. Sort the list alphabetically by three sort keys: Last Name, First Name, and City.
3. Extract a list of commissioned employees.
4. Extract a list of hourly employees.
5. Extract a list of salaried employees who live in Oak Hill.
6. Display all records.
7. Save the file. If requested by your instructor, print two copies of the list, including all records, then close the file.

Applying Your Skills

> In this exercise, students using the **D**ata, **S**ort command to sort a list alphabetically by three sort keys, LastName, FirstName, and City. The **D**ata, **F**ilter, AutoFilter command is used to extract a list of commissioned employees, hourly employees, and salaried employees who live in Oak Hill. Finally, students use the **D**ata, **F**ilter, AutoFilter command to display all records. The solution file is saved as **Employees** on the Instructor's Resource disk.

4. Creating a CD Collection Inventory

Using the worksheet provided, create a database to keep track of the music CDs you keep to play in the coffee shop.

To Create the CD Inventory

1. Open the file Proj0705 and save it as CD Inventory.
2. Change the worksheet into a list by adding field names to the top of each column, as follows: Title, Artist, Price, Type.
3. Use the data form to add the following two records:

    Shaking the Tree, Peter Gabriel, $13.99, Rock.

    Rumours, Fleetwood Mac, $8.99, Rock.

4. Sort the list alphabetically by artist so that you can easily find any CD.
5. Extract a list of all titles that cost more than $12.99 or less than $9.99 so that you can track the most expensive and least expensive titles.
6. Save the file. If requested by your instructor, print two copies, then close the file.

> In this activity, students create an inventory list by adding column field names to an existing worksheet. The **D**ata, **F**orm command is used to add two records. Students sort the list alphabetically by artist, using the **D**ata, **S**ort command. The **D**ata, **F**ilter, AutoFilter command is used to extract a list of titles that cost more than $12.99 or less than $9.99. Once the AutoFilter is displayed, use the Custom option in the Price field to display the Custom AutoFilter dialog box. Insert "is greater than" in the first operator text box and insert "12.99" in the first criteria text box. Choose the OR option, and insert "is less than" in the second operator text box and insert "9.99" in the second criteria text box. The solution file is saved as **CD Inventory** on the Instructor's Resource disk.

5. Using the Data Form to Add Records to a List

In this exercise, you use the data form to add records to a list.

To Use the Data Form to Add Records to a List

1. Open the file Proj0706 and save it as Billing 3.
2. Click a cell within the list to activate it.
3. Choose **D**ata, F**o**rm to display the data form dialog box.
4. Use the scroll bar to move to the end of the records. A blank dialog box should display on your screen.

Project 7 Managing Data

5. Add the following record to the list:

Billing Date:	6/1/97
Company:	Reliable Roofing
Amount:	175.00
Date Paid:	6/15/97
Amt. Rec'd:	175.00

   You cannot enter information into the other fields, because these are calculated automatically.

6. Add the following records to the list using the data form:

Billing Date:	6/8/97	6/7/97
Company:	Craig Concrete	Decks & More
Amount:	292.00	87.00
Date Paid:	6/10/97	6/30/97
Amt. Rec'd:	292.00	87.00

7. Close the data form dialog box.

8. Save the file again, and leave it open for the following exercise.

> In this activity, students use the **D**ata, F**o**rm command to add three records. The solution file is saved as **Billing 3** on the Instructor's Resource disk.

Challenge

The following challenges enable you to use your problem-solving skills. Take time to work through these exercises now.

1. Sorting Data

As part of your job responsibilities, you have been asked to arrange the data in the Billing 3 worksheet by date paid, from the earliest to the latest date.

Select a cell within the list and choose **D**ata, **S**ort to display the Sort dialog box. In the Sort by list, select Date Paid. Sort the list in ascending order. Save the workbook again, and leave it open for the following exercise.

> In this activity, students continue to use the Billing 3 worksheet. Students sort the list alphabetically by Date Paid, using the **D**ata, **S**ort command. The solution file is saved as **Billing 3** on the Instructor's Resource disk.

2. Sorting by Two Fields

Because you can sort a list using up to three sort fields, you decide to sort the billing list by company name and then by billing date—oldest to newest. Remember, Excel sorts by the first criteria you enter, then looks at the second criteria if any of the data in the first field is the same.

Select a cell within the Billing 3 worksheet and display the Sort dialog box. Select Company in the Sort by drop-down list. Sort the list in ascending order. In the Then by drop-down list, select Billing Date. If matching records are found in the first criteria, the records will then be sorted by billing date. Perform the sort and then save the file. Leave the worksheet open for the next exercise.

> In this exercise, students continue to use the Billing 3 worksheet. Students use the **D**ata, **S**ort command to sort the list alphabetically by two sort keys, Company Name, and Billing Date. The solution file is saved as **Billing 3** on the Instructor's Resource disk.

3. Deleting Records

In a large database, you may want to have Excel locate specific records for you. These records can be deleted using the data form. Because you no longer need the records for A-1 construction, you decide to delete them.

Select a record within the list of the Billing 3 worksheet and display a blank criteria data form. In the Company text box, type A-1 Construction. Click the Find Prev button to locate the first record. Click Delete to delete the record from the list. Choose OK when you are prompted to delete the record. Delete all records for A-1 Construction; then close the data form. Save the worksheet and leave it open for the next exercise.

> In this exercise, the Criteria feature of the data form command is used to delete records for the A-1 Construction company. The solution file is saved as **Billing 3** on the Instructor's Resource disk.

4. Using AutoFilter

You have been asked to find only the records of companies that owe your company money. You are then to find the records of those companies to whom your company owes money. You decide to use the AutoFilter to make the task easier.

Select any cell in the Billing 3 worksheet. Choose **D**ata, **F**ilter, AutoFilter to display filter arrows next to each of the field names in the list. Click the Balance field filter arrow and select (Custom...) to display the AutoFilter dialog box. In the first operator text box, select is greater than. Type 0 in the first criteria text box to display all the records with a balance greater than 0. The record for Decks & More should display on your screen.

Now display all the companies that owe your company money. Click the Balance field filter arrow and select (Custom...). In the first operator text box, select is less than. Type 0 in the first criteria text box to display all the records with a balance of less than 0. The records for Wilson General Contractors and Craig Concrete display on your screen. If requested by your instructor, print two copies of the worksheet. Click the Balance filter arrow and select (All) from the list. All of the records are again displayed. Turn off AutoFilter. Save the worksheet before closing it.

> The **D**ata, **F**ilter, AutoFilter command is used to extract a list of Balances that are zero. Once the AutoFilter is displayed, use the Custom option in the Balance field to display the Custom AutoFilter dialog box. Insert "is greater than" in the first operator text box and "0" in the first criteria text box. A second Custom AutoFilter is used to display all records with a balance less than zero. The solution file is saved as **Billing 3** on the Instructor's Resource disk.

5. Displaying Records

Now that you know how to use Excel's database features, you can use them to quickly access information in your checking account file.

Open Proj0707 and save it as Checking Account 7. Add the following checks to the list using the data form:

510	5/1	Jane Smith	15.00
511	5/5	Grocery Store	36.00

You want to see where your biggest expenditures are, so display all the checks that are larger than $100.00. Print a copy of this worksheet. Display all the records in the list. Display all the records for the Grocery Store, so that you can quickly see how much you have spent on groceries. If requested by your instructor, print two copies of this worksheet. Display all the records in the list. Remove the AutoFilter feature. Save the file again, then close it.

> In this activity, students use the **D**ata, **F**orm command to add two records to a list. The **D**ata, **F**ilter, **A**utoFilter command is used to extract a list of checks that are larger than $100.00. Once the AutoFilter is displayed, students use the Custom option in the Check Balance field to display the Custom AutoFilter dialog box. Insert "is greater than" in the first operator text box and "100.00" in the first criteria text box. A second Custom AutoFilter is used to display all records with a description of Grocery Store. The solution file is saved as **Checking Account 7** on the Instructor's Resource disk.

Project 8

Using Excel with Other Programs

Integrating Applications

In this project, you learn how to:
- ➤ Switch among Applications
- ➤ Copy Data between Applications
- ➤ Link Data between Applications
- ➤ Work with Embedded Data
- ➤ Share Data across Applications

Project 8 Using Excel with Other Programs

Why Would I Do This?

While at your desk, you probably do several things in rapid succession: work on a paper, talk on the phone, punch numbers into your calculator, and so on. Similarly, when you work on your computer, you may work for a few minutes on a document in a word processor, take a moment to update a worksheet, then look up a phone number in an electronic phone book.

One of the advantages of using software that runs under Windows 95 is that you have the capability to exchange data among various applications. In Windows 95, you can have more than one application running at once—called *multitasking*—so you can switch among applications as you need to work on different tasks. You can display several applications' documents at the same time, if necessary, and you can exchange data among those documents.

In addition, with Excel 97, you can easily open and work with documents that were created in different applications, such as Lotus 1-2-3. You can also save documents in different file formats so that people using other applications can open and work with worksheets created with Excel. This feature of Windows software is called *integration,* and it makes working with the computer easier and more intuitive.

Multitasking
The execution of more than one program at a time on a computer system.

Integration
Using two or more software applications together to create a single document.

✓ On Your Mark
What types of Windows applications do you use or expect to use? Can you think of situations in which you would share information between several applications, or have access to more than one application simultaneously?

Lesson 1: Switching among Applications

You can use the taskbar to switch among open applications and to start additional programs. The number of applications that you can have open at one time is largely determined by the amount of available memory in your computer.

To Switch among Applications

Tip for Instructors
Begin the topic with a discussion of RAM, and the inherent problems of running several programs simultaneously on computers that have a small amount of RAM.

Tip for Instructors
Remind students that the list of programs shown in the workbook probably differs from the list on their own computers.

Speedy Class
A discussion of how to add programs to the **P**rograms menu may be useful.

❶ In Excel, open the file Proj0801 and save it as Office Expenses.

The worksheet is a version of the office expenses worksheet you have used in earlier projects of this book.

❷ On the taskbar, click the Start button, then move the mouse pointer to the Programs command.

A submenu appears, similar to the one shown in Figure 8.1, listing all the programs installed on your computer.

**Project Time
45 minutes**

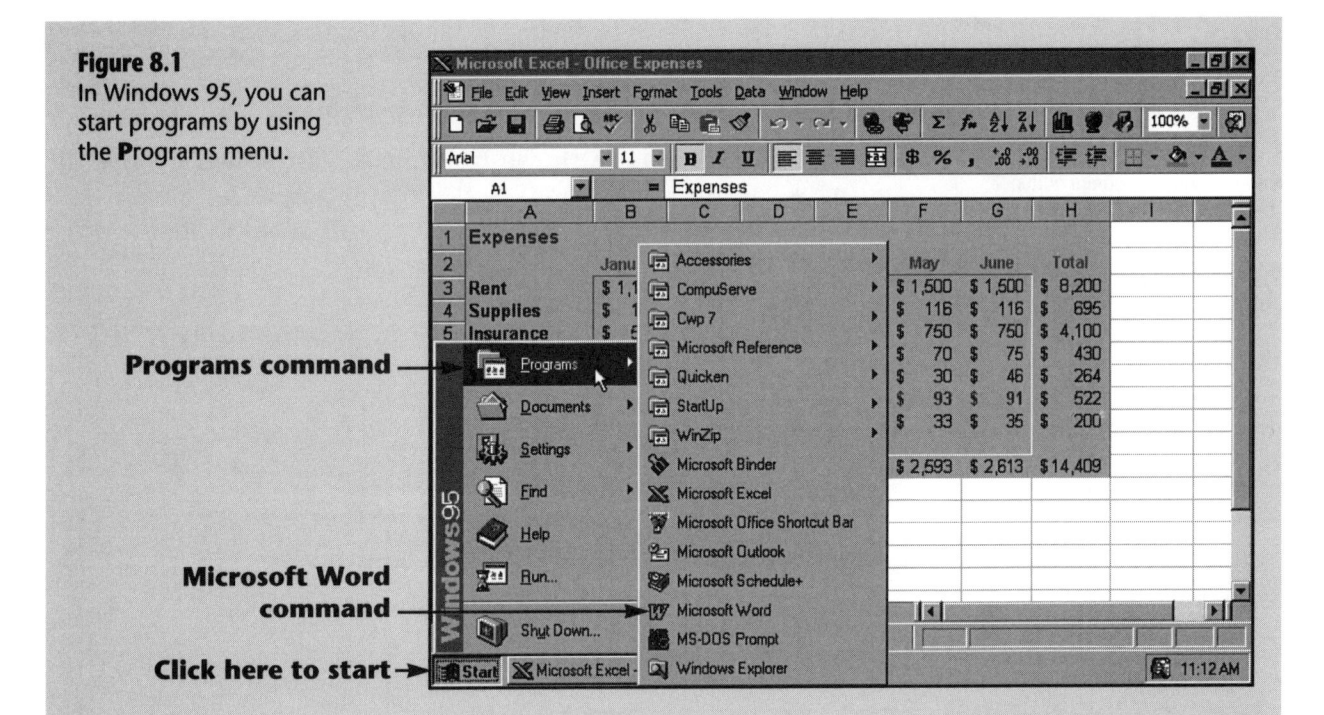

Lesson 1: Switching among Applications

Figure 8.1
In Windows 95, you can start programs by using the **P**rograms menu.

Programs command

Microsoft Word command

Click here to start

If you have problems...

If the taskbar does not appear at the bottom of your screen, it may have been moved to a different edge of your screen, or it may be hidden. If you see it in a different location, you can leave it there or drag it back to the bottom. If it doesn't appear at all, simply slide the mouse pointer down to the bottom of the screen to see if it appears. If you want the taskbar to be visible all the time, you can change the taskbar properties in Windows 95.

Microsoft Word was chosen for this example because it is a popular word processing program that is widely available. If you cannot find Microsoft Word listed in the **P**rograms submenu or if you have a different version of Microsoft Word installed, check with your instructor for information about what to do in this project. Your instructor may have you use a different word processing application to complete the lessons in this project.

Don't worry if you have never used Word or any other word processing software before. The instructions in this project tell you exactly what to do. Remember, just about everything you do with Excel and Word in this project can be done using other Windows 95 applications. However, if you are using a different word processing application, the steps you use to complete the lessons may be slightly different.

continues

To Switch among Applications (continued)

Tip for Students
You can easily switch between open programs by clicking a program button on the taskbar at the bottom of the screen.

3 **Click Microsoft Word on the Programs submenu.**

Microsoft Word opens, as shown in Figure 8.2; Excel remains open and moves to the background. Notice that a button for Microsoft Word has been added to the taskbar. Microsoft Word is often used in conjunction with Excel.

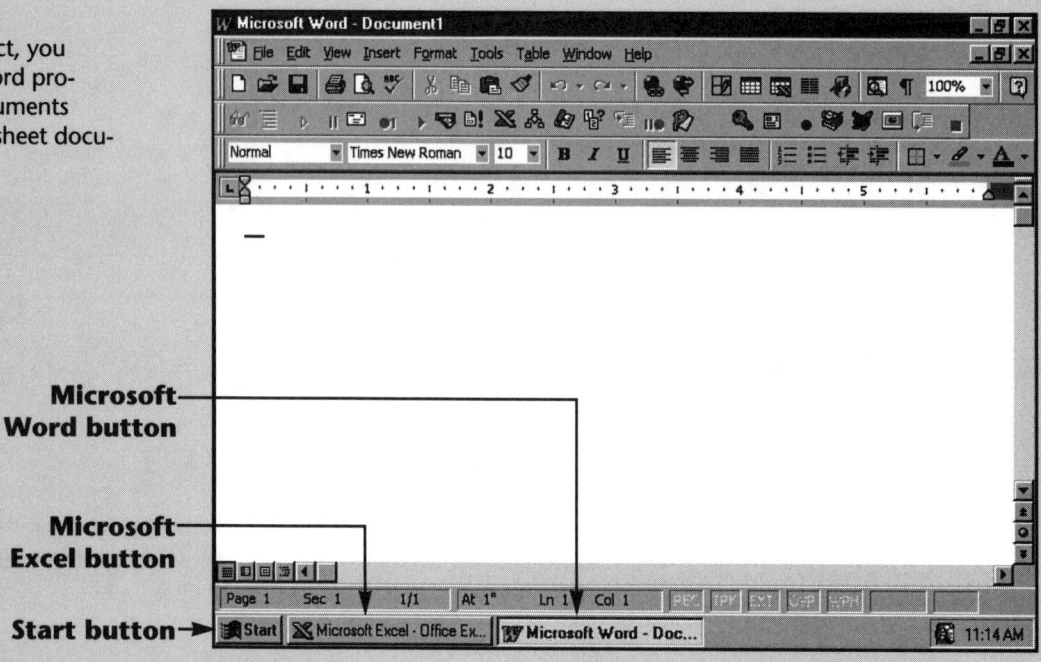

Figure 8.2
In this project, you integrate word processing documents with spreadsheet documents.

Tip for Students
Save the file with a new name in Word by choosing **F**ile, Save **A**s. Saving in Excel is performed the same way.

4 **In Word, open the file `Proj0802` and save it as `Memo`.**

You will use the `Memo` document with the Excel `Office Expenses` document throughout this project (see Figure 8.3).

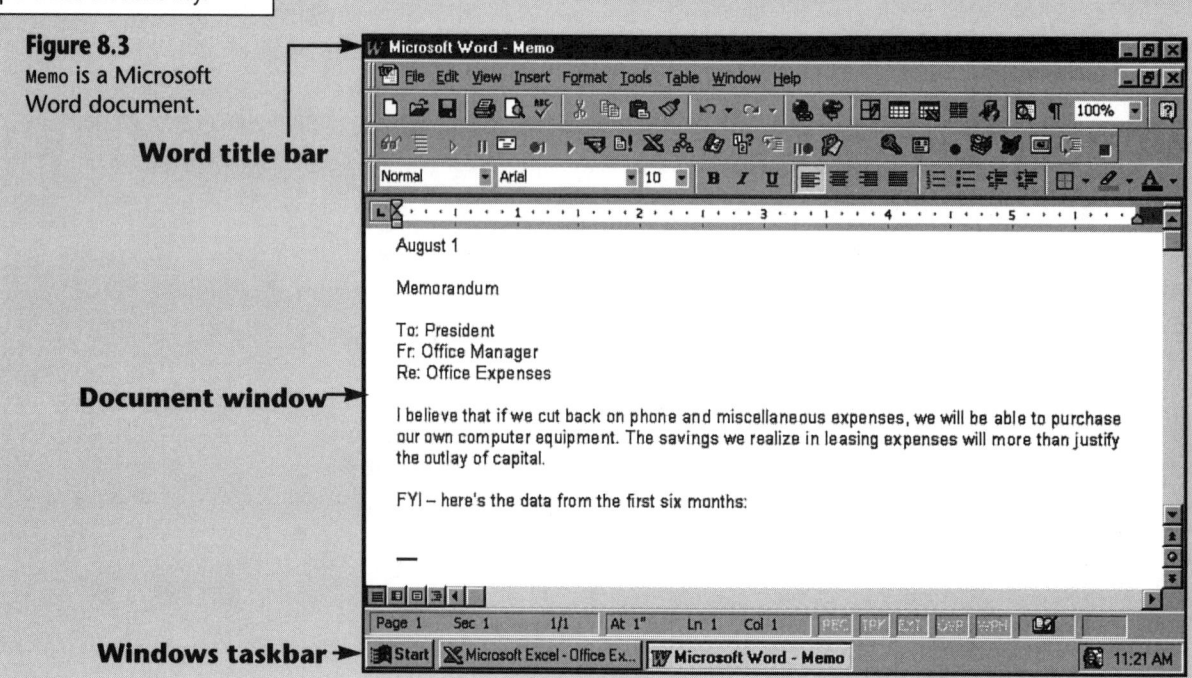

Figure 8.3
`Memo` is a Microsoft Word document.

Speedy Class

You can display all open Windows 95 programs by right-clicking an empty area of the taskbar and then choosing Tile **H**orizontally or Tile **V**ertically. Note that all windows that you want to tile must be open and not minimized.

5 **Click the Microsoft Excel button on the taskbar.**

This switches you back to Excel. Word remains open, running in the background. Keep all these documents and applications open. In Lesson 2, you learn how to copy data from one application to another.

Tip for Students

Check the taskbar at the bottom of the screen to see whether a program is open more than once. There will be a button for each instance of an opened program.

Another quick way to switch among open applications is to press and hold down [Alt] as you press [Tab]. Each time you press [Tab], the name of the next open application appears. When you see the name of the application you want to use, release both keys.

If you are distracted by an open application that is visible on the desktop behind the active application, maximize the active application to fill the desktop. If you want to switch to the application in the background, use the taskbar or press [Alt]+[Tab].

If you are using a suite of applications, such as Microsoft Office, you can use the shortcut bar included with the suite to switch among programs. The shortcut bar usually appears in the title bar of the active applications, and it displays one button for each application in the suite. Click the application button to open or to switch to a different application.

Microsoft Office is a collection of several Microsoft applications sold in one package, which usually includes Excel, Word, PowerPoint (a presentation graphics software package), and Access (a database program). Microsoft Office also includes special features, such as the shortcut bar designed to make integration with other Microsoft applications easier.

If you have problems...

If you find that your system is slow or locking up, you may have unintentionally launched a program twice instead of simply switching to it. (You can launch a program again from the **P**rograms menu, even if it is already running, but not from the taskbar.) To avoid this problem, just check the taskbar before opening a new program to make sure that the program is not already running. If two buttons for the same program appear, right-click one of them and choose Close from the shortcut menu.

On Your Mark

How many ways of copying data can you think of? (*Answers:* Toolbar buttons, **E**dit menu commands, keyboard shortcuts, saving as an object and then embedding the object.)

Lesson 2: Copying Data between Applications

It's easy to copy information from one application to another, and it saves you from having to re-enter data. For example, suppose that you want to include data from a worksheet in a letter to your company's president. You can perform this task easily by using the Windows Clipboard and task-switching capabilities.

To Copy Data between Applications

① In Excel, select cells A6:H9 in the Office Expenses **worksheet.**

This is the data you want to copy to the memo document.

② Click the Copy button on the Standard toolbar.

The data is copied to the Windows Clipboard. You can use the menu commands or the toolbar buttons to copy, cut, and paste data among applications. In short, you can use the Clipboard to copy or move data from one Windows application to another, just as you can copy or move data within a single document. For a refresher on using the Clipboard, refer to Project 2, "Building a Spreadsheet."

③ Click the Microsoft Word button on the taskbar.

The Memo file that you opened earlier in this project should now be on your screen.

④ Press Ctrl+End to move the insertion point to the blank line at the end of the memo.

This is where you want to insert the data you just copied from Excel.

⑤ Click the Paste button on the Standard toolbar.

The data is pasted from the Clipboard into the letter at the insertion point's location (see Figure 8.4). The data is inserted in Word as a table, and retains most of the formatting from Excel. The table is in no way connected to the original data in Excel. If you know how to use Word, you can edit and format the data using the T**a**ble menu features. The changes will have no effect on the worksheet data in Excel. Likewise, if you edit the Excel worksheet, the changes do not effect the table in Word.

To prepare for the next lesson in this project, undo the paste action now to remove the Excel data from the Word document.

Tip for Instructors

Discuss the Clipboard: Only one item resides in the Clipboard at a time; you can paste the content of the Clipboard an unlimited number times; it is accessible to all Windows 95 programs; the content of the Clipboard is erased when you shut off or reboot your computer.

Figure 8.4
Selected data from the Excel worksheet now appears in the Word document.

Tip for Students
Note that this is a simple copy and paste operation. No links exist between the files in Excel and Word. If you change the text or numbers in Excel, the version of the text or numbers that was pasted into Word will remain unchanged.

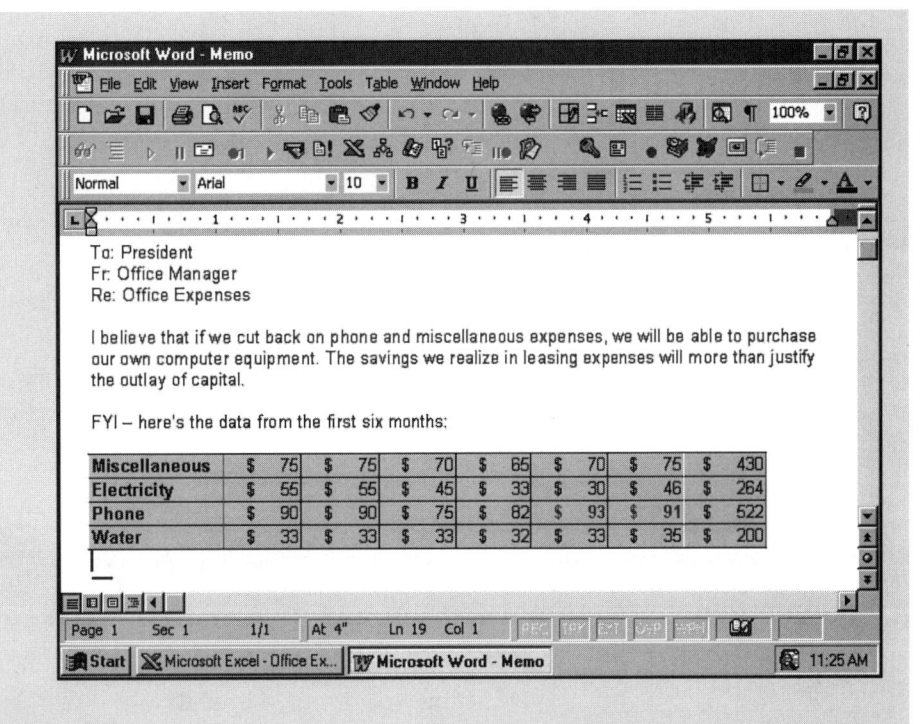

6 In the Memo document, click the Undo button, or press Ctrl+Z.

Word reverses the paste action, and the Excel data is removed from the Memo document.

Save your work, and keep all the current files and applications open. In the next lesson, you learn how to link data between Excel and Word.

To move data from one application to another, use the **C**ut command or its toolbar button rather than the **C**opy command. If you are concerned about losing data, you can use the **C**opy command, then after you paste the data in the new location, return and delete it from the original location. You can also display both worksheets on-screen at the same time, then select and drag the data you want to move from one worksheet to the other.

Lesson 3: Linking Data between Applications

✓ On Your Mark
In what situations would it be useful to connect information between files?

The next level of sophistication in using Excel with other applications is to *link* data from Excel to a document in another program. For example, you can link a range of cells from the expense worksheet to the memo in Word. Then, if you change any values in the worksheet, the information in the Word document is updated automatically. Keep in mind, however, that you cannot edit the linked data in the Word document. (Look for the Jargon Watch at the end of this lesson for more information about the terminology of sharing information between applications.)

Project 8 Using Excel with Other Programs

You can link Excel data to many applications, including Word; presentation programs, such as PowerPoint; and database programs, such as Access. You can even link Excel data to programs that are not part of the Microsoft Office suite, as long as they support linking.

Another benefit of linking Excel data to other applications is that you can double-click the Excel data in the other document to quickly switch to the Excel worksheet where you originally created the data. Also, unlike the copy you made of the chart in the previous lesson, linking the chart updates the document.

You create a link so that you don't have to remember to update the same information in two places: the original worksheet and its representation in the letter.

To Link Data between Applications

> **Tip for Instructors**
> Students can check the source of links in a document by choosing **E**dit, Lin**k**s.

1 **Click the Excel button on the taskbar to switch to Excel, then select cells A1 through H11 in the** `Office Expenses` **worksheet.**

This time, you want to link all of the worksheet data to your letter.

2 **Click the Copy button.**

This copies the selected range to the Windows Clipboard.

3 **Click the Microsoft Word button on the taskbar to switch to Word.**

Word is once again on-screen with `Memo` open.

4 **Press Ctrl+End to move the insertion point to the blank line at the end of the document.**

This is where you want to insert the linked data from Excel.

5 **Choose Edit, Paste Special.**

The Paste Special dialog box appears, as shown in Figure 8.5.

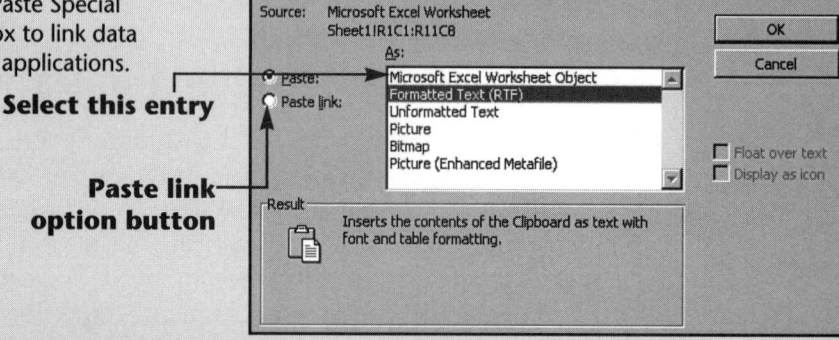

Figure 8.5
Use the Paste Special dialog box to link data between applications.

Select this entry

Paste link option button

6 **Click the Paste link option button.**

This tells Word that you want to link the Excel data to the Word document.

Lesson 3: Linking Data between Applications 219

> **Speedy Class**
> Discuss the other link choices in the Paste Special dialog box (**P**aste, Paste **L**ink, **D**isplay as Icon), as well as the different choices for Paste As.

> **Tip for Instructors**
> Instruct students to display the Word and Excel screens in a tiled format. This way they can make a change in Excel and watch it automatically update in Word.

7 **Select Microsoft Excel Worksheet Object from the As data type list.**

This tells Word that you want to paste the data as an actual Excel worksheet that will be updated any time changes are made in the `Office Expenses` worksheet. Notice that a description of the results of your selections appears in the Result area of the dialog box.

8 **Choose OK.**

The Excel data is pasted into the memo as an actual Excel worksheet object, as shown in Figure 8.6. Notice that Word changes the display view on the screen so that it can show the object in the document. The white boxes around the edges of the worksheet are called *selection handles*. You can drag a handle to change the size of the worksheet in the document.

Now try changing a cell in the Excel worksheet to see how the linked data changes automatically.

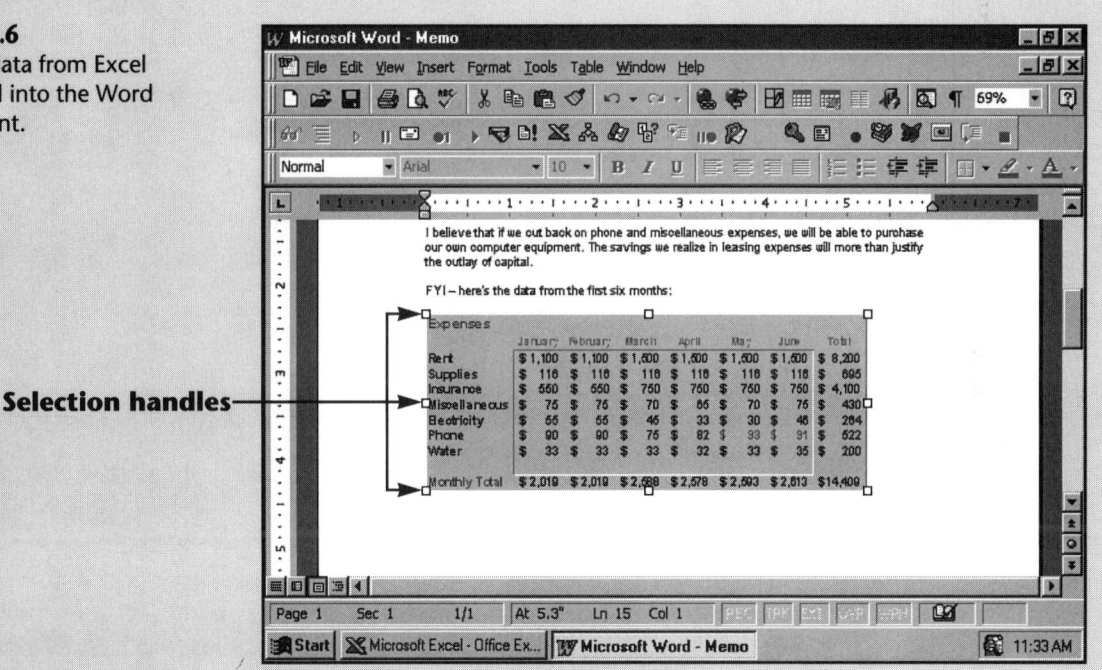

Figure 8.6
Linked data from Excel is pasted into the Word document.

Selection handles

> **Tip for Students**
> Note the change that occurs in the chart when you change the numbers.

9 **Double-click anywhere within the Excel data in the Word document.**

This switches back to Excel with the `Office Expenses` worksheet open. If necessary, maximize the worksheet.

10 **Change cell F8 in the worksheet to $80.00.**

This shows a decrease in the amount spent on phone expenses in May. Make sure that you press Tab or End to update the change to the cell. Notice that Excel automatically updates the conditional formatting, as well as the totals that depend on the data in cell F8.

continues

Project 8 Using Excel with Other Programs

To Link Data between Applications (continued)

⓫ Click the Microsoft Word button on the taskbar.

Word appears, displaying the Memo document. Notice that the linked worksheet has been automatically updated to reflect the changes made in Excel, as shown in Figure 8.7. The May phone expenses, the totals, and the conditional formatting have all changed.

Figure 8.7
The values changed in Excel are updated automatically in the linked data in Word.

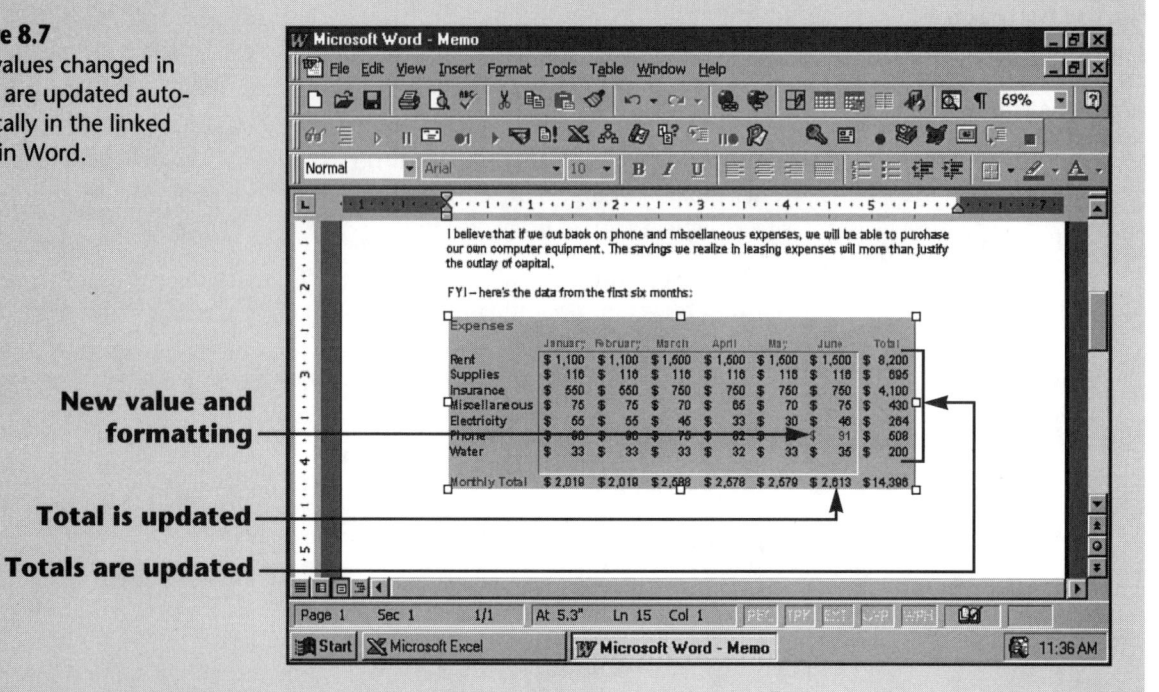

New value and formatting

Total is updated

Totals are updated

Save your work in both the Word document, Memo, and the Excel worksheet, Office Expenses. Keep all the current files and applications open for the next lesson. In Lesson 4, you work directly with the Excel object embedded in Word.

If you have problems...

If the data does not update in Word, you may have just pasted instead of pasting a link. Go back to Excel and copy the spreadsheet again, then switch to Word and make sure you choose **E**dit, Paste **S**pecial.

Also, if you change the location of either the source or the target document, the link between the two is broken. (See the following Jargon Watch for definitions of these terms.) For example, if you move the target document to a different folder or disk and then change the data in the source, Excel cannot automatically update the link. You must repeat the link procedure. If you plan to change the location of either document, you should consider simply copying the data from one to the other or embedding the data, as described in Lesson 4.

Tip for Students

If data is not updating properly, be sure to double check for the existence of a link between the files. Do this by choosing **E**dit, Lin**k**s.

Jargon Watch

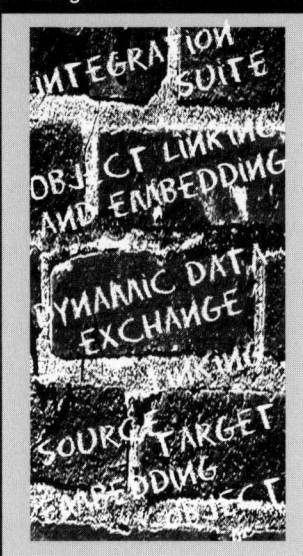

These days, **integration** is a hot buzz word in computing. For example, the Microsoft Office **suite** of applications are referred to as *integrated* because they share many features and standard commands, and because it is easy to integrate data from one program into another.

The common Windows platform enables many Windows applications to easily share data. This feature goes by the catchy names **OLE**, which stands for **object linking and embedding**, and **DDE**, which stands for **dynamic data exchange**.

DDE uses **linking** to set up communication between two files so that when you update the **source** file, the **target** file in the link is automatically updated. `Office Expenses` is the source file in Lesson 3, while `Memo` is the target file.

OLE uses **embedding** to create an **object** in the client file. You use embedding in Lesson 4 to make changes in an Excel object that resides in Word. With embedding, the object is not linked in any way to the source file; you can edit the worksheet data using Excel functions, but the changes do not affect the original data.

Lesson 4: Working with Embedded Data

✓ On Your Mark
In what situations would it be preferable to embed rather than link information?

In Lesson 3, you linked an Excel worksheet object into the Word document `Memo`. This is useful for keeping both the source and target documents current. However, there may be times when you want to keep the two separate—perhaps to experiment with the effects of possible changes in data or when you may not have access to the source file once the target file has been created. In cases such as these, you can embed the Excel worksheet object into the Word document instead of linking it.

Embedding the data enables you to edit the worksheet in the Word document without switching back to Excel. For example, if you want to take a quick look at the effect of decreased leasing costs on your expenses, double-click the embedded Excel worksheet object and make changes directly to the worksheet—without ever leaving the memo you are writing. The original source file, `Office Expenses`, is not affected by the change.

To Work with Embedded Data

Tip for Instructors
If the Excel data has been linked in two places in the Word file (the Excel numbers from the worksheet and the chart), this step will have to be performed on each set of data.

❶ In the Word file `Memo`, click the Excel data and press `Del`.

This selects the data, then deletes it, severing the link between the two applications. Now try embedding an Excel worksheet object into the Word document.

❷ Click the Microsoft Excel button on the taskbar.

This switches you back to the `Office Expenses` worksheet.

continues

Project 8 Using Excel with Other Programs

To Work with Embedded Data (continued)

❸ Select cells A1 through H11, and click the Copy button on the Standard toolbar.

This copies the data you want to embed in the Word document onto the Windows Clipboard.

❹ Click the Microsoft Word button on the taskbar.

This switches you back to Word.

❺ Press Ctrl+End to position the insertion point on the blank line at the end of the memo, then open the Edit menu and choose Paste Special.

The Paste Special dialog box opens.

❻ Choose Microsoft Excel Worksheet Object in the As list box, then choose OK.

Excel embeds the worksheet object at the insertion-point location. Do not choose the Paste **L**ink option button in the Paste Special dialog box. To embed the object, leave the **P**aste option button selected. Now try editing the worksheet.

❼ Double-click the Excel worksheet object in the Word document.

The worksheet appears in its own Excel window within Word, as shown in Figure 8.8. Although the title bar tells you that you are still in Word, notice that the menu bar and toolbars have changed to include Excel commands and options. The formula bar even appears in your Word window now. Next, see what effect removing miscellaneous costs would have on your worksheet.

> **Quicksand**
> Make sure that the Paste Link option in the Paste Special dialog box is not chosen.

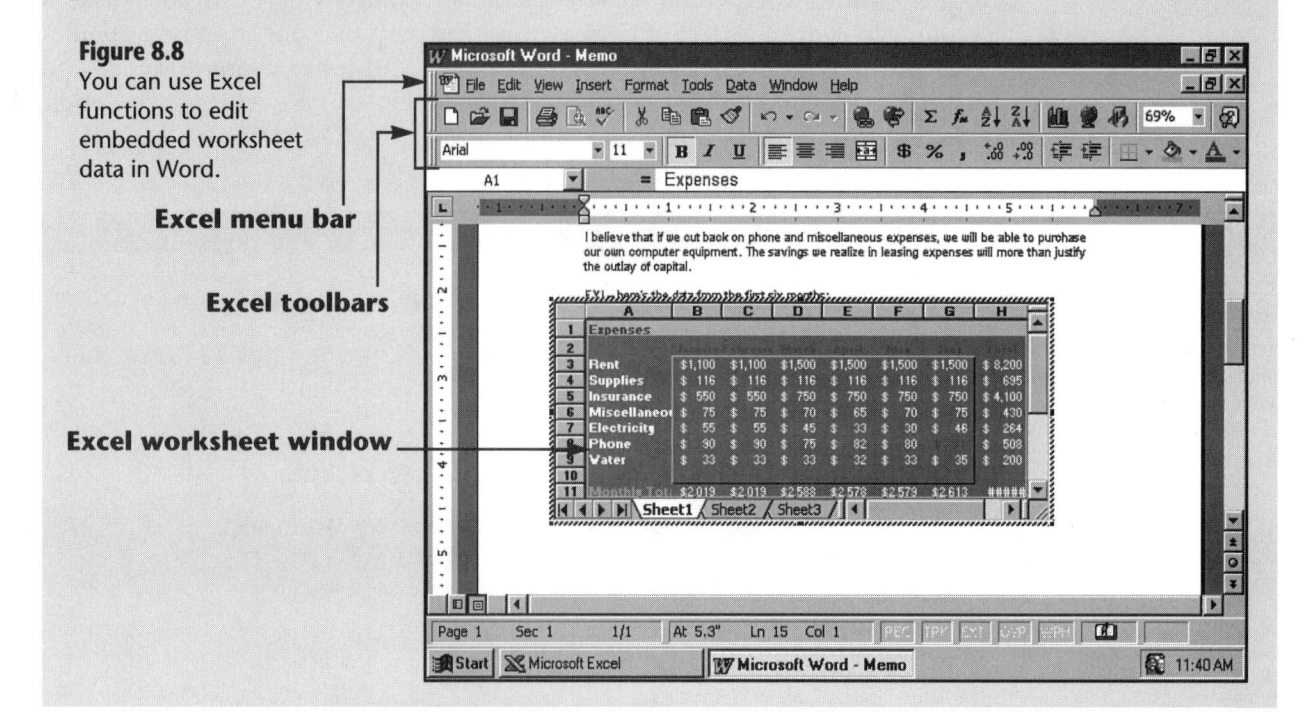

Figure 8.8
You can use Excel functions to edit embedded worksheet data in Word.

Excel menu bar
Excel toolbars
Excel worksheet window

Lesson 4: Working with Embedded Data 223

8 **In the worksheet window, click the row 6 number in the worksheet frame, then choose Edit, Delete.**

This selects then removes row 6 from the embedded worksheet. Notice that the total cells change automatically to reflect that miscellaneous expenses are no longer included.

9 **Click anywhere in the Word document outside the worksheet window.**

This closes the Excel worksheet, and Word returns to its normal state. Notice that the change you made in the data appears in the Word worksheet object, as shown in Figure 8.9. Save the Word document, then switch back to see how the changes affected the original worksheet document.

Figure 8.9
The changes appear in the embedded worksheet, but not in the original Excel file.

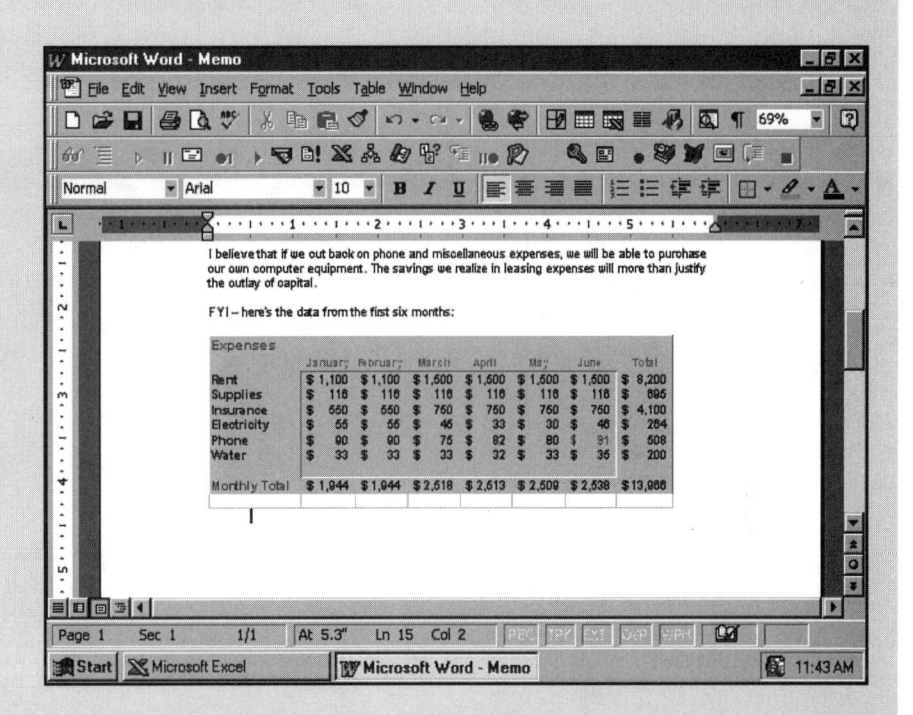

10 **In Word, choose File, Close, then click Yes to save the changes to the Word document** Memo. **Close Word.**

When Word closes, Excel remains open on your screen. In Excel, you can see that no changes have been made to the original data.

Save your Excel work. In the next lesson, you learn how to share data across different applications.

Project 8 Using Excel with Other Programs

Lesson 5: Sharing Data across Different Applications

On Your Mark

In what situations would you save a worksheet in a file format other than Excel's default format?

Sometimes you may need to open files that have been created in a different application. Likewise, you may want to be able to open an Excel file using a different application. For example, you may use Excel at work but have Lotus 1-2-3 at home, or a coworker or client may use a different application.

Excel 97 is able to open and save files in a wide variety of file formats. When you open a file created in a different file format, Excel simply converts the data to the Excel format, so you can easily use all Excel commands and options. When you save the file, you have the option of saving it in its original format or in Excel 97 format. When you save a file in a different file format, Excel converts the file so that you can open it and edit it in the other application. In this lesson, you save the Office Expenses workbook file in a different file format.

To Share Data across Different Applications

❶ In the Office Expenses worksheet, choose File, Save As.

Tip for Students

If others will be using worksheets you create or modify, make sure you save them in the appropriate file format. Consider the spreadsheet program and the corresponding version number others are using when choosing the file format.

The Save As dialog box is displayed. The default file type is Microsoft Excel Workbook. However, you want to save the file so that you can open it with Lotus 1-2-3.

❷ Click the Save as type drop-down arrow.

A list of file formats that you can use to save the file opens, as shown in Figure 8.10.

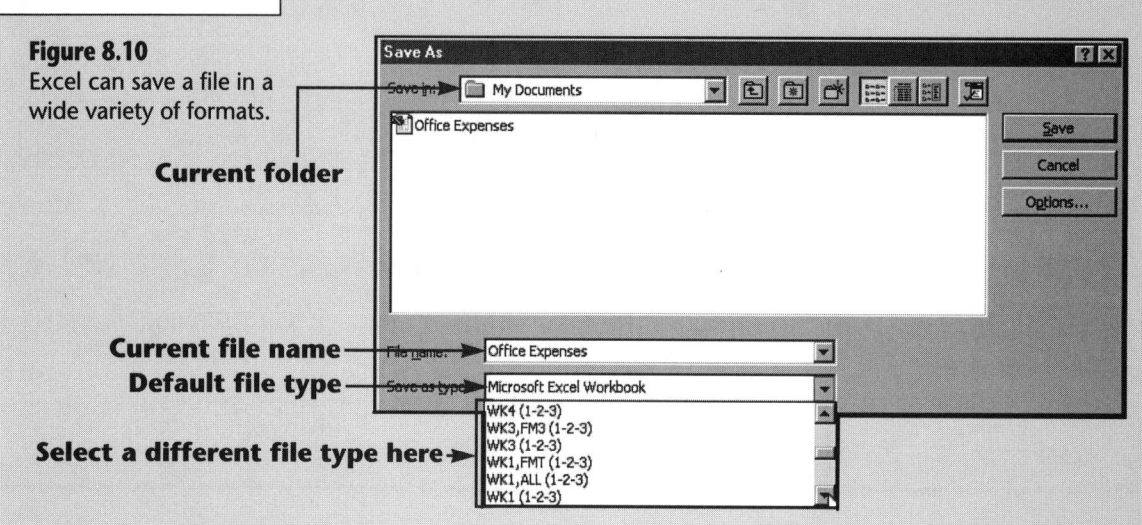

Figure 8.10
Excel can save a file in a wide variety of formats.

- Current folder
- Current file name
- Default file type
- Select a different file type here

❸ Scroll down the list and choose WK4 (1-2-3).

This tells Excel you want to save the file in Lotus 1-2-3 Release 4 format.

Lesson 5: Sharing Data across Different Applications 225

4 **In the File name text box, type** Expenses123.

This changes the file name to make it easier to identify which file is the Excel file and which is the Lotus 1-2-3 file. If necessary, select the folder or disk where you want to save the file from the Save in drop-down list.

5 **Choose Save.**

Excel saves the file in 1-2-3 format and keeps it open on the screen, as shown in Figure 8.11. The Excel Office Expenses worksheet is saved in its original format and closed. All of the data in the Expenses123 file appears as it did in the Excel format file; however, some of the formatting is changed to conform to the 1-2-3 standard. For example, notice that the dollar signs are no longer left-aligned in the cells formatted as currency. Also, notice that the conditional formatting is no longer in effect and that merged cells are split.

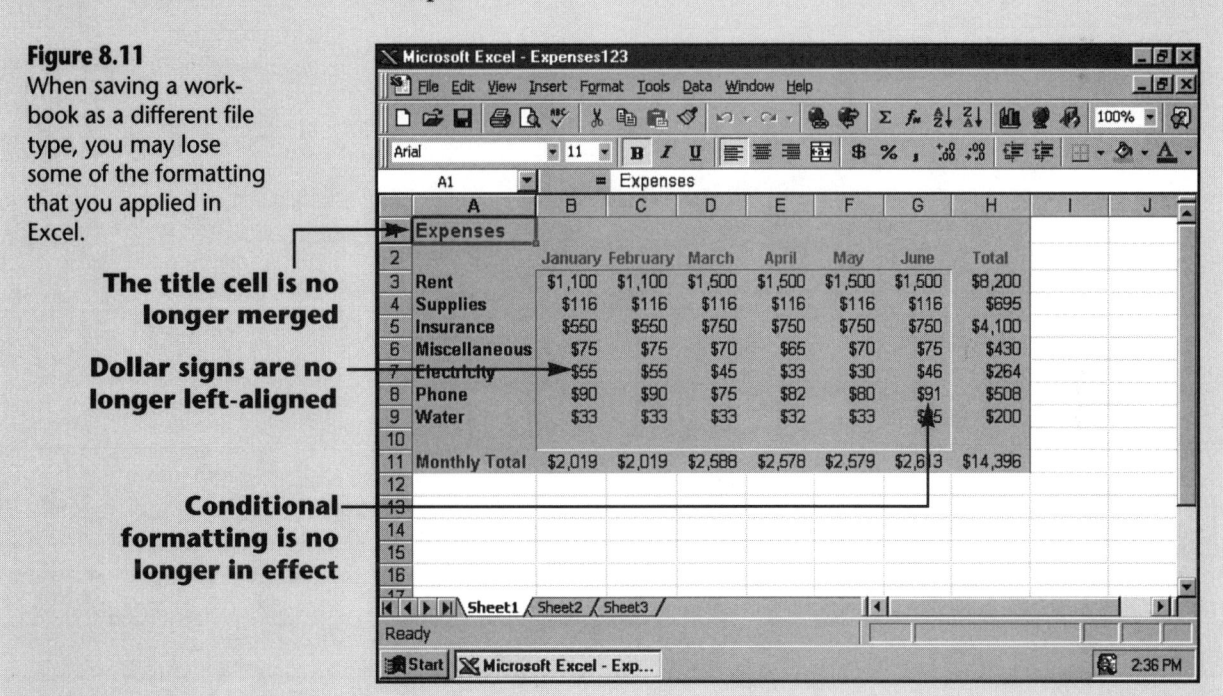

Figure 8.11
When saving a workbook as a different file type, you may lose some of the formatting that you applied in Excel.

The title cell is no longer merged

Dollar signs are no longer left-aligned

Conditional formatting is no longer in effect

6 **Choose File, Close.**

The first time you close a file saved in a different file format, Excel displays a message box asking if you want to convert the file back to Excel format before you close it.

7 **Choose No.**

Excel saves the file in 1-2-3 Release 4 format and closes it. Now, try opening a file saved in a different file format.

continues

Project 8 Using Excel with Other Programs

To Share Data across Different Applications (continued)

8 **In Excel, choose File, Open.**

The Open dialog box is displayed. Notice that only Excel files are listed.

9 **From the Files of type drop down list, choose Lotus 1-2-3 Files.**

This tells Excel to list files saved in the Lotus 1-2-3 format. In the Open dialog box, you see the Expenses123 file name (see Figure 8.12).

Figure 8.12
You can use Excel to open files saved in other file formats.

File name

Files of type text box

10 **Select the Expenses123 file name, then choose Open.**

Excel opens the file.

11 **Close the Expenses123 file.**

You have now completed the lessons in this project. If you have completed your session on the computer, exit all open applications and Windows 95 before turning off the computer. Otherwise, continue with the "Checking Your Skills" section.

With Excel 97, you can save data in the HTML format, which is used to store files on the Word Wide Web. To save data in HTML format, choose **F**ile, Save as **H**TML to start the Internet Assistant Wizard, then follow the instructions that the wizard displays on your screen.

In the Open dialog box, you can display all files stored in the current folder—regardless of file type—by choosing All Files from the Files of **t**ype drop down list.

Project Summary

To	Do This
Switch applications	On the Windows 95 taskbar, click the button for the application you want to make active, or press Alt+Tab.
Copy data between applications	Select the data to copy and click the Copy button on the Standard toolbar. Change to the target document, position the insertion point, and click the Paste button on the Standard toolbar.
Move data between applications	Select the data to move and click the Cut button on the Standard toolbar. Change to the target document, position the insertion point, and click the Paste button on the Standard toolbar.
Link data between applications	Select the data to link and click the Copy button on the Standard toolbar. Change to the target document, position the insertion point, and choose Edit, Paste Special. Click the Paste Link option button, select the object type, and choose OK.
Edit linked data	Double-click the data to open the source document. Make changes, then close the source document.
Embed data	Select the data to embed and click the Copy button on the Standard toolbar. Change to the target document, position the insertion point, and choose Edit, Paste Special. Select the object type, and choose OK.
Edit embedded data	Double-click the data to open an editing window. Edit the document, then close the editing window.
Save a file in a different format	Choose File, Save As. Select the file format from the Save as type drop-down list, then choose Save.
Open a file in a different format	Choose File, Open. Select the file type from the Files of type drop-down list, select the file you want to open, then choose Open.

Checking Your Skills

True/False

For each of the following, check *T* or *F* to indicate whether the statement is true or false.

✔T __F **1.** You can use the Windows taskbar to switch among programs, but not to open them.

__T ✔F **2.** On the taskbar, you click the Start button to start Microsoft Word.

__T ✔F **3.** You cannot use the keyboard shortcuts for copying, cutting, and pasting when you are integrating applications.

✔T __F **4.** If your system slows down, it could be because you have two copies of the same program open.

✔T __F **5.** Use the Edit, Paste Special command to link or embed data between applications.

Project 8 Using Excel with Other Programs

✔T __F **6.** If two documents are visible on your screen, you can drag data from one document to another.

✔T __F **7.** Excel 97 is capable of opening and saving files in different formats, such as Lotus 1-2-3.

__T ✔F **8.** If you use the Copy and Paste commands to copy data from a worksheet to a word processing file, the data will be automatically updated when you make changes to one of the files.

__T ✔F **9.** You cannot link data between programs that are not part of the Microsoft Office suite.

✔T __F **10.** The number of applications you can have open at one time is largely determined by the amount of your computer's memory.

Multiple Choice

Circle the letter of the correct answer for each of the following questions.

1. Which of the following is an easy way to switch among applications?

   a. Press Ctrl+Del

   b. Press Alt+Ctrl

   c. Click the application's button on the Windows taskbar.

   d. Click the application's Start box.

2. Which of the following can be passed over a link between applications?

   a. numbers

   b. charts

   c. ranges of cells

   d. all the above

3. One application opens within the other application when you do what between two applications?

   a. copy

   b. link

   c. move

   d. embed

4. Embedding and linking are part of a Windows feature called what?

   a. OLE

   b. LEO

   c. ELO

   d. LLE

5. You can make a change in the source, and the destination automatically updates when you do what?

   a. link

   b. embed

   c. copy

   d. paste

6. The changes you make in the target document do not affect the source when you do what to the data?

   a. link

   b. embed

   c. copy

   d. paste

7. Which of the following formats is used to store Excel files on the World Wide Web?

   a. WWW

   b. WK4

   c. HTML

   d. INT

8. What occurs when you double-click a linked object?

   a. The object is deleted from the document.

   b. You are switched back to the originating program.

   c. An error message displays.

   d. You can edit the document in the target file.

Checking Your Skills **229**

9. To embed data into a file, you use which dialog box to paste it into the target document?

   a. Paste Special
   b. Paste Object
   c. Embed Object
   d. Embed Data

10. To paste a link into a document, you choose which option button in the Paste Special dialog box?

    a. Paste
    b. Link
    c. Link document
    d. Paste link

Completion

In the blanks provided, write the correct answer for each of the following statements.

1. A link is a(n) _one_-way connection between the source worksheet and the client file.
2. If your system slows when embedding, you may want to consider sharing your data by _copying_ instead.
3. The taskbar displays buttons for all _open_ applications.
4. When pasting data into another program, the data appears at the _insertion_ point.
5. The _source_ application is the one in which the original object was created.
6. To switch to an application in the background, use the taskbar or press _Alt_ + _Tab_.
7. You can use the _Clipboard_ to copy or move data from one application to another.
8. If the taskbar does not appear at the bottom of the screen, it may have been moved or it may be _hidden_.
9. To move data from one application to another, use the _Cut_ command.
10. If you change the location of the source or target document, the link between the two is _broken_.

Matching

In the blank next to each of the following terms or phrases, write the letter of the corresponding term or phrase.

_e_ 1. White boxes around the edges of a worksheet object
_j_ 2. The file in which linked data originates
_g_ 3. The file in which linked data is pasted
_f_ 4. Executing more than one program at a time
_h_ 5. Using two or more software applications together to create a single document
_d_ 6. Embedding is used to create this in a file.
_i_ 7. Uses linking to set up communication between two files.
_a_ 8. Used to switch among open applications and to start additional programs.
_b_ 9. Use this command to paste information from the Clipboard to another application.
_c_ 10. Use this command to paste a link or embed data into a document.

Project 8   Using Excel with Other Programs

a. taskbar
b. Paste
c. Paste Special
d. object
e. selection handles

f. multitasking
g. target file
h. integration
i. dynamic data exchange (DDE)
j. source file

Screen ID

Label each element of the Excel screen shown in Figure 8.13.

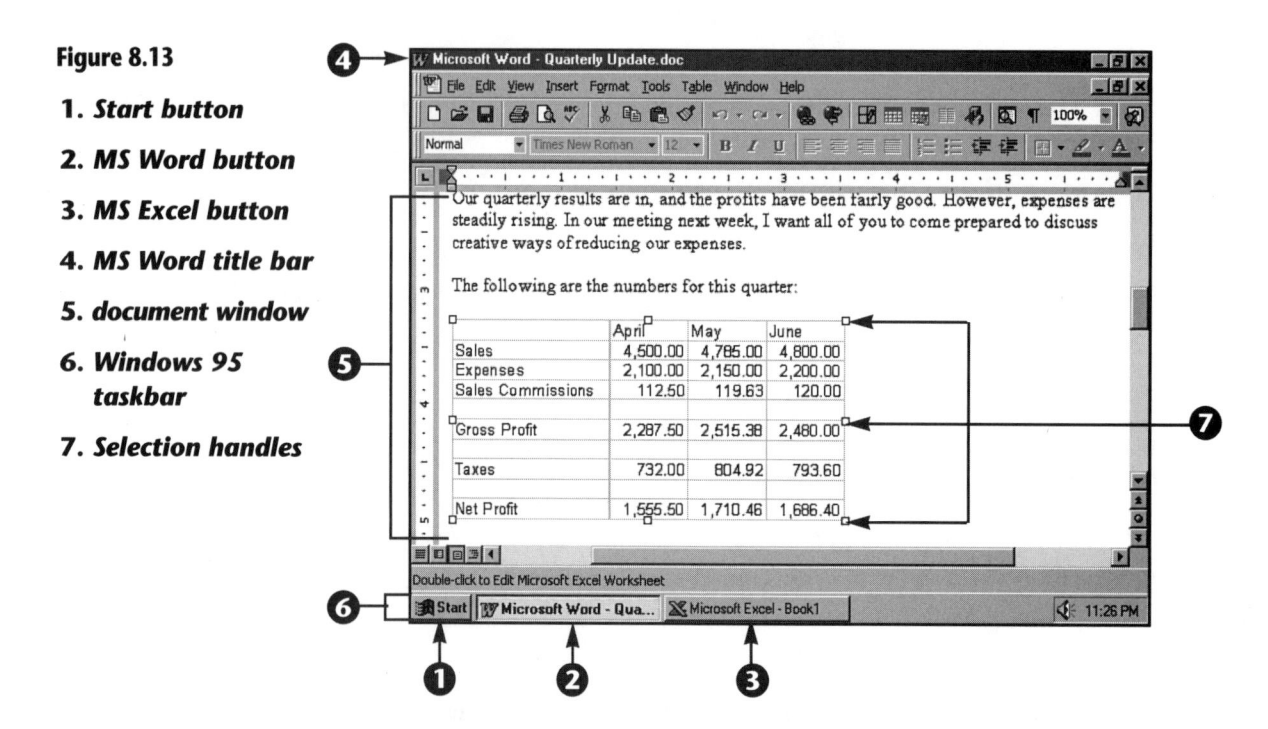

Figure 8.13

1. **Start button**
2. **MS Word button**
3. **MS Excel button**
4. **MS Word title bar**
5. **document window**
6. **Windows 95 taskbar**
7. **Selection handles**

Applying Your Skills

Practice

The following exercises enable you to practice the skills you have learned in this project. Take a few minutes to work through these exercises now.

1. Switching among Applications

In this project, you learned how easy it is to open additional applications and to switch among these applications. In this exercise, you practice switching among applications.

To Switch among Applications

1. In Excel, open the file Proj0803 and save it as Profit Loss 4.
2. Start the Word application using the Start button on the taskbar. If Word is not on your computer, ask your instructor which application to use.

Applying Your Skills

3. Open one more application located in the Accessories submenu. You choose which of these applications to open. Notice that a button for each of these applications displays on the taskbar.

4. Click the Microsoft Excel button to switch to this application.

5. Click the Microsoft Word button to switch to this application.

6. Hold down the (Alt) key and press (Tab⇆) until the name of the Accessories application that you opened appears on the screen. Release both keys to access this application.

7. Close the Accessories application and Microsoft Word. Leave Excel open for the following exercise.

> In this exercise, students open an Excel file, start Microsoft Word, and start Accessories programs. Then, students use the Windows 95 task bar to switch between the open programs. The Excel 97 solution file is saved as **Profit Loss 4** on the Instructor's Resource disk.

2. Creating a Letter

A friend of yours is thinking about relocating to a new state, and has asked you where your company has offices so she can contact them about employment opportunities. You agree to provide a list of the states where your company has offices. Because you already have a list of sites stored in an Excel worksheet, you simply copy the data into a word processing document to send to her.

To Create a Letter

1. In Excel, open the file Proj0803a and save it as Relocate.

2. In Word, open the file Proj0804 and save it as Site Letter.

3. Copy the entire list of offices and locations in the worksheet to the Clipboard.

4. Move to the end of Site Letter in Word, then paste the worksheet data.

5. Save the letter. If requested by your instructor, print two copies before closing both files.

> In this exercise, students open an Excel file and a Microsoft Word file, then use the **C**opy and **P**aste commands to copy the Excel data to the Word document. The solution files are saved as **Relocate** and **Site Letter** on the Instructor's Resource disk.

3. Adding Names to Your Phone List

The company president sends you a file of a memo with the names of four new contacts who he thinks might be interested in your product. You want to add the names to the phone list that you already created in Excel. Instead of retyping the names and phone numbers, copy the data from the word processing document into Excel.

To Add Names to Your Phone List

1. Open the file Proj0805 in Excel, and save it as Contacts.

2. Open the file Proj0806 in Word, and save it as New Names.

3. Select the table in the Word document, then copy it to the Windows Clipboard.

4. Switch to Excel, and paste the data from the Clipboard to the end of the list.

5. Save the worksheet. If requested by your instructor, print two copies before closing both files.

> In this exercise, students open an Excel file and a Microsoft Word file, then use the **C**opy and **P**aste commands to copy the Excel data to the Word document. The solution files are saved as **Contacts** and **New Names** on the Instructor's Resource disk.

4. Creating a Presentation for Potential Investors

Heading into your second year in business, you want to make a presentation to potential investors that will convince them to provide capital so you can open a second coffee shop. To do this effectively, you need to create a report in Word that includes narrative, as well as a worksheet showing strong sales for the current year. Link data from an Excel worksheet to the presentation document in Word, then make some last-minute changes in the Excel worksheet that will be updated in the linked chart.

To Create a Presentation for Potential Investors

1. In Excel, open the file Proj0807 and save it as **Coffee Sales**.
2. In Word, open the file Proj0808 and save it as **Presentation**.
3. In the Coffee Sales worksheet, select the entire worksheet (cells A1:E12) and copy it to the Clipboard.
4. Switch to Word and link the chart to the end of the Presentation document.
5. Switch back to the worksheet and make the following changes: in the January Mocha sales, change the value to **$300**; in the February Espresso sales, change the value to **$250**. Save the worksheet.
6. Switch back to the Word document to view the changes in the chart. Save the Presentation document. If requested by your instructor, print two copies of each file, then save and close all open documents.

> In this activity, students open an Excel file and a Microsoft Word file, then use the **C**opy and Paste **S**pecial, Paste **l**ink commands to copy and link the Excel data to the Word document. Students also make changes in the Excel worksheet, then notice that the changes are also made in the Word document. The solution files are saved as **Coffee Sales** and **Presentation** on the Instructor's Resource disk.

5. Comparing Regional Sales Figures

The New England regional sales manager has submitted sales figures on a disk in Lotus 1-2-3 file format. You want to be able to compare the figures with other regional figures that you have already entered into Excel and then give the comparison back to the sales manager for review. Open the 1-2-3 file, copy the data into the Excel worksheet, then save the Excel worksheet as a new 1-2-3 file.

To Compare Regional Sales Figures

1. Open the file Proj0809 in Excel and save it as **Sales Comparison**.
2. Open the Lotus 1-2-3 file Proj0810 in Excel and save it in 1-2-3 format as **NE Sales123**.
3. Copy the sales data from the NE Sales123 file into cells D2 through E12 in the Sales Comparison Excel workbook file.

Applying Your Skills

4. Adjust the column width so you can read the data, then save the Excel file.

5. Save the Sales Comparison file in 1-2-3 file format with the name Comparison123.

6. If requested by your instructor, print two copies or each file, then close them.

> In this activity, students open an Excel file and a Lotus 1-2-3 file, then use the Copy and Paste commands to copy the Lotus 1-2-3 data to the Excel worksheet. To increase column width, students move the mouse pointer to the line to the right of a column letter, then when the mouse changes to a double-headed black arrow, double-click the left mouse button. Students use the File, Save As command, select the Save as type text box to display WK4 (1-2-3) as the file type, then save the worksheet in the 1-2-3 format with the name **Comparison123** on the Instructor's Resource disk.

Challenge

The following challenges enable you to use your problem-solving skills. Take time to work through these exercises now.

1. Copying Data from One Application to Another

Your boss has asked you to create a document containing data from an Excel worksheet. To save having to reenter the information, you decide to copy the data from one application to another. Open the Word file Proj0811 and save it as Quarterly Update. In the Profit Loss 4 Excel worksheet (created in the previous exercise), copy the data in cells A4:D13 to the Clipboard. Switch back to the Word document and paste the data at the end of the Word document. Save the Word file and keep both Word and Excel open for the next exercise.

> In this activity, students open an Excel file and a Microsoft Word file, then use the Copy and Paste commands to copy and paste the Excel data range (A4:D13) to the Word document. The solution files are saved as **Quarterly Sales** and **Profit Loss 4** on the Instructor's Resource disk.

2. Linking Data

Now that you have copied the data, you realize that you could have linked the data. Then, if you have to make changes to the data in the original application, the target document is automatically changed.

Switch to the Word document, Quarterly Update. Select the information that you copied in the previous exercise, and then delete it. Switch back to the Excel document, Profit Loss 4. Copy the cells A4:D13 to the Clipboard and switch back to the Word document. Use the Paste Special dialog box to link the Excel worksheet object. In the Excel worksheet, change the April sales number in cell B5 to **4,700**. Switch back to Word to see the change in the Quarterly Update document. Save Quarterly Update and leave it open for the following exercise. Switch to Excel and save the Profit Loss 4 workbook. Leave it open for the following exercise.

> In this activity, students open an Excel file and a Microsoft Word file, then use the Copy and Paste Special, Paste link commands to copy and link Excel data to a Word document. Students also make changes in the Excel worksheet, then notice that the changes are also made in the Word document. The solution files are saved as **Quarterly Update** and **Profit Loss 4** on the Instructor's Resource disk.

3. Embedding Data

Because you now want to make some changes in the Word document but don't want to affect the original Excel worksheet, you decide to embed the data instead of linking it.

Switch to the Word Quarterly Update document, and delete the data you linked from the Excel worksheet. Switch back to Excel. Copy the data in cells A4:D13 and use the Paste Special dialog box to embed the data at the end of the Word document. Double-click the Excel worksheet object in the Word document to display the worksheet in its own Excel window within Word. Change the number in cell B5 to **4,500**. Save the Word document before closing it. Switch to Excel. Notice that the value in cell B5 has not changed. Save the Excel workbook and leave it open for the following exercise.

> In this activity, students open an Excel file and a Microsoft Word file, then use the **C**opy and Paste **S**pecial, **P**aste commands to copy and paste Excel data to a Word document. Students also make changes in the spreadsheet data area of the Word document, then notice that the changes are not reflected in the Excel worksheet. The solution files are saved as **Quarterly Update** and **Profit Loss 4** on the Instructor's Resource disk.

4. Sharing Data across Applications

One of your co-workers needs to access some data in one of your Excel worksheets. The only problem is that he doesn't have Excel on his system; only Lotus 1-2-3. You decide to save the Excel file as a Lotus 1-2-3 file so that he can access the information.

In the Profit Loss 4 workbook, choose **F**ile, Save **A**s to display the Save As dialog box. In the Save as **t**ype drop-down list, select WK3 (1-2-3). Choose **S**ave to save the file with the same name, but in the different format. Choose **F**ile, **C**lose. Excel displays a message box asking if you want to convert the file back to Excel format. Choose **N**o. The file is saved in the 1-2-3 format. Choose **F**ile, **O**pen. Because only Excel files display in the dialog box, click the Files of **t**ype drop down list. Choose Lotus 1-2-3 files. Select the Profit Loss 4 file, then choose Open. The file is opened in the Lotus 1-2-3 format. Close the Profit Loss 4 file.

> In this activity, students use the **F**ile, Save **A**s command, select the Save as **t**ype text box to display WK4 (1-2-3) as the file type, then save an Excel worksheet in the 1-2-3 format with the name **Profit Loss 4.**

5. Opening Files Created in a Different Application

Your checking account file was originally saved in Lotus 1-2-3 format. Now you have upgraded to the latest version of Excel, and you want to be able to use this file without having to reenter any information. You open the 1-2-3 file, then save it as an Excel file.

Open Proj0812.wk1. (Hint: You need to display Lotus 1-2-3 files to locate this file.) Save the file as **Checking Account 8** in Microsoft Excel 97 & 5.0/95 Workbook format. Close the file and reopen the Checking Account 8 file, which is now in Excel format. When you have finished, close the Checking Account 8 file.

> In this exercise, students open a file with the Lotus 1-2-3 format, then save the file as Checking Account 8 in the Microsoft Excel format. Students use the **F**ile, Save **A**s command, select the Save as **t**ype text box to display Microsoft Excel 97 & 5.0 as the file type, then save the worksheet in the Excel format with the name **Checking Account 8** on the Instructor's Resource disk.

Appendix A

Working with Windows 95

In this appendix, you learn how to:
- Start Windows 95
- Use the Mouse
- Understand the Start Menu
- Identify the Elements of a Window
- Manipulate Windows
- Exit the Windows 95 Program

Appendix A Working with Windows 95

Why Would I Do This?

Microsoft Windows 95 is a powerful operating environment that enables you to access the power of DOS without memorizing DOS commands and syntax. Windows 95 uses a *graphical user interface* (GUI) so that you can easily see on-screen the tools that you need to complete specific file- and program-management tasks.

This appendix, an overview of the Windows 95 environment, is designed to help you learn the basics of Windows 95.

Lesson 1: Starting Windows 95

The first thing you need to know about Windows is how to start the software. In this lesson, you learn how to start Windows; however, before you can start Windows, it must be installed on your computer. If you need to install Windows, refer to your Windows 95 manual or ask your instructor for assistance.

In most cases, Windows starts automatically when you turn on your computer. If your system is set up differently, you must start Windows from the DOS prompt (such as c:\>). Try starting the Windows program now.

To Start Windows 95

1. Turn on your computer and monitor.

   Most computers display technical information about the computer and the operating software installed on it.

   If Windows starts, you can skip step 2. Otherwise, you will see the DOS prompt c:\>.

2. At the DOS prompt, type **win** and then press ⏎Enter.

   When you start the Windows program, a Microsoft Windows 95 banner displays for a few seconds; then the *desktop* appears (see Figure A.1).

Program *icons* that were created during installation (such as My Computer, Recycle Bin, and Network Neighborhood) are displayed on the desktop. Other icons may also appear, depending on how your system is set up. *Shortcuts* to frequently used objects (such as documents, printers, and network drives) can be placed on the desktop. The *taskbar* appears along the bottom edge of the desktop. The *Start button* appears at the left end of the taskbar.

Graphical user interface (GUI)
A computer application that uses pictures, graphics, menus, and commands to help users communicate with their computers.

Desktop
The background of the Windows screen, on which windows, icons, and dialog boxes appear.

Icon
A picture that represents an application, a file, or a system resource.

Shortcut
Gives you quick access to frequently used objects so you don't have to look through menus each time you need to use that object.

Taskbar
Contains the Start button, buttons for each open window and the current time.

Start button
A click of the Start button opens the Start menu.

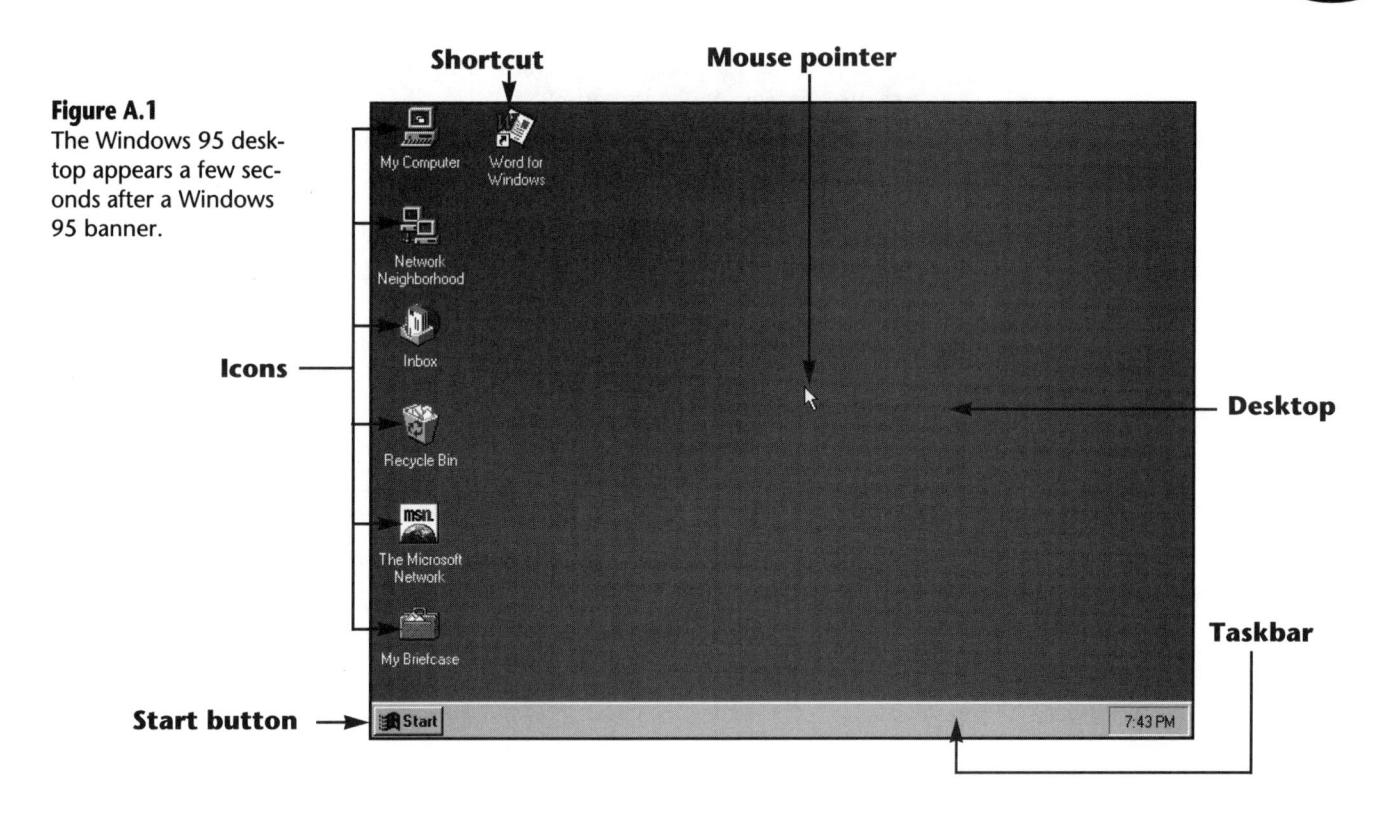

Lesson 2: Using the Mouse

Figure A.1
The Windows 95 desktop appears a few seconds after a Windows 95 banner.

[Screenshot of Windows 95 desktop with labels: Shortcut, Mouse pointer, Icons, Desktop, Taskbar, Start button]

Lesson 2: Using the Mouse

Pull-down menus
Menus that cascade downward into the screen whenever you select a command from the menu bar.

Dialog box
A window that opens onscreen to provide information about the current action or to ask the user to provide additional information to complete the action.

Mouse
A pointing device used in many programs to make choices, select data, and otherwise communicate with the computer.

Mouse pointer
A symbol that appears onscreen to indicate the current location of the mouse.

Mouse pad
A pad that provides a uniform surface for the mouse to slide on.

Windows is designed to be used with a *mouse*, so it's important that you learn how to use a mouse correctly. With a little practice, using a mouse is as easy as pointing to something with your finger. You can use the mouse to select icons, to make selections from *pull-down menus* and *dialog boxes*, and to select objects that you want to move or resize.

In the Windows desktop, you can use a mouse to

➤ Open windows

➤ Close windows

➤ Open menus

➤ Choose menu commands

➤ Rearrange on-screen items, such as icons and windows

The position of the mouse is indicated on-screen by a *mouse pointer*. Usually, the mouse pointer is an arrow, but it sometimes changes shape depending on the current action.

On-screen, the mouse pointer moves according to the movements of the mouse on your desk or on a *mouse pad*. To move the mouse pointer, simply move the mouse.

There are four basic mouse actions:

➤ *Click*. To point to an item, and then press and quickly release the left mouse button. You click to select an item, such as an option on a menu. To cancel a selection, click an empty area of the desktop. Unless otherwise specified, you use the left mouse button for all mouse actions.

Appendix A Working with Windows 95

➤ *Double-click.* To point to an item, and then press and release the left mouse button twice, as quickly as possible. You double-click to open or close windows and to start applications from icons.

➤ *Right-click.* To point to an item, and then press and release the right mouse button. This opens a Context menu, which gives you a shortcut to frequently used commands. To cancel a Context menu, click the left mouse button outside the menu.

➤ *Drag.* To point to an item, then press and hold down the left mouse button as you move the pointer to another location, and then release the mouse button. You drag to resize windows, move icons, and scroll.

If you have problems...
If you try to double-click but nothing happens, you may not be clicking fast enough. Try again.

Lesson 3: Understanding the Start Menu

Program folder
Represented by an icon of a file folder with an application window in front of it, program folders contain shortcut icons and other program folders.

The Start button on the taskbar gives you access to your applications, settings, recently opened documents, the Find utility, the **R**un command, the Help system, and the Sh**u**t Down command. Clicking the Start button opens the Start menu. Choosing the **P**rograms option at the top of the Start menu displays the **P**rograms submenu, which lists the *program folders* on your system. Program folders are listed first, followed by shortcuts (see Figure A.2).

Figure A.2
Click the Start button to open the Start menu. All your programs are grouped together in the Programs submenu.

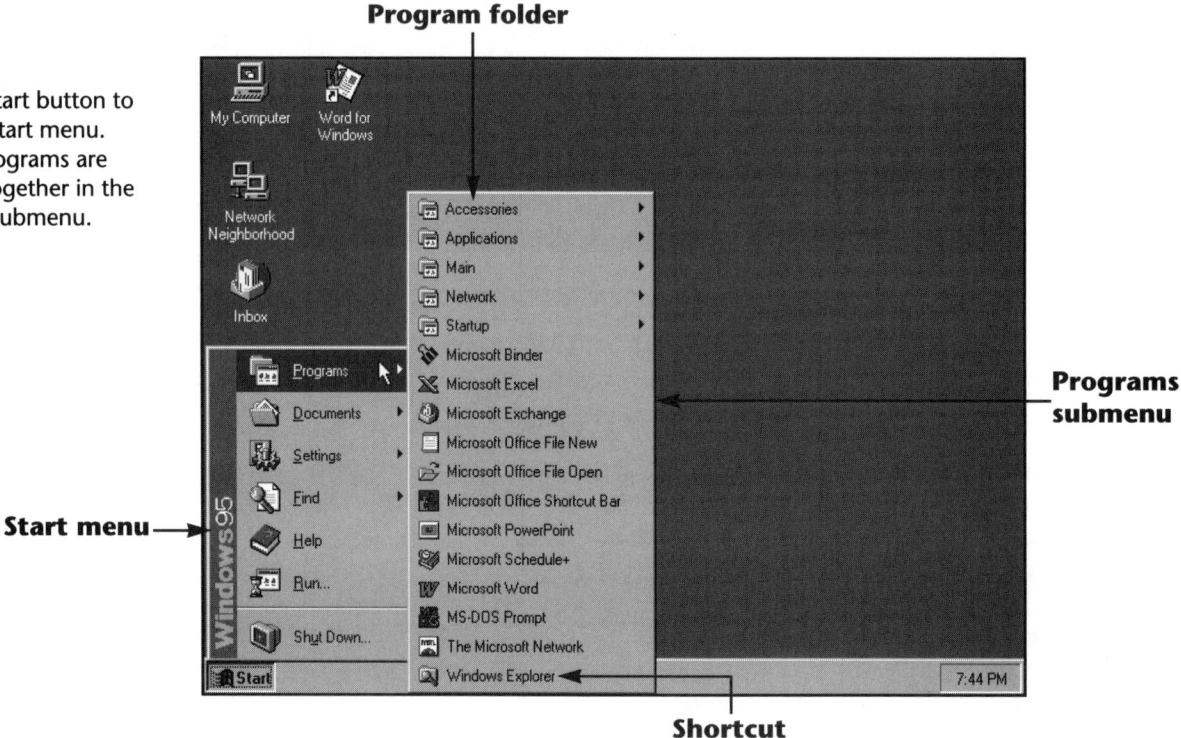

Lesson 4: Identifying the Elements of a Window

When the Start menu is open, moving the mouse pointer moves a selection bar through the menu options. When the selection bar highlights a menu command with a right-facing triangle, a submenu opens. Click the shortcut icon to start an application. If a menu command is followed by an ellipsis (...), clicking that command opens a dialog box.

Lesson 4: Identifying the Elements of a Window

In Windows 95, everything opens in a window. Applications, documents, and dialog boxes all open in windows. For example, double-clicking the My Computer icon opens the My Computer application into a window. Because window elements stay the same for all Windows applications, this section uses the My Computer window for illustration.

Title Bar

Across the top of each window is its title bar. A title bar contains the name of the open window as well as three buttons to manipulate windows. The Minimize button reduces windows to a button on the taskbar. The Maximize button expands windows to fill the desktop. The Close button closes the window.

Menu Bar

The menu bar gives you access to the application's menus. Menus enable you to select options that perform functions or carry out commands (see Figure A.3). The File menu in My Computer, for example, enables you to open, save, and print files.

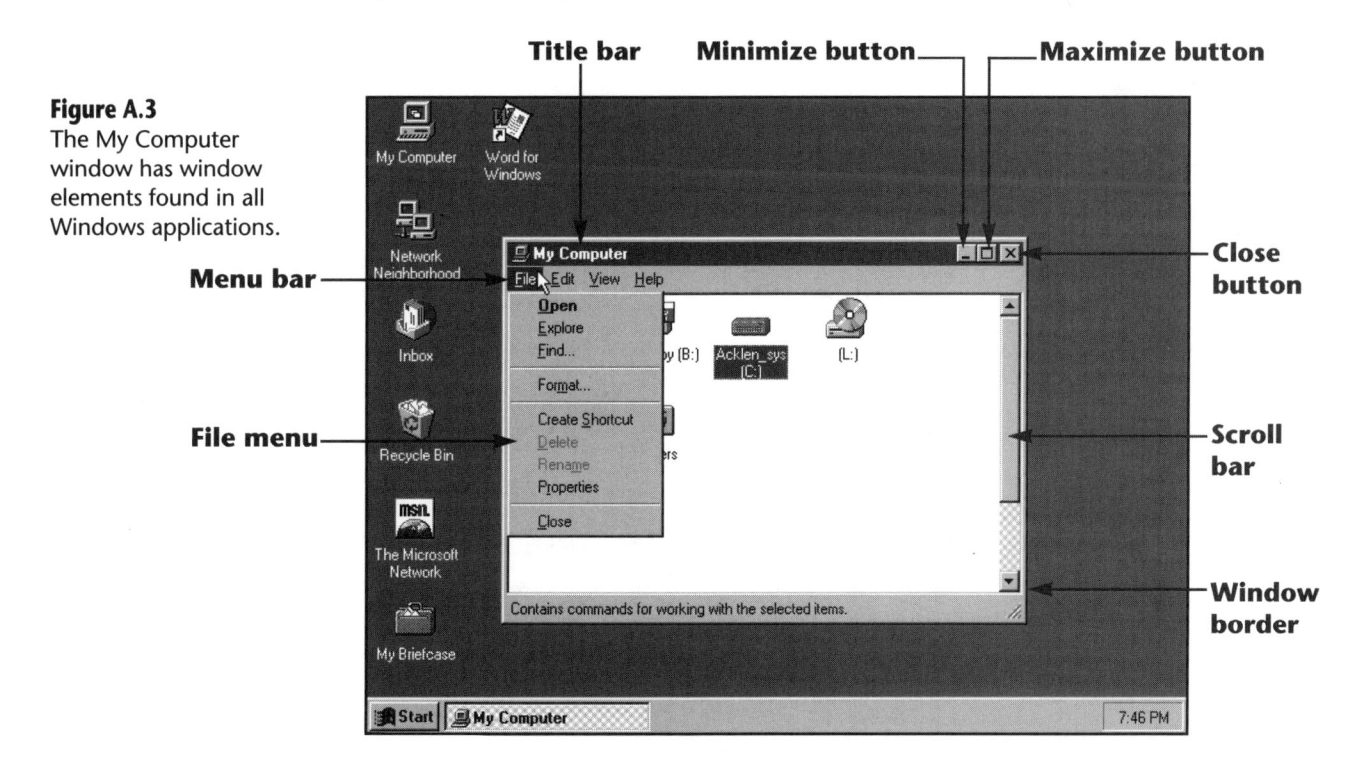

Figure A.3
The My Computer window has window elements found in all Windows applications.

Appendix A   Working with Windows 95

Some menu options require you to enter additional information. When you select one of these options, a dialog box opens (see Figure A.4). You type the additional information, select from a list of options, or select a button. Most dialog boxes have a Cancel button, which closes the dialog box without saving the changes; an OK button, which closes the dialog box and saves the changes; and a Help button, which opens a Help window.

Figure A.4
You can use the options in the Find dialog box to search for a file.

- Enter the name of the file here
- Click here to select this option
- Click here to select from a drop-down list
- Click here to open a dialog box
- Click here to find the file

Scroll Bar

Scroll bars appear when you have more information in a window than is currently displayed on-screen. A horizontal scroll bar appears along the bottom of a window, and a vertical scroll bar appears along the right side of a window.

Window Border

The window border identifies the edge of the window. In most windows, it can be used to change the size of a window. The window corner is used to resize a window on two sides at the same time.

Lesson 5: Manipulating Windows

When you work with windows, you need to know how to arrange them. You can shrink the window into an icon or enlarge the window to fill the desktop. You can stack windows together or give them each an equal slice of the desktop.

Lesson 5: Manipulating Windows

Maximize
To increase the size of a window so that it fills the entire screen.

Maximizing a Window

You can *maximize* a window so that it fills the desktop. Maximizing a window gives you more space to work in. To maximize a window, click the Maximize button on the title bar.

Minimizing a Window

Minimize
To reduce a window to an icon.

When you *minimize* a window, it shrinks the window to an icon on the taskbar. Even though you can't see the window anymore, the application stays loaded in the computer's memory. To minimize a window, click the Minimize button on the title bar.

Restoring a Window

When a window is maximized, the Maximize button changes into a Restore button. Clicking the Restore button restores the window back to the original size and position before the window was maximized.

Closing a Window

When you are finished working in a window, you can close the window by clicking the Close button. Closing an application window exits the program, removing it from memory. When you click the Close button, the window (on the desktop) and the window button (on the taskbar) disappear.

Arranging Windows

Changing the size and position of a window enables you to see more than one application window, which makes copying and pasting data between programs much easier. You can also move a window to any location on the desktop. By moving application windows, you can arrange your work on the Windows desktop just as you arrange papers on your desk.

Use one of the following options to arrange windows:

Tile
To arrange open windows on the desktop so that they do not overlap.

➤ Right-click the taskbar and choose Tile **H**orizontally.

➤ Right-click the taskbar and choose Tile **V**ertically. See Figure A.5 for an example.

Cascade
To arrange open windows on the desktop so that they overlap, with only the title bar of each window (behind the top window) is displayed.

➤ Right-click the taskbar and choose **C**ascade. See Figure A.6 for an example.

➤ Click and drag the window's title bar to move the window around on the desktop.

➤ Click and drag a window border (or corner) to increase or decrease the size of the window.

Figure A.5
The windows are tiled vertically across the desktop.

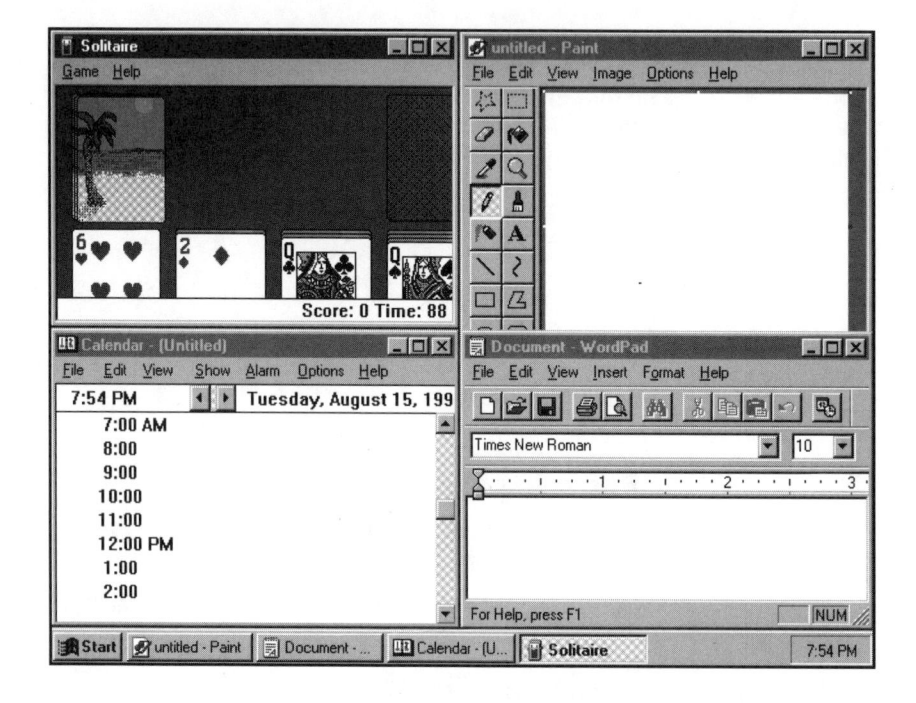

Figure A.6
The windows are cascaded on the desktop.

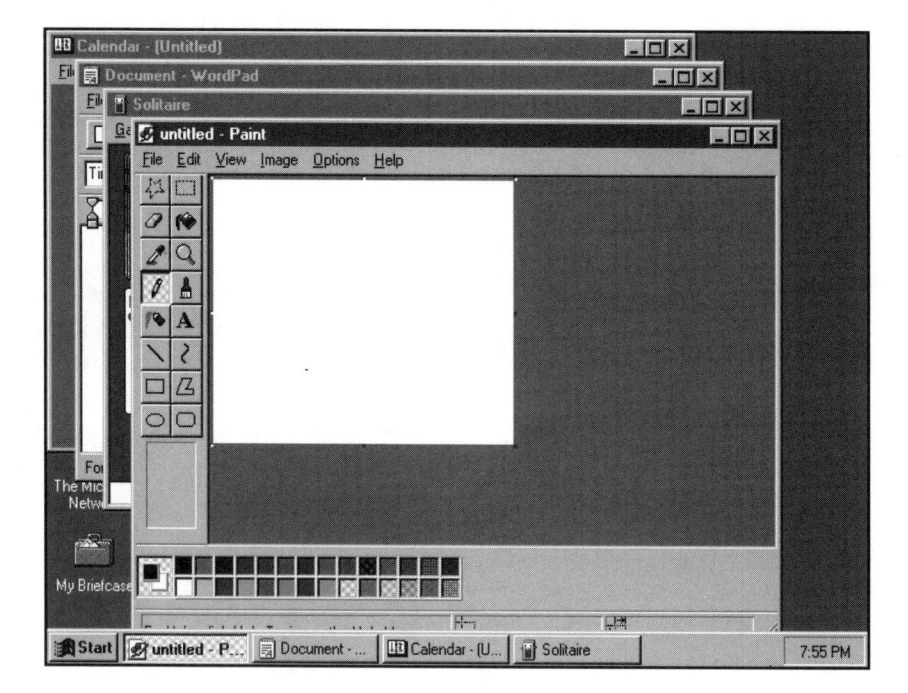

Lesson 6: Exiting the Windows 95 Program

In Windows 95, you use the Sh**ut** Down command to exit the Windows 95 program. You should always use this command, which closes all open applications and files, before you turn off the computer. If you haven't saved your work in an application when you choose this command, you'll be prompted to save your changes before Windows shuts down.

Lesson 6: Exiting the Windows 95 Program

To Exit Windows 95

1. Click the Start button on the taskbar.
2. Choose Sh**u**t Down.
3. Choose **S**hut down the computer.
4. Choose **Y**es.

Windows displays a message asking you to wait while the computer is shutting down. When this process is complete, a message appears telling you that you can safely turn off your computer now.

Appendix B

Project 1

Test Questions

True/False Questions

1. You must load Windows 95 before starting Excel 97.
2. You do not ever need to use a mouse when using Excel.
3. There are three scroll bars on the Excel screen.
4. A worksheet is one page in an Excel workbook.
5. To start Excel, you must click on an Excel icon.
6. The Excel screen displays the scroll bars at the top and left of each screen.
7. The Excel application window has a menu bar that displays twelve menus.
8. The address of the active cell is displayed in the Standard toolbar.
9. Another name for an Excel document is a worksheet.
10. The mouse pointer's shape indicates what you can do with the mouse.

Multiple Choice Questions

1. By default, the Excel application window has a menu bar that displays _____ menus.
    a. 6
    b. 7
    c. 8
    d. 9
2. In Excel 97, the default column width is _____ characters.
    a. 9
    b. 8.43
    c. 12
    d. 10
3. To move to the first cell of an active worksheet, cell A1, press _____.
    a. Ctrl+Home
    b. Home
    c. Home+Home
    d. PgUp
4. To move to column A of the active row, press _____.
    a. Ctrl+Home
    b. Home
    c. Home+Home
    d. PgUp
5. To move up one screen, press _____.
    a. Ctrl+Home
    b. Home
    c. Home+Home
    d. PgUp
6. You can cancel a menu by _____.
    a. pressing Esc
    b. clicking the menu name again
    c. clicking anywhere in the window outside of the menu
    d. any of the above
7. _____ are used to provide a description of a toolbar button.
    a. Tool tips
    b. Screen Tips
    c. Office assistants
    d. Help Tips
8. The shortcut key combination that enables you to go directly to a particular cell in the worksheet is _____.
    a. Ctrl+G
    b. Alt+G
    c. Shift+G
    d. none of the above

9. The extension added to Excel 97 files is _____.
    a. XLS
    b. EXL
    c. XSL
    d. EXS
10. To exit Excel 97, you can press _____.
    a. Ctrl+F4
    b. Break
    c. Alt+F4
    d. none of the above

Completion Questions

1. The formula used to add the contents of cell D5 to the contents of cell E2 is _____.
2. The Status Bar appears at the _____ of the Excel screen.
3. In Excel 97, each cell can contain up to _____ characters.
4. Worksheet tabs are located at the _____.
5. The _____ cell receives the data you type on your keyboard.
6. When referring to a particular cell, you use the cell _____.
7. To save a file on the A drive, select a: from the _____ drop-down list in the Save As dialog box.
8. A new workbook contains _____ worksheets.
9. To activate a cell, place the cell pointer over the cell and _____.
10. When you are working with a worksheet, the data you enter or edit is actually stored in a temporary memory of your computer called _____.

Project 2

Test Questions

True/False Questions

1. When a range is selected, a blue border surrounds the cells in the selected range.
2. You can place up to three items on the Clipboard at a time.
3. Information on the Clipboard is lost when you turn off the computer.
4. The Fill handle is the black square at the lower left corner of a selected cell or range.
5. If you copy more than a single cell, the paste area you select must equal the area of the copied data.
6. Columns cannot be deleted from a worksheet.
7. Rows cannot be inserted into a worksheet.
8. The **E**dit, Cu**t** command enables you to place selected data on the Clipboard.
9. The Edit, Paste command places the contents of the Clipboard in your worksheet.
10. You can use Excel's Cut and Insert Cells command to remove cells from one location in a worksheet and place them in another location.

Multiple Choice Questions

1. Use the **E**dit, _____ command to delete the contents of a cell.
    a. Cle**a**r
    b. **D**elete
    c. **F**ormat
    d. **M**ove
2. To select an entire worksheet, click the _____ button.
    a. Highlight All
    b. Fill
    c. Select
    d. Select All
3. When placed on the AutoFill fill handle, the mouse pointer becomes a _____.
    a. thin, black plus sign
    b. thin, white plus sign
    c. black cross
    d. dark rectangle
4. Because of the _____ feature, after you type the first few characters in the cell that match an existing entry in that column, Microsoft Excel automatically fills in the remaining characters for you!
    a. AutoFill
    b. Fill
    c. Repeat
    d. AutoComplete
5. The default location for storing files is the _____ folder.
    a. Excel
    b. Workbook
    c. My Documents
    d. Spreadsheet
6. Use the **F**ile, _____ command to save a file with a different file name.
    a. **S**ave
    b. Save **A**s
    c. Re**n**ame
    d. **R**ecover

7. In Excel, the standard notation for identifying ranges is to list the first cell in the range, then a(n) _____, then the last cell in the range.
    a. /
    b. -
    c. :
    d. .
8. _____ indicate the data that Excel will use to fill each cell.
    a. Comments
    b. ScreenTips
    c. ToolTips
    d. Macros
9. To quickly undo the most recent action, press _____.
    a. Ctrl+Z
    b. Ctrl+Y
    c. Ctrl+U
    d. Alt+U
10. To quickly redo the most recent action, press _____.
    a. Ctrl+Z
    b. Ctrl+Y
    c. Ctrl+R
    d. Alt+R

Completion Questions

1. The _____ command from the _____ menu will undo an editing change in a worksheet.
2. A(n) _____ is a group of cells in the worksheet.
3. The _____ is a temporary storage area containing data you can place in a worksheet using the **E**dit, **P**aste command.
4. When you use the Copy and Paste method to copy the contents of more than a single cell, the _____ area you select must be only one cell or must be the same size as the area of the copied data.
5. The **E**dit, _____ command removes selected information completely.
6. Moving dashes _____ the area you cut or copy to the Clipboard.
7. To clear the contents of the active cell, you press the _____ key.
8. The worksheet _____ is a horizontal bar containing the column letters and the vertical bar containing the row numbers.
9. Excel always inserts a new column to the _____ of the column you select.
10. The _____ command reverses commands.

Project 3: Test Questions

True/False Questions

1. You can use the AutoSum tool efficiently only when the cell containing the total is at the bottom of a column of numbers or at the end of a row of numbers.
2. You can use the AutoSum tool to sum only one row or column at a time.
3. If you do not type an equal sign at the beginning of a formula, Excel enters the values as text data.
4. You cannot use the Fill handle to copy formulas.
5. You can use the Formula palette to create a formula.
6. To make a cell reference absolute, enter a parentheses in front of the cell address.
7. The operator for exponential calculations is the tilde (~).
8. If you do not use parentheses in a formula, Excel performs multiplication calculations before division calculations.
9. Dragging across cells selects them.
10. You can use the Range Finder to replace cell addresses in a formula.

Multiple Choice Questions

1. To alter the order of mathematical precedence, use _____ around one or more mathematical operations in the formula.
   a. commas
   b. parentheses
   c. colons
   d. apostrophes

2. Considering the order of precedence, which of the following operators would be used first?
   a. *
   b. /
   c. -
   d. ^

3. Cell references that do not adjust to a pasted location are referred to as _____ cell references.
   a. relative
   b. absolute
   c. mixed
   d. combined

4. The AutoSum button automatically enters a formula that uses the _____ function.
   a. ADD
   b. SUM
   c. COMBINE
   d. TOTAL

5. Which of the following is an example of a relative cell reference?
   a. B5
   b. $B5
   c. B$5
   d. $B$5

6. Which of the following is an example of an absolute cell reference?
   a. B5
   b. $B5
   c. B$5
   d. $B$5

7. Press _____ to remove the flashing dotted line from a cell or a cell range.
   a. Enter
   b. Ctrl+Enter
   c. Esc
   d. Delete

8. What is the result of the following calculation: =8+(6*3)-2/2
   a. 20
   b. 22
   c. 25
   d. 18
9. Relative and absolute cell referencing is especially important because of the effects of the _____ command.
   a. Del
   b. Move
   c. Copy
   d. Cut
10. The default type of cell referencing is _____.
   a. circular
   b. absolute
   c. relative
   d. mixed

Completion Questions

1. Whenever you click in the format bar to edit a formula, Excel starts the _____.
2. The results of a formula appear in a cell and the formula itself appears in the _____.
3. _____ are built-in formulas.
4. All formulas begin with the _____ sign.
5. If a formula results in #NAME? instead of a value, it means you made a mistake entering a(n) _____.
6. The _____ is a feature of Excel that helps you locate cell references in a formula by color coding them.
7. To make a reference absolute, enter a(n) _____ in front of the cell address.
8. The _____ sign tells Excel that you are about to enter a formula.
9. The Enter button on the formula bar contains a(n) _____.
10. To remove the contents of a selected cell, press _____.

Project 4

Test Questions

True/False Questions

1. You have only two ways to enter any function into an active cell.
2. There are three ways to access the Paste Function.
3. A34 is an example of an acceptable range name.
4. When you click a function name, the area near the top of the dialog box displays a short description of what the function does and a list of its arguments.
5. The contents of the second dialog box in the Paste Function changes according to the function selected in the first dialog box.
6. You can include spaces in range names.
7. Functions must be entered in all uppercase letters.
8. When entering a function, you can indicate a range of cells used as the argument by clicking and dragging over the cells.
9. Do not use range names as arguments in functions.
10. By default, Excel assumes that the label text from the row in which the active cell is located will be the range name.

Multiple Choice Questions

1. _____ are the values on which a function performs its calculations.
   a. Ranges
   b. Numbers
   c. Arguments
   d. Formulas

2. All functions begin with a(n) _____.
   a. asterisk
   b. parentheses
   c. plus sign
   d. equal sign

3. The _____ function displays the current system date.
   a. DAY
   b. TODAY
   c. CURRENT
   d. SYSTEM

4. Use the _____ to select a function from Function drop-down list.
   a. Function dialog box
   b. Formula Palette
   c. Formula Editor
   d. Revise Function dialog box

5. When using the Formula Palette, you must enter values or cell references for each required _____ before the function will work properly.
   a. argument
   b. range
   c. cell
   d. formula

6. The _____ function shows the correct date only when the computer has the date set properly.
   a. DAY
   b. TODAY
   c. CURRENT
   d. SYSTEM

7. The _____ function returns TRUE if every argument is TRUE.
   a. AND
   b. IF
   c. NOT
   d. OR

8. The AutoSum button is on the _____ toolbar.
    a. Standard
    b. Formatting
    c. Formula
    d. Function

9. _____ errors can occur in you place parentheses in the wrong locations in a function.
    a. Syntax
    b. Name
    c. Logical
    d. Range

10. In the function, =IF(D11>4000, "YES," "NO," the argument is _____.
    a. D11
    b. IF
    c. "YES"
    d. >

Completion Questions

1. When entering functions, two common errors are _____ and _____.
2. A(n) _____ function's result is TRUE or FALSE.
3. When you nest functions in a formula, you _____ them.
4. Worksheet tabs are located at the _____ of a worksheet.
5. The _____ function enables you to set conditions.
6. The _____ function finds the smallest number in a range of numbers.
7. A(n) _____ is a predefined formula.
8. With the TODAY function you do not need to include any _____.
9. When entering a function, the range address appears in _____ in the formula bar.
10. You can quickly check the results of a calculation without actually entering the formula by using the _____ button.

Project 5

Test Questions

True/False Questions

1. You can use the conditional formatting feature to apply shading to cells.
2. When spell checking, make cell A1 the active cell so that Excel will begin checking the spelling at the top of a worksheet.
3. Borders do not have to surround a cell.
4. When using the conditional formatting feature, up to five conditions can be specified in one conditional format.
5. You can apply color only to a cell that has a border.
6. Excel spell checking begins at the active cell location.
7. Before creating a conditional format, you must select a cell range.
8. If you do not select a word or range of words, Excel checks the spelling for all text in a worksheet.
9. The Custom.dic file is used to store words that you add to the Excel spelling dictionary.
10. The Format Painter can be used to copy text formats.

Multiple Choice Questions

1. Conditional formatting can be used to apply _____.
    a. font styles
    b. patterns
    c. shading
    d. any of the above

2. When using the conditional formatting feature, to use the values in the selected cells as the data criteria, click _____ Is in the left-most column of the Conditional Formatting dialog box.
    a. Cell Value
    b. Formula
    c. Label
    d. Text

3. If you want to indent characters from the left edge of the cell, select _____ alignment on the Alignment page of the Format cells dialog box.
    a. Left
    b. Right
    c. Default
    d. General

4. Up to _____ conditions can be specified in one conditional format.
    a. 1
    b. 2
    c. 3
    d. 4

5. Use the _____ option in the Spelling dialog box to add a word to the Excel dictionary.
    a. Add
    b. Insert
    c. Include
    d. Include all

6. Use the Format Painter to copy _____.
   a. text
   b. formulas
   c. values
   d. formats

7. Excel's _____ feature contains several pre-defined table formats.
   a. AutoFormat
   b. Format
   c. Repeat
   d. Edit

8. When aligning text, choose the _____ option when you want to reduce the appearance of the data so it fits within the displayed column width.
   a. Wrap Text
   b. Shrink to Fit
   c. Merge Cells
   d. Decrease Font Size

9. You can use the Format _____ dialog box to align text in a selected cell or cells.
   a. Entries
   b. Ranges
   c. Cells
   d. Columns

10. To quickly open the Format Cells dialog box, press _____.
    a. F1
    b. Ctrl+1
    c. F8
    d. Ctrl+F

Completion Questions

1. When using the conditional formatting feature, formatting criteria can consist of _____ or _____.

2. When using the spell checker, to leave a word unchanged throughout the entire worksheet, select the _____ button.

3. When using the conditional formatting feature, there are eight _____ operators available.

4. To remove conditional formats, use the _____ key.

5. When you select the Format Painter button, a(n) _____ icon is added to the mouse pointer.

6. When values do not fit in the width of a column, a series of _____ appear in the cell.

7. When using the spell checker, to leave a word unchanged, use the _____ button.

8. There are _____ methods available for rotating text.

9. Before assigning a border, you must first _____ the cell range.

10. The Excel default border is a(n) _____ border.

Project 6

Test Questions

True/False Questions

1. Three-dimensional charts have a third axis, the z-axis.
2. Another name for a value axis is an alpha exit.
3. Charts are based on selected data in a worksheet.
4. You can use a function key to create a chart.
5. Excel displays the same shortcut menu when you click a grid line, a chart axis, or a plot area.
6. A legend tells what each color or symbol in the chart's data series represents.
7. After creating a chart with the Chart Wizard, you must indicate where in the worksheet you want to place the chart.
8. To create a chart on its own chart sheet, press F8.
9. Use a radar chart to show a correlation between two data series.
10. Changing the size of a chart will not change the appearance of the chart nor the display of the labels on the axes.

Multiple Choice Questions

1. The horizontal axis on a chart is the _____-axis.
    a. x
    b. y
    c. z
    d. value

2. The space on a chart where the pie, lines, columns, or bars are drawn is called the _____ area.
    a. plot
    b. grid
    c. axis
    d. data

3. Charts and maps are considered to be Excel _____.
    a. pictures
    b. objects
    c. articles
    d. components

4. A(n) _____ chart shows a data segment and its relationship to the whole.
    a. area
    b. bar
    c. pie
    d. 3-D

5. Besides adding height and width, a(n) _____ chart adds depth to a chart.
    a. area
    b. bar
    c. pie
    d. 3-D

6. _____ charts can chart only one set of values.
    a. Area
    b. Bar
    c. Pie
    d. Line

7. Use a(n) _____ chart to show several sets of data.
    a. area
    b. bar
    c. pie
    d. 3-D

8. When you click the Grabber button on the Data Map toolbar, the mouse pointer changes shape to a _____.
    a. small hand
    b. double-headed arrow
    c. small map
    d. pointing finger

9. Use the _____ menu to change the margins of a worksheet and chart.
    a. File
    b. Edit
    c. Format
    d. Style

10. _____ handles surround a chart.
    a. Four
    b. Six
    c. Eight
    d. Nine

10. If you decide that a chart contains too much data and looks cluttered, you can easily delete one or more _____ from the chart.

Completion Questions

1. The default chart type is _____.
2. The labels along the bottom of a chart are the _____ -axis labels.
3. The labels along the left side of a chart are the _____-axis labels.
4. Press DEL to delete a(n) _____ chart.
5. The mouse pointer should be shaped like a(n) _____ on the worksheet cell where you want the upper left corner of a map to start.
6. By using _____, you can move an embedded chart to any location in the worksheet.
7. A(n) _____ is an item on a chart that can be moved, sized, and formatted.
8. Data _____ proportions can be misleading.
9. To print only an embedded chart without the worksheet, double-click the chart to activate it and then click the _____ button.

Project 7

Test Questions

True/False Questions

1. Each entry in a telephone directory is a record.
2. A row in a database worksheet represents a field.
3. Field names must be different from each other.
4. Each column contains one type of information.
5. No blank rows should appear between the row of field names and the first data record.
6. Usually, you should separate each record with a blank row between them.
7. Each row in a database is a field.
8. Field names cannot contain spaces.
9. After you have entered the field names and the data records, you define the Excel list.
10. In a data form, column headings appear as field labels.

Multiple Choice Questions

1. Which of the following is an invalid field name.
    a. 1stName
    b. LastName
    c. FirstName
    d. none of the above are valid names
2. A _____ displays field names, text boxes, and buttons for adding, deleting, and finding records in your list.
    a. data form
    b. record
    c. file
    d. file form
3. You cannot use the data form to _____.
    a. add records
    b. delete records
    c. find records
    d. all of the above can be done with the data form
4. Which of the following is not a comparison operator?
    a. begins with
    b. is greater than or equal to
    c. is greater than
    d. all of the above are comparison operators
5. _____ operators tell Excel the type of comparison you want to use.
    a. Comparison
    b. Logical
    c. Numeric
    d. Financial
6. A _____ is the criteria that tells Excel which database records you want to see displayed.
    a. field
    b. record
    c. filter
    d. range
7. Each _____ represents a field.
    a. column
    b. row
    c. cell
    d. range

8. A field name can be up to _____ characters in length.
   a. 8
   b. 11
   c. 215
   d. 255
9. When you click on a filter _____, a list of criteria options appears below it.
   a. button
   b. knob
   c. arrow
   d. check mark
10. When using a filter, the three criteria that appear at the top of the list are All, Top 10, and _____.
    a. Default
    b. Custom
    c. Natural
    d. Normal

9. When you enter numeric selection criteria in which you search for a range of values, you use _____ operators.
10. The Sort Ascending button in on the _____ toolbar.

Completion Questions

1. A(n) _____ in a database worksheet represents a record.
2. A(n) _____ contains related information.
3. The _____ row of a database must contain labels that identify the database fields.
4. All records in a database contain the same _____.
5. The _____ is a dialog box that shows the contents of all the fields in one data record.
6. If you add records into blank cells or rows, remember to insert the records within the _____.
7. When using the data form, to move from one field to another press _____.
8. You can use any field name in the database as a(n) _____ for reordering the database.

Project 8

Test Questions

True/False Questions

1. When multitasking, you must have at least two programs open.
2. You can move the Windows 95 taskbar.
3. If source workbooks are renamed or moved, the link is lost.
4. Links can be broken.
5. If you move the target document to a different folder or disk and then change the data in the source, Excel can automatically update the link.
6. When you use the Excel 97 Copy and Paste commands to copy worksheet data into a word processing document, if the data in the worksheet changes, the worksheet in the word processing document is automatically updated.
7. You can paste, embed, or link data from one program to another.
8. OLE using linking to create an object in the client file.
9. DDE using linking to set up communication between two files.
10. With embedding, an object is not linked to the source file.

Multiple Choice Questions

1. _____ programs share many features and standard commands.
   a. Integrated
   b. Multitasking
   c. Embedded
   d. Linked

2. _____ data enables you to edit the a worksheet in a Word document without switching back to Excel.
   a. Embedding
   b. Linking
   c. Assigning
   d. Locking

3. Press _____ to switch among open applications.
   a. Ctrl+Tab
   b. Alt+Tab
   c. Ctrl+Alt+Tab
   d. Ctrl+Shift+Tab

4. _____ uses embedding to create an object in the client file.
   a. DDE
   b. OLE
   c. DEE
   d. LEO

5. _____ uses linking to set up communication between two files.
   a. DDE
   b. OLE
   c. DEE
   d. LEO

6. Excel embeds a worksheet object at the _____ of another application file.
   a. top
   b. bottom
   c. insertion point location
   d. none of the above

7. If you find that your system is slow or locking up, you may have unintentionally _____.
   a. disengaged the multitasking feature
   b. failed to select the integration option
   c. saved documents to the drive C: disk
   d. launched a program twice

Appendix B

8. If data is _____, any changes in the source file will automatically be updated in the target document.
   a. embedded
   b. linked
   c. assigned
   d. locked

9. Use the Paste link option to _____ data.
   a. embed
   b. link
   c. assign
   d. copy

10. To save data in the HTML format, choose the File _____ command.
    a. **S**ave as **I**nternet
    b. Save **A**s
    c. Save as WE**B**
    d. Save as HTML

Completion Questions

1. Creating links enables you to use the _____ for more than one worksheet.

2. If you move the source workbook to another directory, the links to your data will be _____.

3. Suites of applications have _____ bars.

4. When you copy data, the data is temporarily stored in the _____.

5. The white boxes surrounding linked data are called _____.

6. In a _____ document, value changes in the source document are updated automatically in the target document.

7. The Clipboard is used to copy, link, and _____ data.

8. Unlike the copy command, _____ data updates a document.

9. You can _____ a selection handle to resize a worksheet.

10. If source workbooks are renamed or moved to other directories, dependent workbooks cannot find the needed _____.

Appendix B 261

Project 1: Test Question Solutions

Note: Numbers in parentheses refer to the objective being addressed.

True/False Solutions

1. T (1)
2. F (4)
3. F (2)
4. T (intro)
5. F (1)
6. F (2)
7. F (2)
8. F (2)
9. F (intro)
10. T (2)

Multiple Choice Solutions

1. d (2)
2. b (1)
3. a (4)
4. b (4)
5. d (4)
6. d (2)
7. b (2)
8. a (4)
9. a (6)
10. c (9)

Completion Questions

1. =D5+E2 (5)
2. bottom (2)
3. 32,000 (5)
4. bottom of the worksheet area (1)
5. active (5)
6. address (2)
7. Save in (6)
8. three (1)
9. click (5)
10. RAM (6)

Project 2: Test Question Solutions

Note: Numbers in parentheses refer to the objective being addressed.

True/False Solutions

1. F (2)
2. F (6)
3. T (6)
4. T (3)
5. F (6)
6. F (4)
7. F (4)
8. T (6)
9. T (6)
10. T (7)

Multiple Choice Solutions

1. a (4)
2. d (2)
3. a (3)
4. d (3)
5. c (1)
6. b (1)
7. c (2)
8. b (3)
9. a (5)
10. b (5)

Completion Solutions

1. Undo, Edit (5)
2. range (2)
3. Clipboard (6)
4. paste (6)
5. Clear (6)
6. indicate (6)
7. Del (6)
8. frame (2)
9. left (4)
10. Undo (5)

Project 3: Test Question Solutions

Note: Numbers in parentheses refer to the objective being addressed.

True/False Solutions

1. T (2)
2. T (2)
3. T (1)
4. F (3)
5. T (1)
6. F (1)
7. F (1)
8. F (2)
9. T (2)
10. T (2)

Multiple Choice Solutions

1. b (1)
2. d (1)
3. b (4)
4. b (2)
5. a (3)
6. e (3)
7. c (3)
8. c (1)
9. c (4)
10. c (3)

Completion Solutions

1. Range Finder (2)
2. Formula bar (1)
3. Functions (intro)
4. equal (1)
5. formula (1)
6. Range Finder (2)
7. dollar sign (4)
8. equal (1)
9. check mark (1)
10. Delete (1)

Project 4: Test Question Solutions

Note: Numbers in parentheses refer to the objective being addressed.

True/False Solutions

1. F (3)
2. F (4)
3. F (1)
4. F (3)
5. T (3,4)
6. F (1)
7. F (3)
8. T (3)
9. F (3)
10. T (1)

Multiple Choice Solutions

1. c (3)
2. d (3)
3. b (3)
4. b (3)
5. a (3)
6. b (3)
7. b (5)
8. a (3)
9. a (4)
10. a (5)

Completion Solutions

1. omitting commas, inserting spaces (3,4)
2. IF (5)
3. combine (4)
4. bottom (2)
5. IF (5)
6. MIN (3)
7. function (3)
8. arguments (3)
9. parentheses (3,4)
10. AutoCalculate (3)

Appendix B

Project 5: Test Question Solutions

Note: Numbers in parentheses refer to the objective being addressed.

True/False Solutions
1. T (6)
2. T (8)
3. T (5)
4. F (6)
5. F (5)
6. T (8)
7. T (6)
8. T (8)
9. T (8)
10. T (1)

Multiple Choice Solutions
1. d (6)
2. a (6)
3. a (3)
4. c (6)
5. a (7)
6. d (1)
7. a (7)
8. b (3)
9. c (3)
10. b (1)

Completion Solutions
1. cell values, formulas (6)
2. I**g**nore All (8)
3. conditional (6)
4. DEL (6)
5. Paintbrush (1)
6. ###### (2)
7. **I**gnore (8)
8. two (3)
9. select (5)
10. bottom

Project 6: Test Question Solutions

Note: Numbers in parentheses refer to the objective being addressed.

True/False Solutions
1. T (3)
2. F (1)
3. T (1)
4. T (1)
5. F (2)
6. T (1)
7. T (1)
8. F (1)
9. F (3)
10. F (1)

Multiple Choice Solutions
1. a (1)
2. a (2)
3. b (1)
4. c (3)
5. d (3)
6. c (3)
7. a (3)
8. a (6)
9. a (5)
10. c (1)

Completion Solutions
1. column (1)
2. x (1)
3. y (1)
4. embedded (2)
5. cross hair (6)
6. Drag and Drop (1)
7. chart object (1,2)
8. series (1)
9. Print (5)
10. data series (1)

Project 7: Test Question Solutions

Note: Numbers in parentheses refer to the objective being addressed.

True/False Solutions
1. T (1)
2. F (1)
3. T (1)
4. T (1)
5. T (1)
6. F (1)
7. F (1)
8. F (1)
9. T (1)
10. T (2)

Multiple Choice Solutions
1. a (1)
2. a (2)
3. d (2,4)
4. d (5)
5. a (5)
6. c (5)
7. a (1)
8. d (1)
9. c (5)
10. b (5)

Completion Solutions
1. row (1)
2. record (1)
3. first (1)
4. fields (1)
5. data form (2)
6. defined database range (2)
7. Tab (2)
8. sort field (3)
9. comparison (5)
10. Standard (3)

Project 8: Test Question Solutions

Note: Numbers in parentheses refer to the objective being addressed.

True/False Solutions
1. T (intro)
2. T (1)
3. T (3)
4. T (3)
5. F (3)
6. F (2)
7. T (2,3,4)
8. F (3)
9. T (3)
10. T (3)

Multiple Choice Solutions
1. a (3)
2. a (4)
3. b (1)
4. b (3)
5. a (3)
6. c (4)
7. d (2)
8. b (3)
9. b (3)
10. d (5)

Completion Solutions
1. same data (3)
2. broken (1)
3. shortcut (1)
4. clipboard (2)
5. selection handles (3)
6. linked (3)
7. embed (4)
8. linking (3)
9. drag (3)
10. data (3)